Studien aus dem Max-Planck-Institut
für Sozialrecht und Sozialpolitik

Band 73

Jihan Kahssay

When NGOs Fulfill State Obligations

How NGO Laws in Africa Can Interfere with Social Rights of Beneficaries

Nomos

Open Access funding provided by Max Planck Society.

The Deutsche Nationalbibliothek lists this publication in the Deutsche Nationalbibliografie; detailed bibliographic data are available on the Internet at http://dnb.d-nb.de

Zugl.: LMU, München., Diss., 2019

ISBN 978-3-8487-6576-8 (Print)
978-3-7489-0692-6 (ePDF)

British Library Cataloguing-in-Publication Data
A catalogue record for this book is available from the British Library.

ISBN 978-3-8487-6576-8 (Print)
978-3-7489-0692-6 (ePDF)

Library of Congress Cataloging-in-Publication Data
Kahssay, Jihan
When NGOs Fulfill State Obligations
How NGO Laws in Africa Can Interfere with Social Rights of Beneficaries
Jihan Kahssay
337 pp.
Includes bibliographic references.

ISBN 978-3-8487-6576-8 (Print)
978-3-7489-0692-6 (ePDF)

1st Edition 2020

Published by
Nomos Verlagsgesellschaft mbH & Co. KG
Waldseestraße 3-5 | 76530 Baden-Baden
www.nomos.de

Production of the printed version:
Nomos Verlagsgesellschaft mbH & Co. KG
Waldseestraße 3-5 | 76530 Baden-Baden

Printed and bound in Germany.

ISBN (Print): 978-3-8487-6576-8A
ISBN (ePDF): 978-3-7489-0692-6

DOI: https://doi.org/10.5771/9783748906926

Onlineversion
Nomos eLibrary

When NGOs Fulfill State Obligations:
How NGO Laws in Africa Can Interfere with Social Rights of Beneficiaries

Jihan A. KAHSSAY

For My Family

Preface

This book is the outcome of my work as a doctoral student of the Ludwig Maximilian University of Munich. My dissertation was submitted to the faculty of law in October 2018 and was approved in April 2019. The research for this book was conducted during my time as a doctoral researcher at the Max Planck Institute for Social Law and Policy and as a guest researcher at the University of California Davis, School of Law.

I thank my doctoral advisor, Prof. Dr. Ulrich Becker, LL.M. (EHI) – the director of the Max Planck Institute for Social Law and Social Policy – whose thoughtful questions and rigorous standards were invaluable to my progress. I thank Prof. Dr. Jens Kersten for providing a second opinion on my dissertation.

I am also indebted to many other people for their encouragement. Prof. Leticia Saucedo, for her mentorship and unending support. My fellow doctoral students, including Ms. Yifei Wang, Dr. Maximilian Kreßner and Dr. Stefan Stegner, for always being willing to lend me an attentive audience, even during late hours into night. The researcher staff of the Max Planck Institute for Social Law and Social Policy and in particular the librarians, for always being able to locate resources – no matter how obscure they might have been.

Finally, I thank my family and friends for their kindness and their compassion during these years. My father, for having encouraged me to chase after whatever makes me feel alive. My mother, for always believing that I am more capable than I might sometimes think I am. My husband, for loving me faithfully from the very beginning. Amalia, for her endless support. My siblings and close friends, for reminding me again and again that our moments together often matter so much more than all that's happened while we were apart.

London, January 2020 — Jihan A. Kahssay

Zusammenfassung

In Afrika zeichnet sich ein gesetzlicher Trend ab, der zivilgesellschaftliche Organisationen, einschließlich Nichtregierungsorganisationen (NRO-en), einschränkt. Viele drücken ihre Besorgnis darüber aus, dass die Eckpfeiler einer freien Zivilgesellschaft - nämlich das Recht, sich zu assoziieren und das Recht auf freie Meinungsäußerung - angegriffen werden. Ein bislang eher weniger beleuchtetes Problem ist jedoch, dass solche staatlichen Maßnahmen auch die sozialen Rechte der Personen betreffen, die durch die NRO-en betreut werden (Begünstigte). In diesem Zusammenhang verpflichtet der Internationale Pakt über wirtschaftliche, soziale und kulturelle Rechte (IPwskR) Staaten Schritte zur vollständigen Verwirklichung der sozialen Rechte, unter Einsatz aller geeigneten Mittel bis zum Maximum ihrer verfügbaren Ressourcen, zu unternehmen. In diesem Sinne lässt sich die soziale Verantwortung von Staaten als ein dynamisches Konzept begreifen. In Abhängigkeit von den gegebenen Umständen, z.B. Ressourcenknappheit, variiert demnach der jeweilige Pflichtenhorizont der Staaten gegenüber den Begünstigten. Diesbezüglich stellt sich jedoch die Frage, wie Menschenrechtsverpflichtungen der Staaten im Bereich der sozialen Rechte bestimmt werden sollen, wenn NRO-en mit externen Finanzierungsquellen in die Gleichung eingehen.

Soweit die gemeinnützigen Aktivitäten von NRO-en ein zentrales Instrument darstellen, um soziale Rechte zu verwirklichen oder zu genießen, besteht ein Dreiecksverhältnis zwischen dem Staat, den NRO-en und den Begünstigten, welches die Rechte und Pflichten der Akteure zueinander bestimmt. Während der Staat soziale Rechte im Rahmen der zur Verfügung stehenden Möglichkeiten schuldet, realisieren NRO-en diese faktisch durch gemeinnützige Aktivitäten. Daher sind die Bedingungen der Rechtsbeziehung zwischen NRO-en und dem Staat zu klären.

Wenn Staaten die Verwirklichung und den Genuss sozialer Rechte nicht bis zu dem Grad garantieren, zu dem sie verpflichtet sind, entstehen Schutzlücken, die NRO-en schließen, indem sie die rechtlichen Verpflichtungen des Staates erfüllen. Daher muss der Staat gemeinnützige Tätigkeiten nicht nur zulassen und erleichtern, sondern auch sicherstellen, dass auch dann noch ein vergleichbarer Zugang zu sozialen Rechten garantiert wird, wenn NRO-en ihre Aktivitäten einstellen. Falls die Leistungen der NRO-en jedoch über den Pflichtenhorizont der Staaten hinausgehen, müssen diese nicht zwingend durch staatliche Institutionen aufrechterhalten werden. Solange sie jedoch durch NRO-en erbracht werden, dürfen Staaten dies grundsätzlich nicht unterbinden. Allerdings muss ein Staat die Rechte der Begünstigten vor Eingriffen Dritter schützen, indem er angemessene Maßnahmen ergreift, um sicherzustellen, dass die NRO den Begünstigten nicht schaden.

Da es zweifellos Zeiten geben wird, in denen es für Staaten angemessen ist, NRO-en einzuschränken, selbst wenn dadurch die sozialen Rechte für ihre Begünstigten verkürzt würden, besteht aus regulatorischer Sicht ein Zielkonflikt. Einerseits müssen Staaten zwar die Aufsicht über NRO-en ausüben, um sicherzustellen, dass Begünstigte weder von skrupellosen NRO-en noch von Betrügern geschädigt oder ausgebeutet werden. Andererseits sollte die regulatorische Kontrolle nicht dazu führen, dass die positiven Auswirkungen von gemeinnützigen Aktivitäten behindert werden. Der rechtliche Rahmen für den Ausgleich dieser gegenläufigen Interessen ergibt sich aus den Artikeln 2 (1), 4 und 5 des IPwskR ergeben. Die vorliegende Dissertation bietet eine systematische Untersuchung dieser Rechtsfragen aus der Perspektive der sozialen Rechte der Begünstigten.

Table of Contents

Table of Figures

Table of Abbreviations

ACHPR	African Charter on Human and Peoples' Rights
ACRWC	African Charter on the Rights and Welfare of the Child
ACmERWC	African Committee of Experts on the Rights and Welfare of the Child
ACmHPR	African Commission on Human and Peoples' Rights
AU	African Union
ECtHR	European Court of Human Rights
ESAP	Economic Structural Adjustment Programme
ESC	Economic, social and cultural
CESCR	Committee on Economic, Social and Cultural Rights
CRC	Committee on the Rights of the Child
CHW	Community health workers
COWE	Caring for Orphans, Widows and the Elderly
HRC	Human Rights Committee
IACrtHR	Inter-American Court of Human Rights
ICCPR	International Covenant on Civil and Political Rights
ICEDAW	International Covenant on the Elimination of All Forms of Discrimination Against Women
ICERD	International Covenant on the Elimination of All Forms of Racial Discrimination
ICESCR	International Covenant on Economic, Social and Cultural Rights
ICJ	International Court of Justice
ICRC	International Covenant on the Rights of the Child
LDC	Least developed country
MNCH	Maternal, newborn and child health
NGO	Non-governmental organization
NSP	Non-state service provider
MEL	Minimum essential level
ODA	Overseas development aid
OP-ICESCR	Optional Protocol to the International Covenant on Economic, Social and Cultural Rights

P-ACHPRRWA	Protocol to the African Charter on Human and Peoples' Rights on the Rights of Women in Africa
UN	United Nations
UNCHR	United Nations Commission on Human Rights
UNESC	United Nations Economic and Social Council
UNGA	United Nations General Assembly
UNHCHR	United Nations High Commissioner for Human Rights
UNSG	United Nations Secretary-General
VCLT	Vienna Convention on the Law of Treaties

1. Introduction

During the decades when the Nuba people of South Kordofan were targeted, marginalized and systematically excluded from all forms of social protection by a hostile government in Sudan, their community developed educational and health services through informal, localized and non-governmental forms of social protection.[1] With "almost no start-up resources whatsoever", the indigenous militarized defense force (the Nuba SPLM) "established networks and systems for rudimentary schools, clinics and agricultural extension centres staffed by voluntary teachers, health workers and individuals with technical backgrounds in crop and animal production."[2] Nonprofit provision can strengthen social rights protection through service delivery and rights advocacy. In the case of the Nuba community, the informal services grew in sophistication over time as international nongovernmental organizations (NGOs) gained access to the area.[3] This story invites us to consider how the triangular relations that bind non-state providers, the state and beneficiaries can be critical to the realization and enjoyment of social rights, and how the configuration of those triangular relations might impact the state's social rights obligations.

In today's interconnected world, social rights in developing countries are – to a significant extent – both realized and injured by non-state actors and through global processes. Within this context, NGOs have become increasingly important to the realization of social rights, at times challenging the centrality of the state in the field of social protection and at other times extending it. Moreover, both states and NGOs in developing countries depend heavily on foreign assistance, allowing foreign donors and international financial institutions to occupy a prominently influential role in domestic policy and politics. These complexities are exaggerated in sub-Saharan Africa, where socio-economic conditions are bleak, public social protection programs are severely underdeveloped, the presence of foreign aid and NGOs is widespread, and human vulnerability is pervasive, severe and often left unmitigated. Under such circumstances – where non-state social

1 Justin Corbett, *Learning from the Nuba: Civilan Resilience and Self-Protection During Conflict,* Local to Global Protection (2011).
2 Ibid 40-41.
3 Ibid 41.

provision is extensive, financially independent of state control, and often essential to the social wellbeing of beneficiaries – evaluating the realization and enjoyment of social rights will require a rather nuanced and multi-faceted understanding of the state's social rights obligations.

The ability of most states in sub-Saharan Africa to ensure the realization and enjoyment of social rights is severely undermined by underdevelopment, resource scarcity or unavailability and inadequate formal social protection systems. In terms of development, 70% of the world's least developed countries (LDCs) are in Africa, and 63% of African countries are LDCs.[4] Low social welfare outcomes indicate that African LDCs, of which there are 33,[5] struggle to provide the basic social needs of their populations. In terms of resources, the World Bank classifies all but 6 of Africa's LDCs as low-income countries.[6] African LDCs depend on foreign aid and foreign NGOs, which complicates the state's ability to direct the domestic development of social welfare by overshadowing their political and economic independence. It has become clear that in order to study service provision in African LDCs, one must depart from the traditional statist model and take account of the substantial involvement of third parties, including nonprofit entities, although many scholars continue to overlook non-state social protection.[7]

The past two decades have seen a dramatic rise in the number of NGOs across the globe as well as their institutional influence.[8] During that time, nonprofit organizations in general and NGOs in particular were hailed as the solution to the world's development problems. They were celebrated

---

4 Triennial Review Dataset (United Nations Committe for Development Policy Secretariat 2000-2015).

5 As of June 2017, these are: Angola, Benin, Burkina Faso, Burundi, Central African Republic, Chad, Comoros, Democratic Republic of the Congo, Djibouti, Eritrea, Ethiopia, Gambia, Guinea, Guinea-Bissau, Lesotho, Liberia, Madagascar, Malawi, Mali, Mauritania, Mozambique, Niger, Rwanda, Sao Tome and Principe, Senegal, Sierra Leone, Somalia, South Sudan, Togo, Uganda, United Republic of Tanzania and Zambia. (*List of Least Developed Countires (as of June 2017)*, U.N Committee for Development Policy, (2017) <https://www.un.org/development/desa/dpad/wp-content/uploads/sites/45/publication/ldc_list.pdf>.).

6 See World Bank List of Economics (June 2017) (World Bank 2017).

7 Nicholas Awortwi and Gregor Walter-Drop, 'Governance Below the State: Non-State Social Protection Services in Africa' in Nicholas Awortwi and Gregor Walter-Drop (eds), *Non-State Social Protection Actors and Services in Africa: Governance Below the State* (Routledge 2018) 1-24, 4.

8 Garry W. Jenkins, 'Nongovernmental Orgainzations and the Forces against Them: Lessons of the Anti-NGO Movement' 37 Brook Journal of International Law 459 (2012) 479-481.

widely as grassroots organization with humanitarian aims that filled social protection gaps for the poor and promoted democracy in the then newly independent states. In recent years, however, alongside growing criticism of NGOs in general, there has been an intensification of state scrutiny directed toward NGOs, and particularly toward those with substantial ties to foreign funders. NGOs have undergone closer examination, resulting in challenges to their legitimacy, accountability, effectiveness and integrity. As non-state actors, they are largely unaccountable under international law, which in turn justifies the passage of restrictive NGO laws.

Increasingly so, some African states have enacted, drafted or threatened to draft restrictive legislation to monitor and regulate the operations of NGOs, including non-state providers of social services. Some of these legislative measures severely limit the ability of NGOs to accept foreign funding. Others forbid them from engaging in human rights advocacy, and at least one law prohibits NGOs from conducting any development work at without prior state approval. Notably restrictive laws and regulations have been enacted in Angola (legislation in 2012; presidential decree in 2015),[9] Eritrea (legislation in 2005),[10] Ethiopia (legislation in 2009)[11], Kenya (legislation in 1990),[12] Sierra Leone (regulations in 2009)[13] and Uganda (legisla-

9 Lei Das Associações Privadas Lei No 6/2012 (Angola 2012)(imposes mandatory registration requirements for NGOs; registration can be denied on public morality grounds; NGOs can be terminated when their activities are contrary to public policy); Decreto Presidencial No. 74/15, No. 74/15 (Angola 2015) (granting government broad powers to direct, control and supervise NGO activities and their financing; geographic limitations for nonprofit activities; burdensome registration requirements whereby international NGOs must register with three separate ministries; restrictions on accessing foreign funding; suspension of nonprofit activities on vague grounds such as protecting the "integrity of the Republic of Angola" or when nonprofit activities are deemed not to have been "beneficial to the community").

10 A Proclamation to Determine the Administration of Non-Governmental Organizations, Proclamation No 145/2005 (Eritrea 2005) (severely limiting the scope of nonprofit activities to emergency service provision, with heavy state supervision).

11 Charities and Societies Proclamation No 621/2009 (Ethiopia 2009) (limits access to foreign funding and restricts human rights advocacy).

12 Non-Governmental Organizations Co-Ordination Act, No 19 of 1990 (Kenya 1990) (as amended by The Statute Law (Miscellaneous Amendemendments) Act, 1991, No 14 of 1991 (Kenya 1991)) (NGO registration is mandatory; registration may be denied on "national interest" grounds).

13 Non-Government Organisations Policy Regulations (Sierra Leone 2009) (requires that all NGO projects are first discussed with government prior to their implementation; grants government power to direct NGO operations by setting guidelines, with which NGOs must ensure their operation conform).

tion in 2006 and 2016; regulations in 2009 and 2017)[14]. Likewise, restrictive NGO bills have been considered in Zimbabwe (2004),[15] Kenya (2013)[16] and Uganda (2015)[17].

Human rights observers commonly characterize this phenomenon as "shrinking civic space",[18] or an "attack" or "crackdown" on civil society.[19] This has spurred growing popular interest in the regulation of NGOs and

---

14 The Non-Governmental Organisations Registration (Amendment) Act, No 25 of 2006 (Uganda 2006) (penalizing the operation of non-registered NGOs with fines) ; The Non-Governmental Organisations Act, No 5 of 2016 (Uganda 2016) (imposing harsher penalties for noncompliance, including up to 3 year of imprisonment; imposing forced dissolution of NGOs on vague grounds such as "threatening national security"); The Non-Governmental Organisations Registration Regulations, 2009 No. 19 (Uganda 2009) (forbidding direct contact with people unless the NGO gives seven days written notice to the government; geographic restrictions on nonprofit activities; forbidden to engage in vaguely defined activities, such as that which is "prejudicial to the interests of Uganda and the dignity of the people of Uganda."); The Non-Governmental Organisations Regulations, No. 22 of 2017 (Uganda 2017) (imposes certain geographical constraints on NGOs).

15 For an analysis of the more restrictive provisions of the bill, see United Nations Development Programme, *The Zimbabwean Non-Governmental Orgnizations Bill 2004 and International Human Rights Law/Standards: Issues, Analysis and Policy Recommendations* (UNDP 2004) (noting restrictions on NGOs regarding access to foreign funding and the ability to involve themselves in governance issues.).

16 Statute Law (Miscellaneous Amendments) Bill. 2013, Bill No 32 (Kenya 2013) (sought to limit foreign funding to 15% of an NGO's budget, as well as to channel funds through government before it reaches an NGO).

17 The Non-Governmental Organisations Bill, 2015, Bill No 10 (Uganda 2015) (would have imposed mandatory registration for all NGOs; would have created an NGO Board, consisting of members appointed by the state, with broad powers to discipline or suspend NGOs, deny registration on any grounds it deemed fit, including in the "public interest", and revoke permits or involuntarily dissolve NGOs on "public interest" grounds; would have imposed geographic limitations on NGO activities; would have vaguely forbidden nonprofit activities that were deemed "prejudicial to the interests of Uganda and the dignity of the people of Uganda".).

18 Resolution on the Situation of Human Rights Defenders in Africa, ACmHPR (May 22, 2017) preamble.

19 Julia Kreienkamp, *Responding to the Global Crackdown on Civil Society*, Global Governance Institute, (2017) <https://www.ucl.ac.uk/global-governance/downloads/policybriefs/policy-brief-civil-society>; 'Maina Kiai Tells Conference That Civil Society Is "under Attack" in Africa' *Freedom Assembly* (Nov. 25, 2013) <http://freeassembly.net/wp-content/uploads/2013/11/Media-statement-Kiai-warns-civil-society-under-attack-in-Africa.pdf>.

other associational organizations in Africa.[20] Many have called for reforms. Most recently, the African Commission on Human and Peoples' Rights (African Commission), which is the treaty body of the African Charter for Human and Peoples' Rights (African Charter), in noting that it was "[c]oncerned by excessive restrictions imposed on the rights to freedom of association and assembly",[21] adopted new guidelines on the rights to freedom of assembly and association on the continent.[22]

Restrictive NGO laws certainly threaten the rights of NGOs to associate, assembly and speak freely. However, in least developed states where nonprofit activities are more likely to be vital to the realization of social rights, such laws may also jeopardize the rights of beneficiaries. Thus, restrictive regulation of NGOs may present an additional legal problem: whether states are complying with their social rights obligations to beneficiaries of nonprofit activities.

Research Objectives and Parameters

From this perspective, the present dissertation examines whether and how the social obligations of the state toward beneficiaries of nonprofit activities give rise to implicit state duties toward nonprofit service providers, particularly in Africa's LDCs. Most legal analysts examining NGO laws have commented on their interference with the rights of NGOs. This body of scholarship focuses mainly on the freedom of association and the right to free speech. However, since NGOs play a significant role in the realization of social rights in Africa's LDCs, highly restrictive NGO laws may significantly limit the realization and enjoyment of social rights. Thus, this dissertation employs a beneficiary-centered approach in order to highlight

---

20 A growing interest in NGO laws has even taken root within popular media. (E.g., Ingrid Srinath and Mandeep Tiwana, 'Civil Society: Only the Clampdown Is Transparent' *The Guardian* (Sept. 12, 2010) <https://www.theguardian.com/commentisfree/libertycentral/2010/sep/12/civil-society-millennium-development-goals>.).

21 Guidelines on Freedom of Association and Assembly in Africa, ACmHPR (African Guidelines on Freedom of Assocation and Assembly) <http://www.icnl.org/news/2017/ACHPR%20Guidelines%20english.pdf>.

22 The Guidelines were adopted by ACmHPR during its 60th Ordinary Session held from 8 May to 22 May 2017 in Niamey, Niger. (*42nd Activity Report of the African Commission on Human and Peoples' Rights,* African Commission on Human and Peoples' Rights, (2017) para. 25 <http://www.achpr.org/files/activity-reports/42/42nd_activity_report_eng.pdf>.).

the social rights obligations that states owe to beneficiaries under human rights law, and then to examine how these obligations might impact the state's regulatory duties toward NGOs.

In determining the state's social rights obligations, I examine relevant international and regional human rights treaties, the interpretive works of supervisory treaty bodies as well as relevant legal scholarship. Domestic statutory law and court decisions are offered as case studies and examples throughout the dissertation. Drawing from the Vienna Convention on the Law of Treaties (Vienne Convention), my interpretations of international law take into account the ordinary meaning of texts, within their contexts and along with the object and purpose of the instrument under examination.

Lastly, a few points of clarification are in order. First, I use the terms duty and obligation interchangeably to refer to the acts or omissions with which an actor's behavior must conform. For a duty or obligation to be legally binding, it must arise from a legal source. As aforementioned, my normative sources for the state's legal obligations will be human rights law in general, and social rights obligations in particular. Second, in order to remain within reasonable analytical limits, this dissertation focuses primarily on the regulation of NGOs, although it goes without saying that NGOs are not the only non-state actors that work toward the realization of social rights in Africa.[23] Third, although NGO laws have become more restrictive in many parts of the world,[24] sub-Saharan Africa warrants special attention due to its underrepresentation in legal scholarship, the fact that African

23 See Mark Robinson and Gordon White, 'The Role of Civic Organizations in the Provision of Social Services: Towards Synergy' in Germano Mwabu, Cecilia Ugaz and Gordon White (eds), *Social Provision in Low-Income Countries* (Oxford University Press 2001) 79 - 100, 80.

24 *E.g., see The 2014 CSO Sustainability Index: Central and Eastern Europe and Eurasia,* United States Agency for International Development (USAID), (2014) 2 (noting legal environments have been deteriorating for CSOs in Azerbaijan, Bulgaria, Hungary, Kazakhstan, Russia, Tajikistan, while legal environments "remained extremely restrictive" in Turkmenistan and Uzbekistan); *The 2013 CSO Sustainability Index: The Middle East and North Africa,* United States Agency for International Development (USAID), (2013) 2-3 (CSO regulations in recent years require CSO with foreign assistance to sign memoranda of understanding with government to declare use of foreign funding); ibid ("Several governments in the [middle east and north African] region took actions to close civic space during 2013, mirroring trends in other parts of the world"); Maina Kiai, *Analysis on International Law, Standards and Principles Applicable to the Foreign Contributions Regulation Act 2010 and Foreign Contributions Regulation Rules 2011,* U.N. Special Rapporteur on the Rights to Freedom of Peaceful Assembly and of Association, (2016) (concluding

governments rely on foreign assistance more than governments in other regions,[25] and the extent of the continent's historical experience with foreign intervention as well as non-state (traditional or informal) means of social welfare. Finally, although the dissertation focuses on African states because of the prevalence of LDCs in sub-Saharan Africa, its ultimate theoretical findings and analyses can be generalized to all states bearing social rights obligations under human rights law. Likewise, these findings can, to a certain extent, cover cases involving other similarly situated non-state actors such as faith based and community based organizations.

State of Research

Scholarship dedicated to understanding NGOs in the developing world covers a wide range of topics and analytical approaches located within the broad strokes of development studies. To begin with, most literature on NGOs tends to evaluate their performance,[26] explain their emergence,[27]

India's restriction of foreign funding to NGOs is a violation of their international right to associate and assemble). *See also* Barbara Lethem Ibrahim, 'States, Public Space, and Cross-Border Philanthropy: Observations from the Arab Transitions' 17 International Journal of Not-for-Profit Law 72 (2015) ; Douglas Rutzen, 'Aid Barriers and the Rise of Philanthropic Protectionism' 17:1 International Journal Not-for-Profit Law 5(2015); Timothy M Gill, 'Unpacking the World Cultural Toolkit in Socialist Venezuela: National Sovereignty, Human Rights and Anti-NGO Legislation' 38 Third World Quarterly 621 (2017); Geir Flikke, 'Resurgent Authoritarianism: The Case of Russia's New NGO Legislation' 32 Post-Soviet Affairs 103 (2016) .

25 Lindsay Whitfield and Alastair Fraser, 'Negotiating Aid: The Structural Conditions Shaping the Negotiating Strategies of African Governments' 15 International Negotiation 341 (2010) 342.

26 Nicola Banks, David Hulme and Michael Edwards, 'NGOs, States, and Donors Revisited: Still Too Close for Comfort?' 66 World Development 707 (2015) ; Kevin Edmonds, 'Beyond Good Intentions: The Structural Limitations of NGOs in Haiti' 39 Critical Sociology 439 (2012) ; Mary Kay Gugerty, 'The Effectiveness of NGO Self-Regulation: Theory and Evidence from Africa' 28 Public Administration and Development 105 (2008) ; T. Jeffrey Scott, 'Evaluating Development-Oriented NGOs' in Jr. Welch, Claude E. (ed), NGOs *and Human Rights: Promise and Performance* (University of Pennsylvania Press 2001) 204-221; James Petras, 'NGOs: In the Service of Imperialism' 29 Journal of Contemporary Asia 429 (1999).

27 Lauren M. MacLean, 'Neoliberal Democratisation, Colonial Legacies and the Rise of the Non-State Provision of Social Welfare in West Africa' 44 Review of African Political Economy 358 (2017) ; Lester M. Salamon, 'Introduction: The

address concerns about their accountability and responsibilities,[28] or prescribe solutions for problems that are common within their sector.[29] Critical voices – not limited to any particular ideological tradition – can be found within the scholarship. One refers to this critical branch collectively as "the anti-NGO movement".[30] Postcolonial critiques shed light on how the objectives of NGOs are entangled with the (sometimes overriding) interests of foreign entities, and how this entanglement tends to undermine the legitimacy and effectiveness of NGOs in Africa, as well as extend parts of the imperialistic tradition of missionaries of the colonial era.[31] A related thread of critical literature narrows in on the diminishing sovereignty of states that accompanies the rise of NGOs.[32] As one writer's emblematic probe asks, when is it reasonable to consider NGOs "state sovereignty destroyers" rather than "human rights defenders"?[33]

Some development studies literature has narrowed in on the regulation of NGOs. One area of research focuses on the political processes of enacting NGO legislation and their consequences. Scholars have provided political explanations for the restrictiveness that characterizes recent trends in

---

Nonprofitization of the Welfare State' 26 Voluntas 2147 (2015) ; Redie Bereketeab, 'Conceptualizing Civil Society in Africa: The Case of Eritrea' 5 Journal of Civil Society 35 (2009); Lester M. Salamon, 'The Rise of the Nonprofit Sector' 73 Foreign Affairs 109 (1994); Lester M. Salamon and Helmut K. Anheier, 'Social Origins of Civil Society: Explaining the Nonprofit Sector Cross-Nationally' 9 Voluntas 213 (1998); Lester M. Salamon, 'Of Market Failure, Voluntary Failure, and Third-Party Government: Toward a Theory of Government-Nonprofit Relations in the Modern Welfare State' 16 Journal of Voluntary Action Research 29 (1987).

28 Maria Nassali, *Beating the Human Rights Drum: Applying Human Rights Standards to NGOs' Governance* (Pretoria University Law Press 2015); Elizabeth Griffin, 'The Ethical Responsibilities of Human Rights NGOs' 15 International Journal of Not-for-Profit Law 5 (2013); Lisa Jordan and Peter van Tuijl (eds), *NGO Accountability: Politics, Principles and Innovations* (Earthscan 2006).

29 Pablo Eisenberg, 'Forum - Looking Ahead: What Is the Future for the Nonprofit World' 8 International Journal of Not-for-Profit Law 81 (2005).

30 Jenkins (2012).

31 Issa G. Shivji, 'The Silences in the NGO Discourse' 31 African Development 22 (2006) ; Firoze Manji and Carl O'Coill, 'The Missionary Position: NGOs and Development in Africa' 78 International Affairs 567 (2002); Makau Mutua, 'Human Rights International NGOs: A Critical Evaluation' in Jr. Welch, Claude E. (ed), NGOs *and Human Rights: Promise and Performance* (University of Pennsylvania Press 2001) 151-166; Petras (1999).

32 Jessica T. Mathews, 'Power Shift' 76 Foreign Affairs 50 (1997).

33 Lina Marcinkutė, 'The Role of Human Rights NGOs: Human Rights Defenders or State Soverignty Destroyers?' 4 Baltic Journal of Law & Politics 52 (2011).

NGO regulations.[34] Others consider how the political process of regulating NGOs can enhance society's understanding of democratic accountability and legitimacy. Susannah H. Mayhew shows how legislative debates about how to regulate NGOs can act as a catalyst to enhance national discourse about the role, accountability, legitimacy and vulnerabilities of NGOs.[35] Another area of scholarship looks more closely at the effect that NGO regulations can have on NGOs. For example, how might such regulatory control promote accountability and legitimacy within the nonprofit sector?[36] Or, from another view, how might restrictive regulatory measures affect the operations and outcomes of NGOs? Ronelle Burger examines the pitfalls of various oversight mechanisms in Uganda, and whether they are likely to improve NGO sector outcomes.[37] Finally, some scholars search for a link between NGO regulations and development outcomes in general. Ada O. Okoye examines whether the regulation of NGOs in Nigeria and South Africa promote or undercut development objectives.[38]

In a sense, Okoye's work is exemplary in that it epitomizes both the strength and shortcomings of development studies research in terms of addressing the legal questions posed by the present dissertation. Like Okoye's contribution, development studies scholarship in this area of research is incredibly valuable for legal scholars because it offers background information and theoretical considerations about the links between NGOs and social development, however such literature does not typically employ legal analysis, nor does it yield significant legal findings. Legal scholarship is still needed in order address the issue of whether states owe any special regulatory duties toward NGOs based on the social rights of beneficiaries.

Within the legal discipline, some scholarship has addressed restrictive NGO regulations, but mainly with the objective of determining whether

---

34 Kendra Dupuy, James Ron and Aseem Prakash, 'Hands Off My Regime! Governments' Restrictions on Foreign Aid to Non-Governmental Organizations in Poor and Middle-Income Countries' 84 World Development 299 (2016).

35 Susannah H. Mayhew, 'Hegemony, Politics and Ideology: The Role of Legislation in NGO-Governmental Relations in Asia' 41 Journal of Development Studies 727 (2005).

36 Jassy B. Kwesiga and Harriet Namisi, 'Issues in Legislation for NGOs in Uganda' in Lisa Jordan and Peter van Tuijl (eds), *NGO Accountability: Politics, Principles and Innovations* (Earthscan 2006) 81-92.

37 Ronelle Burger, 'Reconsidering the Case for Enhancing Accountability Via Regulation' 23 Voluntas 85 (2012) 88.

38 Ada Obianuju Okoye, 'The Role of Law in the Development of Nonprofit Sector in Nigeria and South Africa' (University of Cape Town 2006).

the rights of NGOs – rather than beneficiaries – were violated.[39]Analysts consider how restrictive NGO laws may encroach on the rights to associate, to speak freely and to fundraise.[40]Very little legal scholarship addresses the effect of NGO regulations on the rights of beneficiaries. One example is an article by Akingbolahan Adeniran in which a governmental proposal to delegate the management of secondary schools to nonprofit entities in Nigeria was scrutinized from the perspective of the child's right to education.[41] Although a fine example, this article – due to its limited scope – does not provide a systematic exploration of the legal relations that bind beneficiaries, nonprofits and states. What is needed is a thorough investigation into the legal aspects of this this triangular relationship, with a particular focus on the functional role of nonprofits in the realization of social rights *vis-à-vis* the state. It is this particular issue that the present dissertation aims to address, and in doing so would contribute to an underdeveloped area of scholarship.

Perhaps the most direct way to approach the issue is by examining the human rights obligations of the state regarding the obstruction of private efforts to realize social rights. While commentators agree that the state bears a negative duty to respect socio-economic rights by refraining from interfering with their realization and enjoyment, they often are only concerned with instances in which the state directly deprives people of their rights, or when the state interferes with people's ability to realize their rights by their own means.[42] Very few, are concerned with the scenario in

---

39 Burger (2012) 88 ("...much of the writing on NGO regulation has concentrated on a demonstration of the potential negative consequences of government interventions on the independence and the freedom of the sector.").

40 Livingstone Sewanyana, 'Towards an Enabling NGO Regulatory Framework in Uganda: Comparative Experiences from Eastern and Southern Africa' (Doctoral Thesis Unversity of Capetown 2014) (examines how NGO regulations in Uganda affect the rights of NGOs); Jeanne Elone, 'Backlash against Democracy: The Regulation of Civil Society in Africa' 7 Democracy and Society (2010) (examines how NGO laws in Zambia, Zimbabwe and Ethiopia affect the rights of NGOs).

41 Akingbolahan Adeniran, 'Non-Profit Privatization of the Management of Nigerian Public Schools: A Legal and Policy Analysis' 53 Journal of African Law 249 (2009).

42 See Matthew Craven, *The International Covenant on Economic, Social and Cultural Rights: A Perspective on Its Development* (Ian Brownlie ed, Oxford University Press 1995) 110-111; Nsongurua J. Udombana, 'Between Promise and Performance: Revisiting States' Obligations under the African Human Rights Charter' 40 Stanford Journal of International Law 105 (2004) 131-132; Philip Alston and Gerard Quinn, 'The Nature and Scope of States Parties' Obligations under the Interna-

which the state interferes with the rights provided by third parties.[43] Most legal scholars who are concerned with the regulation of non-state providers from a rights-based perspective miss the mark by focusing on for-profit providers rather than nonprofits. Adam McBeth uses a rights-based approach to make a case for more rigorous regulation of private for-profit providers.[44] He begins from the normative position entrenched in international human rights law that the state must ensure the realization of economic, social and cultural rights such that it continues to progress over time. McBeth then posits that since private providers are incentivized by profits rather than by the progressive realization of social rights, the state must supervise them and impose upon them contractual obligations or provide them with financial incentives to ensure the progressive realization of social rights and equitable access to services, especially for marginalized members of society.[45] Although McBeth's analysis is a valuable contribution to the legal understanding of state regulatory responsibilities in the context of privatization, its legal conclusions cannot be supplanted into the field of nonprofit regulation because his underlying reasoning – that social rights cannot be progressively realized through non-state providers without regulatory controls on profit-seeking behavior – simply does not hold true for the nonprofit sector.

Since each sector is incentivized differently, scholars studying NGO laws should not conflate the regulatory reasoning that concern for-profit providers with that which concern nonprofit providers. Neil Gilbert and Barbara Gilbert note that there are two ways to characterize non-state provision: as private/public or as commercial/non-commercial.[46] They note that while the privatization of social welfare generally involves moving its planning or programming further away from state control and into the private sphere, the process of commercialization on the other hand is asso-

---

tional Covenant on Economic, Social and Cultural Rights' 9 Human Rights Quarterly 156 (1987) 184-185.

43 See, e.g., M. Magdalena Sepúlveda, *The Nature of the Obligations under the International Covenant on Economic, Social and Cultural Rights* (Intersentia 2003) 217-218 (asserting that states must refrain from interfereing with privately provided services, but only addresses this briefly in one paragraph; refers to the CESCR's discussion of the state's interruption of NGO services in Mexico.).

44 Adam McBeth, 'Privatising Human Rights: What Happens to the State's Human Rights Duties When Services Are Privatised?' 5 Melbourne Journal of International Law 133 (2004).

45 Ibid 152-153.

46 Neil Gilbert and Barbara Gilbert, *The Enabling State* (Oxford University Press 1989) 27-53.

ciated with "not only the penetration of profit-motivated providers, but also an infusion of the ethos and method of the economic market into all branches of the social market."[47] In this sense, nonprofits are not typically commercialized like their for-profit counterparts, although a significant emergence of either entity within the domain of social welfare is technically subsumed under the term "privatization". Thus, research on for-profit privatization would address an entirely different set of concerns than those raised by nonprofit privatization. In stressing some of those differences, Gilbert and Gilbert write,

> The noncompetitive service culture traditionally associated with the social market emphasizes concern for adequacy of provision over costs, status rather than contract relationships between consumer and provider, and transfer rather than exchange as the basic model of allocation.[48]

While scholars studying for-profit privatization, such as McBeth, might very well conclude that greater governmental oversight is essential to the realization of social rights, the same may not be true of regulating nonprofit providers. Indeed, existing patterns of governmental oversight appear to acknowledge this distinction, albeit in reverse order. According to a recent report of the Special Rapporteur on the rights to freedom of peaceful assembly and of association, states tend to regulate associations more restrictively than they do businesses.[49]

A similar argument for greater governmental oversight and regulation of private providers has been made by Joshua P. Reading, who examines the provision of health care in Pakistan.[50] Unlike McBeth, Reading's research considers all private providers, including nonprofit providers. However, like McBeth, Reading begins *a priori* from the position that increased regulation of private providers will improve, rather than interfere with, the realization of social rights. He asserts that "with increased government involvement, the level of health care will improve, both in terms of access and quality" and reasons that "increased expenditures lead to improved

47 Ibid 29.

48 Ibid.

49 Maina Kiai, *Annual Report: Comparative Study of Enabling Environments for Businesses and Associations*, U.N. Special Rapporteur on the Rights to Freedom of Peaceful Assembly and of Association, A/70/266 (2015).

50 Joshua P. Reading, (Note) 'Who's Responsible for This? Globalization of Healthcare in Developing Countries' 17 Indiana Journal of Global Legal Studies 367 (2010).

health care."[51] This line of research does not address the legal problems that arise when regulations are so restrictive that they obstruct or reduce nonprofit activities that were essential for the enjoyment or realization of social rights, and whether the state's social rights obligations toward the beneficiaries can act as a check or limit on the extent to which regulatory measures can restrict nonprofit activities.

Another way to distinguish this dissertation's objective from those of McBeth and Reading is through the paradigm of positive/negative duties. When McBeth and Reading argue for greater state oversight and intervention, they are largely extrapolating from the positive duties of the state to *do* something. Readings calls for greater governmental expenditure in health care and coordination with private providers. McBeth urges greater state supervision of private providers and the imposition of certain contractual obligations. The obligation of the state to exert at least some regulatory control on private providers is of course vital to the realization of social rights provided by nonprofits as well. What remains unclear, however, and what constitutes the primary concern of this dissertation, is whether the state bears *negative* duties. That is, whether and to what extent the state must refrain from interfering with the activities of private actors that would advance the realization of social rights, especially in the context of limited state capacity and resource scarcity.

On the peculiarities of the African context, neither McBeth nor Reading is exceedingly relevant. McBeth's article addresses international law rather generally while Reading's research uses Pakistan as an example from which he formulates generalized recommendations for all developing countries. Henry Mwebe's research, however, goes a step further in this regard by focusing on socio-economic rights in the African context.[52] Mwebe examines the impact of water privatization in South Africa on socio-economic rights and services. However, like McBeth and Redding, Mwebe's work addresses for-profit provision and, consequently, is primarily concerned with the problems that arise when the cost-cutting interests of profit-driven firms come into conflict with socio-economic development goals. Although this problem may have an analogy in the increased professionalization and self-preserving interests of NGOs in Africa, it does not address the primary concern of this dissertation: namely, the state's ability to obstruct nonprof-

51 Ibid 386.

52 Henry Mwebe, 'The Impact of Privatisation on Socio-Economic Rights and Services in Africa: The Case of Water Privatisation in South Africa' (Master's Thesis, University of Pretoria 2004).

it provision in scenarios where beneficiaries rely on nonprofit activities for the realization of their social rights.

Writing separately, Joe Oloka-Onyango,[53] Danwood Mzikenge Chirwa[54] and Aoife Nolan[55] examine state responsibility for private interferences with human rights. Although Chirwa examines human rights generally, Nolan and Oloka-Onyango focus their work on interferences with social, economic and cultural rights in particular; moreover Oloka-Onyango's attention turns primarily toward the regulation of transnational corporations. While Oloka-Onyango emphasizes how the "uniqueness of the African experience" and the particularities of African human rights law calls for a more robust protection of economic, social and cultural rights, Chiwa and Nolan employ a broad international scope without focusing extensively on the African context.[56] Ultimately, their respective works make the case that the state is responsible for harmful private conduct rather than considering the scenario envisioned by this dissertation, wherein it is rather the state's conduct that (often inadvertently) threatens social rights.

Ada Okoye Ordor's work on not-for-profit laws in Africa is a meaningful contribution to this area of scholarship.[57] Ordor asserts that comprehensive, simplified and administrable legislative frameworks for regulating the non-profit sector would be most advisable in African countries due to the emphasis on people- and development-focused approaches. While, Ordor's article provides a good overview of various legislative models in Africa for not-for profit law, her work is different than mine in part because she leans on the protection of associational rights as her normative framework. She urges for the "ongoing surveillance and safeguarding of a hard-won enabling legal environment" so as to ensure the protection of associational activities.[58] Moreover, her analysis includes all non-profit organizations

53 Joe Oloka-Onyango, 'Reinforcing Marginalized Rigths in an Age of Globalization: International Mechanisms, Non-State Actors, and the Struggle for Peoples' Rights in Africa' 18 American University International Law Review 851 (2002-2003).

54 Danwood Mzikenge Chirwa, 'The Doctrine of State Responsibility as a Potential Means of Holding Private Actors Accountable for Human Rights' 5 Melbourne Journal of International Law 1 (2004).

55 Aoife Nolan, 'Addressing Economic and Social Rights Violations by Non-State Actors through the Role of the State: A Comparison of Regional Approaches to the 'Obligation to Protect'' 9 Human Rights Law Review 225 (2009).

56 Although Nolan limits his research to the regional level.

57 Ada Okoye Ordor, 'The Non-Profit Sector in the Context of Law in Development in Africa' 58 Journal of African Law 45 (2014).

58 Ibid 68.

generally, while this dissertation brings into sharper focus those nonprofits that are particularly important for the realization and enjoyment of social rights.

Summary of Argumentation

This dissertation builds the following line of argumentation. To begin with, international and regional human rights laws impose certain obligations upon states regarding the realization and enjoying of social rights within their territories. Because Africa's LDCs have limited institutional capacity and resources, they often do to fulfill the basic social needs of their people and sometimes fail to fulfill their own social rights obligations. In such cases, nonprofit activities that fill protection gaps serve as functional substitutes for or supplements of the state's own social welfare activities. Crucially, this means that such some NGOs are fulfilling the social rights obligations of the state. Therefore, the social rights of beneficiaries, which apply against states, give rise to implicit state obligations toward the NGOs. In other words, the legal relationship between the state and the beneficiaries of nonprofit activities can influence the legal relationship between the state and the nonprofits when those nonprofits fulfill the state's social rights obligations. These implicit state obligations toward NGOs include the obligation to facilitate and permit certain nonprofit activities. Finally, judicial review of restrictive NGO laws in LDCs should employ a heightened level of scrutiny if the court concludes that nonprofit providers are discharging the social obligations of the state.

One court in South Africa has already taken this approach to justify extensive judicial oversight of a governmental measure that regulated the funding of NGO services in the province of Free State. The following paragraphs of this introductory chapter are dedicated to summarizing the court's judgment. The keystone in this decision is a finding that nonprofits can sometimes fulfill state obligations. While the South African decision follows a similar line of argumentation to that which is presented in this dissertation, it falls short of conducting a systematic inquiry into the social and legal foundations that support its argument. The present dissertation contributes to the understanding of NGO regulations by filling this gap. The following discussion of the South African decision should serve as a preview that pulls together many of the elements that will be discussed throughout this dissertation in some depth, and offers a hint of the legal and societal relevance of the issues involved.

A Preview: The Decision of a South African Court in Free State

How might courts apply the normative position that certain NGOs are discharging the state's outstanding social obligations? A series of decisions issued by a judge in the Free State province of South Africa demonstrates how judicial recognition of this normative position can trigger rigorous judicial review of NGO regulations in order to protect the social rights of beneficiaries.

The South African court issued multiple decisions over the course of four years, yet they all deal with the same facts, involve the same parties, and bear the same case name. As such, I will refer to them collectively as *National Association of Welfare Orgs. v. Member of the Executive Council for Social Development*.[59] The applicants in all four cases were NGOs in South Africa that provided social services to children, the elderly and people in vulnerable situations within the province of Free State. The respondents were various governmental agencies that were responsible for the distribution of funding subsidies to the applicants and all other qualifying NGOs.

In the province of Free State, the government delivered directly through public institutions only a small portion of the core services that it was obliged to ensure. The remaining core services were either not provided or were delivered by NGOs through a special arrangement with the state. On the one hand, the government incorporated NGOs into part of its plan for delivering social services by granting funding awards to NGOs who provided core services. On the other hand, the government systematically underfunded NGOs through its financial awards program and thus many NGOs provided part of their services as though they were substituting for the government, meaning that they did so without the public financial support. In the worst cases, certain beneficiaries simply did not receive

59 *National Association of Welfare Organisations and Non-Governmental Organisations and Others v. Mec of Social Development, Free State and Others*, 2010 ZAFSHC 73, 1719/2010 (Free St. High Ct. 2010) (S. Afr.); *National Association of Welfare Organization and Non-Governmental Organizations and Others v. Mec for Social Development, Free State and Others* 2011 ZAFSHC 84, 1719/2010 (Free St. High Ct. 2011) (S. Afr.); *National Association of Welfare Organisations and Non-Governmental Organisations and Others v. Mec for Social Development, Free State and Others* 2013 ZAFSHC 49, 1719/2010 (Free St. High Ct. 2013) (S. Afr.); *National Association of Welfare Organisations and Non-Governmental Organisations and Others v. Mec for Social Development, Free State and Others* 2014 ZAFSHC 127, 1719/2010 (Free St. High Ct. 2014) (S. Afr.).

core services because no NGO or public institutions could provide it to them.

Under these circumstances, the court evaluated and supervised multiple revisions of the state's NGO financing policy to determine whether systematically underfunding all NGOs was consistent with the state's obligation to provide core services to the residents of Free State. The court's key finding that legitimized extensive judicial supervision over state financing policy was that NGOs in Free State were fulfilling the social rights obligations of the state.

The provincial government awarded grants to NGOs in accordance with a policy guideline entitled the *Policy on Financial Awards to the Nonprofit Organisations in the Social Development Sector*.[60] Pursuant to policy guidelines, the government would deduct from an NGO's award the amount that it determined the NGO should contribute from its own resources toward the costs of service delivery. In 2010, the applicants sued the state in order to challenge the constitutionality of the government's financing policy on the grounds that it arbitrarily and unreasonably determined how much an NGO should contribute from its own resources toward the provision of social services.

In trial, the government openly admitted that NGOs played a vital role in filling essential service gaps left behind by limited public provisioning. Of the 2000 beds that were needed in child and youth centers in Free State, the government provided only approximately 320 while NGOs provided nearly 800. [61] Most services for street children were also provided by NGOs. [62] Moreover, NGOs provided 40 % of those services that were statutorily required to be performed by social workers, such as safeguarding children in need of care, recruiting foster parents, family reunification and supervision, adoption services, and services regarding alcohol and drug dependence. [63] Remarkably, the delivery of all statutorily guaranteed services in six towns fell squarely on the shoulders of merely one NGO.[64]

The applicants demonstrated that despite the critical role of NGOs in the realization of social rights, the government continuously underfunded their programs. For example, although one NGO provided residential care

60 *National Association of Welfare Organisations v. Mec of Social Development (2010)* para. 19.
61 Ibid para. 13.
62 Ibid para. 15.
63 Ibid para. 18.
64 Ibid para. 17-18.

centers for 1000 older persons, the government funded only 290 of those residents.[65] Another NGO that cared for children in need only received enough funding to provide three basic meals at R11.84[66] per child per day, although a daily minimum of R50.00 was required per child.[67] Likewise, for the care of street children, the NGO received R400-R500 per child per month, which was a far cry from the R2000 per month that was needed for each child. The court found the R1,925 per month received by another NGO for the care of older persons in vulnerable situations was "substantially inadequate".[68] Without enough funding from the government, NGOs would have had to cut back on their services or terminate them all together.

To determine whether the funding policy violated the state's obligations, the court first determined what those obligations were by examining the social rights of children, the elderly and persons in vulnerable situations. The constitution and statutory law (Children's Act, 38 of 2005) guaranteed children the protection of the state when they were removed from the family environment. These protections included the right to "basic nutrition, shelter, basic health care services and social services."[69] The court relied on *South Africa and Others v. Grootboom and Others* to reinforce the primacy of the state's duty to guarantee these basic provisions to children without families.[70] Asserting a reasonableness standard, the court wrote, "…the State is obliged to take reasonable measures to the maximum extent of its available resources to achieve the realization of the rights of children…"[71]

After evaluating the NGO funding policy of Free State, the court concluded that the policy was "fundamentally flawed" because, although the state recognized the importance of NGO services, the funding policy,

---

65 Ibid para. 15.
66 Currency is in South African Rands.
67 *National Association of Welfare Organisations v. Mec of Social Development (2010)* para. 34.
68 Ibid para. 35.
69 Constitution of South Africa (1996) § 28(1) (b)-(d).
70 *National Association of Welfare Organisations v. Mec of Social Development (2010)* para. 40. See also, *Government of the Republic of South Africa and Others v. Grootboom and Others*, 1 SA 46, CCT 11/00 (CC 2000) (S. Afr.) para. 77 ("The State thus incurs the obligation to provide shelter to those children, for example, who are removed from their families.").
71 *National Association of Welfare Organisations v. Mec of Social Development (2010)* para. 44.

> ...fail[ed] to recognize, as a fundamental principle of funding, that NPOs [non-profit organizations] that provide care to children, older persons and vulnerable persons in need as well as statutory services, fulfill constitutional and statutory obligations of the [governmental] department.[72]

In essence, NGOs were discharging the social obligations of the state, and the terms of the government's funding policy needed both to reflect and to be consistent with that notion. The court went on to conclude that while it was reasonable for funding determinations to take into account alternative funding sources that were likely available to NGOs, it needed to do so in accordance with a reasonable and transparent method of determination, which the funding policy lacked.[73]

Furthermore, the court held that the funding guidelines must not systematically underfund NGOs by approving grants amounting to only a fraction of the minimum amount needed by each NGO. In 2010 and 2011, the amount granted to NGOs was 49% less than the amount that they needed.[74] The government should ensure that the amount calculated for each NGO "does not result in the service required by the department not being provided."[75] The underlying reasoning is that inadequate funding is likely to result in inadequate provision of services, or none at all, which pose constitutional problems with respect to the rights of beneficiaries. The court elaborates on this point:

> Imagine now that the financial award allocated to the NPO is 49% less that the amount [required] which the department itself calculated as the reasonable cost to care for these children. This gives rise to many questions. What is the NPO to do in the circumstances? How will the human dignity of the child be maintained? And what about their rights to equality, because they may suffer solely as a result thereof that they happen to be referred to the NPO's child and youth care center and not, for instance, to one of the department's own institutions? Will this not result in the failure of the NPO's programme and resultant effective waste of the financial award to it?[76]

---

72 Ibid para. 47.
73 Ibid para. 48-49.
74 *National Association of Welfare Organisations v. Mec of Social Development (2011)* para. 17.
75 Ibid para. 25.
76 Ibid para. 17.

The court concluded that the funding policy was irrational and unreasonable because it underfunded all NGO-provided services, rather than prioritizing and adequately funding just a few essential NGO services.[77] "There is therefore no reason" writes the court "for the senseless procedures of approval of service plans that cannot be fully funded…and payment of palpably insufficient amounts to all approved NPO's."[78] In concluding that the funding policy guidelines failed to comply with the state's constitutional obligations, the court emphasized that funding guidelines "must not result in merely paying lip service to the fundamental principle of funding that NPOs that care for children, older persons or vulnerable persons in need or provide statutory services fulfill the obligation of the department."[79] In the end, in order to ensure that the funding guidelines complied with the state's social obligations toward the beneficiary, the court recognized a legal claim on the part of NGOs and dedicating no less than four years of close judicial supervision over multiple revisions of the NGO funding guidelines in Free State.

The most important finding of the court was that the NGOs fulfilled the state's social rights obligations to the beneficiaries. This allowed the court to hold the state to a higher standard of care regarding the manner in which it regulates NGOs. Ultimately, the regulation of NGOs was a concern for the social rights of beneficiaries. This dissertation will elaborate on this argument from the perspective of human rights law. The following chapter, chapter 2, briefly provides some background information to help situate the issue within its socio-economic, historical, and political contexts. Chapter 3 then outlines the social rights of beneficiaries under international and regional human rights law and explains how NGO-government relations can affect interference with beneficiaries' social rights. This raises the issue of whether the state's social rights obligations to beneficiaries gives rise to certain regulatory obligations toward NGOs in order to ensure the protection, respect and fulfillment of the social rights of beneficiaries.

Since not all NGOs will fulfill the state's social rights obligations, chapter 4 offers a classification of NGOs based on their propensity to fulfill social rights obligations of the state as well as whether they are essential for the realization and enjoyment of the social rights of beneficiaries. This chapter relies on the law of social rights as it is laid down in the Interna-

77 Ibid para. 22.
78 Ibid.
79 Ibid para. 25.

tional Covenant on Economic, Social and Cultural Rights (ICESCR) and the African Charter.

Chapter 5 looks at how differences in the triangular relations that bind the various types of NGOs to their beneficiaries and to the state reflect differences in the legal relations among them. In particular, the state's social rights obligations to beneficiaries can augment the state's legal relation with NGOs by imposing upon the state special regulatory requirements *vis-à-vis* the nonprofit sector. Different NGO types – as they are presented in chapter 3's typology – enjoy different degrees of freedom from tight regulatory control and varying levels of state support.

Chapter 6 considers when it might be acceptable for a state to restrict and even obstruct NGOs even though doing so would limit the enjoyment of social rights for their beneficiaries. This chapter relies on the general clauses of the ICESCR, which lay out the state's obligations and powers regarding the limitation of Covenant rights. The dissertation closes with a summary and some brief concluding remarks on the role of the judiciary in these matters.

2. Background: Social Development and NGOs in Africa

Many argue that a primary function of the modern democratic state is to promote the welfare of its people, which in turn supports the state's legitimacy.[80] In African countries, where state legitimacy is often contentious, states have garnered acceptance with their populations through social provisioning. Social welfare was an essential component of legitimate governance in pre-colonial African societies.[81] Likewise, expanding social welfare was central to the legitimacy of post-colonial states.[82] Furthermore, when welfare provisioning declined in the 1980s, it undermined the social contract and threatened to unravel social and political stability.[83] If ensuring social welfare is such a core function of the state that is tied to its very legitimacy, then what is to be made of poorer states that struggle to address severe and widespread human suffering? Does the state still bear any responsibilities to ensure social welfare when it lacks the resources or the capacity to provide services directly?

These questions are particularly relevant for African LDCs, where human welfare is quite dim. Many African states claim their failure to alleviate poverty and guarantee human security is justified due to the unavailability of resources. However, a state's resources amount to far more than merely its financial capacity. In African LDCs, where financial resources are indeed scarce, analysts must look beyond whether the state is directly providing social services in order to determine whether it is in fact doing all that it can do to promote social welfare. In particular, since the nonprofit provision of social services is an important avenue of social protec-

---

80 Paul Spicker, *Principles of Social Welfare: An Introduction to Thinking About the Welfare State* (Routledge 1988) 53; Wisdom Gagakuma and Zigiju Samuel, 'Effectiveness of Capacity Building Programs in Fragile States: The Ethiopia Case' in Dele Olowu and Paulos Chanie (eds), *State Fragility and State Building in Africa: Cases from Eastern and Southern Africa* (Springer International Publishing 2015) 113-134, 136-137; Edward Kofi Quashigah, 'Legitimate Governance: The Pre-Colonial African Perspective' in Edward Kofi Quashigah and Obiora Chinedu Okafor (eds), *Legitimate Governance in Africa: International and Domestic Legal Perspectives* (Springer Netherlands 1999) 43-66; Adebayo O. Olukoshi, *The Politics of Opposition in Contemporary Africa* (Stylus Pub Llc 1998).

81 Quashigah.

82 Olukoshi (1998) 19-20.

83 Ibid.

tion in African LDCs, any state measure that has the effect or purpose of obstructing nonprofit activities should raise serious doubt about whether the state is doing all that it can do to promote social welfare.

In order to understand how the regulation of NGOs might interfere with the social rights of beneficiaries, it is helpful first to understand the contexts within which NGOs have emerged in Africa, the role that they have played in the realization of social rights, their relation to foreign aid, and the growing anti-NGO sentiments advanced by their critics. The current chapter will provide this background in preparation for the legal analysis that follows.

2.1. Theory and Context

The following sections provide the theoretical and socio-economic foundations upon which the legal analysis is built. In particular, social development is discussed in relation to law and theory as well as the socio-economic context of Africa's LDCs. In particular, this sub-section examines the existing socio-economic context of African beneficiaries and how states and NGOs have both been involved in the alleviation and exacerbation of social rights. This is meant to provide a factual and conceptual background for a better understanding of the challenges that states face when regulating NGOs and how those regulations can interfere with the social rights of beneficiaries.

2.1.1. Social Development in Theory and Law

Social development theories underlie any understanding of the way that NGOs relate to the governments of least developed African countries, which in turn affects the legal relations between them. The term 'social development' connotes the progress made within a society as measured by indicators of social wellbeing, such as health and education outcomes. Since such indicators continue to reveal a bleak picture of social wellbeing in sub-Saharan Africa, social protection is an important component to development theory and practice in African states. This is particularly true in the context of social service provision, which is considered a key component of the 'solution' to development problems.[84] As such, development scholars, who work in a wide range of disciplines linked to the social sciences, have proposed theories and models to explain and analyze the various social provision arrangements that arise within different societies. Thus, a basic understanding of development theories is helpful to examining the duties of the state toward NGO service providers.

2.1.1.1. Development Theories

Development theories suggest that social provision in developing countries typically involves a variety of non-state and international actors because the capacity of developing countries is constrained by the limited availability of financial and technical resources. So as to properly conceptualize the relationship between government and NGOs in the provision of social service, the following paragraphs briefly summarize the relevant theories and models from development studies.

Early development theories supported state-centered service provision. Development theorists and practitioners initially believed that transplanting a centralized, bureaucratic and top-down model from certain European countries into poorer countries would be the most effective and appropriate way to solve the problems of under-development.[85] In terms of provisioning, this approach would advance centralized service provision by the government. Others refer to these earlier ideas within development studies as structuralist theories because they emphasized the role of the state and of planning.[86] Structuralism relied upon economic theories on

---

84 Armando Barrientos, 'Social Protection' in Bruce Currie-Adler and others (eds), *International Development: Ideas, Experience & Prospects* (Oxford University Press 2014) 188-203, 188 & 191; Lant Pritchett and Michael Woolcock, 'Solutions When the Solution Is the Problem: Arraying the Disarray in Development' 32 World Development 191 (2004) 192 (noting how most development studies scholars agree that key social services should be part of the development agenda).

85 David Williams, 'The Study of Development' in Bruce Currie-Adler and others (eds), *International Development: Ideas, Experience & Prospects* (Oxford University Press 2014) 21-34, 23-26 (noting that development studies has always struggled with how far it can generalize the knowledge generated within its discipline into policy prescriptions for all developing countries.).

86 John Harriss, 'Development Theories' in Bruce Currie-Adler and others (eds), *International Development: Ideas, Experience & Prospects* (Oxford University Press 2014) 35-49, 38-40.

the failure of markets to provide public goods.[87] This theory suggests that, due to the presence of market imperfections such as information asymmetries, moral hazard, externalities and the free rider problem, only government can ensure the provision of certain goods, often referred to as public or collective goods.[88] The market, with its competitive ethos and profit-distributing imperatives, simply could not effectively overcome these imperfections. For some time, structuralist development policies were fairly popular. After years of implementing what Lant Pritchett and Michael Woolcock refer to as "the strategy of 'skipping straight to Weber'", the results yielded some successful cases – however, not without many disastrous failures.[89]

Later, liberalist thinking became prominent in development practice. Liberal policies championed by international financial institutions were implemented in developing countries to pry markets open through slashing government expenditure and privatizing service provision. These policies also failed to deliver meaningful results and were largely criticized by the 1990s. As a result, disarray and disagreement emerged within in development studies, leading one scholar to note that "by the 1990s development theory was in crisis, given the practical failures of both structuralism and of liberalism, and the fact that many developing countries, particularly in Africa, were experiencing violence and civil war."[90] The lesson, it seems, is that development theories needed a more nuanced and perhaps less ideological approach.

---

87 Public goods (or 'collective goods') are goods that, once produced, can be consumed by additional consumers at no additional costs, and from which consumers cannot be excluded. (Paul A. Samuelson, 'The Pure Theory of Public Expenditure' 36 The Review of Economics and Statistics 387 (1954); Randall G. Holcombe, 'A Theory of the Theory of Public Goods' 10 Review of Austrian Economics 1 (1997).).

88 Samuelson (1954) 389; William H. Oakland, 'Theory of Public Goods' in Alan J. Auerbach and Marin Feldstein (eds), *Handbook of Public Economics*, vol 2 (1987) 485-535, 485, 509; Robert P. Inman, 'Markets, Governments, and the "New" Political Economy' in Alan J. Auerbach and Marin Feldstein (eds), *Handbook of Public Economics*, vol 2 (1987) 647-776, 653-672 ("...in many important instances governments are necessary for economic efficiency, and...the central features of those instances is the need for the coercive enforcement of cooperative behavior among self-seeking agents.").

89 Pritchett and Woolcock (2004).

90 Harriss 44-46.

2.1.1.2. Theories on Service Provision in Developing Countries

In terms of achieving the realization of social rights, there is no single development strategy that has worked or will work for all states. Most scholars now agree that the emergence of social welfare in developed countries is primarily a consequence of history rather than the predominance of liberalist or structuralist thinking. Each regime developed over time in response to the particular dynamic socio-political conditions within which it was embedded.[91] Understandably, scholars warn against hastily transferring the approaches used by developed countries into the social policies of today's developing countries, as though they were golden standards of development. As Armando Barrientos remarks, while

> [t]here is a great deal for us to learn from the experiences of developed countries as regards poverty reduction and development... conditions in developing countries strongly recommend against transferring European approaches and institutions slavishly to developing countries.[92]

In terms of service provisioning, scholars reject a "one-size fits all" approach, offering instead a variety of approaches as alternatives to both the centralized-bureaucratic approach and the liberal privatization agenda.[93] Pritchett and Woolcock examined the array of service arrangements currently proposed by development scholars. Their analysis indicates that due to the immense complexity and expense of providing social services, no single service arrangement can be heralded as a universally appropriate solution for service provision in all countries.[94]

Although others might reasonably disagree, these authors argue that the complexities of service provision are inherently incompatible with the log-

91 See Salamon and Anheier (1998); Walter Korpi, 'An Augmented Rational-Action Analysis of the Origins and Path Dependency of Welfare State Institutions in Western Countries' 13 Rationality and Society 235 (2001).

92 Barrientos 192.

93 Ibid 191-193; Pritchett and Woolcock (2004) 203-206.

94 They argue that since providing social services requires a high volume of human-to-human interaction ("transaction intensive") and a great deal of independent decision-making authority on the part of professionalized providers ("discretionary practices"), service provision is extraordinarily difficult for any single sector within a society to perform on its own – let alone any single sector of a developing nation. (Pritchett and Woolcock (2004) 204.).

ic and imperatives of large-scale bureaucratic provisioning.[95] At the same time, they assert that neoliberal calls to "amputate" the state by weakening its role in service provision are shortsighted because some services will not be provided to the population without substantial state support.[96] Neither an amputation of government nor an intensification of the same large-scale Weberian bureaucratic approach to development is appropriate for the provision of services that are transaction intensive and discretionary.[97] Pritchett and Woolcock advocate instead for an approach that models different solutions for different societies based on the peculiarities of their underlying conditions.[98] In particular, societies should strike a cooperative balance between government, private providers and beneficiaries:

> It is in the tension between the interests and incentives of administrators, clients, and front-line providers that the solutions (plural) lie. These tensions—between specialists and the people, planners and citizens, authority and autonomy—cannot be escaped; rather, they need to be made creative rather than destructive.[99]

Third sector scholars bolster this recommendation. They argue that government-private partnership is a staple of modern social policy. Lester Salamon explains why both the state and the voluntary sector are necessary for the effective provision of social services. His third-party government theory posits that the government's involvement in welfare provision is the inevitable consequence of failures in both the market and the voluntary sector.[100] He emphasizes the primacy of private nonprofit provision by arguing that where the government emerges as the solution for failures in the voluntary sector, the government takes on a supportive subsidiary role in partnership with nonprofit providers. Salamon reasons that government and the nonprofit sector benefit mutually from one another and are thus interdependent. He explains that, "governments and nonprofits are the yin and yang of modern social policy, with superbly synched patterns of strengths and weaknesses."[101]

---

95 Ibid 195-196.

96 Ibid 201-202. See also Harriss 43-44 (noting the rise and fall in the 1980s of market-first theories in development studies, as well as the policies they inspired, which precipitated Africa's 'lost decade' of delayed development).

97 Pritchett and Woolcock (2004) 201-202.

98 Ibid 207.

99 Ibid (internal citation omitted).

100 Salamon (1987).

101 Salamon (2015) 2150.

There are some problems with using Salamon's theory in the African context. Having been developed with wealthier states in mind, the third-party government theory presumes that governments have the capacity to provide services neglected by the nonprofit sector. It is questionable whether this presumption holds true for African LDCs, where governments have limited capacity to provide public services each time the voluntary sector fails to do so.[102] Empirical evidence on the collective volunteerism in Africa seems to suggests, at least at the grassroots level, that non-state provision emerges in low-capacity states in order to fill service gaps left behind by government, not the other way around as Salamon theorizes.[103] In other words, in low-capacity states, it is more likely that government failure mobilizes non-state provision, rather than voluntary sector failure tending to inspire the provision of public social services.

Moreover, Wolfgang Seibel's theory of functional dilettantism contests Salamon's underlying premise that the government's interest in collaborating with the nonprofit sector is the potential for improving the effectiveness and efficiency of service provision.[104] More recently, Salamon has written,

> ...in different ways, and in widely differing environments, a significant process of "nonprofitization" of the welfare state is taking place as governments turn increasingly to nonprofit organizations to assist in carrying out publicly funded functions.... suggesting a growing realization of the limitations facing exclusive reliance on state institutions in the delivery of important human services and of the special qualities that nonprofit organization can bring to the social welfare arena as an active collaborator of the state.[105]

In contrast, Seibel posits instead that governments work with nonprofits precisely because nonprofits are prone to voluntary failures. In this way,

---

102 MacLean (2017) (noting that, with Botswana and South Africa as notable exceptions, African governments have weak capacity to deliver or finance social services).

103 Erin Hern, 'In the Gap the State Left: Policy Feedback, Collective Behavior, and Political Participation in Zambia' 52 Studies in Comparative International Development 510 (2017).

104 Wolfgang Seibel, *Funktionaler Dilettantismus: Erfolgreich Scheiternde Organisationen Im "Dritten Sektor" Zwischen Markt Und Staat* (Nomos-Verlag-Ges. 1992).

105 Salamon (2015) 2154.

governments that offload social problems that they cannot or simply desire not to fix can appear to do so legitimately.[106]

Historical perspectives have contributed a different understanding to the emergence of nonprofit service providers in Africa. Burton Allen Weisbrod theorized that nonprofit provision emerged because governments failed to provide services that were in demand.[107] His conclusion is observable in African societies, namely that the nonprofit sector grows in order to fill the service gaps left behind by government failure whenever the third sector has the financial capability to do so, and whenever there is a demand for such services.[108] However, the underlying political mechanisms in his theory do not appear to describe African LDCs very well with respect to both the demand for and supply of nonprofit services.

On the demand side, Weisbrod's theory suggests that minority voters determine the level, nature and quality of services that NGOs will provide. His theory relies on the presence of a functioning democratic system, wherein the government 'hears' voters through fair and competitive elections, and thereafter fulfills the social demand of the median voter. In heterogeneous societies, groups of minority voters, whose political interests were 'unheard' by the government, then come together to provide supplementary services through the voluntary sector. Such an efficient and effective democratic process is far from the reality observed in many African states.[109] Thus, while voter competition is likely a relevant factor to the growth of nonprofit services in electoral democracies, this democratic nar-

106 Wolfgang Seibel, 'The Function of Mellow Weakness: Nonprofit Organizations as Problem Nonsolvers in Germany' in Estelle James (ed), *The Nonprofit Sector in International Perspective: Studies in Comparative Culture & Policy* (Oxford University Press 1989) 177-192; Wolfgang Seibel, 'Successful Failure' 39 American Behavioral Scientist 1011 (1996).

107 Burton Allen Weisbrod (ed), *The Voluntary Nonprofit Sector: An Economic Analysis* (Lexington Books 1977).

108 See, e.g., Jennifer N. Brass, 'Why Do NGOs Go Where They Go? Evidence from Kenya' 40 World Development 387 (2012) 395 (finding that in Kenya, "on a per capita basis, NGOs are more prevalent in [geographic] places where the state is weak" and estimating that nearly a quarter of NGOs worked in health and education sector); Jennifer N. Brass, 'Blurring Boundaries: The Integration of NGOs into Governance in Kenya' 25 Governance 209 (2012) 220-221, 216 (finding that over 90% of NGOs in Kenya focus on service provision, and that the government explicitly relies on NGOs for the funding and delivering of services, including in the education and health sectors.).

109 *Populists and Autocrats: The Dual Threat to Global Democracy,* Freedom House, (Freedom in the World, 2017) 11, 20-24 <https://freedomhouse.org/sites/default/files/FH_FIW_2017_Report_Final.pdf>.

rative alone cannot explain the rise of nonprofits in Africa. Instead, government failure in service provision is likely the consequence of challenges of a more structural nature. As a result of continued economic and political instability, as well as neo-patrimonial political systems, African LDCs likely lack the institutional and financial capacities in addition to the political incentives to deliver the services that are in demand.[110] Furthermore, the demand for NGO services is more likely to reflect the extent to which the needs of beneficiaries coincide with donor interests rather than the outcome of competitive elections. Since many African beneficiaries have little political clout to affect reforms in domestic social law and policy, domestic social institutions and social laws are not likely to offer adequate legal protection for social rights. This suggests that international law and non-state actors are could play an important role for the realization and enjoyment of social rights in African LDCs.

On the supply side, Weisbrod's theory presumes citizens are financially capable consumers who purchase supplementary services delivered through the nonprofit sector. However, the average person in Africa is not the primary source of financial support for nonprofit providers because her personal financial resources are severely limited. People in Africa live in the poorest region of the world. The World Bank reported that in 2013, over 40% of people in Sub-Saharan Africa lived below the international poverty line, and that "the region's poor are, on average, living much further below the US$1.90-a-day extreme threshold" than all other regions of the world.[111] All in all, Sub-Saharan Africa is home to half of the world's poor.[112] When the third sector fills service gaps resulting from government failure, its services are not financed predominantly through user fees paid by minority voters, as Weisbrod's theory presumes. Evidence on foreign

110 See Philippa Bevan, 'The Dynamics of Africa's in/Security Regimes' in Ian Gough and Geof Wood (eds), *Insecurity and Welfare Regimes in Asia, Africa and Latin America: Social Policy in Development Contexts* (Cambridge University Press 2004); Ian Gough, 'Welfare Regimes in Development Contexts: A Global and Regional Analysis' in Ian Gough and others (eds), *Insecurity and Welfare Regimes in Asia, Africa and Latin America* (Cambridge University Press 2004) 15-47; Michael Bratton, *Civil Society and Political Transition in Africa*, Institute for Development Research, 6 (Reports, 1994) 8-9 <https://www.issuelab.org/resources/19673/19673.pdf> 8.

111 *Taking on Inequality*, World Bank, (Poverty and Shared Prosperity) 36 <https://openknowledge.worldbank.org/bitstream/handle/10986/25078/9781464809583.pdf?sequence=24&isAllowed=y> (Note that the international poverty line is set at 1.90 USD per person per day).

112 Ibid 37.

funding[113] suggests rather strongly that the rise of NGO-providers in Africa has been made possible by the availability of *foreign* aid, rather than through the personal resources of the median voter. In other words, nonprofits in Africa receive substantial financial support from foreign donors. This suggests that state efforts to restrict access to foreign funding for nonprofits in African LDCs should raise concerns about the viability of the nonprofit sector, as well as the social rights of beneficiaries that depend on it.

In acknowledgment of the various ways in which nonprofit sectors have developed around the world, more recent scholarship has tried to categorize the different paths of emergence. Taking a historical view, Salamon and Anheier use social origins theory to postulate that country-specific social histories related to class struggles have shaped the scale of the nonprofit sector and its embeddedness within the state's social policy framework.[114] They conclude by offering a typology of nonprofit development based on dominant historical trends. These models characterize the way in which nonprofits are embedded into the state structure.[115]

This work, however, was developed with reference to the social histories of advanced industrial societies with sizeable urban middle classes.[116] As such, it is not evident that such a theory would explain the emergence, scale and embeddedness of African nonprofit sectors.[117] Melanie Cammett

113 See *supra* part 0on the extent to which NGOs in Africa rely on foreign funding.

114 Salamon and Anheier (1998); see also Gøsta Esping-Andersen, *The Three Worlds of Welfare Capitalism* (Princeton University Press 1990) (using a similar analysis to offer three state models prior to Salamon and Anheier's contribution, but without focusing on the emergence of the third sector).

115 They are *liberal* (e.g., U.S. & U.K.), *statist* (e.g., Japan), *corporatist* (e.g., Germany & France) and *social democratic* (e.g., Sweden & Italy). (Salamon and Anheier (1998).).

116 According to Salamon and Anheier, while states in the liberal nonprofit regime serve the interests of the middle class, they predominantly serve their own interests in the statist model. The corporatist regime is the consequence of political compromise between various classes, which forced the state to work with nonprofits in service provision. Social democratic regimes emerged when an organized working class managed to dominate the political reigns of the state. (Ibid.).

117 The majority of LDCs in Africa are predominately service-oriented or agricultural economies. (*Extreme Poverty Eradication in the Least Developed Countries and the Post-2015 Development Agenda,* United Nations Under-Secretary-General and High Representative for LDCs, LLDCs and SIDS, (State of the Least Developed Countries, 2014) 84-88 <http://unohrlls.org/custom-content/uploads/2014/10/State-of-the-Least-Developed-Countries-Report-2014.pdf>.).

and Lauren M. MacLean offer another typology of nonprofit-government relations in service provision, which is comparable to Salamon and Anheier's models, but for the emphasis on historical class struggles.[118] Cammett and MacLean focus instead on the comparative capacities of the state and nonprofit sector to provide social services. They identify four modes of service provision, each characterized by a high or low service capacity for the public and nonprofit sectors.[119]

Others have looked more closely at African histories to examine how colonial-era patterns of administration have persisted and influenced the division of labor in social provision today between non-state actors and the government.[120] Wietzke's examination of the geographically uneven supply of private education in sub-Saharan Africa suggests that the present patterns of distribution and prevalence in private schools was influenced by corresponding patterns of missionary schools during the colonial period.[121] Examining the enduring legacies of colonial public institutions, MacLean argues that differences in colonial administrative approaches[122] can account for at least some of the cross-national variation in the preva-

---

118 Melanie Cammett and Lauren M. MacLean (eds), *The Politics of Non-State Welfare* (Cornell University Press 2014).

119 Low capacity states engage low capacity nonprofit sectors in modes of *appropriation*, whereby nonprofit providers control access to limited state resources and services. Low capacity states can also engage high capacity nonprofits through a *substitutional* relationship, where the nonprofit sector steps in to provide services that the state lacks the capacity to provide. According to MacLean, these are the most common relational modes in Africa because most African states have a limited capacity to provide services themselves. In high capacity states, nonprofit-governmental relations can be characterized as either *state-dominated* (low nonprofit capacity) or as a mode of *coproduction* (high nonprofit capacity). (MacLean (2017).).

120 In explaining the origins of NGOs in developing countries, Cammett and MacLean note that dominant theories focus on market failures, state failures, or pro-market policies and decentralization reforms of the 1980s. Although, as the authors point out, these theories cannot explain variations across different developing countries. They argue instead that "variations in non-state social welfare in many developing counties" can be explained by differences in "the particular historical context of state administrative power." (Melanie Cammett and Lauren M. MacLean, 'Introduction' in Melanie Cammett and Lauren M. MacLean (eds), *The Politics of Non-State Welfare* (Cornell University Press 2014) 1-16, 13.).

121 Frank-Borge Wietzke, 'Historical Origins of Uneven Service Supply in Sub-Saharan Africa: The Role of Non-State Providers' 50 The Journal of Development Studies 1614 (2014).

122 Notably, the indirect rule of British colonial administrations as compared to the centralized administration imposed by French colonial authorities.

lence and emergence of nonprofits within West Africa.[123] Her historical assessment suggests that the nonprofit sector flourishes more broadly today in countries that were once governed by decentralized colonial rule, namely former British colonies, and less broadly in countries that were colonized in a centralized administrative manner, such as former French colonies. [124]

Development theory indicates that the best way to provide social services will differ from country to country. However, third sector scholarship points to a growing dependence upon the nonprofit sector for service provision. This suggests that while many types of NGO-state relations could work for the provision of services, NGOs will likely play a significant role in many developing countries. Thus, it is important to consider how NGO-state relations can affect the social rights of beneficiaries, and what such an affect indicates for the social rights obligations of states.

2.1.2. Socio-Economic Context of African LDCs

The realization of socio-economic rights is an important part of development in Africa. This is reflected in the continent's human rights system. As one scholar has noted, the African Charter "narrows the scope of governments to circumvent their collective rights obligations",[125] and the treaty body that interprets the African Charter "has removed any doubt about the enforceability of collective rights".[126] This has led the same commentator to conclude that, "collective rights have been placed at the centre of the African human rights system."[127] Others posit that the African Charter's emphasis on second-generation rights reflects a particularly African concept of human rights.[128]

It has been further asserted that for the Charter to have any meaningful relevance to the needs of African peoples, its implementation must include

---

123 MacLean (2017).

124 Ibid.

125 Kofi Oteng Kufuor, *The African Human Rights System: Origin and Evolution* (Palgrave Macmillan US 2010) 61.

126 Ibid 80.

127 Ibid.

128 See, e.g., H. W. O. Okoth-Ogendo, 'Human and Peoples' Rights: What Point Is Africa Trying to Make?' in Ronald Cohen, Goran Hyden and Winston P. Nagan (eds), *Human Rights and Governance in Africa* (Univeristy Press of Florida 1993) 74-86, 81-82.

a strong emphasis on collective rights.[129] Okoth-Ogendo insists that such assessments

> ...must go beyond what has become the stock-in-trade of Western human rights activism concerning Africa, namely, the endless recital of civil and political rights violations with very little appreciation of the material conditions under which these occur.[130]

Likewise, the African Commission notes that human rights law must respond appropriately to the distinctive circumstances found in Africa, which compels particular attention is paid to the protection of socio-economic rights. The Commission writes:

> The uniqueness of the African situation and the special qualities of the African Charter imposes upon the African Commission an important task. International law and human rights must be responsive to African circumstances. Clearly, collective rights, environmental rights, and economic and social rights are essential elements of human rights in Africa. The African Commission will apply any of the diverse rights contained in the African Charter. It welcomes this opportunity to make clear that there is no right in the African Charter that cannot be made effective...[131]

Because Africa has sustained a staggering degree of poverty and other social ills, an Africanist approach to addressing the human rights challenges of restrictive NGO laws must emphasize the importance of guaranteeing socio-economic rights. In this regard, a general overview of the societal context in Africa's LDCs will assist in understanding the role and impact of nonprofit provision for beneficiaries in those countries. These circumstances indicate the level of social rights realization and also shape the social rights obligations of states, which in turn affect the legal relations be-

---

129 E.g., see generally, Joe Oloka-Onyango, 'Ngo Struggles for Economic, Social, and Cultural Rights in Utake: A Ugandan Perspective' in Makau Mutua (ed), *Human Rights NGOs in East Africa: Political and Normative Tensions* (University of Pennsylvania Press 2009) 75-111; Makau Mutua, 'Human Rights in Africa: The Limited Promise of Liberalism' 51 African Studies Review (2008); Issa G. Shivji, *The Concept of Human Rights in Africa* (Codesria Book Series 1989).

130 Okoth-Ogendo 82; Mikuin Leliel Balanda, 'African Charter on Human and Peoples' Rights' in Konrad Ginther and Wolfgang Benedek (eds), *New Perspectives and Conceptions of International Law: An Afro-European Dialogue* (Springer-Verlag 1984) 134, 137.

131 *Social and Economic Rights Action Center and Center for Economic and Social Rights v. Nigeria*, Communication No. 155/96 (ACmHPR 2001) para 68.

tween NGOs and the state. For the least developed African countries, the social obligations of the state are defined within a context that is characterized by the state's reliance on foreign aid, its subordinate economic position *vis-à-vis* international markets, its limited use of advanced technologies, its fiscal inefficiencies, and growing inequalities within its territory.[132]

African LDCs struggle to meet the very basic needs of many people.[133] In terms of material possessions and vulnerability, approximately 40% of Africa's population lives in poverty.[134] In six African countries, the poverty rate exceeded 70 per cent in 2011.[135]Although the continent's poverty[136] ratio is lower now than in the 1990s, it is the only developing region in the world that has sustained a significant net growth in the absolute number of people living in extreme poverty.[137] Moreover, from 1995-2012, Africa exhibited the lowest poverty reduction rate of all continents.[138] In 2012, the number of people in Africa who lived in poverty was 330 million; more than two out of five adults cannot read or write; and nearly two out of five children are malnourished. [139] By 2013, the number of people living in poverty increased to 388.7 million.[140] The World Bank reported that all of the top ten countries with the highest poverty ratios in 2013 were in Africa, as well as more than half of the top ten countries with the highest number of poor residents.[141] All but one of these African countries listed

---

132 See J. Ferguson, *Global Shadows: Africa in the Neoliberal World Order* (Duke University Press 2006).

133 See, Nsongurua J. Udombana, 'Social Rights Are Human Rights: Actualizing the Rights to Work and Social Security in Africa' 93 Cornell International Law Journal 181 (2006) 210-221.

134 Zivanemoyo Chinzara and others, 'Growth and Development Finance Required for Achieving Sustainable Development Goals (Sdgs) in Africa' 29 African Development Review 15 (2017) 19.

135 Burundi, the Democratic Republic of Congo, Liberia, Madagascar, Malawi and Zambia. (*The Path to Gradution and Beyond: Making the Most of the Process,* United Nations Conference on Trade and Development (UNCTAD), (The Least Deveoped Countries Report, 2016) 19 <http://unctad.org/en/PublicationsLibrary/ldc2016_en.pdf>).

136 Poverty measures were based on the international poverty line, which is 1.90 USD per person per day.

137 World Bank, *Taking on Inequality* 38-39.

138 Kathleen Beegle and others, *Poverty in a Rising Africa,* World Bank Group, (Africa Poverty Report, 2016) 57 <https://openknowledge.worldbank.org/bitstream/handle/10986/22575/9781464807237.pdf?sequence=10&isAllowed=y>.

139 Ibid 1, 12 & 57.

140 World Bank, *Taking on Inequality* 36.

141 Ibid 41.

by the World Bank are also characterized by the United Nations as least developed countries,[142] indicating that it is particularly difficult for them to break out of 'poverty traps' wherein most people receive just enough or not enough income to meet their basic needs.[143]

Exacerbating Africa's development challenges is the fact that public institutions and services remain weak and fragmented, and government resources are limited.[144] In general, social protection schemes on the continent do not benefit from ample investments.[145] In most cases, these schemes are either nonexistent or have very low coverage.[146] For example, primary education is not universal in Africa, and the continent suffers from the largest shortage of teachers worldwide.[147] This makes it a daunting and challenging task for African LDCs to ensure that even the very basic levels of social rights are realized and enjoyed. As noted by the African Union (AU), most African states have "overstretched social infrastructure and facilities, especially, in health, education and employment sectors". [148] The AU noted further that, "[r]educing inequity in access to basic social services remains a major challenge for many African countries."[149]

142 United Nations Conference on Trade and Development (UNCTAD), *The Path to Gradution and Beyond: Making the Most of the Process* (2016) xiii (a country may be designated LCD status only if it meets certain criteria: a maximum national income per capita threshold of $1,035 and low index results based on indicators relating to population nutrition, health, school enrolment, literacy, and economic vulnerability.).

143 Ibid 18.

144 Brian Levy and Sahr John Kpundeh (eds), *Building State Capacity in Africa: New Approaches, Emerging Lessons* (World Bank Publications 2004).

145 Social Policy Framework for Africa, African Union, CAMSD/EXP/4(1) (Afr U 2008) 17 <http://www.un.org/esa/socdev/egms/docs/2009/Ghana/au2.pdf>.

146 Emerging Issues: Social Protection, Commission for Social Development, U.N. Economic and Social Council, UN Doc. E/CN.5/2011/8 (UN 2010) paras. 8-10.

147 *The World Needs Almost 69 Million New Teachers to Reach the 2030 Education Goals,* United Nations Educational, Scientific and Cultural Organization (UNESCO), (UIS Fact Sheet, 2016) <http://unesdoc.unesco.org/images/0024/002461/246124e.pdf>; Kate Hodal, 'UN Warns Universal Education Goal Will Fail without 69 Million New Teachers' *Guardian* (5 Oct. 2016) <https://www.theguardian.com/global-development/2016/oct/05/un-universal-education-goal-fail-69-million-new-teachers-unesco>.

148 Social Policy Framework for Africa (2008) 13, para. 22.

149 Common African Position (CAP) on the Post-2015 Development Agenda, African Union, (AU 2014) 4 <http://www.uneca.org/sites/default/files/uploaded-documents/Macroeconomy/post2015/cap-post2015_en.pdf>.

Without external assistance, it is doubtful that African states are presently capable of mobilizing sufficient domestic resources in order to ensure the enjoyment of even the very basic levels of social welfare, in addition to financing other important governmental expenditures.[150] Indeed, many African states have become dependent on foreign aid. In 1999, 27 sub-Saharan countries received at least 25% of their governments' expenditures from overseas development assistance.[151] While things have improved since then, there are still a number of countries that depend rather heavily on international aid. In 2011, foreign official aid and assistance amounted to more than 25% of government expenditures in at least eight sub-Saharan countries.[152]

A quick review of basic social outcome indicators also suggests that African LDCs do not ensure the enjoyment of social rights at very basic levels.[153] Consider the performance of African states with regard to achieving the right to health through the provision of essential primary health care services.[154] In 2015, the World Health Organization reported that, "as the result of unsafe health care" in hospitals within the African and Eastern Mediterranean regions between 2009 and 2014, over 10,000 deaths were known to have occurred (although some estimates were in the millions).[155] African states can hardly be said to be fulfilling their social rights obligation when patients are being infected with fatal diseases as a result of

150 See *Mobilizing Domestic Financial Resources for Implementing Nepad National and Regional Programmes & Projects: Africa Looks Within*, NEPAD Planning and Coordinating Agency, UN Economic Commission for Africa (2014) <http://www.un.org/africarenewal/sites/www.un.org.africarenewal/files/DRM_ENGLISH_REPRO_OP.pdf> (noting the potential of Africa's domestic financial resources to lift countries out of the aid dependency cycle if only those resources were mobilized and unobstructed by challenges such as poor governance and illicit financial flows.).

151 Deborah A. Bräutigam and Stephen Knack, 'Foreign Aid, Institutions, and Governance in Sub-Saharan Africa' 52 Economic Development and Cultural Change 255 (2004) 257-258.

152 The World Bank, African Development Indicators, *Net ODA Received (% of Central Government Expenditure)* (2017).

153 See, e.g., Beegle and others (2016) *Poverty in a Rising Africa.*

154 General Comment No. 14: The Right to the Highest Attainable Standard of Health, Committee on Economic Social and Cultural Rights, U.N. Doc. E/C.12/2000/4 (UN 2000) para. 43; General Comment No. 3: The Nature of States Parties' Obligations, Committee on Economic Social and Cultural Rights, U.N. Doc. E/1991/23 (UN 1990) para. 10.

155 *Partnerships for Safer Health Service Delivery: Evaluation of Who African Partnerships for Patient Safety 2009-2014,* World Health Organization, WHO/HIS/SDS/

receiving public health care services that are deemed "unsafe". This is but one example of many that illustrate how resource-strapped African states struggle to ensure the enjoyment of very basic levels of social welfare and, in some cases, might even deprive social rights in their efforts to realize them.

Consequently, many people in African LDCs cannot readily depend on their governments to ensure their social rights are realized and enjoyed. Instead, many rely on informal arrangements such as families and mutual assistance schemes at the community level.[156] However, these informal mechanisms are undermined by limited resources, urbanization and other societal factors.[157] Although the state retains the primary obligation to realize social rights, services and assistance provided by nonprofits have become vital for the realization and enjoyment of social rights in the least developed African countries. This results in a triangular engagement that encompasses NGOs (providers or advocates), beneficiaries (rights bearers), and the state (duty bearer). For many people in sub-Saharan Africa, it is through this triangular relationship that the progressive realization of social rights occurs – or is arrested.

2.1.3. Defining Non-Governmental Organizations

NGOs are notoriously difficult to define. Instead of indicating a category of organizations through an affirmative description of what it contains, the term instead describes only what the category *does not contain*: governmental organizations.[158] Thus the 'NGOs' can take on a variety of meanings,

---

2015.13 (2015) 6 <http://www.who.int/patientsafety/implementation/apps/evaluation-report.pdf>.

156 See generally Stephen Devereux and Melese Getu (eds), *Informal and Formal Social Protection in Sub-Saharan Africa* (Fountain Publishers 2013). E.g., Helmut K. Anheier and Lester M. Salamon, *The Nonprofit Sector in the Developing World: A Comparative Analysis* (Manchester United Press 1998) 162-166 (in Ghana, informal traditional organizatons as well as church groups and modern NGOs have played important roles as providers of social and development assistance, including building schools and hospitals and delivering health and social services.).

157 Emerging Issues: Social Protection (2010) para. 7.

158 There is a similar problem with the term "non-state actors". (See Philip Alston, ''Not-a-Cat' Syndrome: Can the International Human Rights Regime Accommodate Non-State Actors?' in Philip Alston (ed), *Non-State Actors and Human Rights* (Oxford University Press 2005) 3-36.).

depending on the purpose of the analysis. For my purposes, I have excluded the private for-profit sector because the way that they are regulated by the state follows an entirely different line of reasoning. Even if businesses like private hospitals provide social services, the primary regulatory concern is controlling the negative effects of profit-seeking behavior, which is not a problem with non-profit entities. Moreover, the emergence and maintenance of the non-profit sector has its own distinct political and historical trajectory that has shaped its relation to the state *vis-à-vis* protecting and fulfilling the social rights of beneficiaries. Furthermore, since the focus of the dissertation is on the fulfillment and protection of social rights, NGOs that are not socially oriented are excluded, such as cultural groups and political parties. Beyond those limits, the term includes a wide range of actors from international NGOs to local community based organizations and faith-based organizations.

I do not limit my analysis to NGOs that provide social services because advocacy NGOs can also contribute significantly to the fulfillment of social rights by alerting the government and others of areas of deficiencies and social need.[159] The line between advocacy and service provision is not always clear.[160] NGOs that provide services often engage in non-confrontational forms of advocacy.[161] There is some evidence to suggest that even when service-providing NGOs are heavily dependent on the state, financially or otherwise, they still influence state policy and practice implicitly and incrementally "by example and interaction while avoiding confrontation with the government."[162] This evidence led researchers to conclude that,

> By comparison with the blunt view of much of the literature –that collaboration [with the state] in service delivery undermines NGOs' freedom to undertake advocacy—our evidence supports the view that it affects how, not whether, they influence policy and its implementation.[163]

---

159 See, Henry J. Steiner, Philip Alston and Ryan Goodman, *International Human Rights in Context: Law, Politics, Morals* (3d edn, Oxford University Press 2008) 368-369.

160 *See supra* part 0on the beneficiary-centered approach.

161 Richard Batley, 'Structures and Strategies in Relationships between Non-Government Service Providers and Governments' 31 Public Administration and Development 306 (2011).

162 Ibid 316.

163 Ibid.

Moreover, even when advocacy NGOs are in a confrontational relationship with the government, they can still have a positive effect on social rights. Consider the example of Zimbabwe, a country situated within a region where the relationship between NGOs and governments has been strained over the last few decades.[164] NGO-government tensions within East Africa have culminated in the promulgation of regulatory frameworks designed to keep NGOs and civil society in line so as to diminish what governments perceive to be threats to their legitimacy in the areas of governance and service provision.[165] In a study of NGO-government relations in Zimbabwe from 1980 to 2000, Sara Dorman explains how a non-controversial stance among NGOs – which reduced them to need-based service providers – hurt social welfare outcomes.[166]

A main contributing factor in their progression toward taking on a non-confrontational stance *vis-à-vis* the government was the tendency among NGOs to professionalize as they grew. Dorman explains that as "donor funding to NGOs increased staff numbers and strengthened their positions *vis-à-vis* volunteers" so too did the "tendency of so-called voluntary organizations to 'professionalize'" themselves.[167] Increased donor funding led to the expansion and 'professionalization' of NGOs in Zimbabwe, thus strengthen their interest in self-preservation.[168]

Consequently, NGOs of the 1990s focused their attention on social service provision in Zimbabwe and maintained a non-adversarial relationship with the government, in part due to material and ideological restraints. NGOs avoided confrontation with government "[e]ven when legislation was implemented to control NGO activity",[169] and even when the Economic Structural Adjustment Programme (ESAP) of the Mugabe government caused visible social harm to the poor. Dorman writes,

---

164 Chris Maina Peter, 'Coming of Age: NGOs and State Accountability' in Makau Mutua (ed), *Human Rights NGOs in East Africa: Political and Normative Tensions* (University of Pennsylvania Press 2009) 305-318, 312-315 (outlining the historical tension between NGOs and the governments of Uganda, Tanzania and Kenya).

165 Ibid.

166 Sara Rich Dorman, 'Inclusion and Exclusion: NGOs and Politics in Zimbabwe' (Doctoral Thesis, University of Oxford 2001).

167 Ibid 163. This internal transition did not happen smoothly. Dorman explains that ideological conflicts emerged between the new career-oriented staff and the "'old, committed' members" as the organizations professionalized.

168 Ibid.

169 Ibid 163, 193.

> The introduction of health user fees and school fees, in urban areas, coupled by decreases in the availability of drugs and equipment for hospitals, have led to decreasing levels of maternal health, and left many others unable to seek medical care or remain in hospital for treatment. School fees have led to declining enrollment in education in urban areas and the overburdening of rural schools, where poor urban children may be sent since there are no school fees.[170]

Aligned with the government in a non-confrontational relationship, NGOs served beneficiaries by focusing on needs-based provision instead of engaging the government on a policy level, even though it was precisely the government's policy that was causing harm to their beneficiaries. Dorman explains,

> Those organizations which might have been expected to lobby for change, particularly for change in socio-economic policies, did not do so. NGOs stress that ESAP's implementation took them by surprise, that people believed the government when it said that the Social Dimensions Fund would support the poor and that they didn't know how to respond to ESAP. Even the ZCTU [Zimbabwe Congress of Trade Unions], which did publically question the implementation of ESAP, moved from a confrontational engagement with the state, to a much more co-operative one between 1992-5.[171]

NGOs in Zimbabwe did away with the kind of right-based advocacy that might have prodded the government into addressing structural obstacles that undermined the realization and enjoyment of social rights.

Things changed in the mid-1990s, however, when Zimbabwe considered rolling out a second phase of structural adjustment programs. This time, at least one international NGO strongly criticized the government's program. In 1994, OXFAM published a damning report on the government's implementation of user-fees and the decline in funding for health. Dorman describes the government's reaction:

> The government's attack on OXFAM alleged factual inaccuracies in the report and their failure to clear the field research conducted with the Government Research Council. The government hinted that OXFAM had come close to abrogating its agreement to "respect the law and institutions of Zimbabwe and...conduct its affairs in consultation

170 Ibid 167.
171 Ibid 168.

> with the Government, people, and institutions of Zimbabwe." The government was appalled at the unnecessarily public character of OXFAM'S disclosure in New York, without having previously shown the material to the Zimbabwean government. A *Financial Times* report alleged that the Zimbabwean government was threatening to expel OXFAM.[172]

The OXFAM report was a form of advocacy that, although adversarial and confrontational, was made on behalf of beneficiaries and with the ultimate aim of ameliorating their deprived living conditions. More importantly, the report may have been effective: Dorman notes that the government removed user fees for rural residents a year later, "suggesting that the government may have rejected the medium, but accepted the message."[173]

A fiery governmental response, such as the threats and ridicule hurled at OXFAM, coupled with highly restrictive regulations, serves to reinforce a submissive role for NGOs within a non-confrontational relationship with government, and undermines the social rights of beneficiaries. Thus, the efforts by governments to censor NGOs or force them into an exclusively provisioning role should raise concerns about the social welfare of beneficiaries. Finally, although not the primary focus of this dissertation, it is worthwhile mentioning that in contemplating the way that NGO advocacy might lead to pro-poor changes in society, knowing the structural framework of power within a state is just as important as understanding the relationship between NGOs and government.[174]

In summary, for the analytical purposes of this dissertation, the term NGOs will be used in reference to organized individuals who do not distribute profits and are not officials or agents of the state. Furthermore, their objectives are charitable and socially oriented, and their activities include service provision and advocacy. This definition is consistent with the way that NGO laws in Africa have typically characterized NGOs. For example, under Kenya's NGO law, the Non-Governmental Organizations

172 Ibid 170.

173 Ibid.

174 Gathering lessons from the confrontational capacity of NGOs in Zimbabwe, Dorman writes,

> ...the process of challenging authority, whether we call it rebellion, revolution, liberation or democratization, must be understood in the context from which it is derived. It is only by understanding the nature of the authoritarian system that we are able to understand the challenge – or lack of challenge – to it. (Ibid 22.).

Co-ordination Act (1990), an NGO is "a private voluntary grouping of individuals" who organize themselves "for the benefit of the public at large and for the promotion of social welfare, development charity or research".[175]

2.2. *NGOs and Social Development*

NGOs have become thoroughly embedded into all sectors of society, in particular during the last few decades. They often play an important role in social welfare in developing countries due to their nonprofit status and their penchant for social justice and the alleviation of poverty. Conversely, NGOs have the capacity to do harm to their beneficiaries, a point which has been duly noted by their critics. This section aims to provide a background on NGOs in sub-Saharan Africa within the context of social development by outlining their promising emergence and reviewing some of the challenges and criticism they have faced in recent years.

2.2.1. Social Protection and the Role of NGOs in Africa

Social protection is conventionally understood as a function of the state in the fulfillment of its duties toward society.[176] Thus, many governments, including those in African countries, focus mainly on building formal systems of social protection.[177] However, formal social protection programs

---

175 Non-Governmental Organizations Co-Ordination Act, No 19 of 1990 (Kenya) § 2 (as amended by The Statute Law (Miscellaneous Amendemendments) Act, 1991, No 14 of 1991 (Kenya) and The Statute Law (Miscellaneous Amendemendments) Act, 1992, No 11 of 1992 (Kenya 1992).).

176 Borrowing from the UN's notion of social protection, the African Union states that the purpose of social protection is "to ensure minimum standards of well-being among people in dire situations to live a life with dignity, and to enhance human capabilities." Social protection should be aimed at "ensuring a minimum standard of livelihood for all people in a given country" and includes "measure to secure education and health care, social welfare, livelihood, access to stable income, as well as employment." (Social Policy Framework for Africa (2008) p. 9, para. 13.).

177 See Stephen Devereux and Melese Getu, 'The Conceptualisation and Status of Informal and Formal Social Protection in Sub-Saharan Africa' in Stephen Devereux and Melese Getu (eds), *Informal and Formal Social Protection in Sub-Saharan Africa* (Fountain Publishers 2013) 1-8.

in Africa only cover a small fraction of society; some estimates suggest that 90 % of people in the low-income countries of sub-Saharan Africa are not covered by any formal social protection program.[178] Meanwhile, informal or non-state mechanisms are pervasive throughout the continent, as they appear to constitute "primary lines of protection for the majority in developing countries."[179] Perhaps this is why the AU recognizes the important role of private parties, stating that "[s]ocial protection includes responses by the state *and society* to protect citizens from risks, vulnerabilities and deprivations."[180]

Under the strains of urbanism and the limited financial capacity of African LDCs, informal social protection continues to be important for coping with social risks and shocks.[181] The African Union notes that African states observe an "almost complete reliance on informal networks for social protection."[182] Informal social protection schemes take many forms, as illustrated by the following excerpt:

> Informal social security entitlements are offered by traditional solidarity (such as support payments, gifts, dowries and bequests, which are all based on generalised reciprocity), indigenous self-help (such as burial funds, savings clubs and community support, which are all based on balanced reciprocity) and modern self-help, which can be initiated from above, such as cooperatives, trade unions, charities or NGOs. They can also be initiated from below such as through farmers" organisations, religious groups or self-help groups on their own behalf. Unconventional social security may provide food (food for work), loan insurance, employment security (guaranteed employment) and a strengthened capacity for solidarity.[183]

178 Awortwi and Walter-Drop 3.

179 See Mamo Hebo, ''Giving Is Saving': The Essence of Reciprocity as an Informal Social Protection System among the Arsii Oromo, Southern Ethiopia' in Stephen Devereux and Melese Getu (eds), *Informal and Formal Social Protection in Sub-Saharan Africa* (Fountain Publishers 2013) 9-42, 14.

180 Social Policy Framework for Africa (2008) p. 9, para. 13(emphasis added).

181 Devereux and Getu (2013) *Informal and Formal Social Protection in Sub-Saharan Africa.*

182 Social Policy Framework for Africa (2008) 13, para. 22.

183 United Nations Economic Social Commission for Asia the Pacific, *Sustainable Social Development in a Period of Rapid Globalization: Challenges, Opportunities and Policy Options* (United Nations Publications 2002) 146.

In light of Africa's longstanding reliance on foreign assistance and continued significance of informal social protection arrangements,[184] the private nonprofit sector is an important player in the field of social welfare. This is particularly true in the context of LDCs, where limited resources and high levels of poverty present enormous challenges for governments seeking to offer social protection without relying on NGOs to deliver social services.[185] The vital role of NGOs in social protection can also be seen in the context of fragile states.[186]

NGOs in Africa can, and often do, play a crucial complementary role in a country's national social welfare by reaching underserved or excluded communities. One commentator goes so far as to claim,

> In Sub-Saharan Africa the non-state sector has played a significant role in the provision of health and education services since the colonial period despite the imposition of controls by some governments. In no other region has the direct involvement of civic organizations in service provision achieved such prominence, and for this reason it merits more detailed consideration.[187]

One study on NGOs in East African countries suggests that NGOs have a comparative advantage with respect state governments in the realm of service delivery when, among other things, "their work is with groups considered to be 'illegal' or 'victims' and not recognizable by the state – examples would be squatters, street children and petty traders."[188] Moreover, NGOs are said to be better than the governments at providing services that are "innovative or tailored to local circumstances."[189]For example, NGOs supported secondary education in Kenya in the '70s and '80s by equipping eight state schools with computers.[190] Similarly, a Kenyan NGO provided a compact, tailored, flexible and relevant educational curriculum for indi-

---

184 See Bevan.

185 See *Managing Risk, Promoting Growth: Developing Systems for Social Protection in Africa*, World Bank, (2012) 47 <https://openknowledge.worldbank.org/handle/10986/23744>.

186 See ibid 47-48.

187 Robinson and White 82.

188 Alan Fowler, 'NGOs & the Globalization of Social Welfare: Perspectives from East Africa' in Ole Therklindsen and Joseph Semboja (eds), *Service Provision under Stress in East Africa: The State, NGOs & People's Organizations in Kenya, Tanzania & Uganda* (Centre for Development Research 1995), 63.

189 Ibid.

190 B. M. Makau, 'Dynamics of Partnership in the Provision of General Education in Kenya' in Ole Therklindsen and Joseph Semboja (eds), *Service Provision under*

gent urban children, which was meant to equip them with "practical skills (e.g., carpentry, crafts, and tailoring), basic literacy, and social skills."[191]

Consider the provision of health care services in Africa, and the significant role of NGOs therein. One reason that NGOs are particularly important in this regard is that public health care is severely underdeveloped across the continent. One analyst describes the situation in the following way:

> In many African countries the quality of government health facilities is often very poor, coverage is limited, technical capacity is inadequate, decision-making is over centralized, and service provision is plagued by inefficiencies and petty corruption.[192]

Likewise, in *Purohit and Moore v. The Gambia*, the African Commission recognized the overwhelming obstacles that African states face in fulling the very basic needs of African people. Commenting on what it calls a "depressing but real state of affairs", the Commission notes that it is:

> … aware that millions of people in Africa are not enjoying the right to health maximally because African countries are generally faced with the problem of poverty which renders them incapable to provide the necessary amenities, infrastructure and resources that facilitate the full enjoyment of this right.[193]

NGOs play a significant role in the health sector by functioning primarily in the areas of service delivery and health advocacy.[194] This is especially the case in low-income countries and middle-income countries, where NGOs are mostly engaged in delivering services, raising awareness and campaigning about disease prevention.[195] International NGOs respond to global health problems with projects such as vaccination programs and emergency response; they also tend to engage in the establishment of health services and hospitals in developing countries.[196]

Stress in East Africa: The State, NGOs & People's Organizations in Kenya, Tanzania & Uganda (Centre for Development Research 1995) 87, 95-96.

191 Ibid 96.

192 Robinson and White 82.

193 *Purohit and Moore v. Gambia*, 241/01 (ACmHPR 2003) para. 84.

194 Maria Piotrowicz and Dorota Cianciara, 'The Role of Non-Governmental Organizations in the Social and the Health System' 67 Przeglad Epidemiologiczny 69 (2013) 71.

195 Ibid.

196 Ibid 72.

Regarding the provision of health care services in particular, community-based NGOs can provide localized interventions, which are particularly important to ensure timely access to essential health care. In 2007, the World Health Organization (WHO) Regional Office for Africa held a panel discussion on the role of the community in improving maternal, newborn and child health (MNCH) within the region. Emphasizing the need for localized health care services, panel participants reported that "Mothers and children continue to die due to the triple delays in *seeking* appropriate care, *reaching* the health facility and *receiving* the appropriate management at the facility."[197] The report referred to "community empowerment, participation and ownership of community-based interventions" as being "essential for increased utilization and access to services", and called for the "involvement of the community in the planning, implementing and monitoring of community-based health services." [198]

Noting that access to affordable and accessible health services remained a challenge in Africa, panel participants highlighted the importance of foreign funding. They stated that although community-based programs are essential to MNCH programs, domestic financing of health services for mothers and children was inadequate precisely at the community level, which rendered community-based programs dependent upon external funding.[199] Moreover, panel participants emphasized the important contribution of NGOs to MNCH. They indicated that "Nongovernmental organizations working through government structures can play a major role in advocacy and implementation of MNCH programs through capacity building, including institutional strengthening."[200] In summary, the participants of the WHO African Region panel confirmed the vital role of foreign funding, community based services, and NGO communities that work in concert with African governments. The report did not call for tightening NGO operations or severing their ties to foreign funding in health care services. Rather, the report of the panel recommended that

197 The Role of the Community in Improving Maternal, Newborn and Child Health in the Who Africa Region, Regional Committee for Africa, World Health Organization, AFR/RC57/16 (b) (UN 2007) 1 <http://www.afro.who.int/sites/default/files/sessions/working_documents/AFR-RC57-16b%20REPORT%20OF%20THE%20PANEL%20DISCUSSION%20-%20FINAL.pdf> (emphasis in original).

198 Ibid.

199 Ibid 2.

200 Ibid.

"Partnerships at national and global levels should be strengthened to ensure adequate resources for MNCH." [201]

Finally, if they manage to establish and maintain a collaborative relationship with government, NGOs can enhance performance of and access to existing public services. First, they can expand the availability of resources and audit the quality of public services.[202] Second, NGOs can act a bridge between informal and formal services, thereby promoting the formalization process. Poor and vulnerable communities in LDCs typically rely on informal social protection schemes due to the inaccessibility or unavailability of formal services. NGOs activities can be critical in this regard by helping these communities to access semi-formal and then formal systems of protection.[203] As with all their other contributions, they do this through a variety of strategies including community empowerment, political advocacy and involving themselves in the provision of services.

2.2.2. NGOs in Sub-Saharan Africa

It is difficult to know the exact number of NGOs that operate in sub-Saharan Africa today.[204] However, writers have noted their remarkable growth during the post-independence period. [205] Instead of attempting the notoriously difficult task of quantifying NGOs in Africa, this section will provide a brief view into their emergence and relationship with governments. The

---

201 Ibid 3.

202 Tayo O. George and others, 'Effective Service Delivery of Nigeria's Public Primary Education: The Role of Non-State Actors' 15 Journal of African Development 221 (2013) (although these authors also considered corporate bodies in their study, their findings appear to be equally applicable to nonprofit providers.).

203 Edward Mac Abbey, 'Constructive Regulation of Non-Governmental Organizations' 48 The Quarterly Review of Economics and Finance 370 (2008) 372.

204 One international directory of development organizations estimates that civil society organizations have approximately 8600 offices and that international organizations have 1600 offices in Africa (including North Africa), however the directory collects most of its contacts through voluntarily self-reporting. (*Directory of Development Organizations: Resource Guide to Development Organizations and the Internet,* (vol Africa 10th edn, 2010) <https://www.ecoi.net/file_upload/1002_1264767399_uganda.PDF & https://www.ecoi.net/file_upload/1002_1264708453_botswana.PDF>.).

205 See Michael Bratton, 'The Politics of Government-NGO Relations in Africa' 17 World Development 569 (1989) 571; Jenkins (2012) 469-474.

following pages begin by summarizing the historical origins of NGOs in Africa as well as the political and economic context of their subsequent rise to prominence. This prefaces a discussion on the relationship between NGOs and governments as well as some of the criticism lodged against NGOs. These pages are meant not to serve as a comprehensive historical record of NGOs in Africa, or to capture fully the deep and complex dynamics of NGO-government tensions. Rather, it offers a brief overview of certain political and historical aspects in order to provide a contextualized understanding of the rise in recent years of restrictive NGO regulations.

2.2.2.1. History of Associational Life and Non-State Service Provision in Africa

The history of associational life in general is very long.[206] Social provisioning by non-governmental actors is also not new.[207] In Africa, there is a long history of nongovernmental forms of organized social welfare, mainly through extended family networks and civil society. [208] For example, lineage funds of pre-colonial times speak to this heritage. Historians note that these were "corporately owned" funds that were financed by members of a lineage in order "to insure lineage members against enslavement and to use in other crises, especially famine and illness."[209] Likewise, secret societies in parts of West Africa served the function of ensuring the provision of general education and various social services including medical treatment.[210]

During the colonial era, Africans were systematically marginalized within or excluded from the political and economic spheres, and were subjected to racial discrimination in the social service sector.[211] Associational life

206 One anthropologist dates formal common interest associations back to at least the Neolithic era. (Robert T. Anderson, 'Voluntary Associations in History' 73 American Anthropologist 209 (1971).).

207 Cammett and MacLean note that "[m]any NSPs [non-state service providers] were established long ago and have extensive institutional legacies." As an example, they point out that there have been faith-based organizations present Tanzania since at least the colonial period. (Cammett and MacLean, 'Introduction' 14.).

208 Bratton (1989) 'The Politics of Government-NGO Relations in Africa' 570-571.

209 Philip Curtin and others, *African History* (Little Brown 1978) 568.

210 Kenneth L. Little, 'The Role of the Secret Society in Cultural Specialization' 51 American Anthropologist 199 (1949).

211 Bratton (1989) 'The Politics of Government-NGO Relations in Africa' 570-571.

– being suppressed within the political sphere – was predominantly engaged in the provision of social services.[212] A significant contribution of voluntary associations was to promote social welfare for Africans, who were systematically marginalized by the colonial state.

Within the advent of urbanization, larger cities saw the blossoming of social groups around kinship ties into "home-town" or "village" associations.[213] Newcomers from the countryside sought out such ascriptive-based associations for social support in larger cities.[214] Many of these groups served primarily to promote the social and economic wellbeing of their members.[215] They provided members with financial assistance for the cost of medical care and other social expenses.[216] Many also financed the development of their ancestral regions by building schools, clinics and other public structures that promoted social protection, such as water systems and roads.[217]

Voluntary associations also used political advocacy to enhance the socio-economic wellbeing of their members. As members grew discontent with colonial rule, some associations pushed for greater political participation by black Africans.[218] During the Great Depression of the 1920s and 1930s, organized economic strikes spread across colonized African societies.[219] These strikes targeted the entire colonial system as a whole, thereby pressuring colonial authorities to begin investing in economic and social development.[220] As a result, public investments were made into education and

212 Livingstone Sewanyana, *Comparative Experiences of NGO Regulatory Frameworks: Eastern and Southern Africa* (Verlag Dr. Kovac 2017) 170-173.

213 Kenneth L. Little, 'The Organisation of Voluntary Associations in West Africa / Les Associations Volontaires En Afrique Occidentale' 9 Civilisations 283 (1959).

214 Blessing Mberu, Donatien Béguy and Alex C. Ezeh, 'Internal Migration, Urbanization and Slumbs in Sub-Saharan Africa' in Hans Groth and John F. May (eds), *Africa's Population: In Search of a Demographic Dividend* (Springer 2017) 315-332, 317.

215 (2003) *Encyclopedia of Twentieth-Century African History* (Paul Tiyambe Zeleza and Dickson Eyoh eds, Routledge 2003) 96.

216 Ibid ; Little (1959) 'The Organisation of Voluntary Associations in West Africa / Les Associations Volontaires En Afrique Occidentale'.

217 *Encyclopedia of Twentieth-Century African History* 96 ; Dwayne Woods, 'Elites, Ethnicity, and 'Home Town' Associations in the Côte D'ivoire: An Historical Analysisof State-Society Links' 64 Africa: Journal of International African Institute 465 (1994) 471-472.

218 *Encyclopedia of Twentieth-Century African History* 96.

219 Ibid ; see also Curtin and others (1978) 577-579.

220 *Encyclopedia of Twentieth-Century African History* 96.

other areas of social protection.[221] Colonial welfare and development laws emerged in order increase social expenditures on welfare and to expand associational life.[222]

Such an active and critical third sector clearly posed a threat to the efficient execution of colonial projects. Not surprisingly, colonial authorities encouraged the formalization of associations to keep them under state control,[223] and rendered them 'legible' to authorities.[224] Consider the example of Angola under Portuguese rule. Angolans living under the colonial rule of the Portugal began forming political associations in the 20th century and sought to improve the lives of Angolans. By the 1920s, the Portuguese government began restricting these associations by controlling, supervising, censoring and even expelling their leaders. One historian notes that the government viewed this as "a threat from the 'nativist movement' in Angola".[225] In 1935, Portugal began requiring registration of all associations in all of its territories, which included colonial territories in Africa, in order to dissuade and criminalize what its lawmakers deemed to be "secretive" organizations.[226] These earlier associational laws were in many ways the precursors of today's NGO laws in Africa: they typically limited associations to service-based operations—prohibiting political involvement—and kept associations under tight state supervision.[227]Colonial powers formalized, or 'legitimized', civil society by way of legal and institutional mechanisms that imposed registration and operational requirements and monitored compliance.

---

221 Ibid 96-97; Sewanyana (2017) 172-173 ; see also Bratton (1994) Institute for Development Research, *Civil Society and Political Transition in Africa* 10 ("While liberalization may occur at the initiative of a progressive faction that splits the state elite, more commonly it is a response to escalating economic protest…").

222 Sewanyana (2017) 172-173.

223 See Peter 312-315 (Until 2002, Tanzania relied on colonial-era legislation to impose registration requirements on NGOs. That same law was used by British colonialists to restrain civil society organizations that challenged the colonial regime in Tanzania.).

224 James Scott posits that states standardize and regularize social practices that are otherwise 'illegible' and exceptionally complex for officials to keep track of and to regulate. (James C. Scott, *Seeing Like a State: How Certain Schemes to Improve the Human Condition Have Failed* (Yale University Press 1998).).

225 Ronald H. Chilcote (ed), *Protest and Resistance in Angola and Brazil: Comparative Studies* (University of California Press 1972) 74.

226 Associações Secretas, Lei No 1901 (Portugal 1935).

227 *Encyclopedia of Twentieth-Century African History* 97; Sewanyana (2017) 173-174.

William Olsen has studied similar phenomena involving the colonial regulation and registration of traditional medicinal practices of African societies.[228] From these observations, he concludes that the practice of regulating civil society in Africa may have emerged as an adaptive state measure to achieve the unchanged colonial objective of disciplining and controlling indigenous subjects. Olsen writes, "...in the nearly 40 years of colonial engagement with witchcraft and witch-finding movements, the British changed the content of their 'official' orientation towards these practices but their purposes of regulation and discipline remained intact."[229]

Threats to African associational life did not end with colonialism. Voluntary associations were once again under attack after the end of colonial rule, but this time from African regimes.[230] Recounting the historical relationship between voluntary associations and the state primarily in Côte d'Ivoire, Dwayne Woods writes,

> Following independence, Africa's ruling elites sought to suppress all forms of ethnic affiliation and independent associational activity. They justified their actions on the basis that tribalism and ethnicity were detrimental to national unity and economic development. In the Côte d'Ivoire the Parti Démocratique de la Côte d'Ivoire (PDCI) served one function—namely the suppression of all independent associational life... Simply put, the party served as an instrument for President Felix Houphouet-Boigny to limit participation, especially participation based on ethnic ties. A similar process of restricting political input from social groups occurred elsewhere in Africa...[231]

Non-governmental associations in Africa have taken form as professional associations, ethnic welfare groups and churches.[232] But it was not until the rise of foreign aid in the 1980s that NGOs proliferated across the continent in their modern form as institutionalized, foreign-funded organizations that had strong international ties and took on a significant role in humanitarian assistance and social welfare.

---

228 William C. Olsen, 'The Empire Strikes Back: Colonial "Discipline" and the Creation of Civil Society in Asante' 30 History in Africa 223 (2003).

229 Ibid 226.

230 Bratton (1994) Institute for Development Research, *Civil Society and Political Transition in Africa* 5.

231 Woods (1994) 466 (internal citations ommitted) (Woods notes, however, that despite these challenges, associations managed to survive.).

232 Bratton (1989) 570-571.

2.2.2.2. The Rise of Foreign-Backed NGOs

Africa, along with the rest of the world, saw a sharp growth in NGOs during the late 1980s and 1990s, leading one third-sector scholar to declare that time as the beginning of an "associational revolution [that] may prove as significant as the rise of the nation-state."[233] Consider their rise in East Africa. According to one account, there were more than 400 NGOs in Kenya alone by the late 1980s, which is nearly a fourfold increase from the 125 NGOs that were there in 1974. [234] By another account, Kenya is believed to have had 4,000 NGOs by the year 2000, and 6,000 NGOs by 2010.[235] Similarly, the number of NGOs in Ghana increased from 80 in 1980, to 700 in 1990, to 1,300 in 2000, and finally to 4,772 in 2010.[236] Tanzania also experienced an extraordinary rise in NGOs from 25 in 1980 to over 5000 NGOs in 2010.[237] The proliferation of NGOs was observed in other continents as well.[238] In addition to their growing numbers, NGOs were significant in terms of their mobilization of resources. By 1992, international assistance to developing countries that came either from or through NGOs amounted to $8 billion, which represented 13 % of all development assistance, and amounted to more than the UN's contribution to development assistance for the same period.[239]

On a global scale, the world saw a dramatic growth in NGOs during the 1990s.[240] To explain this NGO-boom, scholars point to cultural and political shifts in the 1980s that changed the conditions within which NGOs operated. First, donor countries from the "global north" that championed neoliberal ideologies common in western societies advanced democracy aid campaigns by promoting NGOs in the developing world.[241] Democracy aid campaigns were based on the notion that a strong and active civil society would enhance democratic governance, and northern donor countries tried to accomplish that goal by pumping funding into NGOs.

Second, the advancement of structural adjustment programs through neoliberal pro-market policies backed by international financial institu-

---

233 Salamon (1994) 114.
234 Bratton (1989) 571.
235 Cammett and MacLean (2014) 'Introduction' 8.
236 Ibid.
237 Ibid.
238 Ibid.
239 P. J. Simmons, 'Learning to Live with NGOs' 112 Foreign Policy 82 (1998) 87.
240 Jenkins (2012) 472-474.
241 Ibid 474-477.

tions led to massive cuts in public social spending within developing countries, thereby creating the opportunity for NGOs to expand within the social service sector. [242] By the 1980s, official funding for development aid (that is, direct funding to governments) declined, thus the space for non-state social provisioning steadily widened.[243] Structural adjustment programs ultimately failed to lift people in developing countries out of poverty and eventually came under scrutiny before they were finally abandoned. [244] But by then, the NGOs were already there.

Meanwhile, neoliberal aid packages had urged developing countries toward decentralized models of governance, thus burdening local levels of government with the task of financing and delivering social welfare services.[245] This incentivized local governments to "contract out" their services to NGOs.[246] In some areas, decentralization went even further than the level of local government. In 1994, the World Bank reported that it had "increasingly used nongovernmental organizations (NGOs) in the delivery of services," and that "in several countries, public works agencies [had] been set up with Bank encouragement *outside the structure of government* to manage and implement public works".[247] Today, it is not uncommon for nonprofits to be the only service providers available to certain segments of the population.[248]

As social indicators worsened and public services diminished, NGOs flourished to fill remaining gaps in social protection.[249] They have become rather important for vulnerable and marginalized groups. The U.N. Committee on Economic, Social and Cultural Rights (ESCR Committee) has

---

242 Ibid; Helmut K. Anheier and Lester M. Salamon, 'The Nonprofit Sector in Comparative Perspective' in Walter W. Powell and Richard Steinberg (eds), *The Nonprofit Sector: A Research Handbook* (2nd edn, Yale University Press 2006) 89-114, 92-93.

243 See Jenkins (2012) 476-477.

244 See ibid.

245 Cammett and MacLean, 'Introduction' 13.

246 Ibid 13, n. 10.

247 Mike Stevens and others, *Governance: The World Bank's Experience*, World Bank, (1994) 20 <http://documents.worldbank.org/curated/en/711471468765285964/pdf/multi0page.pdf> (emphasis added).

248 E.g., Concluding Observations on the Initial and Second Period Report of Djibouti, Committee on Economic, Social and Cultural Rights, UN Doc. E/C.12/DJI/CO/1-2 (UN 2013) para. 22 (noting that a large number of children in Djibouti live and work in the streets; regretting that "their care is managed entirely by civil society organizations, whose capacity is limited.").

249 See Jenkins (2012) 476-477.

also recognized their importance in this regard on at least two occasions. First, when it insisted that "States parties should respect and protect the work of human rights advocates and other members of civil society who assist vulnerable groups in the realization of their right to adequate food."[250] And second, when it noted that "States parties should respect, protect, facilitate and promote the work of human rights advocates and other members of civil society with a view to assisting vulnerable or marginalized groups in the realization of their right to health."[251]

As nonprofit sectors in developing countries expanded to fill protection gaps, Northern donors have been there to continue supporting their growth with foreign funding.[252]According to one commentator, NGOs in the 1980s were receiving 22% of total aid funds.[253] During the same period, the growth rate for donor-to-NGO funding was almost five-folds that of total overseas development aid to governments of developing countries.[254] While some understood that a shift in donor funding had occurred, for many there was "a dawning realization" by the late 1980s "that a greater share of North-South resource transfers pass[ed] through NGOs than [was] commonly realized."[255]

Today foreign funding remains a significant and vital source of financial resources for NGOs in Africa.[256] While it is difficult to find comprehensive data on the share of NGOs' resources that come from foreign donors, existing evidence on a few sub-Saharan African countries suggests that NGOs' reliance on foreign funds, rather than household or government resources, is quite substantial. By one estimate, NGOs in Kenya (over 90% of which focus on service provision) receive 91% of their revenues from international sources, while 8% comes from private sources and only 1% from the

250 General Comment No. 12: The Right to Adequate Food, Committee on Economic Social and Cultural Rights, U.N. Doc. E/C.12/1999/5 (UN 1999) para. 35.

251 General Comment No. 14: The Right to the Highest Attainable Standard of Health (2000) para. 62.

252 See Jenkins (2012) 476-477.

253 Tim Brodhead, 'NGOs: In One Year, out the Other?' 15 World Development 1 (1987) 1.

254 Ole Therklindsen and Joseph Semboja, 'A New Look at Service Provision in East Africa' in Ole Therklindsen and Joseph Semboja (eds), *Service Provision under Stress in East Africa: The State, NGOs & People's Organizations in Kenya, Tanzania & Uganda* (Centre for Development Research 1995) 17.

255 Brodhead (1987) 1.

256 Bratton (1994) Institute for Development Research, *Civil Society and Political Transition in Africa* 8.

Kenyan government.[257] In Mozambique, it is estimated that foreign funding accounted for 71% of revenues collected by the nonprofit sector in 2003, while membership fees and service fees collected from private enterprises and households amounted to 10.7% and government subsidies and contracts made up only 3% of total revenues.[258] For all nonprofit organizations in Cameroon that worked in the social, health, education, housing and development sectors, contributions from foreign sources or other nonprofit organizations amounted to 67% of 2011 revenues, while only 17% came from households and 8% came from the government.[259]

Evidence is also available on the share of foreign aid directed toward NGOs worldwide. The OECD reports that in 2011, over $19 billion (or 14.4%) of official development assistance from OECD countries was channeled through NGOs worldwide, with $1.1 billion going to and through NGOs based in developing countries.[260] Social infrastructure and services has been a priority for foreign donors. It is the main sector through which Oversees Development Aid (ODA) is channeled through NGOs. Fifty-one per cent (or $9 billion) of bilateral ODA was directed toward NGOs working in this sector,[261] and at least 24% of all ODA channeled through NGOs in 2011 was dedicated to health, education, water supply and sanitation, other social infrastructures and services, and food aid.[262]

2.2.2.3. Governments Restricting NGOs

African governments and intellectuals also noticed the growth of NGOs, as their resources were significant in size. In Kenya, for example, NGO re-

---

257 Brass (2012) 'Blurring Boundaries: The Integration of NGOs into Governance in Kenya' 210 & 216.

258 Saide Dade, *The Dimension of NPI in Mozambique: A Satellite Account Perspective,* (2009) table 8 <http://ccss.jhu.edu/wp-content/uploads/downloads/2011/10/Mozambique_SatelliteAccount_2009.pdf>.

259 Author's own calculations of percentages from a data reported by the Cameroonian government (*Compte Satellite Des Institutions Sans but Lucratif: De L'année 2011,* Institut National de la Statistique (2014) table 3.1 <http://ccss.jhu.edu/wp-content/uploads/downloads/2015/01/Cameroon_SatelliteAccount_2014.pdf>.).

260 *Aid at a Glance: Flows of Official Development Assistance to and through Civil Society Organizations in 2011,* Organization for Economic Cooperation and Development, (2013) 3 <http://www.oecd.org/dac/peer-reviews/Aid%20for%20CSOs%20Final%20for%20WEB.pdf>.

261 Ibid 10.

262 Ibid 14.

sources between 1980 and 1990 amounted to 31% of government expenditure on education, health, labor and social welfare.[263] Governments grew weary of NGOs as they continued to receive funds that might have otherwise supported government projects.[264] One Africanist scholar insisted that an anti-state stance among donors "was the real push behind the upsurge in NGO activity."[265] Governments across the continent started to pass laws that placed restrictions on foreign aid to NGOs. Proponents of today's restrictive NGO laws continue to express a similar disenchantment and mistrust of the alliance between NGOs and their Northern donors,[266] often recasting the NGO-boom as a political takeover or bombardment by what one Zimbabwean official has referred to as "non-*governable* organisations".[267]

African states that seek to control or direct the nonprofit sector are not likely to do so through financial incentives due to their own financial limitations and due to the fact that NGOs typically rely on foreign funding. Thus, states will likely resort to regulatory and legislative means, despite their limited capacity to do so. Kendra Dupuy *et al* find that in low and medium-income countries, a growing inflow of foreign funding is associated with heighted restrictions on foreign funding to NGOs.[268] Paradoxically, this indicates it is governments with the greatest need for foreign assistance that are restricting foreign aid flows.[269] Dupuy *et al* explain that when governments believe internationally funded NGOs are enabling or empowering political opposition, they will risk economic and reputational

---

263 Fowler (1995) 61.

264 Jephias Mapuva and Loveness Muyengwa-Mapuva, 'A Critique of the Key Legislative Framework Guiding Civil Liberties in Zimbabwe' 15 Potchefstroom Electronic Law Journal 125 (2012) 128.

265 Shivji (2006) 39.

266 A general mistrust of the global North among independent African states predates the emergence of NGOs in Africa. Historians of the 1970s noted "a general fear of 'neocolonialism'" among African states, which included the belief that – despite their independence from colonial rule – industrialized nations still controlled African economic life through direct means of political intervention as well as through indirect means. (Curtin and others (1978) 541.).

267 Staff Reporter, '29 NGOs Banned in Crackdown' *New Zimbabwe* (14 Feb 2012) <http://www.newzimbabwe.com/news-7189-29+NGOs+banned+in+crackdown/news.aspx> (emphasis added) (quoting Governor of Masivingo, Titus Maluleke, after the sudden de-registration of 29 NGOs in Zimbabwe).

268 Dupuy, Ron and Prakash (2016).

269 Ibid.

harm in order to secure themselves against threats to their political survival; this is especially the case after nationally competitive elections.[270]

Consider the recent example of South Sudan as a prototypical scenario in which tensions between NGOs and government have led to tightening controls on NGOs in low-income countries. Not long after its independence from Sudan in 2011, the new state of South Sudan found itself in a dire situation. By May 2016, public services were collapsing. The country's largest public hospital had experienced weeklong power outages, shortages of medical supplies, essential drugs, oxygen supplies and water.[271] Women were giving birth by candlelight, and patients in need of surgery were being turned away. The government had not paid its medical staff for months, and hospitals did not have enough fuel for their generators. Similarly, the educational system suffered from inadequate support.[272] Public university professors went on strike because they had not been paid their salaries for months, and half of the children in South Sudan were out of school.

One explanation for the collapse in public social services was a reduction in oil revenue, which was caused by falling oil prices and declining oil production.[273] Since South Sudan relies mostly on oil revenues, the government's financial capacity to meet social needs had severely diminished. The financial problem was compounded by an armed internal conflict that began in December 2013, which necessitated high military expenditure and resulted in a humanitarian crisis.[274] The government was unable to organize and provide even minimal social protection. Private providers of social services, including NGOs, UN Agencies and community-based organizations, tried to fill the protection gap. Officials felt that nonprofit actors with foreign ties posed a threat to the state's newfound independence. As

---

270 Ibid 300.

271 Jason Patinkin, 'It's Like Florence Nightingale's Time': South Sudan's Public Services Collapse' *The Guardian* (27 May 2016) <http://www.theguardian.com/global-development/2016/may/27/south-sudan-public-services-collapse-juba-teaching-hospital-like-florence-nightingale-time>.

272 Ibid.

273 See 'South Sudan Oil Revenue at $3.38 Bln, Hit by Conflict and Price Falls' *Reuters* (3 Jan. 2015) <http://www.reuters.com/article/southsudan-crude-idUSL6N0UI02D20150103>.

274 Jacey Fortin, 'Power Struggles Stall South Sudan's Recovery' *New York Times* (31 May 2016) <http://www.nytimes.com/2016/05/31/world/africa/south-sudan-struggles-to-collect-taxes-after-years-of-war.html>.

tensions grew between the third sector and the state, the South Sudanese government tried to control NGOs through legislation.

In 2015, aid agencies feared that certain provisions of an NGO bill that was proposed in 2013 and approved by parliament in May 2015 would "not regulate NGO operations, but rather hinder their ability to serve South Sudanese people at a time when needs are escalating".[275] The bill prohibited foreigners from constituting more than 20 percent of an NGO's staff.[276] One government official stated that the law is intended to ensure that more jobs are given to South Sudanese workers. He accused NGOs of employing too many foreigners and warned that their registration would be denied if they did not employ nationals.[277] The minister of Justice, Paulino Wnanawilla, complained that NGOs were uncooperative and ignored the government's efforts to coordinate services. The minister explained, "There is no country where you have free lunch; you go and you do business as you want… You cannot operate in a country under your own conditions." The bill was signed into law in February 2016 along with another act that widens the government's power to monitor NGOs. These new acts are the Non-Governmental Organizations Act of 2016 and the Relief and Rehabilitation Commission Act of 2016.[278]

Restrictive NGO laws have appeared in other parts of Africa as well. Uganda's NGO Registration Act (2009) required NGOs to provide the government with a written notice of their intention to make direct contact with people within their operational area at least one week prior to doing so. [279] NGOs, including those that were wholly owned and operated by Ugandans, could operate only within the particular geographic area that

275 See 'South Sudan Risks 'Catastrophe' with New Aid Agency Law, Warn NGOs' *The Guardian* (14 May 2015) <http://www.theguardian.com/global-development/2015/may/14/south-sudan-aid-agency-law-risks-catastrophe-warn-ngos>.

276 See 'S. Sudan Parliament Passes NGOs Bill, Gives Requirements for Relief Agencies' *Sudan Tribune* (12 Mar. 2015) <http://www.sudantribune.com/spip.php?article54953>; 'South Sudan Risks 'Catastrophe' with New Aid Agency Law, Warn NGOs' (2015).

277 'S. Sudan Parliament Passes NGOs Bill, Gives Requirements for Relief Agencies' (2015).

278 'South Sudanese President Signs NGO Bill into Law' *Sudan Tribune* (11 Feb. 2016) <http://sudantribune.com/spip.php?article57988> ; 'South Sudan Tables NGOs Bill for the Second Time' *Sudan Tribune* (20 Jan. 2016) <http://www.sudantribune.com/spip.php?article57749>.

279 The Non-Governmental Organisations Registration Regulations, 2017 No. 22 (Uganda 2017).

the government had authorized for them.[280] Moreover, the law rather vaguely proscribed NGO activities that were "prejudicial" to the "security of Uganda" or to the "interests of Uganda and the dignity of the people of Uganda".[281] Likewise, it allowed government to involuntarily dissolve NGOs for failure to comply with its provisions, and broadly "for any other reason the [National] Board [of Non-Governmental Organisations] considers necessary in the public interest."[282] The terms "public interest", "security of Uganda", "interests of Uganda" and "dignity of the people" were left undefined by the NGO law. Uganda enacted a new NGO law in 2016 and new NGO regulations in 2017 that maintain many of these features, including burdensome registration requirements and the imposition of criminal sanctions for violations.[283]

2.3. Conclusion

Since their rise in the 1980s, NGOs have become a fixture of social welfare in the least developed countries of Africa. They arose into prominence due to their presumed advantage in service provision and governance. However, as time has passed, scholars and politicians alike have begun to view their role in social development with a critical eye. Of particular concern is their dependence upon foreign sources of aid, which – unsurprisingly – mirrors the dependency among African governments on the same. The conflicting objectives among states to benefit from the resources and activities of NGOs as well as to keep them at arm's length reflect the long and complicated history of social protection in Africa. That history exhibits a compilation of indigenous and familial traditions of informal protection; missionaries entrenched within colonial agendas; and politicized community organizing in the name of social justice. From this historical background of political tension, and within the existing socio-economic context of deep and widespread poverty, emerges the current dilemma: African states are passing restrictive NGO laws that are justified in terms of their sovereignty but have the potential to interfere with the social rights of beneficiaries.

---

280 Ibid § 13(d).

281 Ibid § 13(c), (g).

282 Ibid § 17(3)(e).

283 The Non-Governmental Organisations Act, No 5 of 2016 (Uganda); The Non-Governmental Organisations Regulations, No. 22 of 2017 (Uganda 2017).

3. Beneficiaries' Perspective: How NGO-State Relations Can Affect Social Rights

The analytical framework for this research is a beneficiary-centered approach. This approach is grounded in the fact that human rights law in general and the ICESCR in particular ultimately aim to protect the freedom of individuals and their right to dignified lives. From this angle, the manner in which NGOs and the state interact with one another becomes a potential social rights concern for beneficiaries of the NGOs. This chapter begins by introducing the beneficiary-centered approach and its usefulness as a critical framework for legal analysis. Next, it provides an overview and discussion of social rights as they have been guaranteed in international and regional instruments. Finally, it concludes with a discussion on how NGO-state relations can affect the social rights of beneficiaries.

3.1. A Beneficiary-Centered Approach

A beneficiary-centered approach to human rights analyses of development policies places an emphasis on the wellbeing of the intended beneficiaries of social development. This angle can get lost when analysts use only an NGO-focused approach that takes into account the liberal rights of NGOs who work to alleviate social ills, or only a state-sovereignty approach that is critical of the foreign ties of many NGOs working in Africa as well as the foreign financial support that they enjoy. An NGO-focused approach tends to underestimate the harm that NGOs can do to beneficiaries, while the state-sovereignty approach tends to understate the obligation that states owe to beneficiaries in terms of their socio-economic rights. In contrast, a beneficiary-centered approach to assessing social development in Africa aims toward the empowerment and emancipation of the poor by consciously evaluating the living conditions and lived experiences of African peoples, rather than prioritizing the civil and political rights of NGOs or legitimizing state measures that restrict nonprofit activities.[284]

284 For a discussion on the related concept of client-centered lawyering, see Derrick A. Bell Jr., 'Serving Two Masters: Integration Ideals and Client Interests in School Desegregation Litigation' 85 Yale Law Journal 470 (1976). Bell argues

A beneficiary-centered approach is similar to the human rights based approach to development in that both envision people as rights holders rather than merely quiet recipients of charitable services, standing behind the main stage of law and politics.[285] Evaluations of how NGOs use the human rights based approach indicate that the particular manner in which the human rights based approach is applied will affect its impact on social development.[286] If such approaches are to bring about the realization of social rights, then they must challenge structural inequities in order to achieve the lasting social changes that can actually support the progressive realization of social rights.[287] This is why bringing together the human rights based approach and a beneficiary-centered approach in the assessment of social development policies can address the root causes of poverty.[288] In legal terms, this means ensuring that the state fulfills its social rights obligations toward rights holders, even when the state is not directly involved in the provision of social services. This is unlike the needs-based approach, which

---

that the attorneys who championed civil rights litigation like in *Brown v. Board of Education* risked doing a disservice to their clients when they failed to place substantive equity on the same footing as *de jure* equality. He argues for a client-centered approach to ensure that improved educational quality is at the heart of *de jure* desegregation efforts.

285 See, Katarina Tomaševski, 'International Development Finance Agencies' in Asbjørn Eide, Catarina Krause and Allan Rosas (eds), *Economic, Social and Cultural Rights: A Textbook* (2nd rev. edn, Martinus Nijhoff 2001) 403-413, 409 (explaining that the purpose of a human rights assessment of development programs is to anticipate possible adverse effects of development interventions on human rights, and prevent, reduce and mitigate harmful consequences.).

286 Hans Peter Schmitz, 'A Human Rights Based Aproach (HRBA) in Practice: Evaluating NGO Development Efforts' 44 Polity 523 (2012).

287 Cornwall and Nyamu-Musembi offer a critical perspective of how the rights-based approach to development has emerged and is practiced. They caution that unless such approaches facilitate a global transformation of power relations, mainstreaming human rights discourse into development policy is not likely to result in the meaningful realization of social and economic rights. (Andrea Cornwall and Celestine Nyamu-Musembi, 'Putting the "Rights-Based Approach" to Development in Perspective' 25 Third World Quarterly 1415 (2004).).

288 See, Marius Pieterse, 'Health Care Rights, Resources and Rationing' 124 South African Law Journal 514 (2007) 518 (in response to the argument that rationing decisions are inevitable in poorer countries, Pieterse argues for an approach similar to the beneficiary-centered approach wherein "the interests affected by the outcome of rationing decisions and processes coincide with the objects of fundamental human rights.").

> view[s] development as a need or a gift, motivated by and derived from charitable intentions and patronage relationships, rather than a reflection on rights. Needs-based approaches focus on fulfilling, for example, health care or educational needs, yet stop short of addressing structural conditions and policies that could make systematic change.[289]

In this regard, the beneficiary-centered approach transcends the depoliticization that characterizes the needs-based approach. However, it goes a step further by ensures that the rights of the beneficiaries remain at the center of legal concern. For example, while little doubt remains that severely restrictive NGO laws may interfere with the rights of NGOs, limiting one's legal analysis to the violations of NGOs' rights – and disregarding the rights of beneficiaries – is still technically a human rights based analysis. However, this view belongs to a limited debate that concerns NGOs and the political elites who would benefit from censoring them, rather than the socio-economically vulnerable individuals who depend on them.

Even when resources are severely constrained, states should prioritize the protection of vulnerable members of society. The Committee urges states to do this "by the adoption of relatively low-cost targeted programs."[290] There appears to be evidence in support of an approach that emphasizes the sustained empowerment of marginalized people rather than merely offering piecemeal provision of social services. Research on NGOs that provide services versus those that integrate advocacy into their work offers evidence in support of using a beneficiary-centered approach when seeking to assess or alleviate deprivations related to social rights. Bill Abom asserts that NGOs that provide services without a participatory or critical approach risk undermining sustainable development by breaking down social capital within the community and encouraging a dependency mindset among beneficiaries.[291] On the other hand, NGOs that engage in advocacy, community outreach and education, as well as exposing government to the perspectives of beneficiaries, are more likely to strengthen social capital

289 Susan O'Leary, 'Grassroots Accountability Promises in Rights-Based Approaches to Development: The Role of Transformative Monitoring and Evaluation in NGOs' 36 Accounting, Organizations and Society 21 (2017).

290 General Comment No. 3: The Nature of States Parties' Obligations (1990) para. 12.

291 Bill Abom, 'Social Capital, NGOs, and Development: A Guatemalan Case Study' 14 Development in Practice 342 (2004) 345-346.

and encourage sustainable social development.[292] There is also evidence to suggest that certain forms of participatory human rights advocacy, particularly measuring the state's compliance with its social rights obligations, can have a transformative impact on beneficiaries in terms of both realizing and claiming their social rights.[293]

The dual role that NGOs play in their development work, as well as the legal measures that attempt to segregate NGOs into two broad categories, can also be understood through the opposing paradigms of the human rights based approach and the needs-based approach to development. For example, when NGOs provide services without advocating for or taking into account the social rights of their beneficiaries, they are employing a needs-based approach. While such an approach may appear to ensure harmonious state-to-NGO relations, it may also ensure that the NGO remains embedded within the same structural mechanisms that perpetuate poverty. Likewise, an analysis of NGO laws that does not take into account the rights claims of beneficiaries is not likely to address their concerns in a structural way. A needs-based approach is limited in its capacity to bring about lasting social change because it does not demand structural change. Indeed, when NGO laws include gag-rules that suppress nonprofit advocacy, they tend to push the third sector into a kind of non-confrontational, non-critical and passive role by silencing voices of dissent. These kinds of measures suppress the human rights based approach at a cost to the wellbeing of beneficiaries. Consequently, a beneficiary-centered approach is needed to bring to light that which threatens the social rights and social wellbeing of beneficiaries.

Consider a special feature of the NGO law in Ethiopia, which prohibits rights advocacy among NGOs that receive more than 10% of their funding from a foreign source.[294] Ethiopia's NGO law has been called "one of the most controversial laws in Africa"[295] due to its restrictive funding provisions and its threat of criminal sanctions. The law, referred to as the Charities and Societies Proclamation, targets human rights advocacy by stating that NGOs that receive more than 10% of their funding from foreign sources are forbidden from promoting human rights.[296] In particular, such

292 Ibid.

293 O'Leary (2017).

294 Charities and Societies Proclamation No 621/2009 (Ethiopia).

295 International Center of Not-for-Profit Law, 'Introductory Overview' 12:2 International Journal of Not-for-Profit Law 5 (2010) 6.

296 Charities and Societies Proclamation No 621/2009 (Ethiopia).

organizations may not engaging in, *inter alia*, "the promotion of human and democratic rights; the promotion of equality of nations, nationalities and peoples and that of gender and religion; [and] the promotion of the rights of the disabled and children's rights".

The government of Zimbabwe tried to pass an NGO law in 2004 that had a similar effect. It sought to weed out human rights activities among NGOs by severely restricting the ability of NGOs to involve themselves in governance issues.[297] Foreign NGOs would not be registered if their sole or principal purpose involved issues of governance, and local NGOs were forbidden from receiving foreign funding to carry out activities involving issues of governance.[298] However as one UN report noted, separating activities involving good governance – which undoubtedly includes respecting and protecting human rights – from service provision is a particularly difficult task within the African regional framework of human rights law.[299] Since the African Charter gives both ESC rights and civil and political rights equal legal significance as human rights, NGOs that provide social services are technically involved in the protection and fulfillment of human rights. This would have made them vulnerable to penalization under Zimbabwe's NGO bill.

By effectively censoring most of the non-profit advocacy within the country, Ethiopia's Charities and Societies Proclamation considerably undermines the human rights based approach to social development. Since most nonprofit actors in Ethiopia – including nonprofit service providers – rely heavily on foreign funding, they must be careful not to engage in rights advocacy. In some cases, however, it is unclear whether an NGO's activities constitute rights advocacy or service provision. For instances, social service programs that pursue equal access to education, promote women's health, or protect affordable housing for ethnic minorities could reasonably be interpreted under the Proclamation as forms of rights advocacy. Since some degree of rights promotion could overlap with some amount of service provision, NGOs may decline to pursue certain social programs, or even abandon existing programs, in order to avoid criminal liability under Ethiopian law. Although precise information is unavailable as to the volume of nonprofit social provision in Ethiopia, the presence of nonprof-

---

297 See *The Zimbabwean Non-Governmental Orgnizations Bill 2004 and International Human Rights Law/Standards: Issues, Analysis and Policy Recommendations* (UNDP 2004).

298 See ibid 17-18.

299 Ibid 18.

it service providers is substantial.[300] Moreover, their contributions are important due to the severely limited coverage of public social protection schemes as well as widespread poverty and vulnerability among its population.[301] For beneficiaries whose livelihoods depend on nonprofit activities, Ethiopia's NGO law creates a social rights dilemma by jeopardizing their access to an essential means of realizing and enjoying their social rights.

Nonprofit advocacy can be critical to the realization and continued enjoyment of social rights precisely because such activities prod or otherwise facilitate the state's capacity to honor its social rights commitments through awareness raising and engaging national stakeholders.[302] Indeed, the ESCR Committee has recognized the "essential" and "important role" of human rights NGOs in "the promotion, protection and realization of social, economic and cultural rights" due to their role in "monitoring and evaluating State parties' compliance" with international human rights law.[303] More to the point, the Committee makes it clear that, according to its own interpretation of the ICESCR, censoring or intimidating nonprofits is forbidden. The Committee writes that it

> … considers any threat or violence against human rights defenders to constitute violations of States' obligations towards the realization of Covenant rights since human rights defenders also contribute through their work to the fulfillment of Covenant rights.[304]

In the context of analyzing NGO laws, the beneficiary-centered approach to human rights and development has the advantage of circumventing the deadlock between the defenders of state sovereignty and defenders of NGOs' rights by shedding light on the state's social rights obligations to-

300 Daniel Hailu and Terry Northcut, 'Ethiopia's Social Protection Landscape: Its Surface and Underlying Structures' 56 International Social Work 828 (2012).

301 Amdissa Teshome and others, 'Governance Characteristics and Policy Relevance of Informal Social Protection Services in Ethiopia: When the State Is Willing but Not Able' in Nicholas Awortwi and Gregor Walter-Drop (eds), *Non-State Social Protection Actors and Services in Africa: Governance Below the State* (Routledge 2018) 25-43, 26.

302 See Patrick Mutzenberg, 'NGOs: Essential Actors for Embedding the Covenants in the National Context' in Daniel Moeckli, Helen Keller and Corina Heri (eds), *The Human Rights Covenants at 50: Their Past, Present, and Future* (Oxford University Press 2018) 75-95, 87-89.

303 Human Rights Defenders and Economic, Social and Cultural Rights, Committee on Economic Social and Cultural Rights, U.N. Economic and Social Council, U.N. Doc. E/C.12/2016/2 (UN 2017) para. 1.

304 Ibid para. 5.

ward its own people, thereby contextualizing the entire debate within a beneficiary-based framework. This advantage reflects a critical edge that can accommodate post-colonial concerns by scrutinizing both foreign political entities as well as African political elites for their respective roles in the ongoing distress of African peoples.

The peculiarity of Africa's long-term dependence on foreign aid echoes earlier periods of colonial intervention wherein social programs such as health care and education were provided through missionaries in the service of colonial projects. Placing an emphasis on the rights of socio-economically marginalized individuals and groups – rather than the wellbeing of institutional actors – is a way to remain cognizant of the continent's long experience with subjugation and various forms of imperialism. Moreover, it is an attempt to ensure that human rights law does not serve to perpetuate further exploitation and injury by advancing the rights of a privileged few while neglecting the rights of the vulnerable and marginalized.

Social wellbeing of beneficiaries must also be sustainable in order to alleviate African countries of their dependence on foreign aid. Anything less would leave the realization and enjoyment of social rights vulnerable to the arbitrary contingencies and inevitable conflicts associated with foreign interests. Abdullahi Ahmed An-Na'im cautions against the impulse of the international community to choose "between rushing to 'doing something' [and] passively watching flagrant and systematic violations of basic human rights".[305] He implores those in the west instead to cultivate "the principled and institutionalized application of the same standards everywhere over time" rather than employing "self-help and vigilante justice in crisis situations".[306] In this regard, An-Na'im calls for the "promotion of local capacity", which he writes must be achieved

> ...through the development of national institutions and mechanisms of accountability within the specific context of each country. In other words, such efforts must build on what actually exists on the ground because attempting to impose norms and models developed elsewhere is both objectionable as a colonial exercise of cultural imperialism, and unlikely to be workable in a sustainable manner in practice. Moreover, these efforts should always respect the independent agency and human

305 A.A.A. Na'īm, 'Introduction: Expanding Legal Protection of Human Rights in African Contexts' in A.A.A. Na'īm (ed), *Human Rights under African Constitutions: Realizing the Promise for Ourselves* (University of Pennsylvania Press, Incorporated 2003) 1, 2.

306 Ibid.

> dignity of its intended beneficiaries by gradually diminishing their dependency on external support. [307]

Thus, the central orientation of such human rights analysis should be to seek social wellbeing and reaffirm the dignity of people living in Africa as the central concern when evaluating state action by taking into account the distinctive circumstances found on the continent and aiming for sustainability and longevity in social welfare. The approach needed is one that is concerned not only with guaranteeing the realization of social rights for beneficiaries in sub-Saharan Africa, but also with aiming for the underlying ideal of human freedom that those rights are meant to achieve. As Ashwani Kumar posits, the poor are more than just people who lack material items such as food, income and security, they are also powerless in that they lack "freedom to achieve even minimally satisfactory living conditions."[308] Ultimately, a beneficiary-centered focus within a human rights based approach to development is about empowerment within enormously unfavorable socio-economic circumstances as well as emancipation from oppressive societal structures.[309]

3.2. Social Rights of Beneficiaries

The social rights of beneficiaries can be found in international human rights law as well as regional African human rights instruments. The social rights of beneficiaries correspond to certain state obligations toward the beneficiaries and, ultimately, give rise to additional state obligations toward nonprofit entities that are essential to the realization and enjoyment

---

307 Ibid 3. Elsewhere I have traced how at the end of the twentieth century the primary aim of international humanitarian intervention in Somalia shifted away from humanitarian protection towards an emphasis on top-down state building, consequently undermining the legitimacy of those efforts within Somalia. (Jihan A Kahssay, (Note) 'Lessons Learned from Somalia: Retuning to a Humanitarian-Based Humanitarian Intervention' 19 UC Davis Journal of International Law & Policy 113 (2012).).

308 Ashwani Kumar, 'The Question of the Poor' in Rupert Taylor (ed), *Third Sector Research* (Springer 2010) 281-298, 285.

309 See Tom Inglis, 'Empowerment and Emancipation' 48 Adult Education Quarterly 3 (1997) 4 ("...empowerment involves people developing capacities to act successfully within the existing system and structures of power, while emancipation concerns critically analyzing, resisting and challenging structures of power.").

of social rights. This section will provide some background on the international and regional legal frameworks wherein which social rights are enshrined, and lay out the social rights of beneficiaries that bind African states.

3.2.1. The Human Rights Framework & General Problems with Social Rights

The Universal Declaration of Human Rights recognizes social rights as being indispensable for guaranteeing human dignity and the free development of one's personality.[310] Social rights, found in articles 22, 25 and 26, include the right to social security; an adequate standard of living, including food, clothing, housing, medical care and social services that are necessary for one's health and wellbeing; special rights for the protection of children and mothers; and education. Despite its high ideals, the Declaration is not a legally binding document. There are, however, two major instruments of international law that do in fact impose social rights obligations on African states. These are the ICESCR and the African Charter. The social rights obligations of African states under these two human rights instruments will be discussed in the follow subsections, yet it is worthwhile noting here that there are still several more instruments of international human rights law that recognize social rights and impose corresponding obligations upon states.[311]

Although states are bound by their social rights obligations, the strength of these obligations is overshadowed by the fact that social rights are largely unenforceable at the international level.[312] Moreover, there remains

310 Universal Declaration of Human Rights, UNGA (adopted 10 December 1948) UN Doc A/810 (UDHR) art. 22.

311 E.g., International Covenant on the Elimination of All Forms of Racial Discrimination (adopted 21 December 1965, entered into force 4 January 1969) 660 UNTS 195 (ICERD) art. 5 (e) (iii - v); International Covenant on the Elimination of All Forms of Discrimination against Women (adopted 18 December 1979, entered into force 3 September 1981) 1249 UNTS 13 (ICEDAW) arts. 11 (1) (e), (2) (b) (c), 12 (1 -2), 14 (2) (b - d); Covenant on the Rights of the Child (adopted 20 November 1989, entered into force 2 September 1990) 1577 UNTS 3 (CRC) arts 20, 23-28.

312 The ICESCR establishes the competence of a treaty body (originally the UN Economic and Social Council, but later the Committee on Economic, Social and Cultural Rights) to supervise State compliance, but does not authorize any tribunal to hear or adjudicate individual complaints, and does not propose any

doubt as to their justiciability.[313] At the theoretical level, these concerns are often the consequence of efforts to distinguish economic, social and cultural (ESC) rights from their civil and political counterparts. This is part of a longstanding theoretical debate in law about whether human rights are indivisible and interdependent, or whether they may be arranged in a hierarchical order.[314] To summarize the point, the ESCR Committee wrote,

> In relation to civil and political rights, it is generally taken for granted that judicial remedies for violations are essential. Regrettably, the contrary assumption is too often made in relation to economic, social and cultural rights. This discrepancy is not warranted either by the nature of the rights or by the relevant Covenant provisions.[315]

Yet, any view that arranges human rights norms into a hierarchy would be contrary to the formal position of international[316] and regional[317] law,

---

enforcement mechanism for the recommendations issued by treaty body. (See International Covenant on Economic, Social and Cultural Rights (adopted 16 December 1966, entered into force 3 January 1976) 993 UNTS 3 (ICESCR) arts. 16 - 22).

313 See Michael J. Dennis and David P. Stewart, 'Justiciability of Economic, Social and Cultural Rights: Should There Be an International Complaints Mechanism to Adjudicate the Rights to Food, Water, Housing, and Health?' 98 American Journal of International Law 462 (2004); but see Mónica Feria Tinta, 'Justiciability of Economic, Social and Cultural Rights in the Inter-American System of Protection of Human Rights: Beyond Traditional Paradigms and Notions' 29 Human Rights Quarterly 431 (2007).

314 Formally, there is international recognition of the interdependence, indivisibility and interrelatedness of human rights norms. In practice, however, there is a divergence in the manner in which different human rights norms are treated by states and by the courts. (Dinah Shelton, 'Hierarchy of Norms and Human Rights: Of Trumps and Winners' 65 Saskatchewan Law Review 301 (2002) 302-303, 308-331.).

315 General Comment No. 9: The Domestic Application of the Covenant, Committee on Economic Social and Cultural Rights, U.N. Doc. E/1998/24 (UN 1997) para. 10.

316 UDHR preamble; ICESCR preamble; International Covenant on Civil and Political Rights (adopted 16 December 1966, entered into force 23 March 1976) 999 UNTS 171 (ICCPR) preamble. Vienna Declaration and Programme of Action, (July 12, 1993) U.N. Doc. A/CONF.157/23 para. 5 (endorsed by World Conference on Human Rights, UNGA (Dec. 20, 1993) UN Doc. A/RES/48/121) ("All human rights are universal, indivisible and interdependent and interrelated. The international community must treat human rights globally in a fair and equal manner, on the same footing, and with the same emphasis.").

each of which acknowledge the interconnectedness and interdependence of human rights norms. On this point, the ESCR Committee,

> The adoption of a rigid classification of economic, social and cultural rights which puts them, by definition, beyond the reach of the courts would thus be arbitrary and incompatible with the principle that the two sets of human rights are indivisible and interdependent. It would also drastically curtail the capacity of the courts to protect the rights of the most vulnerable and disadvantaged groups in society.[318]

Despite their questionable justiciability at the level of theory, there is evidence to suggest that jurisprudence on ESC rights continues to develop around the world within the regional and domestic fields.[319] Notwithstanding, in general, domestic law and domestic courts in sub-Saharan African countries have yet to concretize social rights fully into individual entitlements with corresponding state duties.[320] There are of course a few exceptional cases where there has been significant progress, such as the well-known judicial treatment of constitutionally guaranteed socio-economic rights in South Africa.[321] There are also examples where rights have been concretized through legislation. In Kenya, for example, the child's right to free and compulsory education has been made concrete through the Children's Act and the Basic Education Act, although in other areas of social law, such as housing, health and water, individuals still use constitu-

---

317 African Charter on Human and Peoples' Rights (adopted 27 June 1981, entered into force 21 October 1986) 21 ILM 58 (ACHPR) preamble ("...civil and political rights cannot be disassociated from economic, social and cultural rights in their conception as well as universality and that the satisfaction of economic, social and cultural rights is a guarantee for the enjoyment of civil and political rights").

318 General Comment No. 9: The Domestic Application of the Covenant (1997) para. 10.

319 See generally, *Courts and the Legal Enforcement of Economic, Social and Cultural Rights: Comparative Expereinces of Justiciability*, International Commission of Jurists (2008) <https://www.humanrights.ch/upload/pdf/080819_justiziabilitt_esc.pdf> (reviewing the enforcement and justiciability of economic, social and cultural rights at the regional and domestic levels).

320 Manisuli Ssenyonjo, 'Influence of the ICESCR in Africa' in Daniel Moeckli, Helen Keller and Corina Heri (eds), *The Human Rights Covenants at 50: Their Past, Present, and Future* (Oxford University Press 2018) 99-123, 107-108.

321 See Mirja Trilsch, 'What's the Use of Socio-Economic Rights in a Constitution? – Taking a Look at the South African Experience' 42 Verfassung und Recht in Übersee / Law and Politics in Africa, Asia and Latin America 552 (2009).

tional law to claim social goods through litigation.[322] Finally, there seems to be some evidence to suggest that the process of concretization might be able to begin from even as high up as international law. According to one study, the creation of the ICESCR was followed by increased institutionalization of social security laws across 173 countries.[323] While it cannot be said for sure whether the relation is causal,[324] these findings nonetheless leave open the possibility that international recognition of ESC rights might have had a lasting impact on their domestic concretization.

These legally protected rights do not always translate into greater social wellbeing and protection in everyday life. Where social rights legislation does exists, as in the case of social security and social assistance law in Tanzania, coverage can be so limited and the quality of social goods so poor that social rights are effectively no more than privileges.[325] In some countries, such as Botswana, social rights guarantees are left out of the constitution entirely.[326] In other countries, like Namibia, most social rights appear in the constitution as policy directives rather than individual rights *per se*.[327] These constitutional directives are found in a number of African constitutions. To understand how they differ from concrete social rights entitlements, consider the example of Uganda.

---

322 Godfrey O. Odongo and Godfrey M. Musila, 'Direct Constitutional Protection of Economic, Social and Cultural Rights in Kenya's 2010 Constitution' in Danwood Mzikenge Chirwa and Lilian Chenwi (eds), *The Protection of Economic, Social and Cultural Rights in Africa: International, Regional and National Perspectives* (Cambridge University Press 2016) 338-371.

323 Lyle Scruggs, Christian Zimmermann and Christopher Jeffords, 'Implementation of the Human Right to Social Security around the World: A Preliminary Analysis of National Social Protection Laws' in Lanse Minkler (ed), *The State of Economic and Social Human Rights: A Global Review* (Cambridge University Press 2013) 117-134.

324 But see Ssenyonjo 112 (asserting that the adoption of ESC rights in the domestic law of African dualist states was influenced in part, but not explicitly, by the ICESCR.).

325 Tulia Ackson, 'Justiciability of Socio-Economic Rights in Tanzania' 23 African Journal of International and Comparative Law 359 (2015) 365-372.

326 Bonolo Ramadi Dinokopila, 'The Justiciability of Socio-Economic Rights in Botswana' 57 Journal of African Law 108 (2013) 109.

327 John Cantius Mubangizi, 'The Constitutional Protection of Socio-Economic Rights in Selected African Countries: A Comparative Evaluation' 2 African Journal of Legal Studies 1 (2006) 8-10.

Although Uganda is a member to the International Convention on Economic, Social and Cultural Rights,[328] its constitution does not treat ESC rights the same as civil and political rights. The Ugandan constitution declares, as one of the state's objectives, the "guarantee and respect [of] the independence of non-governmental organisations which protect and promote human rights."[329] It also recognizes some social state objectives, including a declaration that the state "shall endeavor to fulfill the fundamental rights of all Ugandans to social justice...and shall, in particular, ensure that...all Ugandans enjoy rights and opportunities and access to education, health services, clean and safe water, work, decent shelter, adequate clothing, food security and pension and retirement benefits."[330] Yet, it remains unclear whether these objectives translate into constitutionally guaranteed social rights.[331] On the other hand, the constitution explicitly and thoroughly sets out constitutional protections of civil and political rights, including the right to a fair hearing.[332]

In general, the realization and enjoyment of social rights in sub-Saharan Africa remains rather weak at the domestic level due to the fact that social rights are not widely concretized. Instead, social rights are guaranteed by the broad strokes of international (and sometimes constitutional) law. However, as suggested early, domestic courts are typically reluctant to concretize social rights directly from constitutional or international law.[333] This reluctance is captured well by Odongo and Musila in their assessment of judicial enforcement of socio-economic rights enshrined in Kenya's 2010 constitution. In their view,

---

328 'Status of International Covenant on Economic, Social and Cultural Rights' (*United Nations*) <https://treaties.un.org/Pages/ViewDetails.aspx?src=TREATY&mtdsg_no=IV-3&chapter=4&clang=_en>; 'Status of International Covenant on Civil and Political Rights' (*United Nations*) <https://treaties.un.org/Pages/ViewDetails.aspx?src=TREATY&mtdsg_no=IV-4&chapter=4&clang=_en>.

329 Constitution of Uganda (1995; rev. 2005) Objective V.

330 Ibid Objective XIV.

331 See *Centre for Health Human Rights & Development & Others v. Attorney General*,UGCC 4, Petition No. 16 of 2011 (CC 2012) (Uganda) (in holding that petitioner's claims represented political questions rather than constitutional challenges, the Constitutional Court of Uganda denied petitioner's request for a declaration that the constitution guarantees a right to health and that the government's health policies violate the right to health of pregnant women.).

332 Constitution of Uganda art. 28.

333 Ssenyonjo 109-122 (noting that in practice, domestic courts in both dualist and monist African states are reluctant to give full effect to ESC rights directly from the ICESCR.).

> ...it appears, as we have argued below, that court's refusal to consider individualised relief is consistent with the general approach adopted by Kenyan courts in ESC rights cases so far: they focus on structural conditions that would enable the state to progressively meet its obligations rather than on providing immediate relief upon demand.[334]

There are doctrinal grounds for the difficulty that courts encounter whenever they are asked to concretize social rights from international and constitutional instruments. First, the language of social rights found in constitutional and international instruments tends to be so broad that their distillation into specific entitlements does not lend itself well to principled legal reasoning. Terms such as 'health', 'education', 'housing' and 'social security' are equivocal in their meaning, and determining the specific content of their essential cores is fraught with unprincipled or incoherent methods.[335] Second, it is difficult for a court to ascertain in concrete terms the state's constitutional or international duties with respect to realizing these social rights because such rights are typically subject to internal[336] and external[337] limitations clauses.[338] Finally, courts hesitate to shape social

334 See, e.g., Odongo and Musila 364-365.

335 See Katharine G. Young, 'The Minimum Core of Economic and Social Rights: A Concept in Search of Content' 33 Yale Journal of International Law 113 (2008); Karin Lehmann, 'In Defense of the Constitutional Court: Litigating Socio-Economic Rights and the Myth of the Minimum Core' 22 American University International Law Review 163 (2006).

336 For example, some commentators view those rights that guarantee mere *access* to a good as having an internal limitation built into the scope of the right itself. See Odongo and Musila 346-347 (*quoting and citing* Japhet Biegon, 'The Inclusion of Socio-Economic Rights in the 2010 Constitution: Conceptual and Practical Issues' in Japhet Biegon and Godfrey M. Musila (eds), *Judiciary Watch Report: Judicial Enforcement of Socio-Economic Rights under the New Constitution : Challenges and Opportunities for Kenya*, vol 10 (Kenya Section of the International Commission of Jurists 2011).).

337 Under international law, social rights are subject to resource limitations and other limitations determined by law for the purpose of promoting general welfare. (ICESCR arts. 2(1) & 4.).

338 See Walter Kälin and Jörg Künzli, *The Law of International Human Rights Protection* (Oxford University Press 2009) 116. Cf. Scott Craig and Patrick Macklem, 'Constitutional Ropes of Sand or Justiciable Guarantees? Social Rights in a New South African Constitution' 141 University of Pennsylvania Law Review 1 (1992) 72-73 (cautioning that the imprecision of social rights "should not be overstated", and calling upon the judicial branch to make constitutionally guaranteed social rights more precise and concrete through "years of repeated applications of practical reasoning to facts at hand".).

rights into individual entitlements for specific goods or to grant judicial remedies because doing so involves addressing questions of a predominantly political nature, which some have argued threatens to upset democratic safeguards against the consolidation of power into the hands of unelected officials, and raises concerns about judicial accountability.[339]

Despite the difficulty in domestically concretizing internationally guaranteed social rights, international human rights law is not irrelevant as it does impose real, albeit not always concrete, duties upon states. Human rights law guarantees certain social rights to individuals, for which the state bears corresponding legal obligations. This gives rise to a legal relationship between the beneficiary and the state. In order to protect, respect and fulfill the social rights of beneficiaries, states must take steps toward the progressive realization of social rights, to the maximum of available resources.[340] One consequence of this distinction between concrete legislation and broadly defined human rights is that people in African do not have a right to a particular service or benefit *per se*, but rather to the progressive realization of their social rights.

Closely related to the issues of justiciability and enforceability is the question of individual entitlements. Some have argued that, because their

339 Navish Jheelan, 'The Enforceability of Socio-Economic Rights' 2 European Human Rights Law Review 146 (2007). See also Shadrack B. O. Gutto, 'Beyond Justiciability: Challenges of Implementing/Enforcing Socio-Economic Rights in South Africa' 4 Buffolo Human Rights Law Review 79 (1998); Jeremy Waldron, 'A Rights-Based Critique of Constitutional Rights' 13 Oxford Journal of Legal Studies 18 (1993). Cf. Larry Alexander, 'What Is the Problem of Judicial Review?' in José Rubio Carrecedo (ed), *Political Philosophy: New Proposals for New Questions* (Franz Steiner Verlag 2007) 173-181, 177 (noting that although legislative interpretations of the constitution boast democratic legitimacy, "legislatures lack the power to entrench their laws against future legislatures. That is why the courts when engaging in constitutional decisionmaking have a settlement advantage over legislatures, at least if the courts follow a moderately strong doctrine of precedential constraint."); International Commission of Jurists, *Courts and the Legal Enforcement of Economic, Social and Cultural Rights: Comparative Expereinces of Justiciability* (2008) 73-77 (pointing out that the boundary separating a legal issue from a political one is rather blurry, and emphasizing that, regarding the justiciability of ESC rights, "[t]he issue is not whether the judiciary should have the leading role in the implementation of public policies intended to comply with constitutional or international ESC rights obligations...[but] Rather, the fundamental question is what role the courts should have to supervise the implementation of these policies, according to constitutional, international human rights or legal standards.").

340 ICESCR art. 2.

realization necessitates the demand for public goods, social rights do not yield individual rights that each person can claim against the state.[341] However, the recent emergence of an individual complaint mechanism for the ICESCR suggests that blanket denials of an individualized component to social rights may be too simplistic.[342] The individual complaint mechanism came into force in 2013 by way of the Optional Protocol to the International Covenant on Economic, Social and Cultural Rights (OP-ICESCR), which allows the ESCR Committee to adjudicate individual complaints against State Parties to the OP-ICESCR.[343]

A key feature of the OP-ICESCR is the CECSR Committee's power to request interim measures from state parties prior to the resolution of a case. These measures require states to perform, or abstain from performing, specific acts meant to prevent exceptional and irreparable damage to the enjoyment of covenant rights.[344] Although some states are reluctant to acknowledge the binding effect of interim measures, international bodies insist that they are legally binding upon state parties.[345] The existence of such a binding mechanism for individual complaints supports the notion that social rights are individual rights, yet the low ratification rate of the OP-ICESCR rather indicates the reluctance among states to recognize the same. As of February 2017, only 22 countries had ratified the OP-ICE-

---

341 See, e.g., Christian Tomuschat, *Human Rights: Between Idealism and Realism* (2d edn, Oxford University Press 2008) 42.

342 See, Martin Scheinin, 'Indirect Protection of Economic, Social and Cultural Rights in International Law' in Danwood Mzikenge Chirwa and Lilian Chenwi (eds), *The Protection of Economic, Social and Cultural Rights in Africa: International, Regional and National Perspectives* (Cambridge University Press 2016) 72-87, 73.

343 See 'UN Lauds New Tool Enabling Individual Complainst on Economic, Social and Cultural Rights' *UN News Centre* (Feb. 6, 2013) <http://www.un.org/apps/news/story.asp?NewsID=44081#.WJMqCZUzVaS>.

344 Optional Protocol to the International Covenant on Economic, Social and Cultural Rights (adopted 10 Dec. 2008, entered into force 5 May 2013) 2922 UNTS 27 (Op-ICESCR) art. 5.

345 See Christian Courtis, *Commentary on the Optional Protocol to the International Covenant on Economic, Social and Cultural Rights*, International Commission of Jurists & Inter-American Institute of Human Rights, (2008) 71 <https://www.icj.org/wp-content/uploads/2009/07/Commentary-OP-ICESCR-publication-2009-eng.pdf>; Viviana Krsticevic and Brian Griffey, 'Interim Measures' in Malcolm Langford and others (eds), *The Optional Protocol to the International Covenant on Economic, Social and Cultural Rights: A Commentary* (Pretoria University Law Press 2016) 293-326, 320-325.

SCR.[346] Likewise, within the African continent, commitment to the OP-ICESCR is extremely low despite efforts of the African Commission on Human and Peoples' Rights to urge African states to ratify the OP-ICESCR.[347] As of September 2018, only three African countries were state parties to the optional protocol.[348] If more African states join the OP-ICESCR in the future, intern measures could be employed to require states to amend problematic NGO laws.

3.2.2. International and Regional Protection for Social Rights

At the international level, social rights are most prominently featured in the ICESCR. As of 2017, the ICESCR enjoys wide acceptance among African states. It has been ratified by all but four African countries (South Sudan, Mozambique, Comoros and Botswana).[349] Ten African states parties to the treaty have filed declarations or reservations to its terms, although two have since withdrawn their reservations.[350] Of the remaining eight, only five state parties make reservations that explicitly limit their obligations regarding social rights. Kenya limits its obligation to provide workers with remunerated maternity leave, while Algeria, Madagascar, South Africa and Zambia restrict their obligations regarding the free and compulsory provision of primary education to all.[351] The withdrawn reservations, previously submitted by Congo and Rwanda, also limited the duties of those states with regard to the provision of education.[352] With the exception of these limitations on the provision of education, almost all African states are bound by all the terms of the ICESCR.

---

346 See 'Status of Optional Protocol to the International Covenant on Economic, Social and Cultural Rights' (*United Nations*) <https://treaties.un.org/Pages/ViewDetails.aspx?src=IND&mtdsg_no=IV-3-a&chapter=4&clang=_en>.

347 Resolution on the Optional Protocol to the International Covenant on Economic, Social and Cultural Rights, ACmHPR (May 2, 2012) (Resolution on the OP-ICESCR).

348 See 'Status of Optional Protocol to the International Covenant on Economic, Social and Cultural Rights'(*United Nations*).

349 'Status of International Covenant on Economic, Social and Cultural Rights' (*United Nations*).

350 Ibid.

351 Ibid.

352 Ibid.

At the regional level, the African Charter recognizes certain social rights, which are enshrined in articles 16 and 17.[353] These include the right to the best attainable physical and mental health, and the right to education. Notably missing are the rights to food, water, housing, social security and an adequate standard of living. However, the African Commission has recognized additional social rights by deriving them from others explicitly guaranteed in the Charter. These will be discussed in detail below.

Additionally, social rights are protected in the African Charter on the Rights and Welfare of the Child (African Children's Charter),[354] and the Protocol to the African Charter on Human and Peoples' Rights on the Rights of Women in Africa (African Women's Protocol).[355] Finally, various 'soft law' documents recognize social rights at the regional level. They include the Pretoria Declaration on Economic, Social and Cultural Rights in Africa[356], the Principles and Guidelines on the Implementation of Economic, Social and Cultural Rights in the African Charter on Human and Peoples' Rights[357] and other resolutions of the African Commission. Although technically non-binding,[358] these documents offer guidance on the normative content of social rights in Africa and are legally significant because the African Commission often relies on them in its opinions.[359] Some international lawyers insist that relying on 'soft law' and other non-binding texts in order to interpret the provisions of a treaty is at odds with

353 African Charter.

354 African Charter on the Rights and Welfare of the Child (adopted 11 July 1990, entered into force 29 November 1999) OAU Doc. CAB/LEG/24.9/49 (ACRWC), arts. 11, 14.

355 Protocol to the African Charter on Human and Peoples' Rights on the Rights of Women in Africa (adopted 11 July 2003, entered into force 25 November 2005) AU Doc. CAB/LEG/66.6 (African Women's Protocol), arts. 12-16.

356 Pretoria Declaration on Economic, Social and Cultural Rights in Africa, ACmHPR (Dec. 7, 2004).

357 Principles and Guidelines on the Implementation of Economic, Social and Cultural Rights in the African Chart on Human and Peoples' Rights, ACmHPR (Oct. 24, 2011).

358 Sibonile Khoza, 'Promoting Economic, Social and Cultural Rights in Africa: The African Commission Holds a Seminar in Pretoria: Recent Developments' 4 African Human Rights Law Journal 334 (2004) 338.

359 See, e.g., *Monim Elgak, Osman Hummeida and Amir Suliman v. Sudan*, Communication 379/09 (ACmHPR 2014) para.134; see also *Purohit v. Gambia, paras. 81-82* (*relying* on Principles for the Protection of Persons with Mental Illness and Improvement of Mental Health Care, UNGA (Dec. 17, 1991).).

the Vienna Convention.[360] However, the African Commission may be justified in doing so due to the broad spectrum of interpretive tools made available to it by Articles 60 and 61 of the African Charter.[361]

As of September 2018, the African Court on Human and Peoples' Rights, which is a judicial body, has not yet issued a decision on the normative content of social rights or the state's social rights obligations under African human rights law.[362] The only two regional bodies that have done so are the African Commission and the African Children's Committee. As such, this chapter will review the jurisprudence emanating only from these two treaty bodies in order to clarify the core obligations of African states regarding the realization and enjoyment of social rights.

3.2.2.1. The Committee on Economic, Social and Cultural Rights

The ESCR Committee serves as the Covenant's treaty body and issues interpretive guidelines through the adoption of general comments.[363] These comments provide normative content to the social rights and corresponding obligations declared in the Covenant. Although the general comments of UN treaty bodies are not legally binding *per se*, they represent the official interpretation of the treaty body and are not without any legal significance or consequence.[364] In international law, treaty interpretation and state practices are important indicators of a norm's legal character. States are not permitted to decide for themselves whether they have violated the ICESCR. As per the purpose of ICESCR, the ESCR Committee has that fi-

---

360 Malgosia Fitzmaurice, 'Interpretation of Human Rights Treaties' in Dinah Shelton (ed), *The Oxford Handbook of International Human Rights Law* (Oxford University Press 2013) 739-771, 765.

361 African Charter arts. 60-61 (permitting broadly the use of "…African practices consistent with international norms on human and peoples' rights, customs generally accepted as law, general principles of law recognized by African states as well as legal precedents and doctrine.").

362 It appears that the primary reason for this is a lack of applications lodged before the courts alleging social rights violations.

363 See Tomuschat (2008) 190-191.

364 Nigel S. Rodley, 'The Role and Impact of Treaty Bodies' in Dinah Shelton (ed), *The Oxford Handbook of International Human Rights Law* (Oxford University Press 2013) 621-648, 639-641; Nihal Jayawickrama, *The Judicial Application of Human Rights Law: National, Regional and International Jurisprudence* (Cambridge University Press 2002) 167-168.

nal responsibility.[365] Regarding state practice, states rarely put forward their own interpretation of specific provisions of the ICESCR.[366] Moreover, they tend to accept interpretations of the ESCR Committee, thereby implicitly endorsing them.[367]

The legal significance of general comments is also characterized by their impact on court opinions. Judicial bodies, including domestic courts, sometimes rely on the interpretation of treaty bodies as though they had persuasive authority. For instance, the International Court of Justice (ICJ) modeled its own interpretation of human rights treaties in accordance with the jurisprudence of treaty bodies. Following the interpretations of the U.N. Human Rights Committee (HRC), which is the supervisory body of International Covenant on Civil and Political Rights, the ICJ writes:

> 66. … Although the Court is in no way obliged, in the exercise of its judicial functions, to model its own interpretation of the Covenant on that of the [Human Rights] Committee, it believes that it should ascribe great weight to the interpretation adopted by this independent body that was established specifically to supervise the application of that treaty. The point here is to achieve the necessary clarity and the essential consistency of international law, as well as legal security, to which both the individuals with guaranteed rights and the States obliged to comply with treaty obligations are entitled.[368]

3.2.2.2. African Commission on Human and Peoples' Rights

The African Commission shoulders the task of interpreting the African Charter through the promulgation of guidelines and principles, which states may use to implement Charter provisions.[369] Its interpretations draw upon relevant international and regional human rights instruments, including the International Covenant for Economic, Social and Cultural

---

365 Alston and Quinn (1987) 163.

366 Kerstin Mechlem, 'Treaty Bodies and the Interpretation of Human Rights' 42 Vanderbilt Journal of Transnational Law 905 (2009) 920-921.

367 Ibid 921.

368 *Case Concerning Ahmadou Sadio Diallo (Republic of Guinea v. Democratic Republic of the Congo)*, 2010 I.C.J. Rep. 639, (ICJ 2010) para. 66-67.

369 African Charter art. 45 (1) (b); Udombana (2004) 'Between Promise and Performance: Revisiting States' Obligations under the African Human Rights Charter' 119.

Rights.[370] The African Charter explicitly permits reliance on a broad range of sources for its interpretation, including "African practices", which do not obviously constitute binding legal sources.[371] Some scholars argue that the Charter even permits the use of 'soft law' or treaties that are not yet in force.[372]

Although it remains doubtful that the Commission's outputs bind African states, some commentators (including, at times, the African Commission) insist that they do.[373] The African Commission's outputs, like those of the ECSCR Committee, nonetheless provide persuasive insight into the normative content of social rights guaranteed by the African Charter, as well as the states' corresponding duties.[374] Moreover, they are legally significant due to their impact on the decisions of judicial bodies. In the same case ICJ cited earlier, the court remarked on its willingness to rely on the interpretations of the African Commission:

> Likewise, when the Court is called upon, as in these proceedings, to apply a regional instrument for the protection of human rights, it must take due account of the interpretation of that instrument adopted by the independent bodies which have been specifically created, if such has been the case, to monitor the sound application of the treaty in question. In the present case, the interpretation given above of Article 12, paragraph 4, of the African Charter is consonant with the case law of the African Commission on Human and Peoples' Rights established by Article 30 of the said Charter…[375]

Although binding legal norms are preferred for the enforcement of law, non-binding 'soft law' can still be effective in improving state compliance. Rachel Murray and Debra Long have gone so far as to argue that the binding/non-binding distinction is an "unhelpful distraction" for the evaluation of state compliance with the Commission's decisions.[376] Their research concludes that the non-binding status of the African Commission's

370 African Charter arts. 60-61.

371 Ibid art. 61.

372 E.g., Fitzmaurice (2013) 765.

373 R. Murray and D. Long, *The Implementation of the Findings of the African Commission on Human and Peoples' Rights* (Cambridge University Press 2015) pp. 52-56.

374 See ibid 58-61.

375 *Case Concerning Ahmadou Sadio Diallo* para. 67.

376 Murray and Long (2015) 58.

findings does not preclude compliance by African States.[377] Indeed, Kofi Oteng Kufur argues that by clarifying the meaning of rights, the African Commission is "making the law more determinate", which in turn "creates the conditions for the [States] parties to fulfill their obligations."[378] Murray and Long assert further that in some cases insisting upon the binding effect of the Commission's decisions may be undesirable because doing so would likely result in political backlash and "undermine the overall authority of the African Commission."[379] As some observers have commented, the "persuasive style" of the African Commission's outputs "takes the law as an invitation to dialogue between more or less equal parties", and "the [state] authorities respond better to something that won't criminalise them and where there will be less public criticism, and this may ultimately result in greater compliance."[380]

3.2.2.3. African Committee of Experts on the Rights and Welfare of the Child

The Committee of Experts on the Rights and Welfare of the Child (African Children's Committee) is the treaty body charged with interpreting and monitoring the implementation of the African Children's Charter.[381] The African Children's Charter guarantees various social rights.[382] Article 11 lays out the right of children to education, including "free and compulsory basic education." Article 14 guarantees children's right to the "best attainable state of physical, mental and spiritual health".

The Committee's findings offer persuasive interpretations of the Charter in at least two meaningful ways. First, they provide clear guidance on the normative content of the state's minimum core obligation. Second, they contribute guidance on the general obligations of states. For instance, in implementing General Comments of the ESCR Committee, the African Children's Committee agrees that states have obligations to "protect, ful-

377 Ibid 56.
378 Kufuor (2010) 72.
379 Murray and Long (2015) 57.
380 Ibid 16-17 (internal quotation marks and citations omitted).
381 African Children's Charter arts. 32, 42; *Michelo Hunsungule and Others (on Behalf of Children in Northern Uganda) v. Uganda*, Communication No. 1/2005 (ACmERWC 2013) para. 39.
382 African Children's Charter.

fill, respect and promote."[383] The Committee notes further that although the "general obligation that States undertake is subject neither to progressive realization, nor to available resources",[384] certain specific provisions of the Charter, including the right to health, are subject to these qualifications.[385] The Committee strongly insists that states must fulfill its obligations effectively in accordance with "due diligence" and "reasonableness" standards.[386] The key question is, has a government "take[n] all reasonable steps necessary to fulfill its obligations under the Charter?"[387]

3.2.3. Social Rights and their Normative Content

The text of the ICESCR explicitly recognizes several social rights. These include rights relating to social security, health, education, housing and an adequate standard of living. Although these rights are enshrined in law, their meaning is rather ambiguous as the Covenant leaves key terms undefined. The right to social security is guaranteed to everyone and includes social insurance, although these terms are not defined.[388] Likewise, the Covenant guarantees the right to an adequate standard of living for each person and his or her family, which includes adequate food, clothing and housing as well as continuously improving living conditions, without explicating what precisely constitutes an adequate standard of living, food, clothing, etc.[389] The same can be said of the remaining social rights, which are "freedom from hunger";[390] and the "enjoyment of the highest attainable standard of physical and mental health".[391] The right to education, however, has been fleshed out a bit more.[392] It includes free and compulsory primary education, as well as some degree of secondary, tertiary and fundamental education.[393] Ultimately, however, the Covenant does not en-

---

383 *Centre for Human Rights, University of Pretoria and La Rencontre Africaine Pour La Defense Des Droits De L'homme v. Senegal*, (ACmERWC 2014) para. 47.
384 *Hunsungule v. Uganda* para. 37.
385 Ibid para. 72.
386 Ibid, paras. 38, 69-70.
387 Ibid, para. 70.
388 ICESCR art. 9.
389 Ibid art. 11 (1).
390 Ibid art. 11 (2).
391 Ibid art. 12 (1).
392 Ibid art. 13 (1).
393 Ibid art. 13 (2).

dow social rights with sufficient normative content to determine what precisely each right entails. This means that their contents are up for interpretation.

The Committee has developed a body of texts – particularly its General Comments – that are dedicated to interpreting the meaning of Covenant rights. These texts tend to use a teleological style of interpret in order to construct social rights in the broadest way possible, which also allows the Committee to take advantage of the Covenant's call for the *full* realization of social rights. While such a broad interpretation seems harmless since states may achieve these lofty goals progressively, such a construction appears to give social rights an idealistic, rather than legalistic, character.

Regarding the right to adequate housing, the Committee has noted that this includes "the right to live somewhere in security, peace and dignity" rather than a more narrowly constructed notion such as "merely having a roof over one's head".[394] While the Committee recognizes that the adequacy of housing will vary in relation to the given circumstances, it insists that certain aspects of adequacy are inherent to the right to housing.[395] These include security of legal tenure, the availability of services, materials, facilities and infrastructure, the affordability, habitability, accessibility and cultural adequacy of housing, and the proximity of housing to employment and social facilities.[396]

The right to adequate food is similarly interpreted in a broad manner so as to be fully realized "when every man, woman and child…have physical and economic access at all times to adequate food or means for its procurement."[397] This is far from a restrictive construction that would limit the right to "a minimum package of calories, proteins and other specific nutrients."[398] The Committee also incorporates the notion of sustainability into the right to adequate food in order to protect the rights of future generations.[399] Finally, the Committee asserts that the right to adequate food implies that dietary needs must be met and that food must be safe to consume, culturally acceptable (or made acceptable for consumers through

394 General Comment No. 4: The Right to Adequate Housing, Committee on Economic Social and Cultural Rights, U.N. Doc. E/1992/23 (UN 1991) para. 7.

395 Ibid para. 8.

396 Ibid paras. 8 (a) - (g).

397 General Comment No. 12: The Right to Adequate Food (1999) para. 6.

398 Ibid.

399 Ibid para. 7.

proper labelling, processing and distribution), and both available and accessible.[400]

The right to education is similarly construed in a broad manner, such that the Committee emphasizes four generic aspects: availability, accessibility, acceptability and adaptability of education.[401] The right to technical and vocational training has received additional attention from the Committee. It is said to include a variety of aspects, such as acquiring knowledge and skills which contribute to one's personal development, self-reliance and employability.[402] Once again, the Committee's broad generalization are a way to universalize some basic standards for social right while leaving intact the discretion of each state to determine the particularities of social rights in accordance with the prevailing conditions within the state.

In the case of the right to health, the Committee is careful not to employ the widest possible interpretation. It notes cautiously that the "right to health is not to be understood as the right to be *healthy*".[403] It notes that the state cannot be the guarantor of good health or provide protection against every possible illness or disease.[404] Instead, the right "must be understood as the right to the enjoyment of a variety of facilities, goods, services and conditions necessary for the realization of the highest attainable standard of health."[405] This includes freedom to control one's body and health, such as sexual and reproductive health,[406] and freedom from bodily interference, such as torture, experimentation and non-consensual medical treatments.[407] The Committee also notes that normative contents of the right to enjoy the highest attainable standard of health is partly defined, or perhaps limited, by the availability of the state's resources.[408]

In other ways, however, the right to health is understood broadly. It includes the right to a system of health protection, as well as the right to un-

---

400 Ibid para. 9-13.

401 General Comment No. 13: The Right to Education, Committee on Economic Social and Cultural Rights, U.N. Doc. E/C.12/1999/10 (UN 1999) para. 6.

402 Ibid para. 16.

403 General Comment No. 14: The Right to the Highest Attainable Standard of Health (2000) para. 8 (emphasis in original).

404 Ibid para. 9.

405 Ibid.

406 General Comment No. 22: The Right to Sexual and Reproductive Health, Committee on Economic Social and Cultural Rights, U.N. Doc. E/C.12/GC/22 (UN 2016).

407 General Comment No. 14: The Right to the Highest Attainable Standard of Health (2000) para. 8.

408 Ibid para. 9.

derlying determinants of health, such as access to water, adequate sanitation, food, housing and healthy occupational and environmental conditions.[409] Moreover, the Committee insists upon the generalizable aspects that it has found in other social rights – the availability, accessibility, acceptability and quality of health care – each aspect being adjustable in accordance with prevailing conditions.[410] Finally, the Committee constructs implicit rights from the Covenant's explicit mandate that states achieve a non-exhaustive list of objectives.[411] These rights, some of which overlap with others previously mentioned, include the right to maternal, child and reproductive health, to healthy natural and workplace environments, to prevention, treatment and control of diseases and to health facilities, goods and services.[412]

Perhaps the Committee's most ambitious interpretation of the Covenant is its construction of the implicit right to water, which is not featured explicitly anywhere in the Covenant. The Committee reasons that the right to water must exist because it is a necessary precondition for the realization of almost every other social right, as well as the right to life and the human dignity.[413] It is as if the right to water lurks in all corners of the Covenant. In terms of its generic aspects, this right entails entitlement to "sufficient, safe, acceptable, physically accessible and affordable water for personal and domestic use," as well as water of a decent quality.[414] More specifically, the right to water includes the freedom to maintain access to existing water supplies, free from interferences such as arbitrary disconnections or contamination, as well as "the right to a system of water supply and management".[415]

Finally, the Committee has weighed in on the right to social security. This is perhaps the most difficult right to interpret because the Covenant provides absolutely no definition or explanation for what social security might entail, except to note that it includes social insurance. As such, the Committee relies heavily on Conventions of the International Labor Organization. It notes that the right to social security is essentially the right to

---

409 Ibid paras. 8 & 11.

410 Ibid para. 12.

411 ICESCR art. 12 (2) (a) - (d).

412 General Comment No. 14: The Right to the Highest Attainable Standard of Health (2000) paras. 13-17.

413 General Comment No. 15: The Right to Water, Committee on Economic Social and Cultural Rights, U.N. Doc. E/C.12/2002/11 (UN 2003) paras. 3 & 6.

414 Ibid paras. 2 & 12.

415 Ibid para. 10.

access benefits in order to secure protection from a variety of social risks.[416] These risks include income unaffordable access to health care; insecurity brought on by sickness, disability, maternity, injury, unemployment, old age, or death of a family member; and insufficient family support.[417] In terms of freedoms and entitlements, the right entails freedom from unreasonable restrictions of existing social security coverage, as well as the right to "equal enjoyment of adequate protection from social risks and contingencies".[418] Finally, the Committee articulates the generic aspects of availability, adequacy, and accessibility, which relate to having a transparent social security system in place that includes social assistance and non-contributory schemes with universal coverage.[419]

Unlike the ICESCR, the African Charter only explicitly recognizes two social rights: the right to "the best attainable state of physical and mental health" and the "right to education."[420] However, the African Commission has expanded the scope of protection rather extensively to include a wide range of social rights, often by relying on the ICESCR and the interpretive work of the ESCR Committee.[421] According to its construction of the African Charter, several social rights are implicitly guaranteed, including access to basic shelter, housing, sanitation and safe water;[422] right to food;[423] electricity;[424] protection from arbitrary and forced eviction;[425] access to affordable and reasonable health facilities, goods and services for

416 General Comment No. 19: The Right to Social Security, Committee on Economic Social and Cultural Rights, U.N. Doc. E/C.12/GC/19 (UN 2007) para. 2.

417 Ibid paras. 2 & 10 (2).

418 Ibid para. 9.

419 Ibid para. 10 (1) - (4).

420 African Charter arts. 16 & 17 (1).

421 Ssenyonjo 101-103.

422 *SERAC v. Nigeria, paras. 51- 52, 59-61*; see also Resolution on the Right to Water Obligations, ACmHPR (Feb. 28, 2015).

423 *SERAC v. Nigeria* para. 65; *Sudan Human Rights Organisation & Centre on Housing Rights and Evictions v. Sudan*, Comm. Nos. 279/03, 296/05 (ACmHPR 2009) para 209.

424 *Free Legal Assistance Group and Others v. Zaire (DRC)*, Comm. Nos. 25/89, 47/90, 56/91, 100/93 (ACmHPR 1996) para. 47.

425 *SERAC v. Nigeria* para. 63; see also Resolution on the Right to Adequate Housing and Protection from Forced Evictions, ACmHPR (Oct. 9-22, 2012).

all;[426] free and compulsory primary education;[427] and affordable vocational training and adult education.[428]

In summary, both the ICESCR and the African Charter enshrine certain social rights but leave much for interpretation, without which the rights would lack substantive content. By means of their interpretive work, the ESCR Committee and the African Commission have stepped in to provide guidance on the normative aspects of social rights. By looking to the object and purpose of their respective treaties, as well as the principle of human dignity, they are able to broaden the scope of protection. The downside is that such broad strokes lend social rights an ambitious and idealistic character. On the other hand, the treaty bodies counterbalance these seemingly lofty goals by leaving states a great deal of discretion to define the concrete peculiarities of each right in accordance with prevailing conditions, especially with regard to what constitutes an adequate amount of benefits. In this way, their interpretive work provides some meaningful normative content while remaining sensitive to the different needs and capabilities among states. It is from this normative framework that the corresponding social rights obligations of states must be understood.

3.2.4. Minimum Essential Levels of Social Rights

The ESCR Committee recognizes that minimum essential levels exist, but often refers to them in rather general terms without specifying precisely their normative contents. Instead, minimum essential levels tend to read like a list of prioritized societal objectives or aims rather than substantive benefit levels. For example, in terms of the right to adequate food, states must act immediately to take "the necessary action to mitigate and alleviate hunger."[429] A state violates its Covenant obligations when, although having the available resources to do so, it "fails to ensure the satisfaction of, at the very least, the minimum essential level required to be free from

426 *Purohit v. Gambia* para. 80 (*reaffirmed* in *Egyptian Initiative for Personal Rights & Interrights v. Egypt* Comm. No. 323/06 (ACmHPR 2011) paras. 261, 264). See also Resolution on Access to Health and Needed Medicines in Africa, ACmHPR (Nov. 24, 2008); Resolution on the Health and Reproductive Rights of Women in Africa, ACmHPR (May 16-30, 2007).

427 Resolution on the Right to Education in Africa, ACmHPR (20 April 2016).

428 Ibid.

429 General Comment No. 12: The Right to Adequate Food (1999) para. 6.

hunger."[430] Here, the prioritized objectives are mitigating and alleviating hunger, although it is not clear what quantity or quality of nutritional intake is needed in order to mitigate or alleviate hunger. Some commentators have noted the wisdom in leaving these normative determinations to the judgement of judicial bodies.[431]

The work of the ESCR Committee has, however, provided some insight into the matter by requiring states to include the results of specified assessments into their regular reporting duties. In this way, the ESCR Committee establishes certain normative standards with respect to each right, which all states must either report to have achieved or explain the reasons for failing to do so. Likewise, the African Commission and the African Children's Committee have also weighed in on the issue, however in slightly different ways. While the Children's Committee has provided normative content for a few social rights, the African Commission has conceptualized minimum essential levels predominately as state duties to respect existing social rights achievements, namely by refraining for destroying them or obstructing one's access to existing resources that are necessary for the enjoyment of social rights. As such, this subsection will discuss the jurisprudence of the Children's Committee as well as the ESCR Committee, but will leave out much of the African Commission's findings.

The Committee asserts that states have an immediate core obligation to ensure non-discriminatory and physical access to minimum essential amounts of safe water that is sufficient to prevent disease, affordable for vulnerable and marginalized groups, within a reasonable distance from the household, available in equally distributed facilities, and can be accessed without a threat being posed to one's personal security.[432] Here, the prioritized objectives are preventing disease, affordability for all, and reasonable and equitable accessibility. Again, the normative specificity is left open for

---

430 Ibid para. 17.

431 Scott and Alston note that,

> While *precise* identification of the minimum… as some objective measures is of course an illusory quest, the responsibility to exercise best judgement in the national and local context cannot be avoided. Courts will of course have to balance reaction to deprivation on a 'calling it as we see it' case-by-case basis with a pragmatic sense of what remedies are desirable and likely to prove effective.
>
> (Craig Scott and Philip Alston, 'Adjudicating Constitutional Priorities in a Transnational Context: A Comment on Soobramoney's Legacy and Grootboom's Promise' 16 South African Journal on Human Rights 206 (2000) 250 (emphasis added).).

432 General Comment No. 15: The Right to Water (2003) para. 37.

interpretation. It is unclear, for example, how much water is needed to prevent disease, or what price point is considered affordable.

The right to adequate housing also corresponds to certain core obligations, though the Committee is much more precise here as to the normative content of these obligations. States must refrain from forcibly evicting people from their homes, which amounts to a *prima facie* violation, and they must take adequate measures to prevent and punish forced evictions carried out by third parties.[433] The Committee notes in *Ben Djazia and Bellili v. Spain* that a forced eviction can occur even when the eviction is due to the expiration of the term of a rental lease between private parties if the State does not guarantee the eviction is compatible with Covenant rights and duties.[434] Moreover, "evictions should not render individuals homeless", since the State must "ensure, where possible, that adequate alternative housing, resettlement or access to productive land, as the case may be, is available."[435] The Committee found Spain violated the authors' right to adequate housing because it did not sufficiently demonstrate why no alternative housing was made available for the authors and their small children to prevent homelessness after they were evicted from their rental property.[436] Here, is it quite clear that the minimum essential level for the right to adequate housing is to be free from forcible eviction and homelessness, which includes the right to receive adequate notice about legal action that could result in the loss of housing.[437]

The Committee also sets objectives for minimum essential levels regarding the rights to education and the highest attainable standard of health. As for the right to health, the state must ensure, *inter alia*, equitable access to health services and goods without discrimination, access to minimum essential food and freedom from hunger for everyone, and providing essential drugs.[438] Likewise, objectives are set for the right to education, such

---

433 General Comment No. 7: The Right to Adequate Housing - Forced Evictions, Committee on Economic Social and Cultural Rights, U.N. Doc. E/1998/22, annex IV (UN 1997) paras. 8-9; General Comment No. 4: The Right to Adequate Housing (1991).

434 *Ben Djazia and Bellili v. Spain*,U.N. Doc. E/C.12/61/D/5/2015, Communiciation No. 5/2015 (CESCR 2017) (U.N.) paras. 14.1 - 14.2.

435 Ibid para. 15.2.

436 Ibid paras. 17.1 - 17.8.

437 *Idg v. Spain*,U.N. Doc. E/C.12/55/D/2/2014, Communiciation No. 2/2014 (CESCR 2015) (U.N.).

438 General Comment No. 14: The Right to the Highest Attainable Standard of Health (2000) para. 43.

as, *inter alia*, access to public educational programs that are free from discrimination, provide compulsory and free primary education for all, and ensure that – subject to minimum educational standards – education may be chosen freely without state or third party interference.[439] Moreover, the text of the Covenant also sets objectives regarding the right to education, such as the full development of the human personality and the sense of dignity, strengthening respect for human rights, enabling people to participate effectively in a free society, promoting tolerance and friendship among all national, ethnic, racial and religious groups, and furthering the activities of the UN with respect to maintaining peace.[440] Once again, these minimum essential levels do not indicate what quality of health or education is required to guarantee that the prioritized objectives will be obtained.

The African Children's Committee provides further guidance on minimum essential levels for the rights of children to health and education. In *Centre for Human Rights and Other v. Senegal*, [441] the African Children's Committee considered a case involving a certain group of Senegalese children, referred to as *talibés* students, who were allegedly in the care of exploitive private entities called *daraas*. The African Children's Committee concluded that the state violated the rights of these children to health and education in part by failing to provide them with adequate education and primary health services.

Regarding the right to the best attainable health, the African Children's Committee noted that a "[f]ailure to provide safe drinking water amounts to a violation",[442] of the African Children's Charter, and that states must "ensure the provision of adequate nutrition".[443] The African Commission has echoed the same in *Social and Economic Rights Action Center and Other vs. Nigeria,* whereby the Commission announced that a "failure of the Government to provide basic services such as safe drinking water and electricity and the shortage of medicine… constitutes a violation of Article 16" of the African Charter.[444]

As for the right to education, states must provide "free and compulsory basic education without any discrimination", which the African Children's

439 General Comment No. 3: The Nature of States Parties' Obligations (1990) para. 5; General Comment No. 13: The Right to Education (1999) paras. 51 & 57.

440 ICESCR art. 13 (1).

441 *Centre for Human Rights v. Senegal.*

442 Ibid, para. 52.

443 Ibid, para. 51.

444 *SERAC v. Nigeria, para. 47.*

Committee notes is a position supported by the African Commission's construction of the African Charter on Human and Peoples' Rights.[445] The education provided must be of acceptable quality and "should be directed toward the child's personality, talents and mental and physical abilities to their fullest potential". [446] The *daraas* did not provide the *talibés* children with an adequate education. Additionally, rather than charge school fees, *daraas* forced *talibés* students to meet daily begging quotas, which kept students away from their studies for many hours per day, thereby depriving them of an adequate education.

The African Children's Committee concluded that Senegal failed to provide "necessary sanitation and nutrition to the *talibés*", in violation of their right to the best attainable health,[447] and failed to fulfill its obligation "to provide free and compulsory education to all children". [448] The Committee reasoned:

> The Respondent State, however, has failed to provide free and compulsory education to all children in accordance with the Charter. Consequently the *talibés* are forced to attend in the *daaras* where they are not subject to school fees except for the daily quota they should bring by begging. Nevertheless, the children do not get the necessary education they are entitled to in the *daraas*… as they spend more time in begging to fulfill their daily quota. In addition, the government failed to provide the necessary curriculum and facilities in which the *daraas* function in delivering education.[449]

In an earlier decision, the African Children's Committee fleshed out in greater detail the rights of children to health and education. That decision, which was supported in part by a parallel case decided on the same facts by the African Commission,[450] is *Institute for Human Rights and Development in Africa and Other v. Kenya*.[451] There, the African Children's Committee dealt with the discriminatory denial of nationality to Kenyan-born chil-

---

445 *Centre for Human Rights v. Senegal, para. 46.*

446 Ibid, para. 46.

447 Ibid, para. 56.

448 Ibid, para. 48.

449 Ibid, para. 48.

450 *The Nubian Community in Kenya v. The Republic of Kenya*, 317/06 (ACmHPR 2015).

451 *Institute for Human Rights and Development in Africa and Other on Behalf of Children of Nubian Decent in Kenya v. Kenya*, No. 002/Com/002/2009 (ACmERWC 2011).

dren of Nubian descent. The complainants argued that without nationality cards, Nubian-descendent children were systematically excluded from public services, including essential health and education services. Although the Committee found Kenya had violated the rights of Nubian children on discriminatory grounds, this case is nonetheless relevant because it contributes persuasive guidance on the normative content of the state's core obligation with respect to health and education.

After reaffirming that the state must provide "free and compulsory basic education", the Committee went further to clarify what tangible provision must be made in terms of education. The Committee noted that providing basic education "necessitates the provision of schools, qualified teachers, equipment and the well recognised corollaries of the fulfillment of this right."[452] Regarding the right to health, the Committee expands the notion to include the provision of services necessary for health, namely electricity, water and medicine. Reasoning that "the underlying conditions for achieving a healthy life are protected by the right to health", the Committee concludes that "the lack of electricity, drinking water and medicines amount to a violation of the right to health."[453]

Regarding the right to social security, states must, at the very least, "respect existing social security schemes and protect them from unreasonable interference",[454] which includes protecting "self-help or customary or traditional arrangements for social security" as well as "institutions that have been established by individuals or corporate bodies to provide social security."[455] In *Rodríguez v. Spain*, the Committee noted that the minimum essential level associated with the right to social security is "access to a social security scheme" for all people that will "enable them to acquire at least essential health care, basic shelter and housing, water and sanitation, foodstuffs, and the most basic forms of education."[456] Non-contributory schemes or assistance must be provided to those who "are unable to make sufficient contributions for their own protection."[457] With regard to welfare benefits in particular, the right to social security entails access to social welfare benefits, whether in cash or in kind, that are "adequate in amount and duration in order that everyone may realize his or her rights to family

452 Ibid, para. 63.

453 Ibid, para. 59.

454 General Comment No. 19: The Right to Social Security (2007) para. 59.

455 Ibid paras. 44-45.

456 *Rodríguez v. Spain*,U.N. Doc. E/C.12/57/D/1/2013, Communiciation No. 1/2013 (CESCR 2016) (U.N.) para. 10.3.

457 Ibid para. 10.4.

protection and assistance, an adequate standard of living and adequate access to health care."[458] Again, the Committee provides a list of prioritized objectives, such as enabling people to access basic shelter, but does not specify what amount or duration of benefits is necessary to achieve these objectives.

3.3. NGO-Government Relations: How Things Can Go Wrong For Beneficiaries

Here, the chapter turns to the relationship between NGOs and governments in order to examine how that relationship might interfere with the social rights of beneficiaries. Although drawn mostly from sociological and political disciplines, this information provides my legal analysis with the theoretical framework that is necessary in order to deduce that the regulation of nonprofit entities might in fact interfere with the social rights of beneficiaries. Political and social scientists have examined and evaluated the relationships of the government with non-state service providers (NSPs), as well as NGOs in general. This body of research also examines the regulatory measures that govern NSPs. Literature from these disciplines supports two key assertions. First, that in low-income countries that depend on the charitable provision of services, such as African LDCs, the relationship between NSPs and the government can have a significant impact on the social wellbeing of beneficiaries. And second, that a balanced regulatory framework for NSPs is essential to the wellbeing of beneficiaries. This section will review these findings in order to position my legal analysis within a theoretical background that explains why legal environments that enable and permit nonprofit provision are necessary for the realization of social rights in African LDCs.[459]

Because scientific studies demonstrating a clear causal link between poor NGO-government relations and deteriorating social rights of beneficiaries are unavailable or simply too difficult to find, anecdotal evidence is relied upon at times to illustrate that, in general, soured NGO-government relations tend to, or at least *could*, be detrimental to the realization of social rights in countries where nonprofit entities provide essential service. The objective here is to provide empirical evidence for the claim that NGO-

458 Ibid paras. 10.1 - 10.2.

459 See Ordor (2014) (providing a law and development perspective on how an enabling legal environment for nonprofit organizations also promotes development objectives in Africa.).

government relationships, and particularly those of a regulatory nature, matter for the realization of social rights in African LDCs, and thus that the social rights of beneficiaries should be taken into account when evaluating the legality of NGO laws.

3.3.1. NGO-Government Relations

In countries where NGOs are major players in the delivery of social services,[460] the relationship between NGOs and the government is more likely to affect the social rights of beneficiaries. If NGO-government relations harden, deteriorate or become combative, beneficiaries' wellbeing and their access to social services are at risk.[461] If, on the other extreme end, their relations are too tangential and the government does without basic regulatory measures, then beneficiaries are vulnerable to abuse or neglect by unrestrained private entities. In order to evaluate whether the state is fulfilling its social rights obligations in countries that depend on the nonprofit sector for service provision, one must take into account how the relationship between the NSPs/NGOs and the government might promote or interfere with those rights. I will be using the terms NSPs and NGOs interchangeably to refer generally to not-for profit nongovernmental service providers.

---

460 See, e.g., Gaspar K. Munishi, 'Social Services Provision in Tanzania: The Relationship between Political Development Strategies and NGO Participation' in Ole Therklindsen and Joseph Semboja (eds), *Service Provision under Stress in East Africa: The State, NGOs & People's Organizations in Kenya, Tanzania & Uganda* (Centre for Development Research 1995) 141, 149-150;Abel G. M. Ishumi, 'Provision of Secondary Education in Tanzania: Historical Background and Current Trends' in Ole Therklindsen and Joseph Semboja (eds), *Service Provision under Stress in East Africa: The State, NGOs & People's Organizations in Kenya, Tanzania & Uganda* (Centre for Development Research 1995) 153, 156-157; Fabius Passi, O., 'The Rise of Peoples' Organizations in Primary Education in Uganda' in Ole Therklindsen and Joseph Semboja (eds), *Service Provision under Stress in East Africa: The State, NGOs & People's Organizations in Kenya, Tanzania & Uganda* (Centre for Development Research 1995) 209, 220-221.

461 An extreme example of this occurred between the '60s and '80s when the Tanzanian government took over secondary schools operated by NSPs as part of a socialist nationalization agenda. Since the government lacked the resources needed to operate all the schools, its forcible acquisition severely limited access to secondary education. Analysts mark this period as "an irreparable secondary education setback in school and enrolment expansion, which has continued to cause Tanzania to lag behind its neighbours." (Ishumi 156-157.).

3.3.1.1. Complications of the NGO-Government Relationship

Several developmental and political factors influence the relationship between NSPs and the government because that relationship sits within a larger web of relationships. At the core of most academic literature on this issue is an acknowledgment that NSPs are part of a wider social network that influences their relationships with government agencies.[462] As Mina Silberberg notes, "Nongovernmental organizations operate within a specific context that conditions the choices they can make and the effects of those choices."[463] This context includes other NSPs, various public bodies, donors, internal NSP staff, members and beneficiaries. NSPs rely on their social capital, which means they draw on their social networks for resources.[464] Developing and maintaining fruitful social networks is essential for raising capital in the nonprofit world. Complications can arise when the interests held by different actors with their networks come into conflict with one another.

The wide-reaching network of NGOs is implicated within the commonly debated themes in African politics relating to the defense of state sovereignty and maintenance of national independence.[465] In part, the NGO's relationship with government depends on the particular composition of the NGO's social network. Critics express concern that NGOs serve the interests of foreign entities that lay beyond the government's control, rather than their beneficiaries.[466] In other words, NGOs can appear to serve many masters. Some states call into question the autonomy and trustworthiness of NGOs that have strong ties to foreign donors. From both a technical and political perspective, the more robust that an NGO's social capital is, the less dependent the NGO is upon the government as a fund-

---

462 See Kelly Teamey, *Whose Public Action? Analysing Inter-Sectoral Collaboration for Service Delivery* (2007) 16, 36.

463 Mina Silberberg, 'Balancing Autonomy and Dependence for Community and Nongovernmental Organizations' 72 Social Service Review 47 (1998) 49.

464 Social capital is "the sum of resources, actual or virtual, that accrue to an individual or a group by virtue of possessing a durable network of more or less institutionalised relationships of mutual acquaintance and recognition." (Teamey (2007) 16 (citing Pierre Bourdieu and Loïc J. D. Wacquant, *An Invitation to Reflexive Sociology* (University of Chicago Press 1992)).).

465 Bratton (1989) 'The Politics of Government-NGO Relations in Africa' 573; Sangeeta Kamat, 'The Privatization of Public Interest: Theorizing NGO Discourse in a Neoliberal Era' 11 Review of International Political Economy 155 (2004) 159.

466 Kamat (2004) at 160.

ing source, and the less regulatory influence the government can exert on the NGO through funding contingencies and financial incentives. Since many NGOs rely on foreign funding, they may be pressed into subservient roles in relation to donors rather than serving national social policy objectives. Under such circumstances, the only prominent regulatory tool that remains at the government's disposal, other than its penal law, is a supervisory framework that imposes strict registration and programming requirements.

3.3.1.2. The Peculiarities of Regulating NGOs in Informal Security Regimes

To understand how the regulation of NSPs might require special attention in the context of Africa's LDCs, it is helpful to borrow Ian Gough's concept of informal security regimes, which is an effort to model welfare systems in developing countries.[467] Gough contends that scholars can no longer apply the welfare state regime paradigm to developing countries without "a radical reconceptualization"; meaning "there must be a broadening of focus from *welfare state regimes* to *welfare regimes*."[468] He proposes a broader analytical framework than the more narrowly constructed notion of the *welfare state regime* so as to generalize the latter away from its Western liberal philosophical underpinnings. Gough explains,

> In particular, the welfare mix must be extended beyond "the welfare state," financial and other markets, and family/household systems. The important role of community-based relationships must be recognized, ranging from local community practices to NGOs and clientelist networks. In addition, the role of international actors cannot be ignored as it often has been in the welfare state literature: this embraces aid, loans, and their conditions from international governmental organizations, the actions of certain transnational markets and companies, the interventions of international NGOs, and the cross-border spread of

---

467 Others have also noted the limited capacity of African states to implement and enforce their rules in the field of social policy, as well as the need for further research on the role of non-state social protection in governance within the context of limited state capacity. (Awortwi and Walter-Drop at 5-7.).

468 Ian Gough, 'Mapping Social Welfare Regimes Beyond the OECD' in Melanie Cammett and Lauren M. MacLean (eds), *The Politics of Non-State Welfare* (Cornell University Press 2014) 17-30, 19.

> households via migration and remittances. The result is an extended *welfare mix* or *institutional responsibility matrix*...[469]

While, in theory, the classical welfare state regime is generally thought of as a "relatively autonomous" institutional landscape characterized by the "welfare mix of market, state and family", the informal security regime features a state that is "weakly differentiated from other power systems" and is situated within a "broader institutional responsibility matrix with powerful external influences".[470] Hence, for the informal security regime, it is presumed from the outset that "people rely heavily on *non-state* institutions and relationships ... to meet their security needs",[471] which resonates with the circumstances in African LDCs. Gough's work also includes a third regime type for developing countries, which he refers to as the "insecurity regime". Statistical analysis of empirical data appears to confirm Gough's assertion that welfare regimes in developing countries tend to cluster into these three meta-types.[472]

In the welfare state regime, restrictive NGO laws may cause little or no harm to the social rights of beneficiaries, because the state ensures social rights more or less autonomously through the welfare mix of market, state and family. Even if NGOs provide services within the welfare state regime, the state is capable of replacing their services in the event that the NGO is dissolved. In such cases, the liberal rights of NGOs are understandably the primary human rights claims of concern. In an informal security regime, however, restrictive NGO regulations are much more likely to have an amplified effect on the social rights of beneficiaries because non-state actors can play a much bigger role in the realization of social rights. [473] A rather extreme example of this scenario occurred in Sudan within the last decade.

Sudan is an example of an informal security regime (or even what Gough refers to as an *insecurity* regime). As such, its institutional responsibility matrix includes external actors like international NGOs, and people rely heavily on non-state institutions, including the informal and nonprof-

469 Ibid.

470 Gough, 'Welfare Regimes in Development Contexts: A Global and Regional Analysis' 32, Figure 1.3.

471 Gough, 'Mapping Social Welfare Regimes Beyond the OECD' 19 (emphasis in original).

472 Ian Gough and Miriam Abu Sharkh, 'Global Welfare Regimes: A Cluster Analysis' 10 Global Social Policy 27 (2010).

473 Geof Wood, 'Informal Security Regimes: The Strength of Relations' in Ian Gough and others (eds), *Insecurity and Welfare Regimes in Asia, Africa and Latin America* (Cambridge University Press 2004) 49-87, 50.

it sectors, so social protection. Any reduction in social services would be especially dire because its institutions already struggle to provide adequate and sufficient services. For example, one study describes the inadequacy of emergency and basic health services in Sudan:

> Prolonged conflict in Sudan has disrupted the health system; much of the infrastructure has either been destroyed or needs to be repaired. As a result of the use of dilapidated buildings and a lack of necessary equipment, many health facilities are not currently functional. This situation also applies to various programs as well. The referral system between the different levels is still rudimentary.
> Despite governmental requirements, overall basic health service coverage is low. There are also significant urban, rural, and regional disparities in the availability of health resources and services. Many of the health facilities either do not function or do not satisfy minimum requirements. [474]

Within this context, in 2009, the Sudanese government expelled several international humanitarian NGOs, citing criticism of NGO accountability and credibility.[475] Commentators insist the "expulsions were plainly retaliatory" against international NGOs and the international community in general since they occurred the very next day after the International Criminal Court indicted Sudanese President Omar Hassan al-Bashir for crimes allegedly committed in Darfur.[476] Aid agencies, including the United Nations,[477] warned that the expulsions would have a devastating impact on

474 A. A-Rahman, Gabrielle A. Jacquet and Nada Hassan, 'The State of Emergency Care in the Republic of the Sudan' 4 African Journal of Emergency Medicine 55 (2014) 57-58; see also, *Oncology Services in Sudan: Realities and Ambitions, Conference Report,* Sudanese Medical Association UK & Ireland, (2013) (recent decades have seen a rising cancer epidemic in Sudan); Yousra Elbagir, 'Patients over Politics: Sudanese Breast Cancer Clinic That Beat Sanctions' *The Guardian* (1 Oct. 2016) <https://www.theguardian.com/world/2016/oct/01/patients-over-politics-sudanese-breast-cancer-clinic-that-beat-sanctions> (reporting that there are only two radiotherapy machines in the country).

475 See 'Sudan Expels 10 Aid NGOs and Dissolves 2 Local Groups' *Sudan Tribune* (4 Mar. 2009) <http://www.sudantribune.com/spip.php?article30382>.

476 Jenkins (2012) 494-499.

477 'Statement Attributable to the Spokesperson for the UN Secretary-General' *United Nations Secretary-General* (5 Mar. 2009) <https://unamid.unmissions.org/statement-attributable-spokesperson-un-secretary-general-0>.

the delivery of social services and humanitarian aid in Sudan.[478] And, in fact, it did. According to one report, the expulsion reduced access to health care, water, sanitation, hygiene and food aid to over 1 million people.[479] Informal security regimes are severely limited and open systems of social protection with heavy reliance on external resources and actors. For this reason, the realization and enjoyment of social rights within such regimes are particularly sensitive to shocks within the informal and non-state sectors.

The emergence of non-state service provision in African states must be viewed with a certain degree of caution, and warrants the state's imposition of at least a minimal regulatory scheme to ensure the protection of social rights. As Geof Wood has stressed in his analysis of Gough's informal state regimes, "there cannot be a naïve optimism about the role of a 'progressive' civil society as compensating for the state." Wood explains the pitfalls of non-state provision by building upon Gough's concept of an informal security regime and employing what he terms "a peasant analogue".[480] He argues that the relationships between non-state institutions and the poor are often themselves hierarchical and asymmetrical, particularly in sub-Saharan Africa and South Asia.[481]This tends to lead to problematic inclusion, whereby (informal) rights are embedded into hierarchical relationships, and operate "within relations of adverse incorporation and clientelism".[482] This structural mechanism perpetuates the very same preconditions of poverty that have long undermined the sustained and meaningful resilience of the poor.[483] Hence, "poorer people acquire some short-term assistance at the expense of longer-term vulnerability and dependence."[484]

Ultimately, Gough's and Wood's conceptualization of informal security regimes presents a challenging conundrum for social rights lawyers and

---

478 See, Louis Charbonneau, 'Sudan Expulsion of NGOs Leave Aid Gap - UN' *Reuters* (9 Mar. 2009) <https://www.reuters.com/article/idUSN09481219>; 'NGO Expulsion to Hit Darfur's Displaced' *IRIN News* (Khartoum, 9 Mar. 2009) <http://www.irinnews.org/news/2009/03/09/ngo-expulsion-hit-darfurs-displaced>; 'Health Fears as Sudan Expels NGOs' *Aljazeera* (5 Mar. 2009) <http://www.aljazeera.com/news/africa/2009/03/200935174114968814.html>.

479 U.S. Dep't of State, 2009 Human Rights Report: Sudan (Mar. 11, 2010), http://www.state.gov/g/drl/rls/hrrpt/2009/af/135978.htm.

480 Wood 55 (internal quotation marks omitted).

481 Ibid 72-79 ; see also Bratton (1994) Institute for Development Research, *Civil Society and Political Transition in Africa* 8-9.

482 Wood 77.

483 Ibid.

484 Gough, 'Mapping Social Welfare Regimes Beyond the OECD' 20.

development policymakers: pro-poor regulatory frameworks within informal security regimes should neither leave the social rights of the poor in the unbridled hands of non-state actors, nor overwhelm existing informal systems of security. A law that regulates nonprofit providers must—if it is to remain vigilant against social rights violations—strike an appropriate balance between promulgating burdensome regulations on the one hand, which invites corruption, clientelism and non-compliance, and failing to provide an adequate regulatory framework on the other, which leaves beneficiaries vulnerable to the outcomes of uncontrolled (and likely hierarchical) relations with NSPs. The following sub-sections offer further discussion on how a failure to strike this balance within LDCs can result in interferences with the social rights of beneficiaries.

3.3.1.3. NSP-Government Relations can interfere with Social Rights

All forms of government-NSP relations, even celebrated official partnerships, can result in an interference with the social rights of intended beneficiaries if the due care is not taken to prioritize the rights of beneficiaries. A Kenyan example, in which the government partially funded certain community-operated schools, is a case in point. There, community-level NSPs partnered with the government to open *harambee* primary schools, of which only some were supported by public funds.[485] *Harambee* schools served to minimize the enrollment gap left by government schools in underserved communities, yet they were poorly funded and the quality of their education was quite modest in comparison to government schools. However, the problem did not arise from a lack of state resources to fund the *harambee* schools. Rather, it was that the private provision of primary education freed up government resources that were then invested into Universities, leaving primary students underfunded.[486] This contravenes the state's core obligation to prioritize primary education over higher forms of education, and to ensure that such basic education is compulsory and free.[487] Although *harambee* schools were run by community-based organizations, the state retained the primary obligation to fulfill the right to free and compulsory primary education.

---

485 Makau 99-100.

486 Ibid.

487 This obligation of the state is discussed later in greater detail in part 0on the minimum essential levels of social rights.

Often when government-NSP relations pose a threat to the realization or enjoyment of social rights, that improper interference disproportionately impacts vulnerable groups of beneficiaries. This is evident in the Kenyan example above. By rerouting public funds into Universities and leaving the *harambee* schools in the underfunded hands of community based organizations, the government was deepening structural poverty and perpetuating inequitable access to education, especially since *harambee* students were also less likely to gain admission into Universities and thus less likely to benefit from the redirected educational funds.[488] This is inconsistent with the obligation of states to prioritize the most vulnerable members of society, even as they take steps towards progressively realizing social rights.

Because NSP-government relations involve dynamic two-way exchanges, relationships that get stuck in a damaging feedback loop will likely serve to reinforce, rather than to alleviate, the deterioration of social rights. For instance, a government that mistrusts NGOs might hamper service provision by passing restrictive NGO laws. As discussed earlier, this is especially burdensome for structurally marginalized or vulnerable groups in LDCs because they are most in need of charitable services. However, since the continued marginalization of vulnerable groups tends to indicate governmental neglect or abuse, efforts by NGOs to assist vulnerable communities through addressing structural barriers might position them in a critical or confrontational stance *vis a vis* the government. In other words, the NGOs' focus on serving vulnerable groups by tackling structural obstacles tends to highlight the need for greater governmental accountability and redress. This could deepen an NGO-government relationship based on the exchange of mistrust, confrontation and avoidance, which, when entrenched within a system of structural marginalization, tends to reinforce – rather than alleviate – the social risks faced by the most vulnerable members of society. Consider briefly, as an example, how a climate of mistrust and criticism growing between NGOs and the government of Egypt recently affected the provision of services used by a group that was particularly vulnerable to structural impediments: victims of police torture. Albeit not an example from an African LDC, the following incident in Egypt is conceptually useful as an illustration of the rather generalizable mechanism that was elaborated above.

After the protests and subsequent regime change of 2011, the Egyptian government clamped down on NGOs with foreign funding. The government froze NGOs' accounts and arrested and prosecuted their key leaders,

488 Makau 99-100.

some of whom faced lifetime sentences under the foreign funding law of 2014.[489] By July 2016, the government had dissolved over 400 NGOs, in some cases claiming that NGOs had maintained ties with terrorist organizations.[490] Some estimated that over 1,300 NGOs had been dissolved, including schools and hospitals.[491] In February 2016, the government ordered the closure of an anti-torture NGO called the El Nadeem Center, which was the country's leading institution for the rehabilitation of torture victims and victims of violence.[492] In addition to providing torture victims with counselling and legal assistance, the NGO regularly issued reports on torture perpetuated by the Egyptian police as part of its efforts to address structural problems relating to police brutality.[493] In its attempt to shut down the El Nadeem Center, the government accused it of violating licensing laws, which the NGO vehemently denied.[494] Representatives of the NGO believe it was being targeted because it was a "voice of dis-

---

489 'Egyptian Court Approves Asset Freezes in High-Profile NGO Trial' *Thomson Reuters Foundation* (Sept. 17, 2017) <http://news.trust.org/item/20160917125847-us9sg>; 'Civic Freedom Monitor: Egypt' (*International Center for Not-for-Profit Law*) <http://www.icnl.org/research/monitor/egypt.html#analysis>.

490 'Social Solidarity Ministry Shutters at Least 39 More NGOs, over 400 Closed This Year' *Mada Masr* (July 8, 2015) <https://www.madamasr.com/en/2015/07/08/news/u/social-solidarity-ministry-shutters-at-least-39-more-ngos-over-400-closed-this-year/>.

491 'Egypt Dissolves 57 NGOs for Brotherhood Links' *Middle East Monitor* (Sept. 7, 2015) <https://www.middleeastmonitor.com/20150907-egypt-dissolves-57-ngos-for-brotherhood-links/>; 'Egypt Government Seizes More Hospitals, Firms Owned by Muslim Brotherhood' *Ahram Online* (June 23, 2016) <http://english.ahram.org.eg/NewsContent/1/64/226670/Egypt/Politics-/Egypt-government-seizes-more-hospitals,-firms-owne.aspx>; 'Three International Schools Shut Down, 28 Warned' *Egypt Independent* (Apr. 20, 2016) <http://www.egyptindependent.com/news/three-international-schools-shut-down-28-warned>.

492 'Egypt: Unprecedented Crackdown on NGOs' *Amnesty International* (Mar. 23, 2016) <https://www.amnesty.org/en/press-releases/2016/03/egypt-unprecedented-crackdown-on-ngos/>; 'Egypt's Health Ministry Orders Shutdown of Anti-Torture NGO El-Nadeem' *Ahram Online* (Feb. 17, 2017) <http://english.ahram.org.eg/NewsContent/1/0/187869/Egypt/0/Egypts-health-ministry-orders-shutdown-of-antitort.aspx>.

493 Amro Hassan, 'This Group Stood up to Egypt's Crackdown on Human Rights Organizations' *Los Angeles Times* (Apr. 5, 2015) <http://www.latimes.com/world/middleeast/la-fg-egypt-dissident-crackdown-20160405-story.html>.

494 'Anti-Torture NGO El-Nadeem Rejects Health Ministry's Reasons for Shutdown' *Ahram Online* (Feb. 25, 2016) <http://english.ahram.org.eg/NewsContent/1/64/188500/Egypt/Politics-/Antitorture-NGO-ElNadeem-rejects-health-ministrys-.aspx>.

sent".[495] In the end, it was the NGO's provision of services and assistance to this vulnerable group of torture victims that drew public attention to the government's responsibility for their injuries, and it was the same vulnerable beneficiaries who bore the brunt of this volatile relationship between the NGO and the government when the NGO's operation came under attack.

3.3.2. Regulating Nonprofit Providers: Challenges and Pitfalls

The protection of social rights in African LDCs requires a balanced and clear regulatory framework for nonprofit providers. Both inadequate and burdensome regulations undermine the social rights of beneficiaries. The former leaves NGOs unchecked while the latter limits their capacity for service. Salamon and Toepler use supply-side and demand-side economics to theorize how regulatory mechanisms can enhance the nonprofit sector or cause it to shrink and deteriorate.[496] For example, laws that restricted many activities, set up barriers to establishment or burdened the financial viability of nonprofit organizations were likely to increase the transaction costs to nonprofits of coming into existence or persisting. On the demand side, laws that forbid nonprofit entities from distributing profits, as well as laws that establish reporting, transparency, registration and public participation requirements make it easier for beneficiaries to trust, approach and engage nonprofit entities.

Edward Mac Abbey refers to this balanced approach as "constructive regulation", and insists upon the government's use of varying degrees of regulatory control over NGOs depending on the capacity of the NGOs to bear compliance costs and the risk that they might cause injury to beneficiaries.[497] From an empirical perspective, Sophie Trémolet *et al.* found that the regulation of non-state water and sanitation provision in certain developing countries demonstrated that

> ...regulation...can play a decisive role in making water and sanitation services more accessible to the poor in providing private operators with the right incentives to serve them. But ... regulation can [also] in-

495 Hassan (2015).

496 Lester M. Salamon and Stefan Toepler, Center for Civil Society Studies, *The Influence of the Legal Environment on the Development of the Nonprofit Sector* (2000).

497 Abbey (2008) 375-376 (articulating three levels of regulatory control: minimal regulation, self-regulation and formal regulation).

troduce obstacles to serving the poor, for example when small-scale private providers are relegated to illegality and are thereby not encouraged to further develop services to fill the gap opened by insufficient coverage by the main operator.[498]

Overly burdensome or complicated regulations are also particularly problematic for LDCs because they are difficult for the state to enforce and implement. States that lack the administrative capacity or the political will to implement all regulations that they promulgate are susceptible to corruption and clientelism, which in turn undermines the enjoyment and realization of social rights. Since, the complexity and sheer quantity of regulatory measures placed upon nonprofit providers can have as deleterious an effect on the welfare of beneficiaries in African LDCs as the lack of regulatory oversight, a balance must be struck between the two forms of regulatory control. Susannah H. Mayhew contends that striking a balance within the regulatory framework will depend on the government's accountability and capacity to develop and enforce regulation, NGOs' legitimacy and capacity to meet objectives, and the political will of both parties to engage one another constructively.[499] The follow sections will similarly review various pitfalls and challenges of regulatory control over NGOs with special reference to the relative capacities of the government and NGOs.

3.3.2.1. Irrationality, Corruption and Arbitrary Implementation

Laws and regulations must be rational as a basic requirement of the rule of law. Irrational regulations open the door to unreasonable or even corrupt implementation because they invite administrators to act arbitrarily. Consider again the South African case from Free State, which was discussed at length in the opening chapter.[500] This case illustrates how irrational or unreasonable funding regulations can pose a real danger to the enjoyment and realization of social rights. Having recognized NGOs as partners and key players in the delivery of social services, the government of South Africa chose to extend its social services by providing funding to service-

---

498 Sophie Trémolet, *Adapting Regulation to the Needs of the Poor: Experience in 4 East African Countries*, Building Partnerships for Development in Water & Sanitation, (BPD Research Series, 2006) 2 <https://www.ircwash.org/sites/default/files/Tremolet-2006-Adapting.pdf>.

499 Mayhew (2005) 749-754.

500 See *supra* chapter 0.

oriented NGOs.[501] The court in the province of Free State evaluated the constitutionality of the NGO funding policy guidelines promulgated by the provincial government. It found that irrational funding measures enabled arbitrary funding outcomes, leading to the loss of precious resources that were urgently needed for the realization and enjoyment of social rights in Free State. The court concluded that the irrationality of the NGO funding policies had a deteriorating effect on the realization of social rights, and it was upon this rationale that it ordered the government to revise its funding policy and supervised the revision process with a high level of scrutiny.

Corruption at the stage of implementation certainly undermines the realization of social rights. In another South African example concerning the funding of community health workers (CHWs) in the province of Gauteng, poor implementation of the government's funding model resulted in the interruption of services that were sorely needed for the protection of health. CHWs are vital to the health care system in South Africa because they connect vulnerable and poor households to the health care and social services that they need but would otherwise have difficulty accessing.[502] However, without proper support, the CHWs are unable to do their work. State funding in this particular province was offered to NGOs who in turn hired CHWs, but the funding mechanism of the state was inadequate and fell into disorder. One court found that the government's funding model become "increasingly unworkable, occasioning extended work-stoppages".[503] The court noted that, "The factors contributing to this included widespread corruption…includ[ing] the funding of NPOs [non-profit organizations] operated by officials and non-payment or underpayment of CHWs."[504] The negative impact on the social rights of households was evident. The CHWs in Gauteng were less effective than their counterparts in

501 Policy on Financial Awards to Service Providers, Department of Social Development, Ministry of Social Development, (S Afr 2003) <http://www.dsd.gov.za/index2.php?option=com_docman&task=doc_view&gid=34&Itemid=39> ("Historically, social welfare services have been a joint responsibility of government and civil society, with government providing financial support to organisations through subsidisation.").

502 Maryse C. Kok and others, 'Optimising the Benefits of Community Health Workers' Unique Position between Communities and the Health Sector: A Comparative Analysis of Factors Shaping Relationships in Four Countries' 12 Global Public Health 1404 (2017).

503 *Mokoena and Others v. Mec Gauteng Department of Health: Mahlangu N.O*, 2016 ZALCJHB 98, J 352/16 (Labour Ct. Johannesburg 2016) (S. Afr.).

504 Ibid.

the province of Eastern Cape largely due to the fact that Gauteng CHWs were funded irregularly and inadequately through the province's funding model, while those in Eastern Cape received the support they needed through NGOs that paid them from private funding sources.[505] Without proper implementation of nonprofit regulations, inefficiencies and corruption are likely to threaten the realization of social rights.

3.3.2.2. Limited State Capacity to Implement Regulations

When a public body has promulgated more regulations than it has the capacity to enforce, a dysfunctional bureaucratic setting emerges wherein more rules exist than can be implemented.[506] Under such circumstances, administrators will need to choose which regulations to enforce at any particular moment. This leaves them with vast executorial discretion and increases the risk that dysfunctional practices will arise from a conflict of interests, such as clientelism and corruption.[507] The problem of overregulation is pronounced whenever the interests of the government come into conflict with the social rights of beneficiaries. This can occur when the government aims to suppress political dissent, or control and redirect foreign funds intended for NGOs.[508] Richard Batley asserts that 'pro-service' regulations are most likely to occur when the state regulates within its capacity.[509] These problems are particularly challenging for LDCs in Africa

505 Nonhlanhla Nxumalo, Jane Goudge and Lenore Manderson, 'Community Health Workers, Recipients' Experiences and Constraints to Care in South Africa – a Pathway to Trust' 28 AIDS Care 61 (2016).

506 Gregor Dobler, 'Private Vices, Public Benefits? Small Town Bureaucratisation in Namibia' in Anne Peters and Lukas Handschin (eds), *Conflict of Interest in Global, Public and Corporate Governance* (Cambridge University Press 2012) 217-232, 222-226.

507 Ibid.

508 See Richard Batley and Claire Mcloughlin, *State Capacity and Non-State Service Provision in Fragile and Conflict-Affected States,* Governance and Social Development Resource Centre (2006) 34 <http://www.gsdrc.org/docs/open/eirs3.pdf>; Mayhew (2005) 782.

509 Batley and Mcloughlin (2006) 21 ("…cases of effective (pro-service) regulation were likely to occur where the regulator had information, was capable of enforcing standards, had no incentive to repress non-state providers, and where providers have incentives to comply").

where governments lack the capacity to enforce all regulatory requirements imposed upon non-state providers.[510]

Richard Batley and Claire Mcloughlin offer a conceptual framework for evaluating the risks associated with heavy regulations in states that have low capacity for implementation. Batley and Mcloughlin temper the "obligatory nature of [the state's] engagement with specific NSPs" by taking into account "the risk of doing harm through poor or unsustained interventions".[511] Their model suggests that a "less is more" model is better for low-capacity states. They observe that non-obligatory engagements, such as dialogue and mutual agreements between the state and non-state providers, pose lower risks than more obligatory engagements, such as regulation and contracting.[512] The "government's capacity to plan, co-ordinate, organize, regulate and finance the non-state sector" is key to their analysis because governments must make "strategic choices about how to deploy their limited capacity…without risk to pro-poor and pro-service outcomes."[513]

Notably, Batley and Mcloughlin do not recommend that states with low capacity levels forgo all NSP regulations. Rather, they recommend *restrained* regulations, such as "[m]utual planning of standards" by the government and non-state providers, as well as "[e]stablishing (but minimizing) 'entry' requirements based on service inputs".[514] They explain that the problem is primarily with "command and control regulation", which were often "unnecessarily elaborate and input-focused, placing unrealistic capacity requirements on both the implementing agency and the NSP, with the result that this sort of regulation is often unenforced or avoided."[515] The implication for African LDCs is that rigid, complicated and burdensome NGO laws, which the state often cannot properly enforce, will likely lead to more harm than good for the beneficiaries of nonprofit provision.[516]

---

510 See Richard Batley, 'Engaged or Divorced? Cross-Service Findings on Government Relations with Non-State Service-Providers' 26 Public Administration and Development 241 (2006) 245; Trémolet (2006) 8.

511 Batley and Mcloughlin (2006) 33.

512 Ibid 31.

513 Ibid 36.

514 Ibid 31.

515 Ibid 34.

516 Youssef Tawfik, Robert Northrup and Suzanne Prysor-Jones, *Utilizing the Potential of Formal and Informal Private Practitioners in Child Survival: Situation Analysis and Summary of Promising Interventions,* Academy for Educational Development (2002) 10-11 <http://pdf.usaid.gov/pdf_docs/Pnacp202.pdf>.

This supports Ada Ordor's call to establish and protect enabling legal environments for non-profit organizations in Africa. [517]

3.3.2.3. Burdensome Rules and Noncompliance

The issue of how best to ensure regulatory compliance is complicated by the myriad ways in which the state seeks to achieve compliance through varying degrees of control.[518] Thus, this issue cannot be addressed here in great detail. Instead, the assertion is simply that burdensome regulations – understood here in terms of the impact on the financial and operational ability of the entity subject to regulation – can overwhelm the capacity of nonprofit providers. This occurs when the regulatory requirements imposed upon nonprofit providers are so burdensome that they cannot comply without significantly diminishing their capacity to provide social services. If the capacities of a significant portion of them are diminished, then many beneficiaries are likely to encounter deteriorating social services in places where nonprofit provision is important for the realization of social rights. In some cases, nonprofit providers may leave the sector all together due to high regulatory pressure.

On the other hand, many of them will remain in the sector but simply forgo compliance.[519] A certain degree of noncompliance is unavoidable. However overly burdensome laws, in which the costs of compliance render the continuation of service too difficult to sustain,[520] can incentivize further noncompliance.[521] Summarizing the findings of a comparative study on the regulation of non-state providers in six sub-Saharan African and South Asian countries, Batley concludes, "[i]n the face of burdensome rules, providers ignore regulations or circumvent them often finding it preferable to remain unrecognized." [522] Moreover, widespread noncompliance may undermine the social rights of beneficiaries if it leads to non-

517 Ordor (2014).

518 See Peter N. Grabosky, 'Using Non-Governmental Resources to Foster Regulatory Compliance' 8 Governance 527 (1995).

519 Salamon and Toepler (2000) 2.

520 Ibid 4 (describing law can create high transaction costs and "affect the extent to which nonprofit institutions come into existence and persist".).

521 See, e.g., Ann P. Bartel and Lacy Glenn Thomas, 'Direct and Indirect Effects of Regulation: A New Look at Osha's Impact', 28 The Journal of Law and Economics 1 (1985) 5-7.

522 Batley (2006) 245.

state providers ignoring regulations that are meant to control the quality of services. These issues are especially problematic for African LDCs where the state already struggles with its capacity to enforce law, let alone ensure compliance in all cases.

3.3.2.4. Inadequate Regulatory Oversight

Bately posits that "[b]ad regulation is worse than none", reasoning that a lack of regulation would afford non-state providers a welcomed degree of innovative freedom. [523] However, a rights-based approach rejects the notion that the state can sit idly by while the social rights of its people are subject to unbridled interference by non-state providers. Inadequate regulatory oversight threatens to undermine the social rights of beneficiaries in at least two ways.

First, the total absence of regulation would invite and tolerate fraudulent, unscrupulous or otherwise harmful non-state entities into the sector, for which the state retains responsibility. In *Centre for Human Rights, University of Pretoria and Other v. Senegal*, the African Children's Committee on the Rights and Welfare of Children heard a case involving a group of children referred to as *talibés* who attended private schools called *daaras*. Although the students were not required to pay school fees at the *daaras*, they were forced to meet daily begging quotas.[524] The Committee found that Senegal violated its social rights obligations under the African Children's Charter because it did not provide adequate regulatory oversight to ensure the right to education for these children. [525]

Second, creating a weak regulatory framework around a widespread and deeply embedded nonprofit sector carries with it the risk of state capture or capture of the policy process. As the regulatory distance increases between the state and nonprofit providers, the government becomes more "hollow" in terms of its separation from service outputs.[526] Peter Grabosky cautions, "To the extent that these private interests dominate the public agenda, there is a risk that they will pursue their own interests and priori-

523 Ibid.

524 *Centre for Human Rights v. Senegal*, para. 48.

525 Ibid paras. 48-50 (the court concluded that the state failed to provide "the necessary curriculum and facilities in which the daaras function in delivering education.").

526 H. Brinton Milward and Keith G. Provan, 'Governing the Hollow State', 10 Journal of Public Administration Research and Theory 359 (2000).

ties." African LDCs are experience a great deal of hollowness as a practical consequence of their limited capacity and resources, therefore they are vulnerable to state capture. Their regulatory capacity must be put to use efficiently in order to reduce these risks.

Third, abdication by the state is particularly troublesome because it would weaken the political relationship between citizen and state, which is an essential pillar of democracy. Geof Wood coins such a scenario "The Franchise State" and warns that it "renders democracy meaningless and toothless".[527] He asks rhetorically,

> ...do citizens lose basic political rights if the delivery of universal services and entitlements is entrusted to non-state bodies which would at best only be accountable to the state rather than directly to those with service entitlements? Can the state devolve responsibility for implementation without losing control over policy (since practice is policy) and therefore losing responsibility for upholding the rights of its citizens? If the answer to the first question is 'yes' and to the second 'no', then we have states without citizens.[528]

A legal human rights approach would suggest that inadequate regulatory oversight over nonprofit providers occurs when the state does not ensure that its own social rights obligations are fulfilled. States must act with due diligence to ensure the protection of social rights whenever private parties are involved. In *Zimbabwe Human Rights NGO Forum v. Zimbabwe*, the African Committee on Human and Peoples' Rights followed the Inter-American Court of Human Rights to declare that due diligence required the state to "organize the governmental apparatus, and in general, all the structures through which public power is exercised, so that they are capable of juridically ensuring the free and full enjoyment of human rights."[529] Therefore, inadequate regulatory measures would amount to due diligence, and the state would be responsible for any harm caused by nonprofit providers.

---

527 Geof Wood, 'States without Citizens: The Problem of the Franchise State', in David Hulme and Michael Edwards (eds), NGOs, *States and Donors: Too Close for Comfort?* (Macmillan 1997) 79-92, 81.

528 Ibid.

529 *Zimbabwe Human Rights NGO Forum v. Zimbabwe*, 254/02 (ACmHPR 2006) 143, 147 ("Thus, an act by a private individual and therefore not directly imputable to a State can generate responsibility of the State, not because of the act itself, but because of the lack of due diligence to prevent the violation..."); see also *Velasquez Rodriguez v. Honduras*, (Ser. C) No. 4 (IACrtHR 1988).

Therefore, providing sufficient regulatory oversight would mean ensuring that beneficiaries' social rights are indeed being realized, and not violated, by the private provision of services. On the one hand, regulatory measures must protect beneficiaries against unprincipled or predatory organizations that would pose as benevolent nonprofit providers. On the other hand, they should target the quality of services, as well as the equitable provision thereof, so as to ensure that service provision is aligned with constitutional and human rights norms and principles.

3.3.2.5. The Concurrence of Burdensome and Inadequate Rules

In many cases, nonprofit providers are subject to both burdensome and inadequate regulatory measures. They are often burdened as to their inputs or entry into the service provision sector, while they are simultaneously subject to inadequate regulation as to the quality of their outputs. This combination can undermine the protection of social rights because it diminishes the capacity of NSPs to provide services while concurrently neglecting the quality of those services. In this regard, Batley writes,

> Whether there is elaborate and inappropriate *entry* regulation as in education or little if any in the case for water and sanitation, monitoring and control of the quality of *performance* is largely absent in all service sectors, except in South Africa. Entry standards have the effect of restricting formal permission to operate, and therefore also access to markets, subsidies and donor funding, but they rarely set a practicable basis on which standards of operation can be assessed. The non-state providers that are approved are then able to operate without regard to quality of output, while the unapproved continue to operate in any case. [530]

This finding may explain why, as previously discussed, Batley and Mclouglin concluded in a separate study that regulations in fragile or low-capacity states are more likely to be 'pro-service' if they sought to incentive – rather than control – NSPs, and emphasized output standards rather than entry requirements.[531] Political theory may provide one explanation for such poor regulatory design. The government's interest in maintaining power and control over the polity can lead it to use NGO regulations as a

530 Batley (2006) 245 (emphasis in original).
531 Batley and Mcloughlin (2006) 34.

means of silencing critical or oppositional voices.[532] Ronelle Burger explains that this political motivation reflects "indifference towards the outcomes of the NGO sector" and could explain the poor design of NGO regulations.[533] Rather than protecting the political elites through an assertion of state sovereignty, the objective of NGO regulations should be protecting the welfare of beneficiaries. In this regard, the World Bank and others calls for a "compact" between government and NGOs, which is based on incentivizing NGOs through strong relationships of accountability.[534]

Although the "perfect" regulatory balance is nothing short of an idealistic notion, it remains within the providence of law to carve out analytical boundaries for permissible and impermissible regulatory control over NGOs, even if the specific details regarding the margins of those boundaries are fated to proceed through ceaseless litigation. Enhancing social protection of beneficiaries and ameliorating social risks should serve as guiding principles for the regulatory design of NGO laws where nonprofit entities are essential to the realization of social rights. In legal terms, the analytical boundary between lawful and unlawful regulatory control could be fixed by the (admittedly flexible) limits that are set through social rights law. Therefore, lawful NGO regulations are those that aim to protect social rights and support their progressive realization.

3.4. Conclusion

While nonprofit providers have been immensely instrumental to strengthening social protection in Africa, they have exhibited their own flaws and weaknesses, as their integrity remains vulnerable to corruption and other organizational vices. On the other hand, African states remain wary of foreign political influence and some suspect that NGOs might facilitate such interference. These tensions present a challenge for regulators that seek to retain and foster the benefits of an active nonprofit sector while simultaneously stemming its shortcomings. Indeed, studies on the regulation of non-

532 Salamon and Toepler (2000) 1 (citing Julie Fisher, *Nongovernments: NGOs and the Political Development of the Third World* (Kumarian Press 1998).).

533 Burger (2012) 105.

534 *Making Services Work for Poor People,* The World Bank, (World Development Report, vol 2004 2004) 95-110 <https://openknowledge.worldbank.org/bitstream/handle/10986/5986/WDR%202004%20-%20English.pdf?sequence=1&isAllowed=y>; Ritva Reinikka and Nathanael Smith, *Public Expenditure Tracking Surveys in Education* (International Institute for Educational Planning 2004).

profit providers suggest that governments, and particularly those in low-capacity states, tend to have poor NGO laws that impede rather than promote nonprofit provision. This dissertation suggests that a key normative guideline for balancing the regulation of nonprofit providers is the realization and protection of social rights. International and regional human rights law guarantee a number of social rights relating to social security, housing, health, education, food and water, an adequate standard of living and continuously improving living standards. Additionally, certain minimum essential levels have been articulated by treaty bodies that are tasked with providing interpretive guidance. By ensuring that NGO laws are promoting, rather than hindering, the realization of these social rights, states can protect individuals against unscrupulous NGOs without deterring the beneficial outcomes of NGO activity. In this way, human rights law can serve as the normative framework with which to evaluate whether NGO laws are balancing the positive potential of nonprofit provision against its risks.

4. Classifying NGOs: Who Fulfills Social Rights, Who Fulfills State Obligations?

If NGOs fulfill the social rights obligations of the state, then social rights law should shape the way that the state regulates NGOs. Within the least developed countries of Africa, where structural and financial limitations prevent even well-meaning governments from eradicating widespread poverty and properly managing social risks, and where nonprofits are major players in the realization and enjoyment of social rights, understanding the state's regulation of nonprofits is crucial to evaluating whether the state is fulfilling its social rights obligations. The ECSR Committee has recognized how governmental restrictions on NGOs can interfere with the social rights of beneficiaries, but it has not gone so far as to conclude that such restrictions constitute violations of the states' social rights obligations, or to develop its reasoning with some depth.[535] What is missing is an examination of how the state's social rights obligations toward the beneficiary can give rise to implicit state obligations regarding the manner in which they regulate nonprofit actors. The present chapter builds upon this idea in order to classify the various ways that NGOs might advance the realization of social rights in relation to the state's own efforts and obligations to do so.

Although typologies already exist that categorize NGOs based on their relationship to the state, they do not take into account the state's social rights obligations. In the present chapter, NGO-state relationships are categorized in accordance with the propensity of NGOs to fulfill the state's social rights obligations and bring about the realization of social rights. Each category represents a different functional role for NGOs and is associated

---

535 E.g., Concluding Observations on the Third Period Report on Angola, Committee on Economic, Social and Cultural Rights, UN Doc. E/C.12/AGO/CO/3 (UN 2008) para. 13; Concluding Observations on the First through Third Period Reports on Ethiopia, Committee on Economic, Social and Cultural Rights, UN Doc. E/C.12/ETH/CO/1-3 (UN 2012) para. 7; Concluding Observations on the Initial Period Report of Uganda, Committee on Economic, Social and Cultural Rights, UN Doc. E/C.12/UGA/CO/1 (UN 2015) para. 11; Concluding Observations on the Fourth and Fifth Period Report of Angola, Committee on Economic, Social and Cultural Rights, UN Doc. E/C.12/UGA/CO/4-5 (UN 2015) paras. 17-18.

with a distinct set of regulatory duties that are imposed upon the state by social rights law. The next chapter then outlines the specific obligations of the state that arise in the context of certain NGO types that is essential for the advancement of social rights and fulfillment of state duties. The chapter after that considers how far states can go to restrict such essential NGOs.

4.1. Existing NGO Classifications in the Literature

Although there are many classifications in academic literature of NGOs and their relationships with government, none of these groupings appears to be based on the legal obligations of states. This is mainly due to the simple fact that the analysts are predominantly scholars from non-legal disciples. The way in which NGOs and governments relate to one another has been theorized from at least four perspectives:[536] the *alignment* of aims and strategies;[537] how *embedded* NGOs are within the state's social policy framework;[538] the relative *capacity* of each sector to deliver and finance social services;[539] and the relative *function* of NGO services vis-à-vis the state's own provision of services.[540]

Of the four perspectives listed above, two provide meaningful insight into how various groups of NGOs might advance the realization of social rights or fulfill state obligations. These two perspectives are the relative *capacity* and relative *function* of the nonprofit sector. As will be demonstrated later, the social rights obligations of a state under international human rights law are defined by the state's *capacity* to advance the realization of social rights. However, some states do not ensure the level of achievement that they are required to ensure, thereby leaving behind a service gap where nonprofits step in. This suggests that understanding the relative ca-

---

536 There is some overlap among these four dimensions. In reality, NGO-government relations can occupy multiple forms within each dimension at any particular time. These models offer heuristic value as analytical tools.

537 Adil Najam, 'The Four-C's of Third Sector-Government Relations: Cooperation, Confrontation, Complementarity, and Co-Optation' 10 Nonprofit Management & Leadership 375 (2000).

538 Salamon and Anheier (1998).

539 Cammett and MacLean (2014) *The Politics of Non-State Welfare.*

540 Dennis R. Young, 'Alternative Models of Government-Nonprofit Sector Relations: Theoretical and International Perspectives', 29 Nonprofit and Voluntary Sector Quarterly 149 (2000).

pacity and function of NGOs *vis-à-vis* the government will be important for determining whether nonprofit activities fulfill the state's obligations. How restrictive nonprofit regulations can be will depend on the extent to which NGOs perform state-like functions, and how important those functions are for the realization of social rights. Unfortunately, the existing taxonomies of NGOs that are based on relative capacity and relative functions do not provide much insight into how restrictive NGO laws are allowed to be, thereby highlighting the need for a distinctively legal-based classification of NGO-government relations.

4.1.1. Classification Based on Relative Capacity

Melanie Cammett and Lauren M. MacLean developed a classification of NGO-to-state relations based on their relative capacity to provide services.[541] The categories are co-production (high state capacity; high NGO capacity), state domination (high state capacity; low NGO capacity), substitution (low state capacity; high NGO capacity) and appropriation (low state capacity; low NGO capacity).[542] The authors' are concerned with the manner in which service provision can take place in each scenario, rather than the degree to which NGOs fulfill state obligations or advance realization *per se*.

While Cammett and MacLean's work cannot be used to address legal issues that are symptomatic of nonprofit provision in Africa's LDCs, it can be helpful in problematizing them in the first place by explaining how service provision methods vary according to the relative capacities of state and NGOs. The substitution and appropriation modes represent two scenarios commonly found across the continent because the vast majority of African states have low capacity for service provision.[543] What legal issues can arise from a social rights perspective when the state's capacity to provide services is rather low?

In substitutional relationships, non-state entities exhibit a high capacity to provide services while the state's own capacity is rather low. Here, NGOs can provide services in areas neglected by the state. This raises concerns about how the social rights of beneficiaries might be affected if the state severely restricts the activities of NGOs that substitute for state provi-

---

541 Cammett and MacLean (2014) *The Politics of Non-State Welfare.*

542 MacLean (2017) table 1.

543 Ibid 4-5.

sion. In the appropriation mode, both the state and non-state providers exhibit low capacity for service provision. The authors hypothesize that NGOs in this scenario will act as brokers of the services that are in limited supply by appropriating access to these services. This kind of relationship has been theorized by Geof Wood as a potential feature of low-capacity states, which he refers to as informal security regimes. He describes this arrangement as a collection of hierarchical "relations of adverse incorporation and clientelism", which can be detrimental to beneficiaries since it tends to reproduce patterns of poverty and oppression.[544]

This raises concerns about the capability of NGOs to interfere with social rights rather than advance them. NGOs would become the culprits rather than the benefactors if they take advantage of their organizational capacity to control or distort access to services. In such cases, the state certainly has some obligation to protect the rights of beneficiaries. Moreover, it is worth noting that the appropriation model does not capture comprehensively all instances in which the state must protect beneficiaries from NGOs. For example, NGOs may harm beneficiaries even when both the state and the NGO enjoy high capacities for service provision.

By considering the relative capacities of states and NGOs to provide services, Cammett and MacLean's work offers a framework that is useful for thinking about the legal relations between parties. It provokes the relevant legal questions, but this is a consequence rather than an aim of their work. What is still missing is a categorization of NGOs that indicates how different types of NGOs should be protected against restrictive regulatory measures. Moreover, the narrow focus of Cammett and MacLean's work on the provision of services does not take into consideration NGOs that bring about the realization of social rights through advocacy rather than service provision. Finally, a focus on comparative capacity is limited in its utility because it measures the *potential* for NGOs to provide services, but says nothing about how much NGOs in fact provide compared to the state. It is of legal significance whether an NGO law restricts nonprofit activities that are essential for the existing enjoyment of social rights, or whether they limit the potential for NGOs to execute activities that have not yet brought about the enjoyment of social rights. A new taxonomy is needed that is based on the degree to which NGOs in fact realize social rights, rather than merely their potential to provide services, in order to understand how restrictive an NGO law is allowed to be.

544 Wood, 'Informal Security Regimes: The Strength of Relations' 77. See also *supra* at part 0on the peculiarities of regulating NGOs in informal security regimes.

4.1.2. Classification Based on Relative Function

Another non-legal classification of NGOs that provides some useful insight for shaping a legally based taxonomy comes from the work of Dennis Young, who – unlike Cammett and MacLean – accounts for advocacy NGOs and not just nonprofit service providers. Young proposes three models of government-to-nonprofit relations that represent the relative function of NGOs *vis-à-vis* government.[545] In his view, nonprofits and government can engage one another in complementary, supplementary or adversarial relations. His model relies on socioeconomic factors derived from various economic theories developed by third sector scholars.[546] Young's model captures a variety of generic roles that NGOs might take in relation to the state's social policy plan, thereby inspiring certain legal inquiries. However, his work does not examine the legal character or consequences of these NGO-to-state relations.

To begin with, Young posits that NGOs that prod and criticize the state for inadequate service provision are in an adversarial relationship with the state. Such NGOs attempt to hold governments accountable and demand policy changes. This relationship is present in many African states, as evidenced in part by governmental efforts to silence NGO advocacy. In an adversarial NGO-government relationship, the key legal question is whether the state's duty to realize social rights progressively indicates a state obligation to permit NGO advocacy. This depends on whether NGO advocacy can be construed as advancing the realization of social rights. Young's work does not address this question because he is not concerned with the effect that NGOs have on the realization of social rights, but rather with their impact on the state's social policy.

In a complementary relationship, the state has incorporated NGOs into its own service provision scheme, often at the stage of delivery. NGOs are a component of the state's plan for service provision. The fact that the state has elected to incorporate NGOs into service provision suggests that the legal relationship between NGOs and the state will be characterized by close regulation and a high level of governmental support. Young's complementary relationship is based on Salamon's third-party government theory of voluntary associations, which posits that the government's weaknesses are

545 Young (2000).

546 However, the complementary model also represents relationships involving for-profit providers.

complemented by the strengths of voluntary associations, and *vice versa*.[547] Thus, the two actors work together in a complementary manner toward the implementation of social policy. Young asserts that in a complementary relationship, the government contracts or otherwise partners with providers by financing the delivery of services.

In states where the complementary arrangement is rather dominant, the underlining principle is to enhance efficiency and efficacy in service provision. Proponents of the complementary arrangement believe that efficiency and efficacy is best achieved through collaboration between government and private providers whereby, as Salamon has hypothesized, a symbiotic relationship can form.[548] The idea is that the private sector has the institutional capacity that government needs in order to delivery services; and government has the political authority to regulate sector-wide pricing and quality, thereby ensuring the suitability and accessibility of services. Government also has the institutional capability to funnel mandatory contributions or taxes into national funds, thereby ensuring that sufficient resources are available to finance the delivery of services by private providers. Complementary relations raise their own set of legal issues with respect to social rights law. The primary concerns are whether private providers are adequately fulfilling the social rights of beneficiaries, and whether the government is adequately reimbursing and regulating private providers in order to ensure that the state's social rights obligations to beneficiaries are fulfilled in a proper manner.

Young's supplementary relationship is characterized by NGOs that provide services that are not ensured by the state. In this regard, NGOs act as the functional equivalent of the state because they step into fields of provision where the state is absent. Young based his model of the supplementary relationship on the economic theory of Burton A. Weisbrod, which posits that whenever governments failed to supply services that voter demanded, nonprofit provision would expand in order to fill the unmet demand.[549] Young likewise imagines the beneficiaries collectively as power-

547 Salamon (1987).

548 Ulrich Becker and others, 'Strukturen Und Prinzipien Der Leistungserbringung Im Sozialrecht' 5 Vierteljahresschrift für Sozialrecht (VSSR) 323 (2011) 341-342. This is also in line with the principle of subsidiarity, which has a long history in German social provision and has been described as "the economic backbone of the German nonprofit sector." (Helmut K. Anheier and Wolfgang Seibel, *The Nonprofit Sector in Germany: Between State, Economy, and Society* (Manchester University Press 2001) 72, 96-98.).

549 Weisbrod (1977).

ful actors with substantial financial capabilities and political influence over the provision of services, which does not describe reality in many African countries.[550] Although Young's theoretical reasoning for how a supplementary relationship emerges within a society does not explain the emergence of nonprofits in African countries, his notion of a supplementary relationship is indeed similar to the types of relationships found in many African states. In these states, where governments lack the resources to provide all the public goods that are needed, the legal implications of a supplementary relationships is that NGOs might be fulfilling the state's social rights obligations. Young's model, however, does not address this issue because his criteria do not take into consideration what the state's social rights obligations might be in the first place. Thus, in his view, NGOs are always substituting for the state when they provide services that the state does not provide, even if the state was never obliged to provide those services in the first place.

The existing categorizations based on relative functions and capacities serve inquiries that derive from sociological, political and economic sciences. While these categories are useful for problematizing the legal issues concerned, they are not appropriate for examining the legal relationship between the various types of NGOs and the state, and how restrictive NGO laws might inhibit the state's social rights obligations. A legal inquiry grounded in a beneficiary-centered approach would be concerned with the manner in which the regulation of NGOs complies with the state's social rights obligations, how various types of NGOs might be protected differently from restrictive regulatory measures, and how the state may need to employ restrictive regulatory measures in order to protect the rights of beneficiaries from harmful NGO practices.

4.2. Deriving New Criteria from Social Rights Law

A beneficiary-centered approach to examining the legal relations between the state and different types of NGOs would be to define the relationships

550 Young does not appear to be thinking of nonprofit sectors like many in Africa that are financed predominantly through foreign funders, who in turn typically exert great influence over the content and direction of service provision. He concludes, "[i]n areas such as social services where citizens' preferences can be volatile, we can expect nonprofit provision to respond to ebbs and flows of public sentiments and consensus." (Young (2000) 152.).

on the bases of social rights law. This section reviews the social rights obligations of states according to international human rights law in order to derive from them implicitly the obligations of states toward nonprofits. These implicit obligations indicate which factors are relevant for categorizing the various NGO-state relationships. The categories should reflect whether NGOs bring about the realization of social rights in an appropriate manner, whether they work in concert with the state to do so, whether they advance minimum essential levels of social rights, and whether they fulfill the state's social rights obligations.

4.2.1. Theoretical Framework

When NGOs are significant players in the field of social welfare, whether states fulfill their social rights obligations will depend on how essential NGOs are for the realization and enjoyment of social rights, and on how states regulate essential NGOs.[551] Thus, distinguishing among NGOs in terms of their role in the fulfillment or discharging of a state's obligations, as well as whether they are essential for the realization or enjoyment of social rights, is critical to evaluating whether the state has gone too far in restricting nonprofit activities.

This theoretical framework is derived from doctrinal and normative foundations. The present section begins by discussing the legal theory of implicit duties, namely how some duties can be derived implicitly from the explicit recognition of other duties. The implication is that the social rights obligations of states, which are explicitly stated within international human rights law, give rise to implicit obligations regarding the regulation of nonprofit entities. Then, this section considers the principle of subsidiarity, which offers normative guidance on the extent to which governments should interfere with nonprofit activities that are essential for the realization or enjoyment of social rights. Together, these components indicate that highly restrictive NGO laws may very well be incompatible with the state's social rights obligations toward beneficiaries. Moreover, they provide the foundation for developing a new set of criteria for categorizing NGOs that differentiates nonprofits by their contribution to the fulfill-

551 The Committee has noted that when it examines the state's ability to meet its own Covenant obligations, it will consider the effects of assistance provided by all other actors. (General Comment No. 15: The Right to Water (2003) para. 60; General Comment No. 19: The Right to Social Security (2007) para. 84.).

ment of state duties and the realization and enjoyment of social rights. This allows for an analysis of whether regulatory measures are likely to interfere with the social rights of beneficiaries.

4.2.1.1. Doctrinal Foundations: Recognizing Indirect or Implicit Duties

The interpretive practice of recognizing implicit or indirect rights and duties allows for the construction of state obligations toward nonprofit entities that are essential for the realization and enjoyment of social rights. This is done by recognizing that such obligations arise implicitly from the social rights of beneficiaries as correlative duties that are necessary for their effective realization and enjoyment. Thus, an implicit duty is any conduct (or omission) that is necessary in order to remain in compliance with an obligation explicitly recognized under the law.

A few examples from the work of the ESCR Committee illustrate different ways in which implicit duties have already been interpreted from the ICESCR. For instance, covenant obligations explicitly recognized in one state-to-state interaction could indicate implicit obligations in another. The Committee urges,

> In relation to the negotiation and ratification of international agreements, States parties should take steps to ensure that these instruments do not adversely impact upon the right to education.[552]

Another type of implicit obligations relates to the methods of realization. These are a generic set of actions that each state should take in order to bring about the realization of covenant rights because they are necessary for the achievement of its objectives. For example, in order to fulfill their social rights obligation to achieve full realization progressively, states must understand where they are on the path to full realization, and what can be done to advance further along that path. Without some way of monitoring and assessing social welfare conditions, states cannot possibly determine how to fulfill their Covenant obligations. This indicates that regularly monitoring social welfare conditions and access social welfare interventions is part of each state's methodological obligations, although these

552 General Comment No. 13: The Right to Education (1999) para. 56.

obligations are not explicitly stated in the ICESCR.[553] Other necessary methods of implementation include creating and adopting a detailed plan of action based on the results of regular assessments,[554] ensuring adequate budgetary support, and requesting international assistance when needed.[555] Finally, an implicit obligation can also arise conditionally from the voluntary conduct of the parties. For example, a party's extensive voluntary interference with the enjoyment or realization of rights may ultimately result in that party bearing implicit responsibility for the protection of the same. In relation to the use of economic sanctions by state parties to the ICESCR, the ESCR Committee noted,

> When an external party takes upon itself even partial responsibility for the situation within a country…it also unavoidably assumes a responsibility to do all within its power to protect the economic, social and cultural rights of the affected population.[556]

The notion of implicitly derived obligations has its analogue in a separate but related interpretive practice of tribunals whereby certain rights are implicitly derived from explicitly recognized rights. Martin Scheinin demonstrates that treaty bodies have used an integrated approach that indirectly protects ESC rights through the direct protection of civil and political rights.[557] Such reasoning is employed in order to conclude that whenever an act or omission is necessary for the realization and enjoyment of an explicitly enshrined right, then that act or omission may be protected as an implicit right in order to give effect to the right that has been explicitly enshrined.[558] A simple example of this would be that the right to free speech

---

553 General Comment No. 1: Reporting by States Parties, Committee on Economic Social and Cultural Rights, U.N. Doc. E/C.12/1989/5, Annex III (UN 1989) para. 3.

554 Ibid paras. 4 & 8.

555 General Comment No. 6: The Economic, Social and Cultural Rights of Older Persons, Committee on Economic Social and Cultural Rights, U.N. Doc. E/C.12/1995/16 (UN 1995) para. 18; General Comment No. 5: Persons with Disabilities, Committee on Economic Social and Cultural Rights, U.N. Doc. E/1995/22 (UN 1994) para. 13.

556 General Comment No. 8: The Relationship between Economic Sanctions and Respect for Economic, Social and Cultural Rights, Committee on Economic Social and Cultural Rights, U.N. Doc. E/C.12/1997/8 (UN 1997) para. 13.

557 Martin Scheinin, 'Economic and Social Rights as Legal Rights' in Asbjørn Eide, Catarina Krause and Allan Rosas (eds), *Economic, Social and Cultural Rights: A Textbook* (2nd rev. edn, Martinus Nijhoff 2001) 41-62, 44-52; Scheinin (2016).

558 Fitzmaurice (2013) 761.

implicitly gives rise to a right to associate or assemble with others, otherwise the speaker would not be able to exercise her free speech right because there would be no one around her with whom she could speak.[559]

This is an approach based on the principle of effectiveness, which requires laws to be interpreted in such a way as to ensure that their objectives are capable of being achieved.[560] By emphasizing the object and purpose of a law, the effectiveness principle appears to stray from the interpretive rules of the Vienna Convention. Normally, treaty interpretations should, in good faith, rely on the ordinary meaning of the text within its full context and in relation to its object and purpose, rather than overemphasizing a teleological approach.[561] However, many have argued that the distinctive features[562] of human rights treaties sets them apart so much so that they may be interpreted through a primarily teleological lens that seeks to render their object and purpose effective.[563] For example, one commentator argues that the ICESCR's underlying aim of improving the lives of people by protecting their ESC rights supports the assertion that effectiveness of law as a basic principle of interpretation.[564] Despite criticism about the ways in which this interpretative approach deviates from the rules of the Vienna Convention, Daniel Moeckli maintains that this approach is nonetheless legitimate.[565] It has also been asserted that the princi-

---

559 See, e.g., *Griswold v. Connecticut*, 381 U.S. 479, (Supreme Ct. 1965) (U.S.).

560 Fitzmaurice (2013) 761; Manisuli Ssenyonjo, *Economic, Social and Cultural Rights in International Law* (2d edn, Hart Publishing 2016) 79-80; Craig Scott, 'Interdependence and Permeability of Human Rights Norms: Towards a Partial Fusion of the International Covenants on Human Rights' 27 Osgoode Hall Law Journal 769 (1989) 781-781 & 786 ("It is important to remember that the idea of interdependence [of rights] has been developed not for the sake of rights but for the sake of people.").

561 Vienna Convention on the Law of Treaties (adopted 23 May 1969, entered into force 27 January 1980) 1155 UNTS 331 (Vienna Convention on the Law of Treaties) art. 31.

562 Namely their long-term objectives, the presence of asymmetrical duties whereby rights bearers are not parties to the treaties, and their use of equivocal and broadly stated terms.

563 Sepúlveda (2003) 77-79.

564 Sepúlveda (2003).

565 Daniel Moeckli, 'Interpretation of the ICESCR: Between Morality and State Consent' in Daniel Moeckli, Helen Keller and Corina Heri (eds), *The Human Rights Covenants at 50: Their Past, Present, and Future* (Oxford University Press 2018) 48-74.

ple of effectiveness is reflected within the good faith requirement for treaty interpretations, which is also found in the Vienna Convention.[566]

In this way, ESC duties of the state have evolved and expanded through the interpretive work of the ESCR Committee.[567] Likewise, the African Committee on Human and Peoples' Rights has used this style of interpretation in order to expand the definitions of social rights.[568] Other interpretive bodies such as the European Court of Human Rights have done the same.[569] In these ways, explicitly recognized obligations and rights can give rise implicitly to other obligations and rights in order to ensure the effectiveness of law.[570]

Based on such a teleological interpretation of human rights law, certain duties of the state toward NGOs may arise implicitly from those duties toward beneficiaries that are explicitly recognized under law, particularly when NGOs are heavily involved in the realization of social rights. States are fully capable of harming the social rights of beneficiaries indirectly by obstructing access to nonprofits that are essential to the realization and enjoyment of social rights. The regulation of NGOs may interfere with not only the associational and free speech rights of NGOs, but also the social rights of their beneficiaries and – by extension – the social rights obligations of the state. If NGO regulations become increasingly more restrictive

---

566 See Ian Brownlie, *Brownlie's Principles of Public International Law* (8th edn, Oxford University Press 2012) 380.

567 The principle of human dignity is central to its expansive interpretive approach, whereby ESC rights take on a broad normative meaning in order to ensure a life in dignity rather than merely limiting ESC rights guarantees to the basic minimums needed for human survival. (See, e.g., General Comment No. 12: The Right to Adequate Food (1999) para 4 ; General Comment No. 4: The Right to Adequate Housing (1991); General Comment No. 14: The Right to the Highest Attainable Standard of Health (2000) para. 1; General Comment No. 18: The Right to Work, Committee on Economic Social and Cultural Rights, U.N. Doc. E/C.12/GC/18 (UN 2006) para. 1; General Comment No. 21: The Right of Everyone to Take Part in Cultural Life, Committee on Economic Social and Cultural Rights, U.N. Doc. E/C.12/GC/21 (UN 2009) para. 40; General Comment No. 19: The Right to Social Security (2007) para. 1 ; General Comment No. 15: The Right to Water (2003) para. 3.).

568 See, e.g., General Comment No. 15: The Right to Water (2003) para. 3; *SERAC v. Nigeria.*

569 *Golder v. United Kingdom*, Application no. 4451/70 (ECtHR 1975) (Europe).

570 Craig Scott refers to this as 'organic interdependence' and offers a hypothetical example: the right to an adequate standard of living can be interpreted as constituting part of the right to life, and therefore the former can be directly protected through the latter. (Scott (1989) 780-781.).

in countries where nonprofits are essential for social rights, there could be a point at which – in theory – the social rights of beneficiaries are compromised. As such, the social obligations of states may provide an upper limit on how restrictive NGO laws can be, thereby giving rise to an implicit obligation of states to respect and permit essential nonprofits.[571]

4.2.1.2. Normative Foundations: The Principle of Subsidiarity

The principle of subsidiarity offers a normative basis for whether and how far states should interfere with nonprofit entities that advance the realization of social rights and support their enjoyment. The principle is particularly instructive because it is anchored in the overarching purpose of human rights law in general, and the Covenant in particular, to achieve and support human freedom. Without this normative principle, states would generally be free to interfere with nonprofit activities as long as they were able to provide the benefits of those activities through state measures. However, by viewing the enjoyment and realization of social rights as a necessary and significant stepping stone toward achieving human freedom, the principle of subsidiarity puts the individual's freedom at the core of the entire human rights project, and thereby promotes a normative tendency toward supporting individual and group efforts to realize and enjoy social rights.

Broadly stated, the term 'subsidiarity' is used in this context to characterize a relationship between two entities whereby one supports the other while imposing only very little or no limitations on the autonomy of the other. The supporting party is called the "subsidiary" entity, while the supported party is referred to as the "subordinate" or "principle" entity. The subsidiary principle seeks to maximize the benefits of a supportive relationship while preserving the autonomy of the subordinate entity. Paolo Carozza argues that the principle of subsidiary circumvents human rights debates that juxtapose the sovereignty of states against the rights of individ-

571 In the context of the right to adequate food, the ESCR Committee similarly asserts, "States parties should respect and protect the work of human rights advocates and other members of civil society who assist vulnerable groups in the realization of the rights to adequate food." (General Comment No. 12: The Right to Adequate Food (1999) para. 35.).

uals, and that rely primarily on the language of rights and authority.[572] Instead, the principle emphasizes the abilities (and vulnerabilities) of each entity within the social hierarchy as well as the interests of smaller units of society. It provides guidance on when state intervention is necessary and when it should be withheld based on the underlying values of human dignity and the individual autonomy.[573]Thus, whether the state should interfere in private or community-level affairs is inextricably linked to maintaining a balance between two risks: the risk that the primary entity will fail in its task without some or additional assistance from the subordinate entity, and the risk of it being dominated by the latter.

There are two normative aspects of the subsidiary principle that deal with the appropriateness of intervention: positive and negative subsidiarity.[574] Negative subsidiarity serves as the starting point for the relationship between the state and the community. In general, the subsidiary entity should refrain from interfering in the activities of the subordinate entity in order to preserve the freedom of the subordinate. In some cases, however, state intervention may become necessary as a form of support for the subordinate entity. Positive subsidiarity denotes the expectation that a subsidiary entity comes to the aid of a subordinate entity when the former is unable to accomplish its goals without such assistance.

Carozza has argued rather persuasively that the subsidiarity principle is a structural component of international human rights law.[575] This would indicate that it could guide the interpretation and development of social rights law, which would seem appropriate. Drafters of the ICESCR, for example, expressed a strong desire to restrain international interference in

---

572 Paolo G. Carozza, 'Subsidiarity as a Structural Principle of International Human Rights Law', 97 American Journal of International Law 38 (2003) 58, 66-67.

573 Although, there appears to be some evidence to suggest that the subsidiarity principle may have facilitated greater state-dependency among nonprofits in Germany's social and health services sectors. The state's implementation of subsidiarity, such that public bodies must finance and assist nonprofit providers, has resulted in a growing nonprofit sector within health and social service provision that relies predominantly on public funds for its revenues. This has prompted analysts to hypothesis that "organizations subsumed under the subsidiarity principle…may well have developed a state orientation, particularly in the field of social services and health". (Anheier and Seibel (2001) 96-97, 108-109.).

574 Gerald L. Neuman, 'Subsidiarity' in Dinah Shelton (ed), *The Oxford Handbook of International Human Rights Law* (Oxford University Press 2013) 345-359, 363.

575 Carozza (2003).

the states' national fields of competence.[576] The same concern extended to protecting individuals and groups from state interference.[577] Moreover, the principle of subsidiarity has already become operationalized through at least one area of international human rights law. The ICESCR recognizes families as the basic units of society and protects them against invasive state intervention, thus applying negative subsidiarity.[578] On the other hand, other international instruments of human rights law, such as ICEDAW and ICRC impose a duty upon the state to intervene within the family to support the family as well as to protect vulnerable members within the family.[579]

4.2.1.2.1. As a Component of the ICESCR's Overarching Purpose

The tenants of the subsidiarity principle are virtually identical to the overarching purpose of the Covenant, which emphasizes the value of human freedom and autonomy. Like the subsidiarity principle, the Covenant aims to strike a balance between promoting and protecting human freedom, and requiring states to intervene in private affairs in order to ensure the realization and enjoyment of ESC rights.

The object and purpose of the Covenant can be gleaned from its texts. The preamble emphasizes the aim of achieving human freedom through means that respect and encourage human empowerment and personal autonomy. In addition to aligning the Covenant with the overarching principles and objectives of the U.N. Charter,[580] the preamble declares that the

576 Draft International Covenants on Human Rights: Report of the Third Committee, U. N. General Assembly, UN Doc. A/5655 (UN 1963) paras. 97-101 (drafters concerned that specific measures aimed at achieving freedom from hunger would be better enumerated at the national level.).

577 Draft International Covenants on Human Rights: Report of the Third Committee, U. N. General Assembly, UN Doc. A/3525 (UN 1957) paras. 25-26, 39, 47, 48 (r)-(s) (drafters added paragraph 4 of article 14, which emphasizes the liberty of individuals and groups to establish and direct educational institutions.).

578 ICESCR art. 10.

579 Neuman (2013) 366.

580 These are to secure freedom, justice and peace in the world, as well as to respect the territorial integrity of states and to recognize equally their political sovereignties. (ICESCR preamble. See also, Draft International Covenants on Human Rights: Report of the Third Committee, U. N. General Assembly, UN Doc. A/3077 (UN 1955) (while drafting the ICESCR preamble, members agreed that "in accordance with the principles proclaimed in the Charter" was intend-

Covenant's overarching objective is to reach an "ideal of free human beings", characterized as "freedom from fear and want" through the realization and enjoyment of ESC rights. It notes that human freedom is only achievable if "conditions are created" that allow everyone to enjoy their ECS rights as well as their civil and political rights. This statement holds out individual autonomy (freedom from want) and personal security (freedom from fear) as the ideal forms of freedom while simultaneously recognizing that human vulnerabilities and suffering (i.e., being deprived of one's human rights) cannot be overcome without support from the state.

Another part of the preamble that supports this notion is the suggestion that the participation and cooperation of non-state actors is vital to realizing Covenant rights. It notes that "the individual" is "under a responsibility to strive for the promotion and observance of the rights recognized in the present Covenant." Allowing states wide discretion to limit the freedom of individuals to realize social rights through their own means or through other non-state means would appear inconsistent with the overarching objective of the Covenant to achieve both human freedom and human security. Implicitly, the state takes on a subsidiary role in order to fulfill the Covenant's overarching aim to achieve and protect human freedom.

The preamble reveals that the Covenant seeks to realize human rights not simply for their own sake, but for the ultimate purpose of achieving human freedom. What is the point of having food, housing, education, health or shelter if it cannot be enjoyed freely but instead must be used up under oppressive conditions? Are not human rights meant to be enjoyed rather than stomached? This would seem to suggest that, in general, social policy measures that have the effect or purpose of contracting human freedom are not consistent with this overarching purpose of the ICESCR. For example, it would be difficult to interpret the Covenant to mean that – absent exceptional circumstances – states are permitted to fulfill their social rights obligations by forcing people to accept state-provided social service and denying them the freedom to realize ESC rights by their own means. Offering direct state provision is certainly necessary in some cases in order to enable the enjoyment of ESC rights. However, there is also an element of personal freedom that the Covenant clearly values and a degree of which it attempts to protect against state interference. This suggests that the Covenant has envisioned an essentially subsidiary role for the state.

ed to include both the principles of article 2 and the purposes of article 1 of the UN Charter).).

Support for this claim can also be found in the articles of the Covenant. Of particular relevance is the rejection of a general state right to destroy ESC rights or an unrestricted state power to limit them. Article 5 (1) prohibits any interpretation of the covenant that would recognize a right for states to destroy or limit ESC rights "to a greater extent than is provided for in the present Covenant". This implies that – as a general rule – states are not free to limit ESC rights. Rather, they are only permitted to do so whenever the Covenant allows them to do so. Although article 4 recognizes a general state power to limit ESC rights, its provisions carefully restrict the permissible scope and application of limitations. The underlying suggestion is that human freedom is protected as a boundless range of ESC rights, while the power of states to restrict that freedom is limited. The *travaux préparatoires* appear to support this understanding. Drafters seem to have understood article 4 as a provision that primarily *restricted* the ability of states to limit ESC rights in order to avoid any suggestion that states possess infinite power to limit ESC rights.[581] The boundlessness of human freedom is further supported in the way that article 2 (1) appears to contemplate the full realization of ESC rights as an undefined and ever-expanding target, and that the rights themselves are broadly defined using limitless language such as "highest attainable standard of physical and mental health" and "continuous improvement of living conditions".

Other more specific provisions of the Covenant similarly point to an ideal of human freedom as the overarching purpose of the Covenant. Contemplating a subsidiary role for the state, these provisions require states to enable various non-state actors in their efforts to realize the rights of others, rather than to dominate or control private efforts through excessive state interference. States must enable the efforts of families, parents and guardians to realize the rights of their children. Article 10 (2) states that the "widest possible protection and assistance should be accorded to the

---

581 The drafting members of the 307th and 308th meeting of the Commission on Human Rights were concerned that the discretion of states to limit ESC rights might be too wide due to the practical consequences of trying to fulfill broadly stated obligations. They adopted the general limitations clause in order to restrict states' power to limit ESC rights and to preclude any interpretation of the Covenant that would suggest states have wide discretion to impose limitations on ESC rights. (Summary Record of the 307th Meeting, Commission on Human Rights, U. N. Economic and Social Council, UN Doc. E/CN.4/SR.307 (UN 1952) 4-6; Summary Record of the 308th Meeting, Commission on Human Rights, U. N. Economic and Social Council, UN Doc. E/CN.4/SR.308 (UN 1952) 5-6.).

family...particularly for its establishment and while it is responsible for the care and education of dependent children." Article 13 (3) envisions the support of parents and guardians so that they may realize the right of children to a religious or moral education. The same kind of language is found in other areas of rights, such as freedom from hunger, the right to health and the right to education. Article 11 (2) (a) enables parties involved in the production, conservation and preservation of food in order to realize the right to food. Article 12 (2) (d) mirrors part of the language found in the preamble in order to enable healthcare providers through the "creation of conditions which would ensure to all medical service and medical attention in the event of sickness." Article 13 (2) (e) requires that states enable educators through continuously improving the "material conditions of teaching staff". Under the provisions of article 13 (4), private educational institutions must be allowed to realize the right to education for their students without being shut down by the government, given certain education standards are met.

Finally, the drafting history of the ICESCR also supports the claim that promoting human freedom is an overarching value of the Covenant and that the principle of subsidiarity is among its underlying principles. In preparation for drafting the ICESCR and the International Covenant for Civil and Political Rights (ICCPR), the U.N. General Assembly affirmed the importance of economic, social and cultural rights for human freedom. In a resolution issued in 1950, the General Assembly emphasized that, "when deprived of economic, social and cultural rights, man does not represent the human person whom the Universal Declaration regards as the ideal of the freeman."[582] Drafters of the ICESCR likewise agreed that the denunciation of paternalism was important. In relation to realizing the right to freedom from hunger, they stressed that,

> ...freedom from hunger had to be assured with full respect for the liberty of the developing peoples: they should be given not only enough to eat but also, *and above all*, the possibility to provide for their needs through their own efforts.[583]

582 Draft International Covenant on Human Rights and Measures of Implementation: Future Work of the Commission on Human Rights, UNGA (Dec. 4, 1950) UN Doc. A/RES/421(V) part E.

583 Draft International Covenants on Human Rights: Report of the Third Committee (1963) para. 102 (emphasis added.).

Human freedom is the central value of the Covenant, as well as both the means and end that it contemplates. The Covenant aims for an ideal level of state support whereby people are still able to live dignified lives of their own choosing, rather than a scenario wherein human survival is merely sustained by the state for some other purpose. The ideal of free human beings is not achieved merely by giving a person enough food so that she does not starve, but rather by also ensuring that she is able to acquire the types and amount of food that she reasonably believes will nourish her. It is by expressing this overarching objective that the Covenant reveals the subsidiarity principle as one of its underlying principles. Ensuring that the enjoyment of social rights is at the service of achieving human freedom indicates that states must support human freedom in the enjoyment of social rights. Consequently, in addition to providing direct state support where it is needed, states must permit and facilitate the efforts of individuals and groups of individuals to advance the realization of social rights by private means. This is particularly critical whenever the state does is not capable of ensuring the enjoyment and realization of social rights by public means. But even if the state advances the realization of rights through its direct state provision, it is important that the state maintains a subsidiarity role because non-state activities that advance the realization of rights are valuable in and of themselves as expressions of and potential precursors to human freedom and personal agency.

4.2.1.2.2. As Appropriate in the African Legal Context

The principle of subsidiarity, as it has been understood within the European context, has its roots in the Catholic Church.[584] There are, however, limitations to implanting into the African legal context the particular way in which subsidiarity has been conceptualized and operationalized within Europe.[585] One who is mindful of the imperialistic implications of blindly transferring legal concepts and practices,[586] or simply one who notes the vast differences between Africa and Europe, must acknowledge that at times each region will require different solutions to seemingly similar

584 Neuman (2013) 361-362.

585 As African legal philosophers have cautioned, African jurists should tread lightly when borrowing from Euro-Christian doctrines. (John Murungi, *An Introduction to African Legal Philosophy* (Lexington Books 2013).).

586 Shivji (1989).

problems. In thinking about how the principle of subsidiarity offers a normative foundation for the way in which states may regulate NGOs in Africa, this sub-section examines whether the various tenants of the principle are compatibility with African legal thinking, in particular with respect to the concept of human rights.

The subsidiarity principle is compatible with African legal thought and practices, particularly with the principle of self-determination, which has been emphasized as a central aspect of the African conception of human rights.[587] The two components of subsidiarity (territorial and social) appear to align with the two aspects of self-determination (external and internal). Territorial subsidiarity refers to the subsidiary relationship between political units, wherein the geographical jurisdiction of one subsumes the other. In this aspect, the principle aims to maintain a balance between supporting the smaller political unit through assistance offered by the larger political unit, as well as protecting the autonomy and independence of the smaller unit against being dominated by the larger unit. For example, regarding its application in human rights law, international efforts to protect human rights are typically subsidiary to national efforts to do the same. Territorial subsidiarity is consistent with the external aspect of self-determination, which legitimizes African resistance against foreign domination, undue political influence and imperialistic control.[588]

External self-determination aims to preserve the democratic processes from foreign domination in order to support African peoples in the establishment and maintenance of their own systems of political and socio-economic organization.[589] The external aspect of self-determination is particularly important to the concept of human rights in Africa. In international human rights law, the right to self-determination is enshrined in the first

587 Self-determination is a central part of concepts of human rights that are dominant in Africa. This is due in large part to its historical significance in African struggles for rights. Some argue that the very concept of human rights emerged in Africa through organized struggles against oppressive and colonial regimes, rather than by flowing down from the international law that enshrines them. (See Firoze Manji, 'The Depoliticisation of Poverty' in Firoze Manji (ed), *Development and Rights* (Oxfam GB 1998) 12-33, 143.).

588 Shivji (1989) 76-77.

589 Ibid; Allan Rosas, 'The Right of Self-Determination' in Asbjørn Eide, Catarina Krause and Allan Rosas (eds), *Economic, Social and Cultural Rights: A Textbook* (2nd rev. edn, Martinus Nijhoff 2001) 79-86, 79-80.

article of the ICESCR.[590] However, in African human rights law, there is an emphasis on the external aspect of self-determination. Article 19 of the African Charter condemns the domination of peoples by other people, while article 20 recognizes the right to self-determination and freedom from "foreign domination, be it political, economic or cultural."[591] In practice, subsidiarity norms – such as state sovereignty, territorial integrity, non-intervention, etc. – have emerged as external self-determination claims made by less powerful states, including African states. Amitav Acharya notes that less powerful states that are dissatisfied with the international order make solidarity claims in order to consolidate power and autonomy at the regional and sub-regional levels.[592] These states can claim subsidiarity norms in order to challenge their exclusion from global norm-making processes, their own growing entanglement within the international political order, and the seemingly ever-expanding reach of international law. Subsidiarity norms can also be claimed somewhat symbolically in order to point out and respond to the hypocrisy of greater powers that circumvent or openly violate international norms.[593]

An important role for the state in the protection of the peoples' right to self-determination is guarding against intrusive political influence or imperialistic threats to the domestic order. Shivji argues that such threats can manifest within Africa through foreign NGOs or foreign-funded NGOs.[594] Others have similarly raised concerns that African NGOs have taken up a compradorial role in terms of promoting foreign interests in exchange for securing their share of foreign aid.[595] This risk would suggest that observing territorial subsidiarity and external self-determination would require a certain degree of NGO regulations in order to that NGOs with foreign ties do not pose a threat to the freedom of African peoples to determine their own political and socio-economic systems. However, if such regulations

590 See Inclusion in the International Covenant or Covenants on Human Rights of an Article to the Right of Peoples to Self-Determination, UNGA (Feb. 5, 1952) UN Doc. A/RES/545 (VI).

591 African Charter art. 20 (3).

592 Amitav Acharya, 'Norm Subsidiarity and Regional Orders: Sovereignty, Regionalism, and Rule-Making in the Third World' 55 International Studies Quarterly 95 (2011) 101 ("system-dissatisfied weak states/powers tend to be more prone to norm subsidiarity than system-satisfied weak states/powers.").

593 See Julie A. Mertus, *Bait and Switch: Human Rights and U.S. Foreign Policy* (2d edn, Routledge 2008) 107-156.

594 Shivji (2006).

595 See Julie Hearn, 'African NGOs: The New Compradors?' 38 Development and Change 1095 (2007).

are overly burdensome in that they do not remain strictly limited to those measures that are necessary for the protection and freedom of African peoples, then they run the risk of obstructing nonprofit activities that are essential to the social rights of beneficiaries, by excessively limiting access to foreign funding, foreign NGOs or their services. This highlights a problem with the second aspect of subsidiarity, social subsidiarity, which aligns with the second aspect of self-determination, internal self-determination.

Social subsidiarity is consistent with African legal thought through its alignment with internal self-determination, as demonstrated by their shared affinity for democratic values, personal freedom and pluralism. Unlike territorial subsidiarity, which is concerned with different political units, social subsidiarity applies the subsidiarity norms to relationships between societal units with different capabilities that are located *within the same political unit*. Dinah Shelton describes social subsidiarity as a principle that "calls for non-interference with the activities of individuals or smaller groups when these are capable of the tasks appropriate to them, and assistance to individuals and lesser societies when these are not able to perform appropriate or necessary tasks."[596] For instance, social subsidiarity would insist that charities and other social associations should be free to act with limited governmental intervention, even as they are subject to governmental supervision. This promotes pluralism and social participation within society by enhancing the capabilities and freedom of communities and other sub-state units.

Internal self-determination is similar to social subsidiarity in that it emphasizes the right of people to resist an oppressive government and to organize themselves and their society in accordance with their own will.[597] This is also an important aspect of African conception of human rights from the perspective of individuals and groups in Africa. For Shivji, internal self-determination is an essential part of guaranteeing a democratic order, the legitimacy of the African state, and the ability of people to claim their rights.[598] He notes the risk that African governments align more closely with the interests of elite classes rather than popular masses. Dinah Shelton holds social subsidiarity in high regard as the structural backbone

596 Dinah Shelton, 'Subsidiarity and Human Rights Law' 27 Human Rights Law Journal 4 (2006) 5.

597 Shivji (1989) 76-77; Allan Rosas, 'Internal Self-Determination' in Christian Tomuschat (ed), *Modern Law of Self-Determination* (Martinus Nijhoff 1993) 225-252.

598 Shivji (1989) 76-77; Rosas (1993).

of the subsidiarity principle and even of international human rights law because it serves as a precondition for democratic rule,[599] which is consistent with the principle of internal self-determination. In essence, the notions of social subsidiarity and internal self-determination both arise from recognizing the democratic value of human freedom that is innately promoted by enabling communities and individuals to advance their own interests and realize their own goals, within the limits of a democratic society. As with the beneficiary-focused approach, the ability of individuals and groups to realize their rights is always of primary concern, and it is this prioritization of the wellbeing and freedom of smaller and more vulnerable units of society over that of larger and more powerful entities that highlights the compatibility of the subsidiarity principle in the African legal context. The indication from both is that the rights and wellbeing of individuals and peoples should not be sacrificed in order to pursue grand ideological state and inter-state projects such as modernism, developmentalism or globalism, or to advance exclusively the interests and rights of foreign donors, foreign entities or nongovernmental organizations within the state. The subsidiarity principle, the right of self-determination and the beneficiary-centered approach all indicate that these various interests must be balanced in a manner that nonetheless emphasizes protection of individual freedom, autonomy and self-sufficiency.

In summary, in the wake of intensified governmental intervention in the affairs of NGOs, the regulation of nonprofits would likewise benefit from the principle of subsidiarity. Since subsidiarity marks the degree of deference that a subsidiary entity must exercise with respect to the autonomy and self-sufficiency of a subordinate entity, the principle indicates that African states should exercise both restrictive and supportive regulatory control over the nonprofit entities in order to protect the rights and wellbeing of individuals. In concrete terms, African states should give way to NGO action when NGOs are capable of protecting the social rights of individuals, but remain critical of the impact that their foreign ties can have on African peoples' rights without generally obstructing their activities. On the other hand, states must step in to protect the social rights of African peoples against neglectful, marginalizing or harmful nonprofit activities.

599 Shelton (2006) 'Subsidiarity and Human Rights Law'; Carozza (2003) 38.

4.2.1.2.3. As Appropriate for the Regulation of NGOs

Subsidiarity has negative and positive aspects, which provide normative guidance on how states should regulate nonprofits that are essential for the realization and enjoyment of social rights. Negative subsidiarity indicates that states bear some obligation to refrain from obstructing nonprofit activities, while positive subsidiarity ensures that states are not reduced to passive bystanders to the interaction between NGOs and their beneficiaries. To be sure, the subsidiarity principle does not expect states to stand idly by while nonprofit entities involve themselves in the realization and enjoyment of social rights any more than it would expect states to stand aside while communities organize their own methods of retribution and punishment in lieu of a state-organized criminal justice system. Indeed, positive subsidiarity indicates that states may not completely step back from their regulatory or supervisory role because communities and individuals cannot be expected to exercise self-determination outside of a legal and political framework that enables, supports and protects their efforts.

Moreover, negative subsidiarity does not indicate that states must refrain from participating in the realization or enjoyment of social rights. To the contrary, states that provide services in a way that does not obstruct the parallel provision of private services can expand the overall availability of services.[600] Similarly, international human rights law does not appear to relegate states to providers of last resort. For example, neither the ICESCR nor the African Charter discourage states from providing social services that private organizations could have provided or that individuals could have acquired on their own. The law merely requires that state provision and non-profit provision be allowed to coincide.

This raises the question, when is it appropriate for states to interfere with nonprofit activities? The normative position of positive subsidiarity suggests that states bear an ongoing obligation to *monitor* and *regulate* nonprofit activities for the protection of individuals who benefit from those activities as well as of those individuals who do not. It is only by monitoring at the community and individual levels that the state becomes aware of the need for its subsidiary interference in the first place. Thus, it is always nec-

600 For an example of similar reasoning from the United States see *Pierce v. Society of Sisters*, 268 U.S. 510, (Supreme Ct. 1925) (U.S.), wherein the Supreme Court found that state law requiring all children to attend public schools violated constitutionally guaranteed liberties of individuals because it effectively obstructed access to education provided by private schools.

essary for the state to take on a supervisory role. Moreover, while the state's non-interference can empower communities and individuals by affording them the freedom to achieve their goals, it does not guarantee to do so equitably. Vulnerable individuals or minority groups within a community are particularly vulnerable if the state takes on a passive role because they are exposed to the risk of being marginalized by more powerful or privileged groups within their society. As such, the principle of positive subsidiarity indicates that there are times when the state's interference will be necessary to protect those who might otherwise be neglected or marginalized by nonprofits.

The subsidiarity principle also indicates that the right regulatory balance will depend on the size and function of the NGOs being regulated. The size of NGOs varies immensely in terms of their impact – namely the number of people for whom they can support the realization and enjoyment of social rights – and in terms of their ability to comply with multifaceted legal requirements and cope with their complexity. NGOs that are considered large in terms of impact can affect the social rights, autonomy and self-sufficiency of individuals more tremendously than smaller NGOs. Since individuals are subject to the pervasive scrutiny of nonprofit providers,[601] what remains of their autonomy should be protected by the state. To that end, positive social subsidiarity would justify strengthening NGO laws to ensure that high-impact NGOs do not inhibit or injure the social rights of individuals. NGOs that exhibit a high capacity to cope with complex regulations are less likely to be burdened by NGO laws and can enjoy a greater degree of freedom from state interference. For these NGOs, advanced regulatory schemes aimed at protecting social rights would not pose a problem in terms of negative subsidiarity.

Smaller NGOs usually feature low impact and low capacity. They will achieve only small gains for smaller units of society – such as families and individuals – and pose little threat to them. Additionally, smaller NGOs likely need greater support – rather than scrutiny – from the state due to their low capacity for complying with and coping with complex regulatory requirements. Thus, the subsidiarity principle would indicate that smaller NGOs and community based organizations, should not be regulated as though they were larger pseudo-state entities. Broad and burdensome regulatory control in this context can serve to subvert the principle's humani-

601 For example, indirectly steering individual behaviors and beliefs by enforcing certain eligibility requirements for nonprofit benefits or by executing outreach programs that disseminate political, religious or ideological information.

tarian purpose: namely, to protect the exceedingly limited autonomy and rights of individuals and communities against the overwhelming control of large and powerful state bodies. Instead, the principle of positive subsidiarity should be operationalized such that state agencies and larger NGOs work together to support and enable smaller NGOs in their efforts to provide services and protection to beneficiaries.

Administrative efficiency is one of the widely valued aims of the subsidiarity principle. When states with limited regulatory capacity, such as African LDCs, use heavy-handed regulatory measures on NGOs, corruption is enabled, and administrative efficiency is undermined. In a context of 'overregulation',[602] one would observe inefficiencies in executing and enforcing rules that govern NGOs – including delays in registration, licensing and releasing of funds – which would in turn encourage selective or arbitrary enforcement, corruption, bribery and clientelism between NGOs and state administrators.[603] The Gregor Dobler argues that, in the long term, such as a constellation might result in increased institutional stability and reduced corruption.[604] However, the immediate consequences for beneficiaries of nonprofit providers could prove to be devastating. Consider the case of Kenya in this regard. In October 2015, the NGO Coordination Board suddenly attempted to exercise its power to deregistered nearly 1000 NGOs at once, partly on allegations that some NGOs were supporting terrorism in Kenya.[605] This alarmed donor countries and raised among them "serious concerns and questions about regulation of the sector"; these countries pointed out in a joint statement to Kenya that "regulations must be fair, reasonable, and justly administered."[606] The Board ultimately recalled its notice to deregister these NGOs.[607] In December of the previous year, however, it deregistered hundreds of NGOs – freezing bank accounts and revoking work permits for many of them. [608] In terms of reg-

602 Described by Dobler in analytical (rather than normative) terms as a scenario wherein "more rules apply in theory than can be implemented in practice". (Dobler (2012) 222.).

603 The administrative practice of overregulation leads to "a selective application of regulations and thus increases the power of those who decide which rules to implement", thereby enabling corruption and political clientelism. (Ibid.).

604 Ibid 217.

605 'Non-Governmental Organizations Suspensions' (4 Nov. 2015) <https://ke.usembassy.gov/non-governmental-organizations-suspensions/>.

606 Ibid.

607 Ibid.

608 'Kenya 'Deregisters' NGOs in Anti-Terror Clampdown' *BBC* (19 Dec. 2014) <https://www.bbc.com/news/world-africa-30494259>.

ulating small NGOs, the subsidiarity principle would indicate that states should provide some regulatory oversight to ensure human rights are being respected, but that they should take care not to 'overregulate' smaller NGOs since such NGOs would not likely lack the capacity to cope with erratic or unpredictable regulatory enforcement.[609]

Where large NGOs appear analogous to state agencies in terms of their functional, financial and operational capacities, the subsidiarity principle would permit broader regulatory control in order to ensure the protection of beneficiaries' rights. However, if a state were limited in its regulatory capacity, then its government would not be able to ensure the protection of social rights against potential injuries that might be caused by large NGOs. In this scenario, overregulation could become a problem as states struggle to regulate larger NGOs, thereby enabling corruption between large NGOs and governmental administrators. Since this would be the result of limited state capacity to regulate large NGOs, the subsidiarity principle would indicate that an entity even larger than the state would need to step in to support it. One way to do this would be to recognize the horizontal application of human rights law so that larger NGOs can be held directly liable for human rights abuses even if the state is unwilling or unable to hold them accountable.[610]

---

609 In principle, this normative prescription based on the subsidiarity principle should apply equally to the regulatory practices of larger NGOs that exercise control over smaller NGOs, such as high-value donors and international NGOs.

610 The direct application of international human rights obligations upon larger NGOs would ensure that these entities could not easily evade legal scrutiny if ever a state lacked the capacity (or will) to govern them. Moreover, with direct international oversight of both the state and large NGOs, corruption at the state level would be subject to international review, which could provide a deterrent for both parties. However, although the horizontal application of social rights is clearly relevant for investigating restrictive NGO laws, it remains beyond the scope of this dissertation, which focuses on the regulatory relation between state and NGOs rather than between NGOs and international organizations. Further reading on the horizontal obligations of NGOs and other non-state actors includes: Andrew Clapham, 'Non-State Actors' in Daniel Moeckli and others (eds), *International Human Rights Law* (Oxford University Press 2010) 561-582; Andrew Clapham (ed), *Human Rights and Non-State Actors*, vol 5 (Edward Elgar Publishing Limited 2013); Anne Peters, *Jenseits Der Menschenrechte: Die Rechtsstellung Des Individuums Im Völkerrecht* (Mohr Siebeck Tübingen 2014); Anne Peters, *Beyond Human Rights: The Legal Status of the Individual in International Law*, vol 126 (Cambridge University Press 2016); Rephael Harel Ben-Ari, *The Normative Position of International Non-Governmental Organizations under International Law: An Analytical Framework* (Martinus Nijhoff 2012).

In order to establish a set of criteria for categorizing NGOs based on social rights law, it is critical to look to a legal framework that supersedes the authority of state law, priorities the rights of the beneficiary or at least addresses them on equal footing with that of NGOs and with state sovereignty, and allows for the implicit derivation of the state's regulatory duties from its social rights obligations to beneficiaries. The following sub-sections look to the terms of the ICESCR and the African Charter to derive such a set of criteria, based on the normative guidance offered by the subsidiarity principle and the doctrinal foundations relating to the recognition of implicit rights and duties.

4.2.2. General Social Rights Obligations of the State

States' international human rights obligations are a particularly useful framework for examining the legality of restrictive NGO laws because states are bound to fulfill their international agreements in good faith,[611] which precludes the use of national law to circumvent international obligations – a view shared by the African Commission.[612] Thus, most African states, having ratified the ICESCR and the African Charter, may not pass restrictive NGO laws that would be incompatible with the social rights obligations imposed upon them by those instruments of international law.

It is widely accepted that human rights law imposes three kinds of obligations upon states: the duties to respect, protect and fulfill human rights.[613] The duty to fulfill includes within it the duties to facilitate, provide and promote human rights.[614]The nature of these duties is progressive and forward-looking. They generally rule out a deterioration of the conditions necessary for the realization or enjoyment of social rights. The Com-

---

611 Udombana (2004) 'Between Promise and Performance: Revisiting States' Obligations under the African Human Rights Charter' 126-128 (referring to the principle of *pacta sunt servanda.*).

612 See ibid.

613 See General Comment No. 14: The Right to the Highest Attainable Standard of Health (2000) para. 33; General Comment No. 13: The Right to Education (1999) para. 46; General Comment No. 12: The Right to Adequate Food (1999) para. 15. See also Martin Scheinin, 'Core Rights and Obligations' in Dinah Shelton (ed), *The Oxford Handbook of International Human Rights Law* (Oxford University Press 2013) 527-540, 536.

614 General Comment No. 14: The Right to the Highest Attainable Standard of Health (2000) para. 37; General Comment No. 15: The Right to Water (2003) para. 25.

mittee has recognized the same,[615] and has gone further to insist that there is a strong presumption against the permissibility of retrogressive measures.[616] In very general terms, these duties call for the use of measures that progress realization, protect enjoyment, and alleviate or withdraw retrogressive effects on social rights.

4.2.2.1. Duty to Fulfill Social Rights: Realizing Social Rights Through NGOs

The duty to fulfill social rights can limit the degree to which states may restrict nonprofit activities. The duty to fulfill encapsulates the duties to facilitate, provide and promote. The nature and extent of African states' obligation to fulfill social rights are laid out in article 2 (1) of the ICESCR and article 1 of the African Human Rights Charter. These are considered general obligations because they apply equally to all rights guaranteed by the respective instruments. In simple terms, the duty to fulfill social rights is equated with the duty to realize them, which can be done by providing and promoting rights directly or facilitating their realization and promotion through non-state means. The ESCR Committee notes in particular that the duty to facilitate the fulfillment of social rights "means the State must pro-actively engage in activities intended to strengthen people's access to and utilization of resources and means to ensure their livelihood".[617]

Article 2 (1) of the ICESCR relates to the state's obligation to realize Covenant rights. It requires states to take steps toward the full realization of rights, but allows them a great deal of flexibility in determining precisely how and when they will accomplish this task. However, in interpreting

615 General Comment No. 4: The Right to Adequate Housing (1991) para. 11 ("[A] general decline in living and housing conditions, directly attributable to policy and legislative decisions by States parties, and in the absence of accompanying compensatory measures, would be inconsistent with the obligations under the Covenant.").

616 General Comment No. 13: The Right to Education (1999) para. 45; General Comment No. 3: The Nature of States Parties' Obligations (1990) para. 9; General Comment No. 14: The Right to the Highest Attainable Standard of Health (2000) para. 32.

617 General Comment No. 12: The Right to Adequate Food (1999) para. 15; see also, General Comment No. 14: The Right to the Highest Attainable Standard of Health (2000) para. 37.

the Covenant, it is critical to ensure that states' obligations retain some meaningful content consistent with the functional objective of the Covenant, which is to impose legal obligations upon states that would effectively bring about the full realization of social rights. Therefore, article 2 (1) also limits states' margin of flexibility by imposing a set of conditions that states cannot easily circumvent. The text of article 2 (1) of the ICESCR is as follows:

> Each State Party of the present Covenant undertakes to take steps, individually and through international assistance and cooperation, especially economic and technical, to the maximum of available resources, with a view to achieving progressively the full realization of the rights recognized in the present Covenant by all appropriate means, including particularly the adoption of legislative measures.[618]

At its core, article 2 (1) imposes an obligation of conduct (to "take steps") as well as an obligation of results (to achieve the "full realization" of social rights). At the very least, this means states must take concrete and deliberate steps.[619] The covenant also imposes an obligation of intent, which requires states to take steps "with a *view* to achieving progressively"[620] the full realization of covenant rights.[621]

Most of the difficulty with interpreting article 2 (1) arises from the conundrum that while the obligation of conduct must be fulfilled straightaway, the desired results need not be attained immediately thereafter, but rather progressively over time.[622] However, the allowance for progressive realization is not a license for states to drag their feet or circumvent their obligations. Rather, it is an acknowledgement of the limitations that states encounter in their efforts to realize social rights, and a requirement that they offer nothing less than their full effort, up to the limits of feasibility.[623] The term progressively creates a dynamic state obligation, which ex-

618 ICESCR art. 2(1).

619 General Comment No. 3: The Nature of States Parties' Obligations (1990) para. 2.

620 Emphasis added.

621 General Comment No. 3: The Nature of States Parties' Obligations (1990) para. 9.

622 See ibid.

623 The *travaux preparatoires* of the ICESCR reveal the same. Members of the drafting committee (Third Committee) agreed that the term "progressive" was not intended to permit delaying tactics that, in particular, impeded efforts of less developed countries. Some understood article 2 to require maximum speed of realization, even though it is progressive. (Draft International Covenants on Hu-

pands over time. As one state representative aptly noted during the drafting of what eventually became the ICESCR,

> The idea expressed in the word 'progressively', which must be taken in conjunction with the words 'full realization of the rights', was not a static one. It meant that certain rights would be applied immediately, others as soon as possible.[624]

Rather than progressing, however, some LDCs in Africa see stagnation in their socio-economic outcomes, while others even experience regression.[625] Another reason that constructing concrete social rights obligations can be rather challenging is that such considerations touch upon political issues. Since a multitude of social policies can bring about the full realization of social rights, it is difficult to articulate legal principles that would guide what is essentially a political determination about which social policy is best suited for any particular country. Moreover, determining whether a

---

man Rights: Report of the Third Committee, U. N. General Assembly, UN Doc. A/5365 (UN 1962) para. 52.) Even members of the drafting commission (UN Commission on Human Rights) who opposed the adoption of a general clause that allowed for progressive realization agreed that states were only expected to do all that they could feasibly do – and not more – in order to achieve full realization of ESC rights. (See, e.g., Summary Record of the 237th Meeting, Commission on Human Rights, U. N. Economic and Social Council, UN Doc. E/CN.4/SR.237 (UN 1951) (speaking about the situation of lesser developed countries, Mr. Jevremović of Yugoslavia noted "...no one would censure them if their economic circumstances hampered the full implementation of the Covenant by them.").).

624 Summary Record of the 237th Meeting (1951) (comments of Mr. Whitlam of Australia); see also Summary Record of the 363rd Meeting, Third Committee, U. N. General Assembly, UN Doc. A/C.3/SR.363 (UN 1951) paras. 14-15 (state representative Mr. Cassin of France - whose delegation drafted the original version of what became art. 2 - expressed his view that the term "progressive" did not preclude the immediate implementation of certain ESC obligations.).

625 In terms of poverty outcomes, for example, data made available between 1996 and 2016 indicates that the percentages and absolute numbers of people living at or below the international poverty level in Benin, Comoros, Djibouti, Guinea Bissau, Madagascar, Malawi and Sao Tome and Principe has either increased or remained the same, despite their governments having received substantial foreign development aid. (See Poverty Equity, Number of Poor at $1.90 a Day (2011 PPP) (Millions) (World Bank 2017); Poverty Equity, Poverty Headcount Ratio at $1.90 a Day (2011 PPP) (% of Population) (World Bank 2017); World Development Indicators, Net ODA Received (% of Central Government Expense) (World Bank 2017); World Development Indicators, Net ODA Received (% of GNA) (World Bank 2017).).

particular social policy plan is within the maximum of a state's available resources also involves resolving contentious political questions. Consequently, it seems reasonable that states retain a wide margin of flexibility in deciding how they will achieve the full realization of covenant rights. Yet, their discretion is not absolute. It is incumbent upon states to repeal legislative measures that are inconsistent with the state's article 2 (1) obligations.[626]

The Committee interprets the Covenant conservatively and in accordance with the principle of subsidiarity to conclude that a state's obligation to provide social rights is triggered "whenever an individual or group is unable, for reasons beyond their control, to enjoy the right".[627] In some cases, the state is also unable (or unwilling) to provide the rights. In such cases, nonprofit activities that provide social rights are assisting the state in fulfilling its duties. As long as this is the case, it appears that the state's duty to fulfill social rights would require it, at the very least, to permit these nonprofit activities. The simple fact that nonprofit activities might fulfill the state's duties does not alleviate the state of its obligation to ensure that those underlying social rights are being fulfilled. Indeed, international law addresses states rather private parties. This means that in some cases the state might bear an additional obligation to facilitate and support nonprofit activities unless and until it ensures those social rights by alternative means.

Perhaps what is most striking about the state's obligation under article 2 (1) is its dynamic and customizable character.[628] The full extent of one state's article 2 (1) duties will be distinct from those of another because they expand (and, theoretically contract) in accordance with the state's particular capacity to advance the realization of social rights within the maximum of its available resources. It is as if article 2 (1) imposes upon each

626 See Alston and Quinn (1987) 167.

627 General Comment No. 12: The Right to Adequate Food (1999) para. 15; see also, General Comment No. 14: The Right to the Highest Attainable Standard of Health (2000) para. 37; see also, General Comment No. 15: The Right to Water (2003) para. 25.

628 During deliberations regarding the drafting of what eventually became the ICESCR, one state representative (Mr. Sörensen of Denmark) noted that the word "progressively" encapsulated a "dynamic element, indicating that no final fixed goal had been set in the implementation of economic, social and cultural rights, since the essence of progress was continuity." (Summary Record of the 236th Meeting, Commission on Human Rights, U. N. Economic and Social Council, UN Doc. E/CN.4/SR.236 (UN 1951).).

state its very own duty horizon that tracks an (ideally) ever-expanding feasibility frontier.[629] From the outset, one can already anticipate that nonprofit activities that fall within the duty horizon should be regulated differently than those taking place beyond that which the state is obliged to ensure. The central argument of this thesis is that restricting nonprofit activities that advances the realization of social rights beyond what the state is willing and able to ensure may be incompatible with the state's Covenant obligations. The state's duties are also limited by the appropriateness of the means available to it. The area where feasibility and appropriateness overlap marks the expanding horizon of the state's article 2 (1) obligations.

Figure 4.1. The Duty Horizon of Article 2 (1)

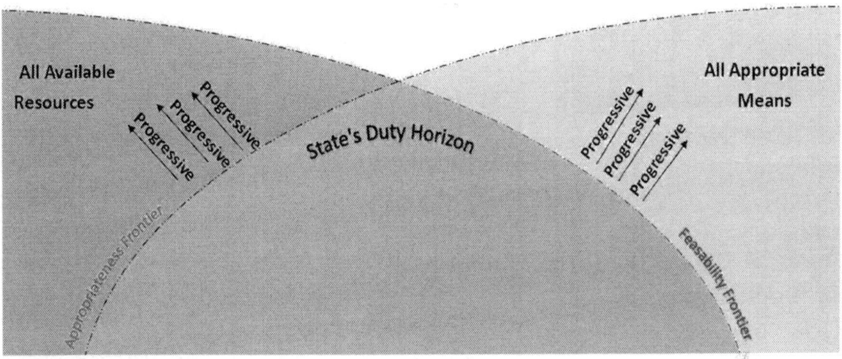

It is notable that the Covenant requires the use of not merely any but *all* appropriate means that are also feasible to adopt (i.e., within the maximum of available resources). The ordinary and full meaning of "all" implies that states may not forgo the implementation of any feasible measure that is deemed appropriate.[630] Whenever a measure would be necessary for the realization of Covenant rights, it is reasonable to conclude that implementing such a measure would fall squarely within the state's article 2 (1)

629 Some members of the Commission on Human Rights that were drafting article 2 of ICESCR understood the term "progressive" to have placed upon states a duty to achieve ever higher levels of fulfillment. (Report to the Economic and Social Council on the Eigth Session of the Commission, Commission on Human Rights, U. N. Economic and Social Council, UN Doc. E/CN.4/669 (UN 1952) para. 107.).

630 The Vienna Convention requires texts to be given their ordinary meaning. (Vienna Convention on the Law of Treaties, art. 31.).

obligation to "take steps...by all appropriate means...". Thus, all feasible measures relating to nonprofit entities must be adopted if doing so is appropriate for the full realization of social rights. Conversely, states are under no obligation to take up *inappropriate* means, indicating that states need not tolerate nonprofit activities that employ inappropriate means of realizing social rights. The key inquiry for this sub-section is, under what circumstances might repealing a restrictive NGO regulation be considered both a feasible and appropriate means of achieving the full realization of social rights, and thus an act required by the Covenant? The following subsections will examine in further detail the state's duty to adopt all appropriate means and the duty to use the maximum of available resources.

4.2.2.1.1. Appropriateness

The lack of a definition for the term 'appropriate' within the Covenant has left commentators baffled as to its meaning.[631] However, the Covenant provides some limited guidance in this regard. Among what some have referred to as a "panoply of appropriate means",[632] article 2 (1) singles out legislative measures as a particularly important type of appropriate means.[633] The Committee asserts further that appropriate means may also include judicial, administrative, financial, educational and social mea-

631 In their seminal work, *The Nature and Scope of States Parties' Obligations under the International Covenant on Economic, Social and Cultural Rights*, leading human rights scholars Philip Alton and Gerard Quinn ask rhetorically and critically, "If legal measures are not required, what other means might be 'appropriate' and ... who shall determine whether the means that have been adopted are both comprehensive ('all') and 'appropriate'?" (Alston and Quinn (1987) 166.) Similarly, in examining socio-economic rights adjudication in South Africa, Nick Ferreira laments, "The world 'appropriate' in the existing dicta is responsible for much of the interpretive challenge, as it is a difficult normative question what level of provision and from which sources is appropriate." (Nick Ferreira, 'Feasibility Constraints and the South African Bill of Rights: Fulfilling the Constitution's Promise in Conditions of Scarce Resources' 129 South African Law Journal 274 (2012) 294.).

632 Ben Saul, David Kinley and Jacqueline Mowbray, *The International Covenant on Economic, Social and Cultural Rights: Commentary, Cases and Materials* (1 edn, Oxford University Press 2014) 157 (internal quotation marks omitted).

633 ICESCR art. 2 (1) ("...by all appropriate means, including particularly the adoption of legislative measures.").

sures.[634] Nonetheless, the role of legislative measures is especially pertinent to the realization of social rights, where, as the Committee has recognized,

> [i]n such fields as health, the protection of children and mothers, and education, as well as in respect of matters dealt within articles 6 to 9 [which include labor, employment and social security rights], legislation may also be an indispensable element for many purposes. [635]

Article 5 of the covenant offers some outer limits for the term "appropriate means" by indicating what types of activities are not permitted by the Covenant. Article 5 (1) forbids any interpretation of the Covenant that would imply that acts aiming at the destruction or extensive limitation of Covenant rights are permissible. This would rule out any reading of article 2 (1) that would suggest that "appropriate means" include aiming at destroying or extensively limiting ESC rights. Article 5 (2) offers a limit on what is considered appropriate *vis-à-vis* the effect that state measures can have on fundamental rights guaranteed by other laws or customs, but that are not fully recognized in the Covenant. Article 5 (2) prohibits derogating from such rights or restricting them on the pretext that the Covenant does not recognize them or recognizes them to a lesser extent. This provision still leaves open the possibility that states may permissibly restrict the enjoyment or realization of unenumerated rights when it is done on some other pretext or for some legitimate purpose, thereby leaving the regulation of such limitations to those legal instruments that fully recognize those affected rights. There are instances when state measures might result in derogations from or restrictions upon unenumerated rights and would still be considered appropriate for the progressive realization of social rights, especially since the ICCPR already permits limitations and derogations *vis-à-vis* civil and political rights. For example, making primary education compulsory for children would still be an appropriate means of realizing the right to education, although it imposes a restriction upon the right to liberty of movement and freedom of association since children would not be free to leave the classroom or associate with other students freely during lectures.[636]

---

634 General Comment No. 3: The Nature of States Parties' Obligations (1990) paras. 5 & 7.

635 Ibid para. 3.

636 ICCPR arts. 12 (right to freedom of movement) & 22 (right to freely associate with others).

Article 5 thus provides guidance on what constitutes the very outer boundaries of "appropriate means" by excluding – at the very least – acts aimed at the destruction and extensive limitation of rights recognized by the Covenant, as well as the use of the fact that the Covenant does not fully recognize certain fundamental rights that are protected elsewhere as a pretext for derogating from or restricting those rights. In other words, aiming at destroying or extensively limiting Covenant rights is never appropriate for the realization of social rights, while derogations from or restrictions of unenumerated fundamental rights are considered inappropriate only if they are taken on the pretext that the Covenant does not fully recognize them. Within the wide limits set by article 2 (1) and 5, it appears that states have a great deal of space to maneuver.

Other texts of Covenant (articles 6 (2), 11 (2), 12 (2), 13 (2), and 15 (2)) provide some insight into what might be considered appropriate means through a set of examples.[637] Particularly instructive for the appropriateness of social rights measures are articles 11 (2) (on food rights), 12 (2) (on health rights) and 13 (2) (on educational rights). These provisions direct states to take measures that aim at specific objectives, indicating that these types of objectives constitute "appropriate means". Regarding the right to the highest attainable standard of health, states must achieve the full realization of this right through measures that are "necessary" for (1) improving the population's health according to certain indicators such as infant mortality, healthy child development, and environmental and industrial hygiene, (2) "the prevention, treatment and control" of diseases, and (3) "the creation of conditions" that would assure medical care for all people who are ill.[638] Article 13 (2) specifies in rather precise language that the right to education shall be achieved through compulsory and free primary education that is made available to all, as well as higher levels of education that is made available gradually and in accordance with the limits of feasibility.[639] Finally, the right to be free from hunger must be protected through "specific programs" that are "needed" in order to,

> ... improve methods of production, conservation and distribution of food by making full use of technical and scientific knowledge, by disseminating knowledge of the principles of nutrition and by develop-

637 Craven (1995) 116.
638 ICESCR art. 12 (2).
639 Ibid art. 13 (2).

ing or reforming agrarian systems in such a way as to achieve the most efficient development and utilization of natural resources. [640]

While these provisions neither define the term 'appropriate means' nor specify their particular form,[641] they clearly indicate what the objective of the state's measures should be, and what results they should bring about. It does not appear to be permissible, for example, for states to achieve freedom from hunger without also aiming to improve methods of production or to disseminate knowledge of nutrition; or to guarantee the right to education without also ensuring free and compulsory primary education for all. Moreover, these objectives and results are directed by the use of terms such as "necessary", "needed" and "shall", which the *travaux préparatoires* reveal are intended to be binding mandates rather than merely illustrative recommendations relating to merely hypothetical needs.[642] As such, states that do not employ any measures to bring about these results, or that employ measures that are deleterious with respect to these aims, are likely noncompliant in terms of their article 2 (1) obligation to make use of all appropriate means, assuming it is within the availability of their resources to do so. Therefore, NGO laws that obstruct private efforts to reach these mandated objectives could amount to inappropriate means that are inconsistent with article 2 (1) obligations if the state does not or cannot pursue alternative means of reaching these objectives.

Another indication of what may be considered appropriate comes from the object and purpose of the Covenant, which can be gleaned from its preamble, as well as the overarching principles of human rights law. Consistent with the aims of the subsidiarity principle, the Covenant seeks to realize ESC rights not for their own sake, but in order to achieve the ideal of human freedom and personal autonomy.[643] This indicates that appropriate means cannot include measures that undermine human freedom or personal autonomy.

640 Ibid art. 11 (2) (a).

641 For example, legislative form, judicial form, administrative form, etc. (with the exception, perhaps, of article 13 (2)'s requirement that states use "specific programs" to bring about freedom from hunger).

642 Draft International Covenants on Human Rights: Report of the Third Committee (1963) para. 105 (A drafter found unacceptable a proposal that would replace "which are needed" with "if and where needed" in reference to the use of measures to improve food production, conservation and distribution methods. The proposal was ultimately withdrawn.).

643 See *supra* part 0on the subsidiarity principle as a component of the ICESCR's overarching purpose.

Through years of reviewing country reports, the Committee has developed a few conceptual parameters for the term 'appropriate means'.[644] In her review of the Committee's work, Magdalena Sepúlveda concludes that certain criteria for "appropriateness" have emerged.[645] She posits that the means of a state are appropriate if they are reasonable and effective.[646] Sepúlveda found that in deciding what is reasonable for a particular state, the Committee tends to consider the country's level of development.[647] In assessing effectiveness, on the other hand, it considers whether the allocation of resources is sufficient to meet Covenant targets.[648] Thus, reasonableness and effectiveness are relative terms that can only be specified in terms of the particular context and circumstances of each state. Sepúlveda also notes that the results of a particular measure appear to matter such that measures are inappropriate if they do not produce results compatible with Covenant obligations.[649] This is consistent with the Covenant's mandate that social rights measures must aim for a particular set of objectives.[650]

Due to the fact that the 'appropriateness' of any measure depends on the socio-economic circumstances of each country, defining 'appropriateness' in clear and universal terms is a rather difficult task.[651] As such, it seems

644 An obvious drawback of the Committee's use of concluding observations is that they are particularized, non-binding recommendations that are determined on a case-by-case basis, which makes it difficult to draw universal themes from them about the meaning of the term 'appropriate means'. (Saul, Kinley and Mowbray (2014) 169-170.) However, the Committee's work can still provide some meaningful insight into what criteria matter for determining whether a particular measure is appropriate for the realization of Covenant rights.

645 Sepúlveda (2003).

646 Ibid 337-338.

647 Ibid.

648 Ibid.

649 Ibid. See also General Comment No. 9: The Domestic Application of the Covenant (1997) para. 5 ("...the means used should be appropriate in the sense of producing results which are consistent with the full discharge of its obligations by the State party.").

650 See ICESCR arts. 11 (2), 12 (2) & 13 (2).

651 See Saul, Kinley and Mowbray (2014) 170-172.

sensible that the Committee[652] and The Limburg Principles[653] have left it to each state to determine whether a particular measure is appropriate.[654]The Committee has cautioned, however, that "the 'appropriateness' of the means chosen will not always be self-evident".[655] Thus, while states determine whether a particular measure is appropriate, the Committee notes that "the ultimate determination as to whether all appropriate measures have been taken remains one for the Committee to make."[656] While a state may take a handful of measures that it deems appropriate, that alone does not ensure noncompliance unless it takes *all* means that are appropriate in relation to its country's socio-economic context, assuming it is feasible to do so.

At the domestic level, courts have tried to tackle the problem of defining appropriateness. To provide an African example: the Constitutional Court of South Africa has developed a rich source of doctrinal material on the reasonableness of social welfare measures, which allows South African courts to consider a wide range of factors including social, economic, historical and constitutional contexts, institutional capacity of the state, and the flexibility, balance and comprehensiveness of the measure in question.[657] The problem remains, however, that the term 'reasonable' is

---

652 General Comment No. 9: The Domestic Application of the Covenant (1997) para. 5; General Comment No. 3: The Nature of States Parties' Obligations (1990) para. 4.

653 The Limburg Principles on the Implementation of the International Covenant on Economic, Social and Cultulral Rights, UN Comm's Hum Rts (Jan. 8, 1987) UN Doc. E/CN.4/1987/17 (The Limburg Principles) para. 20.

654 For an historical view from the preparatory work of Covenant drafters and the Committee members see Saul, Kinley and Mowbray (2014) 158-163 (on whether the Covenant should mandate the use of any particular form of appropriate means such as legislative or constitutional incorporation of Covenant provisions), and Craven (1995) 115-116 (on whether it should be the states or the Committee members that determine whether a state measure is an appropriate means).

655 General Comment No. 3: The Nature of States Parties' Obligations (1990) para. 4.

656 Ibid. See also General Comment No. 9: The Domestic Application of the Covenant (1997) para. 5 ("The means chosen are also subject to review as part of the Committee's examination of the State party's compliance with its obligations under the Covenant."); The Limburg Principles, para. 20 ("The appropriateness of the means to be applied in a particular State shall be determined by that State party, and shall be subject to review by the United Nations Economic and Social Council, with the assistance of the Committee.").

657 *South Africa v. Grootboom*, paras. 41-44.

just as vague as the term 'appropriate' and thus requires additional normative content.

To limit the risk of the judiciary acting as a super-legislature within the all-too political realm of socio-economic policymaking, one could lean toward a more narrowly constructed version of the term "appropriate means". Certainly, and at the very least, all measures that are indispensable for the realization of social rights and that remain consistent with the text, object and purpose of the Covenant will also be considered to be "appropriate means" and therefore must be adopted by the state.[658] This is consistent with the Covenant's mandated objectives that require states use measures that are "necessary" or "needed" to bring about certain desirable outcomes, such as lowering infant mortality and improving methods of food production.[659] In other words, while all appropriate means may not be necessary for the realization of social rights, all measures that are necessary for the realization of social rights are undoubtedly appropriate means if they remain consistent with the text, object and purpose of the Covenant.

4.2.2.1.2. Essentiality as a Measure of Appropriateness

In my view, repealing, striking and refraining from adopting laws that obstruct nonprofit activities always constitute appropriate measures whenever nonprofit activities are *essential* to the realization or enjoyment of social rights in a manner that is *consistent* with the norms and principles of human rights law. 'Essentiality' thus refers to the extent to which nonprofit activities are necessary for the realization or enjoyment of social rights, or for the fulfillment of states' Covenant obligations. NGOs become necessary in this regard when their activities are the sole significant cause of enjoyment or realization for an individual or groups of individuals, such that alternatives are not readily available to these beneficiaries. This definition fits the criteria for appropriateness because it relates to the necessity of realizing/enjoying social rights or fulfilling state duties, but it is only a partial fit.

On the one hand, if NGOs are necessary for realization or enjoyment, then state measures that enable their activities would normally be consid-

658 See General Comment No. 3: The Nature of States Parties' Obligations (1990) para. 3.

659 ICESCR arts. 11 (2) (a) & 12 (2) (a).

ered appropriate means that, according to article 2 (1), a state would normally be required to employ if it is feasible for the state to do so. On the other hand, I have stopped short of claiming that the state must always enable NGOs that are necessary for social rights because unless such NGOs are also compatible with human rights norms and principles they cannot be considered appropriate for realization or enjoyment. Ethnic-based discriminatory practices by NGOs, for example, would undermine the overall objectives of human rights in general and the ICESCR in particular. In these instances, the state would be under no obligation to enable the nonprofit entities because, although they are necessary, they are nonetheless inappropriate for the realization and enjoyment of social rights. To the contrary, states would be obliged to restrain egregiously inappropriate nonprofit activities, even if they are essential to the realization of social rights, in order to uphold the overarching principles and objectives of human rights law. Thus, in order to align essentiality with appropriateness, the essentiality of nonprofit activities is marked by both how necessary these activities are for the realization/enjoyment of Covenant rights or the fulfillment of states' Covenant obligations, as well as whether they are compatible with human rights norms and principles.

The necessity of nonprofit activities is measured by reference to two dimensions of NGO-government relations: their relative *functions* and their relative *capacities*.[660] The more involved NGOs are in the provision of services that contribute to the realization of social rights (functional dimension), and the less capable or willing the state is to provide those services (capacity-related dimension), the more essential the NGO's role is in the realization of the beneficiaries' social rights. This can take place in a number of ways but generally occurs whenever nonprofit activities are the only recourse for people to realize or enjoy their social rights. For example,

660 By selecting relative functions and capacities as the key criteria for essentiality – rather than the need for the services in question or their social significance – essentiality takes on a distinctly *legal* analytical character. The critical requirement for essentiality is not whether the service fulfills basic human needs, which can only be determined through political or philosophical inquiry, but rather whether the service reasonably contributes to the realization of social rights. This is a more inclusive definition that is derived from international human rights law, rather than a restricted notion of which of the very basic services are needed for human survival. Social rights envision a dignified life for each person, not merely human survival. Therefore, when determining whether a nonprofit service is essential, the brunt of the analysis is done on the state's capacity to provide the nonprofit service in question.

when the state does not provide adequate or comprehensive assistance, but NGOs provide the same, then the NGOs are essential for the realization and enjoyment of the rights related to those services.

The crucial point is that under these circumstances, but-for the NGO's contributions, the social rights of beneficiaries would not be realized or enjoyed through reasonably accessible means. Since, by definition, states are unwilling or incapable of replacing essential nonprofit activities, state measures that enable these activities are appropriate for satisfying a state's obligation to fulfill social rights in accordance with article 2 (1). Conversely, obstructing essential nonprofit activities would likely constitute inappropriate regressive measures that breach the state's obligation both to fulfill the realization of rights and to respect their enjoyment.

In developing and using the concept of essentiality of the purposes of this dissertation, a few caveats and comments are in order. First, not all NGOs that are essential for realizing and enjoying social rights are essential in the same way. Some are essential for the enjoyment of social rights that stand at a level of realization beyond what the state is capable of achieving, while others are essential for the enjoyment of very basic rights that are necessary for sustaining human life and fall squarely within the state's duty horizon. In general, the more essential nonprofit activities are, the more they appear to be performing public functions,[661] sometimes even to the point of discharging or fulfilling state duties. Second, the degree to which nonprofit activities are essential to the realization/enjoyment of social rights can impact the way that states try to fulfill their social rights obligations because political decision-making does not take place within a social or legal vacuum. For example, in deciding how to fulfill its outstanding obligations, a state with limited resources may forgo providing services directly to a community that is already serviced by nonprofit providers. In this way, the contours of state action are likely influenced by the extent of nonprofit activities within the country.[662] Finally, since what makes nonprofit activities essential in the first place is the state's reluctance or inability to ensure those social rights being protected or promoted by the nonprofit entity, essentiality can serve as an indirect indication of the govern-

661 See Jonathan Garton, 'The Judical Review of the Decision of Charity Trustees' 20 Trust Law International 160 (2006).

662 Due to the diffused nature of institutionalized political power and political performance, the balance between governmental (formal) and nonprofit (informal) functions is itself an endogenous organizational property of the real-world political structure. (See Philip Abrams, 'Notes on the Difficulty of Studying the State (1977)' 1 Journal of Historical Sociology 58 (1988) 64 & n. 18.).

ment's reliance on or acquiescence to the fulfillment of their state obligations through nonprofit activities. This in turn justifies imposing limits on the way that governments may regulate nonprofit providers.

The notion of essentiality can help us formulate the state's regulatory obligations *vis-à-vis* nonprofits, the specificities of which can be measured on a matrix that represents the extent to which nonprofit actors are essential for the realization of new social rights, the enjoyment of existing rights, the fulfillment of standing state duties, or the discharge of state obligations that have not yet ripened into standing duties but will do so in the reasonably foreseeable future. Consequently, the power of governments to restrict essential nonprofit activities should be restricted and defined according to their essentiality, and courts should employ higher levels of scrutiny when examining whether NGO laws are consistent with the state's social rights obligations whenever they restrict essential nonprofit activities.

4.2.2.1.3. Feasibility

A key qualification of the duty to use all appropriate means is the provision within article 2 (1) that relates to the use of maximum available resources. States must dedicate the maximum of their available resources toward the realization of social rights. When interpreted in light of the primary purpose of the Covenant, which is to recognize and protect ESC rights, the ESCR Committee notes that the use of the term "maximum" indicates an implicit obligation to "strive to ensure the widest possible enjoyment of the relevant rights under the prevailing circumstances."[663] This suggests that states must do nothing less than what they are in fact capable of doing to achieve the full realization of social rights. In this regard – setting aside momentarily a consideration of what precisely constitutes *available* resources – states have no discretion as to how much effort or how much of their available resources they dedicate to achieving full realization.

Even if certain measures are deemed appropriate for the full realization of social rights, states bear no obligation to implement those measures if they lack the available resources to do so. This suggests that the state's duty to use all appropriate means is not yet ripe until the resources to do so be-

663 General Comment No. 3: The Nature of States Parties' Obligations (1990) para. 11.

come available. Nick Ferreira terms this latent obligation to adopt an appropriate (yet infeasible) measure a 'conditional duty', which he argues ripens into an immediate duty once it becomes feasible to adopt the appropriate measures.[664] Based on his assessment of the jurisprudence of the South African Constitutional Court, he goes a step further to assert that states bear 'enabling' duties, which require them to take measures that would increase the availability of resources and feasibility of implementing appropriate means,[665] or as the Constitutional Court put it in *South Africa v. Grootboom*, "legal, administrative, operational and financial hurdles should be examined and, where possible, lowered over time."[666]

In terms of restrictive NGO laws, among the least costly measures that a state can take are (1) refraining from obstructing nonprofit provision and (2) removing existing obstacles to nonprofit provision. These measures very likely fall within the available resources of all states, rendering them feasible. If refraining from obstructing nonprofit provision or removing such obstacles is also necessary for the realization or enjoyment of social rights – in other words, if nonprofit provision is essential for the realization or enjoyment of social rights – then taking such measures would also constitute appropriate means. Under such circumstances, obstructive nonprofit laws would be inconsistent with a state's obligation under article 2 (1) to take all appropriate measures to the maximum of their available resources.[667] Furthermore, this would give rise to an immediate state obligation to repeal the offending NGO law.[668]

Feasibility also relates to the state's ability to regulate and steer NGOs. While refraining from obstructing essential nonprofit activities is certainly

---

664 Ferreira (2012) 299.

665 Ibid 299-300. Seeing as the Covenant already explicitly recognizes at least one enabling duty, Ferreira's assertion does not seem so farfetched when placed within an international legal context. (See ICESCR art. 13 (2) (d) ("The steps to be taken...shall include those necessary for...the creation of conditions which would assure to all medical service and medical attention in the event of sickness.").).

666 *South Africa v. Grootboom*, para. 45.

667 See, The Limburg Principles, para. 70 ("A failure by a State party to comply with an obligation contained in the Covenant is, under international law, a violation of the Covenant.").

668 See ibid paras. 18 & 72 ("...article 2 (1) would often require legislative action to be taken in cases where existing legislation is in violation of the obligations assumed under the Covenant", and a state violates the covenant if "it fails to remove promptly obstacles which it is under a duty to remove to permit the immediate fulfillment of a right").

located within the state's feasibility frontier, regulating and steering them in a manner that is appropriate for the realization/enjoyment of social rights may not be. This depends on how limited a state is in its regulatory and enforcement-related capacities, which is highly relevant for low-income LDCs in Africa. Ultimately, whether the state must employ or forgo employing a particular regulatory scheme regarding nonprofit activities will depend on whether doing so lies within its duty horizon – that is whether it is both feasible and appropriate to do so.

4.2.2.1.4. Maximizing Availability: Public Spending, Private Resources and Accepting Foreign Funding

Given the reality of resource scarcity, major issues of concern are how much a state should spend on realizing ESC rights, what kinds of resources should be considered, and what its obligations if additional funds are made available through an external source? These are issues of particular concern in African LDCs where the availability of resources is severely limited. It is doubtful whether most sub-Saharan countries in Africa – being among the world's least developed nations – can achieve widespread social wellbeing and eradicate poverty in the foreseeable future without an extraordinary upsurge in the availability of resources at their disposal.[669] Chinzara, et al. estimate that, in order to eradicate poverty in Africa by the year 2030, Africa must sustain an economic growth rate of at least 16%, and lower-middle-income countries and lower-income countries would need external funding in the amounts of 56% and 76% of their respective GDPs.[670] After concluding that "these requirements are nearly impossible to achieve", the authors of the study note,

> ... to facilitate future progress in battling extreme poverty, initiatives, especially in low-income countries in the form of social protection, investment in education, and redistribution, need to be pursued with sustained political commitment and at a scale never seen before.[671]

The obvious yet vital point here is that in the least developed countries of Africa, states simply lack the resources needed to eliminate widespread

669 See Robinson and White 82.
670 Chinzara and others (2017) 23-24.
671 Ibid 25.

poverty within the lifespan of people who are currently alive, and probably for some generations to come as well.[672]

In the context of such resource scarcity, it is critical that the governments of LDCs are managing their resources in a proper manner. Not only is squandering scare resources incompatible with article 2 (1) obligations, but improper governmental spending will contribute to the essentiality of nonprofits by reducing the state's capacity to ensure the realization/enjoyment of social rights in relation to that of nonprofits. This raises the question of *how* states should manage limited resources in terms of rationing and compromising through spending trade-offs? In this regard, issues of particular concern are, firstly, the amount of resources that states should make available for social spending; and, secondly, whether courts are competent to evaluate such choices, which are predominantly political in nature.

Since it is impossible to fix a social spending target based merely on the state's article 2 (1) obligations, Robert E. Robertson proposes using a comparative approach instead. He suggests comparing expenditures of countries with comparable economies to determine what a reasonable social spending amount would be.[673] If most countries with comparable economies can spend a specified amount on social rights, then it is reasonable to expect that it is also feasible for all similarly situated countries to do the same. On the other hand, a state could fall into non-compliance if, for example, its military spending exceeded its social spending by an extraordinary amount compared to its peers. [674] In response to the inevitability of such compromises and trade-offs in government spending, scholars like Marius Pieterse offer a critical view.[675] Writing with South African constitutional rights in mind, Pieterse argues that although trade-offs and rationing are an accepted part of reality in developing countries, the discourse of inevitability and compulsion that pervades discussions on rationing "isolate individual rationing decisions from the broader context in which they are taken and hence 'de-politicizes' them".[676] This happens by

672 There are certainly other important factors at play, such as political will and governance. Thus, the availability of adequate resources is a necessary but certainly not sufficient requirement for the progressive realization of social rights.

673 Robert E. Robertson, 'Measuring State Compliance with the Obligation to Devote the "Maximum Available Resources" to Realizing Economic, Social and Cultural Rights' 16 Human Rights Quarterly 693 (1994) 711-712.

674 Ibid.

675 Pieterse (2007) 516-518 ; see also Ferreira (2012).

676 Pieterse (2007) 516-518.

normalizing what are otherwise extraordinary sacrifices of social wellbeing, and by minimizing the need for "institutional scrutiny" of the political or otherwise societal decisions that have contributed to the need for such sacrifices in the first place. [677] Pieterse concludes similarly to Robertson and others in arguing that courts should not shy away completely from scrutinizing the financing and budgeting decision of government,[678] especially in cases involving the frivolous or otherwise unreasonable government spending of scare resources that could have been dedicated to realizing or enjoying social rights.[679] Moreover, evidence of emerging domestic jurisprudence across the globe casts doubt on blanket assertions that courts cannot or do not question the lawfulness of trade-offs in government expenditures.[680]

Even when states are managing scarce resources in a proper manner, they may still need more resources in order to ensure basic or minimum subsistence levels. For African LDCs, additional resources often take the form of foreign funding. Some take the position that developing states with fewer resources must accept financial assistance when it is made available to them from external sources. [681] There is support for this argument in the text of the Covenant, its drafting history, as well as the interpretive work of the ESCR Committee. The Covenant contemplates the use of resources made available to the state by external funders when it imposes obligations of international cooperation through financial and technical assistance,[682] suggesting that perhaps it is indeed impermissible for poorer states to close themselves off from international assistance without good

677 Ibid.

678 Ibid 527-536; Robertson (1994) 711-712; Ferreira (2012); Darrel Moellendorf, 'Reasoning About Resources: Soobramoney and the Future of Socio-Economic Rights Claims' 14 South African Journal on Human Rights 327 (1998).

679 Ferreira (2012) 295. See also, Karl Klare, 'Critical Perspectives on Social and Economic Rights, Democracy and Separation of Powers' in Helena Alviar García, Karl Klare and Lucy A. Williams (eds), *Social and Economic Rights in Theory and Practice: Critical Inquiries* (Routledge 2015) 3-22; Jeff King, *Judging Social Rights* (David Dyzenhaus and Adam Tomkins eds, Cambridge University Press 2012) 316-320.

680 Lucy A. Williams, 'Resource Questions in Social and Economic Rights Enforcement: A Preliminary View' in Helena Alviar García, Karl Klare and Lucy A. Williams (eds), *Social and Economic Rights in Theory and Practice: Critical Inquiries* (Routledge 2015) 43-64.

681 Robertson (1994) 712-713.

682 ICESCR arts. 2 (1) & 23; see also General Comment No. 3: The Nature of States Parties' Obligations (1990) paras. 13-14 (relying on Articles 55 and 56 of the U.N. Charter to emphasize the obligation of states to cooperate with one anoth-

cause. The Covenant similarly emphasizes the "essential importance of international cooperation based on free consent", particularly regarding the right to an adequate standard of living and continuously improving living conditions.[683] The ICESCR's drafting history also seems to support the suggestion that states have an obligation to make use of resources made available from external sources, including foreign funding. [684]

On this basis, the ESCR Committee takes the position that in order for states to make use of *all* available resources, they must "avail themselves of international cooperation and technical assistance",[685] and even request that the same be made available through "resources from the international community".[686] Seeking out and securing such assistance is important for the fulfillment of Covenant obligations in developing countries.[687] Particularly when the realization of social rights – like the right to social security – calls for resource-intensive measures, which "carr[y] significant financial

er); see also Draft International Covenants on Human Rights: Report of the Third Committee (1962) para. 50 (drafting history for art. 2 of the ICESCR reveals members emphasized the importance of international assistance and cooperation in the form of economic and technical cooperation.).

683 ICESCR art. 11 (1). See also Draft International Covenants on Human Rights: Report of the Third Committee (1957) para. 142 (drafting members of the ICESCR noted that recognizing the importance of international assistance for the realization of an adequate standard of living was "particularly essential" for lesser developed countries.).

684 During drafting deliberations at the UN Commission on Human Rights, Mr. Cassin, the state representative from France, proposed amending the phrase "their available resources" – which referred only to the resources of the state – to the unspecified language found in the version that was ultimately adopted: "of the available resources." (Summary Record of the 236th Meeting (1951) (emphasis added) (see also comments from Mr. Azmi of Egypt, Mrs. Roosevelt of USA, and Mr. Sörensen of Denmark, all understanding "available resources" to include international resources made available to developing countries).).

685 General Comment No. 19: The Right to Social Security (2007) para. 41; see also General Comment No. 6: The Economic, Social and Cultural Rights of Older Persons (1995) para. 18.

686 General Comment No. 3: The Nature of States Parties' Obligations (1990) para. 13.

687 See General Comment No. 6: The Economic, Social and Cultural Rights of Older Persons (1995) para. 18 ("...international cooperation...may be a particularly important way of enabling some developing coutnries to fulfill their oblgiations".).

implications".[688] Finally, the ESCR Committee insists that states that were unable to secure the international assistance that they needed must demonstrate to the Committee that they were unsuccessful in doing so.[689] Where NGOs are essential for the realization / enjoyment of social rights, this would of course call into question the legality of NGO laws that broadly limit or obstruct access to foreign funding in countries where resources are already scarce.

Critics have pointed out some problems with the Committee's interpretation of the Covenant. Some scholars note that the initial fervor with which drafting members tried imposing upon richer states obligations to provide technical and financial assistance to poorer states has since been downplayed.[690] Consequently, the Committee emphasizes the duty of poorer states to seek out and accept international assistance, but falls short of addressing *how* international assistance is to be made available and *who* is responsible for ensuring that it is made available to poorer states in the first place.[691]

What about the scenario in which foreign assistance for advancing social rights is being offered to nonprofit organizations instead of directly to the state? This is precisely what happens in sub-Saharan Africa, where many nonprofits are supported predominantly by foreign funding. Thus, one might ask whether the obligation to use the maximum of available resources requires the state to allow or even enable such transactions? This depends on how broadly the terms 'available resources' and 'use' are interpreted.

Among scholars, there is no clear agreement as to the types of resources that qualify under article 2 (1) as "available resources". Some interpret the term 'resources' in narrowly such that it primarily concerns financial resources of the state.[692] Others like Robertson and Sigrun Skogly assert that the state should also mobilize a broader array of resources including hu-

688 General Comment No. 19: The Right to Social Security (2007) para. 41; see also General Comment No. 6: The Economic, Social and Cultural Rights of Older Persons (1995) para. 18.

689 General Comment No. 4: The Right to Adequate Housing (1991) para. 10; General Comment No. 12: The Right to Adequate Food (1999) para. 17.

690 Saul, Kinley and Mowbray (2014) 137-140.

691 Ibid.

692 Audrey R. Chapman and Sage Russell (eds), *Core Obligations: Building a Frameowrk for Economic, Social and Cultural Rights* (Intersentia 2002); Craven (1995).

man, natural, technological, informational and regulatory resources.[693] A wider interpretation is consistent with the ordinary meaning of the term "resources", and falls in line with the related terms within article 2 (1) that are also broadly stated, such as maximal use and international cooperation and assistance. Foreign-funds funneled into a country through NGOs for the purpose of advancing social rights are certainly 'resources' for beneficiaries in the proper sense of the word. However, are they resources in the legal sense of article 2 (1) obligations such that the state can "use" them?

Since these funds are not provided to the state, they are not resources that the state can 'use' in the sense of directing their expenditure. Nonprofit funds that are dedicated to social welfare and development do not constitute resources that are made available to the state *per se*; rather they are a part of those resources that are made available to the people in the state, but not necessary to the government. The legal consequence of this distinction is significant: the property and associational rights of all NGOs proscribes state attempts to take control of nonprofit operations or resources. A question that remains, however, is whether the obligation to 'use' available resources can also mean an obligation to 'permit others to use' available resources.

On the one hand, such an expansive interpretation of the Covenant admittedly stretches the word 'use' beyond its ordinary meaning. On the other hand, the social rights of beneficiaries – which it is the objective of the Covenant to protect and promote – are jeopardized in least developed countries if the state is generally permitted to block the use of private resources that are essential for the realization or enjoyment of social rights. Thus, although the obligation to use the maximum of available resources does not explicitly forbid the state from blocking access to foreign funds granted to NGOs, its emphatic insistence on not wasting resources that are needed for the realization of social rights does seem to suggest that the Covenant would not favor an interpretation whereby states are generally permitted to block foreign funding without adequate justification.

Some have gone a step further to argue that states must, or at least should, not only permit private giving, but also facilitate and encourage it. Relying on Danilo Türk's argument that governments must enable non-governmental actors to dedicate resources to ESC rights, Robertson notes that while governments lack direct control over private donations, they do

693 Robertson (1994) 695-703; Sigrun Skogly, 'The Requirement of Using the 'Maximum of Available Resources' for Human Rights Realisation: A Question of Quality as Well as Quantity?' 12 Human Rights Law Review 393 (2012).

have the power to encourage and allow private giving.[694] Likewise, Nick Ferreira has argued from a South African perspective that the state bears 'enabling duties' with respect to ensuring that resources are made available for the realization of socio-economic rights. He writes,

> Even if it is truly infeasible to provide a certain good now, there are often measures that can be taken which will enable its provision in the future. Such measures might include, for example: alterations to the tax system; saving; the creation of enabling infrastructure (eg building roads and public transport to enable people to access existing services); training people to address skills shortages (eg educating teachers); and re-designing and reforming state institutions to equip them to be able to deliver in future. [695]

Although Ferreira was writing with the South African Constitution in mind, the requirement in article 2 (1) of the ICESCR that *all* appropriate means be used supports his assertion that states bear enabling duties. However, I would add to Ferreira's list of enabling duties the obligation of states to permit private foreign sources of funding to reach nonprofits that are essential to the realization / enjoyment of social rights.

Just as a state should not block essential nonprofits from receiving foreign funding and assistance, it should take care not to obstruct their activities or access to their services without justification because doing so would amount to blocking the external resources that flow through the NGOs. This is a consequence of the state's duty to respect social rights of beneficiaries, which implicitly gives rise to an obligation to refrain from restricting access to available resources that are essential for their realization or enjoyment, such as adequate food, shelter, healthcare and educational services.[696]These nonprofit activities can be thought of as external resources that are made available to beneficiaries through the nonprofit organization. The Committee has noted that, in the area of education, "a State must respect the availability of education by not closing private schools".[697] The African Commission has also used this approach. It asserts that the state's duty to respect social rights includes the duty "to respect the free use of resources owned or at the disposal of the individual alone or in

---

694 Robertson (1994) 713.

695 Ferreira (2012) 299-300.

696 General Comment No. 12: The Right to Adequate Food (1999) para. 15; *SERAC v. Nigeria* para. 45.

697 General Comment No. 13: The Right to Education (1999) para. 50.

any form of association with others, including the household or family, for the purpose of rights-related needs."[698] This language is broad enough to include the free use of resources owned by NGOs that are essential to the realization or enjoyment of social rights.

Thus, state measures that obstruct foreign-funded NGOs whose activities are essential for the realization or enjoyment of social rights should be subject to judicial scrutiny as measure that potentially circumvent article 2 (1) obligations. Without proper justification, obstructing the activities of essential NGOs or denying them access to foreign funding likely contravenes the state's obligation to use the maximum of its available resources and all appropriate means. Moreover, since foreign-funded NGOs do not draw on state resources, courts would not need to address the uncomfortable political questions about state budgeting and apportionment that would normally accompany judicial assessments of whether a state has used the maximum of its available resources.

There must, however, be some exceptions to a general duty to permit externally supported NGOs or to accept foreign assistance. Critics of the ESCR Committee's line of reasoning on this point have argued that it suggests rather unfairly that African states are required to accept foreign aid, which could undermine their sovereignty and independence.[699] Each time a state avails itself to significant amounts of external funding it also exposes itself to foreign control and political influence. Thus, the obligation to accept external resources must be balanced against the risk of foreign political interference. Article 2 (1) allows analysts to balance these risks by implying that states are not required to accept external resources if it would be inappropriate for them to do so. However, since there is not much guidance on what constitutes appropriate means, it remains debatable whether such an assessment is judicially operational. Thus, at least in theory, nonprofit activities that are essential for the realization or enjoyment of social rights cannot be restricted simply because they are backed by foreign funders, unless the state can demonstrate that being backed by foreign funds somehow reduces such activities to inappropriate measures. If, for instance, the conditions placed on accepting foreign funding render nonprofit activities inappropriate, then the social rights obligations of the state

698 *SERAC v. Nigeria* para. 45.

699 See, e.g., Lilian Chenwi, 'Unpacking "Progressive Realisation", Its Relation to Resources, Minimum Core and Reasonableness, and Some Methodological Considerations for Assessing Compliance' 46 De Jure 742 (2013) 752-753.

do not compel it to support those activities or their acceptance of such funds.

Despite the lack of clarity about the meaning of "appropriate", there are some clear instances when enabling foreign-backed nonprofit activities will not be appropriate for the realization of social rights. If, in extreme cases, foreign funding causes nonprofit activities to become harmful to the human rights of beneficiaries or others, the Covenant would allow or even require that states block these nonprofit services or their access to these foreign funds. The potential influence of foreign donors in domestic affairs and their growing entanglement with nonprofit entities certainly raises legitimate concern for the state's political independence and the people's right to self-determination. For example, the state may legitimately subject NGOs and their foreign funders to restrictive regulatory measures if they seek to use nonprofit provision as a means of discriminating against people on account of their ethnicity. The legal grounds for permitting such restrictive regulations, despite their obvious interference with the social rights of the NGO's beneficiaries, is the finding that these nonprofit activities are both inappropriate and harmful, and thus article 2 (1) does not compel the state to enable them but rather requires the state to prevent the discriminatory harm that such activities are likely to inflict on people within the its territory.

4.2.2.1.5. As Compared to State Duties under the African Human Rights Charter

Like the ICESCR, the African Charter incorporates a measure of flexibility into states' Charter obligations, with some limitations. It imposes upon ratifying members an obligation to recognize rights and undertake to adopt effective measures:

> ...parties to the present Charter shall recognize the rights, duties and freedoms enshrined in this Charter and shall undertake to adopt legislative or other measures to give effect to them.[700]

Although the term "recognize" appears to be a weakening of state's duties when compared to the ICESCR's requirement to "take steps", the African Commission insists that article 1 of the African Charter imposes upon states "a positive obligation" to "define the legal framework for the enjoy-

700 African Charter art. 1.

ment of the rights and freedoms contained in the Charter..."[701] It emphasizes the critical function of article 1 as the provision that legally binds each state, and refers to it as "the root of the Charter".[702]

The Charter also imposes duties of promotion:

> States parties to the present Charter shall have the duty to promote and ensure through teaching, education and publication, the respect of the rights and freedoms contained in the present Charter and to see to it that these freedoms and rights as well as corresponding obligations and duties are understood.[703]

Finally, states parties to the African Charter have certain obligations toward judicial and institutional actors that protect Charter rights. In this regard, article 26 of the Charter announces the following:

> States parties to the present Charter shall have the duty to guarantee the independence of the Courts and shall allow the establishment and improvement of appropriate national institutions entrusted with the promotion and protection of the rights and freedoms guaranteed by the present Charter.

In a case concerning the government's involvement in an attack on protestors that took place in Egypt, the African Commission interpreted article 26 in conjunction with article 7 (the right to a fair trial) and concluded that states bear a duty to establish not only courts but also the "institutions which also have the mandate to create mechanisms for protection."[704] This is essentially a positive obligation to "provide the structures and mechanisms necessary for the exercise of the right to fair trial."[705] Article 26, however, is not restricted in its application to the right to fair trial. The commission's reasoning can be applied analogously to ESC rights as well. In that regard, the state would be bound to provide structural support to institutions – meaning to permit and facilitate their establishment and improvement – when those institutions have a national character and when they are – as the Commission has noted elsewhere – "institutions

701 *Groupe De Travail Sur Les Dossiers Judiciaires Stratégiques v. Democratic Republic of Congo*, Comm. No. 259/2002 (ACmHPR 2015) para. 62.

702 *Sir Dawda K. Jawara v. Gambia (the)*, Comm. No. 147/95-149/96 (ACmHPR 2000) para. 46.

703 African Charter art. 25.

704 *Egyptian Initiative for Personal Rights and Interights v. Egypt*, Comm. No. 323/2006 (ACmHPR 2013) para. 235.

705 Ibid.

which are essential to give meaning and content to that right".[706] It would seem that if a state fails to establish such institutions, although it is obliged to do so, it must at the very least enable the establishment and improvement of nonprofit institutions that might take its place.

Notably absent in the African Charter's statement of duties are those qualifying conditions found in the ICESCR. The Charter makes no mention of the maximal use of available resources or the appropriateness of means, which would have restricted both the discretion of states as well as the scope of their duties. The African Charter also excludes the language of progressive realization, which relieves states of the obligation to maintain the particular intention of progressing rather than regressing in the achievement of full realization. At first glance, it may appear that the African Charter provides less protection than the ICESCR, or that African states are bound by less rigorous obligations than other states. However, that would be an erroneous conclusion.

The African Charter should be interpreted in light of the ICESCR,[707] and in a way that is consistent with the object, purpose and terms of each treaty. Thus, the fact that the African Charter is silent with regard to the more stringent obligations found in the ICESCR cannot be taken to mean that the African Charter negates the duties imposed by the ICESCR. Indeed, the more protective provisions of either treaty should trump the less protective provisions of the other.[708] As such, African states are still obliged to fulfill all state obligations found in article 2 (1) of the ICESCR, namely using the *maximum* of available resources, taking *immediate* steps, adopting *all* appropriate means and acting with the intention of realizing social rights *progressively* rather than regressively or stagnantly. In addition, African states are obliged by the African Charter to recognize Charter rights and to ensure that their adopted means are *effective* for the realization of rights. Furthermore, African states must ensure that Charter rights are known and understood by rights bearers. Lastly, African states are

706 *Civil Liberties Organisation v. Nigeria*, Comm. No. 129/94 (ACmHPR 1995) para. 15.

707 African Charter art. 60.

708 Scott and Alston argue that "a principle of greatest protection…should govern interpretive harmonisation amongst human rights treaties." They reason that "[s]uch a principle flows from the best reading of the combined normative signals...and the general principle of treaty interpretation in art 31 (3)(c) of the Vienna Convention of the Law of Treaties which calls for a treaty term to be read in light of other relevant international law applicable in the relations between states." (Scott and Alston (2000) 229.).

bound to guarantee the independence of the judiciary, and to refrain from interfering with the establishment and improvement of national institutions that promote and protect Charter rights.

4.2.2.2. Duty to Respect Social Rights: Permitting Essential NGOs

When the state's duty to respect social rights is characterized as a negative duty, it requires state to refrain from doing anything that would deprive a person of his or her rights.[709] This becomes relevant when states try to restrict private efforts to bring about the realization or enjoyment of social rights.[710] The ESCR Committee refers to this negative aspect when it insists that the duty to respect forbids the implementation or continued use of state measures that result in the prevention or limitation of access to things like adequate food and water, private schools, and preventative, curative and palliative health services (including traditional healing practices).[711] For example, with respect to the right to health, the Committee has asserted, "obligations to respect include a State's obligation to refrain from prohibiting or impeding traditional preventive care, healing practices and medicines."[712] For the regulation of nonprofits, the negative aspect of the state's duty to respect social rights would indicate that it should not obstruct the efforts of nonprofits that are essential for realization or enjoyment.

The positive dimension of the duty to respect imposes another obligation upon states. When viewed through the lens of the duty to respect, the positive obligation of states to take steps toward the progressive realization of social rights through the use of all appropriate means, and particularly

709 See, Sandra Liebenberg, *Socio-Economic Rights: Adjudication under a Transformative Constitution* (Juta & Co. 2010) 214-218 (describing jurisprudence in South Africa that recognizes negative state duties of non-intereference with respect to socio-economic rights.).

710 See, Rosas, 'The Right of Self-Determination' (noting that the internal aspect of the right of self-determination indicates "a right of non-intereference" and "a certain basic freedom to economic, social and cultural activities indepenedent of government policies.").

711 General Comment No. 12: The Right to Adequate Food (1999) para. 15; General Comment No. 13: The Right to Education (1999) paras. 47 & 50; General Comment No. 14: The Right to the Highest Attainable Standard of Health (2000) para. 34; General Comment No. 15: The Right to Water (2003) para. 21.

712 General Comment No. 14: The Right to the Highest Attainable Standard of Health (2000) para. 34.

legislative means, indicates that states bear a standing obligation to repeal existing laws that interfere with or undermine the progressive realization of social rights, unless their retention can by fully justified. If the manner in which a state regulates nonprofit providers is inconsistent with that state's social rights obligations, then the state must withdraw that regulation.

The ESCR Committee has supported this view in its interpretive work. It has noted that states violate their Covenant obligations not only with the "formal repeal or suspension of legislation necessary for the continued enjoyment" of social rights, but also with "the failure to reform or repeal legislation which is manifestly inconsistent" with social rights.[713] In a General Comment on the right to water, the ESCR Committee maintains that "[e]xisting legislation, strategies and policies should be reviewed to ensure that they are compatible with obligations arising from the right to water, and should be repealed, amended or changed if inconsistent with Covenant requirements."[714] The duty to respect the right to social security has been interpreted in a virtually identical manner.[715]

While the imposition of restrictive NGO laws may indicate that the state has breached its duty to respect social rights, the failure to repeal such provisions when they are inconsistent with the state's Covenant obligations may also constitute a breach of the duty to respect. If the content of a restrictive NGO law is an affront to the realization or enjoyment of social rights, then the state breaches its duty to respect social rights not only at the moment that it passes the offensive legislation but also continuously thereafter because it remains in breach until it repeals the offensive law.

4.2.2.3. Duty to Protect Social Rights: Controlling Harmful NGOs

In addition to their duties to fulfill and respect, states also bears a duty to protect social rights from third party interference. The obligation to protect social rights is implicated whenever nonprofit activities are involved in, or could potentially interfere with, the enjoyment and realization of

713 General Comment No. 12: The Right to Adequate Food (1999) para. 19; General Comment No. 13: The Right to Education (1999) para. 59; General Comment No. 14: The Right to the Highest Attainable Standard of Health (2000) paras. 48 & 50; General Comment No. 15: The Right to Water (2003) para. 42; General Comment No. 19: The Right to Social Security (2007) paras. 64 & 65.

714 General Comment No. 15: The Right to Water (2003) para. 46.

715 General Comment No. 19: The Right to Social Security (2007) para. 67.

beneficiaries' social rights.[716] In order to restrain nonprofit activities that pose a threat to human rights, states must – at the very least –exercise adequate regulatory and supervisory oversight. In theory, although NGOs have a right to free speech and free association, the state may limit their conduct so as to protect the social rights of beneficiaries, though such limitations would need to be legitimized with sound and lawful justifications.

States bear primary responsibility for the realization of social rights.[717]While states may delegate tasks towards the fulfillment of their social rights obligations, they may not alienate themselves entirely from their duties. As such, private acts that interfere with the enjoyment of social rights are sometimes attributable to the state.[718] In *Social and Economic Rights Action Center and Other v. Nigeria*, the African Commission concluded that the Nigerian government's treatment of the Ogoni people, and its acquiescence to the destructive conduct of a private oil company, constituted violations of socio economic rights.[719] In that communication, the Commission laid out the state's minimum core obligations under regional and international human rights law for certain social rights. In general, the minimum core obligations of states are twofold: first to refrain from violating social rights, and secondly to refrain from interfering with the efforts of people to fulfill those social rights. With respect to housing and shelter, the Commission notes that states must "refrain from destroying housing

716 In relation to private for-profit providers, Marius Pieterse draws out the state's obligation to regulate private providers from its constitutional obligation toward the social rights of beneficiaries. He asserts,

> Given that private providers of essential social goods and services are in the business of rendering access to the objects of constitutional rights, the limitation of their commercial liberties through such public intervention is not only constitutionally justified, but called for.
>
> (Marius Pieterse, 'Relational Socio-Economic Rights', 25 South African Journal on Human Rights 198 (2009) 208.).

717 Robert McCorquodale, 'Non-State Actors and International Human Rights Law' in Sarah Joseph and Adam McBeth (eds), *Research Handbook on International Human Rights Law* (Edward Elgar 2010) 91-114, 100-103; General Comment No. 13: The Right to Education (1999).

718 This is the case when private parties act on behalf of the state, have some claim to governmental authority, are controlled by the state, carry out government-like conduct in the absence of the state, or exercise conduct that is subsequently acknowledged and adopted by the state. (Responsibility of States for Internationally Wrongful Acts, UNGA (Jan. 28, 2002) U.N. Doc. A/RES/56/83 (Annex) arts. 4-11.).

719 *SERAC v. Nigeria* para. 66.

and obstructing efforts of people to rebuild lost homes."[720] Likewise, the Commission expounds that "the minimum core of the right to food" requires that a state "should not destroy or contaminate food sources" and it should not "prevent peoples' efforts to feed themselves."[721] According to the Commission, Nigeria violated the right to food in part "through terror", by which it had "created significant obstacles to the Ogoni communities trying to feed themselves." [722] These minimum obligations extend to the state's obligation to protect social rights against violations and interferences perpetuated by private actors.[723]

Similarly, in *Sudan Human Rights Organisation and Other v. Sudan*, the Commission held that states could be indirectly responsible for the deprivation of rights by third parties who are "insufficiently regulated by States".[724] Private attacks by state-supported "nomadic tribal gangs of Arab origin"[725] on civilian populations in the Darfur region constituted a violation of the rights to health and the right to food.[726] The Committee noted that "the destruction of homes, livestock and farms as well as the poisoning of water sources, such as wells exposed the victims to serious health risks and amounted to a violation of Article 16 of the Charter", which guarantees the right to health. [727]

Yet even when third party interference cannot be attributed to a state, it is still required to protect individuals against such interference.[728] This is why states must monitor the effects of privatization on the social rights of

---

720 Ibid, para. 61.
721 Ibid, para. 65.
722 Ibid, para. 66.
723 Ibid, paras. 61 & 65.
724 *Sudan Human Rights Organisation v. Sudan*, para. 210.
725 Ibid, para. 5.
726 Ibid, paras. 1-14.
727 Ibid, para. 212.
728 General Comment No. 31: The Nature of the General Legal Obligation Imposed on States Parties to the Covenant, Human Rights Committee, U.N. Doc. CCPR/C/21/Rev. 1/Add.13 (UN 2004) para. 8 (stating that "positive obligations on States Parties to ensure Covenant [ICCPR] rights will only be fully discharged if individuals are protected by the State, not just against violations of Covenant rights by its agents, but also against acts committed by private persons or entities that would impair the enjoyment of Covenant rights in so far as they are amendable to application between private persons or entities."). See also, *X and Y v. The Netherlands*, 8 EHRR 235, 8978/80 (ECtHR 1985); *Velasquez Rodriguez Case*; *Mouvement Burkinabé Des Droits De L'homme Et Des Peuples v. Burkina Faso*, 204/97 (ACmHPR 2001) § 42; Clapham, 'Non-State Actors' 566-568.

beneficiaries with vigilance.[729] The benefits derived from privatization should not be acquired by diminishing the rights of beneficiaries.[730]

The African Children's Committee has also weighed in on the matter of protecting social rights. Its jurisprudence recognizes the duty to protect beneficiaries against unscrupulous NGOs as one of the state's core obligations. In *Centre for Human Rights and Other v. Senegal*, a case referenced in an earlier section about *talibés* students in Senegal who were in the care of private *daraas* schools,[731] the African Children's Committee found a violation of not only the duty to provide minimum essential levels for education and health services, but also the duty to protect the children against the misconduct of the *daraas*. The Committee noted that the duty to protect the right to education from third party deprivation requires the state to "set minimum standards for all educational institutions", including privately run schools like the *daaras*.[732] The African Children's Committee found that the Senegalese state failed to fulfill its obligation to protect because it did not provide "the necessary curriculum and facilities in which the *daaras* function in delivering education." [733] The African Children's Committee wrote:

> The government must enforce its own laws to protect *talibés* from this abuse and ensure that the education received in *daaras* equips these children with a rounded education, and does not allow forced begging... But the authorities have largely failed to take concrete steps to enforce the law and end the exploitation and abuse of the *talibés*. Therefore, the Government of Senegal has violated the right to education of the *talibés* by failing to ensure the availability, accessibility and acceptability of the education and supervising the *daaras*.[734]

Regarding the right to the best attainable health, the African Children's Committee found that the obligation to protect requires states "to assure that children are not deprived of access to health care services", that the state "should not tolerate any practice which violates the right to health of

729 Neuman (2013) 368. See also, General Comment No. 14: The Right to the Highest Attainable Standard of Health (2000).

730 General Comment No. 5: General Measures of Implementation of the Covenant on the Rights of the Child, Committee on the Rights of the Child, U.N. Doc. CRC/GC/2003/5 (UN 2003).

731 Supra note 441 and accompanying text.

732 *Centre for Human Rights v. Senegal*, para. 47.

733 Ibid, para. 48.

734 Ibid, para. 50.

children", and that it "must assert that third parties do not deprive children of their right to access medical services."[735] Each of these obligations is relevant for third party deprivations of social rights, and they indicate that the state must, at the very least, protect against such interferences. The Committee concluded that Senegal violated the right to health by failing to take measures against those private entities that "accommodated *talibés* in squalid health conditions."[736]

The ESCR Committee, the African Commission and the African Children's Committee have all strongly indicated that the destruction, by non-state actors, of objects necessary for the realization of social rights may constitute a breach of the state's duty to protect social rights. These opinions support the claim that the government should protect the social rights of beneficiaries against harmful nonprofit activities. From this perspective, a beneficiary-centered analysis offers a critical approach that renders visible the potential harm that NGOs could cause to beneficiaries in a way that an analysis based exclusively on the rights of NGOs would not have detected. The state's concerns about abusive, negligent or otherwise harmful nonprofit activities can be addressed within a paradigm that takes into account the state's duty to protect the human rights of beneficiaries. For example, from the beneficiary's perspective, the ICESCR can accommodate the claim among some African states that NGOs with foreign ties pose a threat to the political independence of the African state because it guarantees the right to self-determination.

4.2.2.4. Concluding Remarks

It cannot be said in specific terms when a state must fully realize social rights, or by what particular collection of means or with how large a budget it must go about achieving that goal. Instead, the Covenant imposes upon states the task of doing all that they can do in order to achieve the realization of social rights. It does this by requiring that states dedicate the maximum of their available resources, and that they make use of all appropriate means. Then if after having offered all that they can offer toward the realization of social rights states are only able to reach full realization progressively, they do not fall out of compliance for failing to achieve full realization immediately.

---

735 Ibid, para. 54.
736 Ibid, para. 56.

States are bound to adopt all appropriate and feasible measures. Appropriate measures include those that are necessary for the realization of social rights with respect to the particular social and economic context of each country. When nonprofit activities become essential for the realization or enjoyment of social rights, or for the fulfillment of state obligations, then state measures that enable such activities will be considered appropriate means. In the least developed countries of Africa, where the state's own resources are inadequate for the progressive realization of social rights,[737] nonprofit activities are more likely to be essential for the realization / enjoyment of social rights and the fulfillment of state duties. This suggests that the Covenant likely prohibits state measures that obstruct nonprofit activities in African LDCs. Moreover, appropriate and feasible measures would include repealing and refraining from enacting obstructive NGO laws.

NGO laws that forbid or limit the use of foreign funding can cause significant harm to the enjoyment and realization of social rights in countries where essential nonprofits rely heavily on foreign funding. The Covenant and the ESCR Committee seem to suggest that poorer states must accept external resources, and their reasoning seems to extend to foreign-backed nonprofit activities as well. However, whether states must enable or obstruct NGOs with foreign funding depends on whether accepting the foreign funding renders the nonprofit activities inappropriate for or harmful to the realization or enjoyment of Covenant rights. When nonprofit activities are appropriate and foreign funding does not render them inappropriate, then there is an obligation to enable and support them and their access to foreign funding. Otherwise, states bear no obligation to enable or support inappropriate services from a social rights perspective. Lastly, if the activities pose a threat to human rights, then the state has a positive obligation to prevent the harm in order to protect the rights of beneficiaries and others. In this case, the threatening nonprofit activities and their access to foreign funds may be restricted or obstructed.

737 It is questionable whether LDCs can progress without the assistance of external resources. The United Nations agency for least developed countries has stressed how critical external support and, in particular, overseas development aid has been for efforts to eliminate extreme poverty in LDCs. (See (2014) United Nations Under-Secretary-General and High Representative for LDCs, LLDCs and SIDS, *Extreme Poverty Eradication in the Least Developed Countries and the Post-2015 Development Agenda*, 25 & 42.).

4.2.3. Minimum Core Obligations

The term 'minimum core obligations' refers to the notion that states bear certain critical duties that must be fulfilled as a matter of priority because they correspond to the minimum essential level of ESC rights. The term 'minimum essential level' (MELs) refers to the basic core of a right that is inviolable because it reflects the very nature of the right. Despite the lofty ideals that underpin MELs, they are not described with enough precision or normative content to render them legally determinable. What, for example, constitutes adequate housing in Mali? How might adequate housing differ in South Africa? Where does one draw the line between inadequate housing and adequate housing? And, finally, how does one go about determining whether the state has ensured adequate housing? Thus, there is a great deal of controversy about whether the ICESCR guarantees or even recognizes MELs. Since, however, it is clear that the Covenant forbids the total destruction of ESC rights, presumably at the very least adequate housing must exclude homelessness, basic health care must exclude being denied medical attention or services when one is very ill, compulsory and free primary education must exclude fee-based enrollment, access to adequate foodstuffs must exclude chronic hunger and malnutrition, and basic social security must exclude widespread poverty and income insecurity. Therefore, at the very least, MELs reflects a legal guarantee that people are entitled to some level of protection beyond the total deprivation of ESC rights.

As a consequence, the minimum core obligation of states would be to refrain from totally destroying ESC rights or to bring about at least some meaningful degree of realization for all ESC rights whenever it is possible to do so. Although states have a great deal of discretion as to how they will achieve the realization of ESC rights, that discretion does not extend to deciding whether they will all together forgo realizing a particular right when it would otherwise be feasible and appropriate for them to do so. Proponents of the minimum core would insist that it provides greater protection for ESC rights than merely adopting a more-than-nothing rule for the realization and enjoyment of rights. Yet even this very basic assertion would still have considerable legal consequences in least developing countries where the total deprivation of ESC rights is not an uncommon occurrence, and even more so when that deprivation is being alleviated by nonprofit entities.

Accepting the notion of core obligations augments the legal relationship between nonprofits and regulatory bodies. In countries where nonprofit entities realize minimum essential levels in lieu of the state, the nonprofits are fulfilling those core obligations of the state. Thus, any state measures that restrict NGOs that are essential for the realization or continued enjoyment of minimum essential levels may constitute a violation of the state's core obligations. The implication is that such NGOs would enjoy a special level of legal protection from state interference, above and beyond that enjoyed by other NGOs. This kind of legal intervention would in turn incentive greater nonprofit activity in the areas of service that are prioritized by the core obligations approach. In least developed countries, where NGOs are often essential for the realization and enjoyment of very basic ESC rights and where governments have sometimes targeted NGOs through restrictive regulatory measures, the recognition of core obligations could reshape the very landscape of the nonprofit sector, to the benefit of rights bearers. In this section, I will consider what core obligations – if any – states may bear in relations to ESC rights. From these core obligations, I draw out criteria for further classifying NGOs in accordance with their propensity to fulfill minimum essential levels of beneficiaries or the core obligations of states.

4.2.3.1. ICESCR Recognizes Minimum Essential Levels

The notion that states bear minimum core obligations is not found explicitly within the Covenant. Yet these basic duties may be derived implicitly because their fulfillment is necessary for the realization of ESC rights. They are derived first and foremost from the Covenant's indication that the MELs of ESC rights – whatever they may be – cannot be violated. However, while there are conceptual difficulties in demarcating a core or minimum level of realization and enjoyment for each right that constitutes its very nature or essence, the notion of a minimum core is easier to conceptualize for state duties. The existence of minimum core obligations is consistent with the Covenant, at least to the extent that these core obligations condition the way in which article 2 (1) obligations should be operationalized. Thus, although the particular content of MELs is difficult to deduce from the ICESCR, core obligations can be legally defined to a certain extent. The following paragraphs will expound on this point.

As noted earlier, core obligations can be derived from the Covenant's implicit recognition of MELs. Any interpretation of the Covenant that supports the recognition of MELs and core obligations must be consistent with the ordinary meaning, purpose and object of the Covenant, within its context.[738] The text of the Covenant supports the view that ESC rights contain an essential core that must be protected. For example, although article 4 permits limitations on covenant rights, it also requires that those limitations remain "compatible with the nature of these rights". Article 5, which prohibits "any act aimed at the destruction of any of the rights", similarly appears to suggest that a non-derogable core exists within each right. Therefore, MELs exist because, at the very least, the Covenant forbids the total deprivation of ESC rights; and this acknowledgement – without even having yet defined the contents of those MELs – is already enough to give rise to certain determinable core obligations.

A teleological reading of the treaty confirms that MELs, and consequently core obligations, exist. This approach reasons that interpreting the ICESCR as though it does not guarantee the protection of minimum essential levels would effectively wipe out the covenant's objective function, which is to create ESC rights and correlative state duties. The ESCR Committee goes so far as to conclude, "If the Covenant were to be read in such a way as not to establish such a minimum core obligation, it would be largely deprived of its *raison d'être*." [739] If the Covenant does not implicitly recognize MELs for each right, then, although it appears to be a binding instrument of international law, the Covenant would nonetheless have the same practical effect as a recommendation or declaration. Consequently, without imposing certain implicit core obligations to ensure protection for MELs, the Covenant will have created merely illusory state duties. This would suggest that the corresponding rights are reduced to legal principles or, at worst, hollow promises. Since, however, the Covenant is indeed a legal instrument that protects certain human rights by imposing legal restraints and obligations upon states, it must create at the very least some protection against the total deprivation of the rights guaranteed therein.

Martin Scheinin makes a convincing case for the minimum essential levels approach from the perspective of giving effect to the Covenant. His treatment of Robert's Alexy's theory on rules and principles distinguishes between rights as legal principles, which may be balanced against competing principles, and rights as legal rules, which – when applied – determine the outcome of a case without the need for balancing.[740] Scheinin favors a

738 Vienna Convention on the Law of Treaties, art. 31.

739 General Comment No. 3: The Nature of States Parties' Obligations (1990) para. 10.

740 See Martin Scheinin, 'Terrorism and the Pull of 'Balancing' in the Name of Security', EUI Working Papers Law 55 (2009).

minimum essential core approach to human rights in which "every human right contains a core with the quality of a rule", rather than merely a principle, and that the proper scope of application of each right is defined in such a way that "there can never be a genuine conflict between rules".[741] In agreement with Alexy's critics, Scheinin doubts the efficacy of a judicial process that only ever balances rights against one another without recognizing an inviolable core within. Such a system "does not *exclude* its erosion to irrationality, arbitrariness and insufficient protection of the rights of the individual".[742] He asserts that, in an era of global terrorism and the resulting limitation on rights in the name of national security, those judicial bodies in "even the finest democracies of the world" run the risk of "accept[ing] too many compromises in the name of balancing".[743]

The human rights context of the ICESCR also supports the existence of MELs for ESC rights. The ICCPR, being the sister covenant to the ICESCR and having been drafted alongside it, constitutes part of the context within which the ICESCR should be interpreted, especially in view of the interdependence of each set of rights. From this perspective, the existence of MELs in relation to ESC rights can be derived from the right to life, which is protected in the ICCPR. Some proponents of core obligations argue that states must refrain from wrongfully ending life, and must take all possible measures to ensure survival. [744] The African Charter is also part of the human rights context that is relevant for African LDCs. The African Commission's interpretive work features multiple references to core obligations and MELs for social rights,[745] although core obligations as they are recognized by the African Commission are sometimes conflated with the negative duty of states to refrain from destroying existing social rights achievements.

4.2.3.2. The Contents of Core Obligations May Be Legally Determined

Much of the debate and controversy around core obligations is centered around whether and how the specific normative content of MELs can be

741 Scheinin (2013) 535.

742 Scheinin (2009) 57 (emphasis in original).

743 Ibid (emphasis in original).

744 E.g., Bertrand G. Ramcharan, 'The Concept and Dimensions of the Right to Life' in Bertrand G. Ramcharan (ed), *The Right to Life in International Law*, vol 3 (Martinus Nijhoff 1985) 1-32, 8-10.

745 *SERAC v. Nigeria.*

legally defined.[746] Some doubt the conceptual integrity of MELs.[747] Others question whether the MELs concept is even capable of advancing social justice.[748] Despite the difficulties presented by the concept of MELs, their legal determinability is not a prerequisite for beginning to define the contents of core obligations. Although it remains unclear whether one can legally deduce the normative contents of MELs, their mere existence of MELs indicates that some core obligations must also exist. Indeed, core obligations remain intact in their functional form: they exist to the extent that they refine the state's general obligations under article 2 (1), even if it is not possible for law to define in a normative manner the MELs of each ESC right.

The Covenant appears to protect at least some positive, albeit legally indeterminable, degree of MELs for ESC rights. At the very bare minimum, there is protection against the total deprivation of ESC rights. From there, certain generally applicable core obligations can be defined as a consequence of the mere existence of MELs, without the need to first attribute any particular level of realization or enjoyment to the inviolable minimum core of ESC rights. The key is in accepting that, at the very least, the Covenant forbids the total deprivation of ESC rights.

The ESCR Committee appears to have taken this view in some of its interpretive work. Its construction of the substantive contents of MELs and core obligations is based on the need to alleviate and prevent total deprivations of ESCs. They include the following duties: to ensure access to minimal essential food and freedom from hunger to everyone; to ensure equal, secure and affordable access to safe water; to refrain from committing and to protect against forced eviction; to respect and protect existing formal and informal social security schemes; to provide and ensure access to free and compulsory basic education for everyone; to provide essential drugs and to ensure equitable access to health services and goods.[749] The African Children's Committee has expanded upon these core obligations, as they relate to children's rights to health and education. In doing so, it adds the following duties: to establish and enforce minimum educational standards for private schools; to provide schools, qualified teachers, equipment and

746 E.g., Lisa Forman and others, 'Conceptualising Minimum Core Obligations under the Right to Health: How Should We Define and Implement the 'Morality of the Depths''. 20 The International Journal of Human Rights 531 (2016).

747 E.g., Lehmann (2006).

748 E.g., Young (2008).

749 See *supra* part 0on the minimum essential levels of social rights.

other "corollaries" of the right to education; and to provide electricity, adequate nutrition, safe drinking water and medicine.[750] The African Commission has similarly asserted that states bear a core obligation to provide electricity, safe drinking water and adequate medicine.[751] These standards are directed toward preventing and alleviating the total deprivation of ESC rights, signaling that at the very least core obligations should be understood as duties to prevent and alleviate total deprivation.

From the perspective of alleviating and preventing total deprivation, the core obligation of states consists of a negative duty to refrain from causing or facilitating the total deprivation of ESC rights, as well as a positive duty to prevent such deprivations in the first place. Hunger, extreme poverty, homelessness and the widespread unavailability of education or medical services all constitute total deprivations of social rights that are not uncommon in least developed countries. The mere presence of such deprivations within a state raises suspicion of a breach of its core obligation.

4.2.3.3. Reconciling Core Obligations and Progressive Realization

There appears to be some problems reconciling core obligations with the allowance for progressive realization found in article 2 (1), and this has created a great deal of confusion among analysts. The inconsistent manner in which the ESCR Committee has developed its concept of core obligations is partly to blame. At times, the Committee has limited core obligations to achieving those minimum essential levels that the state's available resources will allow for. Other times, it omits this qualifier, insisting that minimum essential levels of social rights – unlike *full* realization – must be achieved immediately.[752] This assertion has become a contentious point among commentators who try to reconcile the ESCR Committee's interpretation with the clear language of article 2 (1). Complicating things even further, the ESCR Committee has stressed that minimum core obligations are non-derogable, and that noncompliance cannot be justified,[753] thereby

---

750 See *supra* part 0on the minimum essential levels of social rights.

751 See *supra* part 0on the minimum essential levels of social rights.

752 General Comment No. 15: The Right to Water (2003) paras. 37 & 40.

753 Ibid. The Committee has insisted that a "State party cannot, under any circumstances whatsoever, justify its non-compliance with the core obligations…which are non-derogable". (General Comment No. 14: The Right to the Highest Attainable Standard of Health (2000) para. 47. See also General Comment No. 15: The Right to Water (2003) para. 40.).

leaving analysts wondering whether all poorer states fall into noncompliance simply because they are less wealthy than their peers.

Criticism of the minimum core approach is largely, and understandably, directed at the Committee's inconsistent and rather confusing assertions.[754] One scholar among these critics is Kerstin Mechlem, who posits that expanding the concept of core obligations such that they are understood to have immediate effect or that noncompliance is unjustifiable is an unfounded interpretation of the ICESCR.[755] She argues that such interpretations are inconsistent with Articles 31 and 32 of the 1969 Vienna Convention[756] on the grounds that they ignore the object and purpose of the Covenant, which includes allowing states to realize social right progressively and up to *but not beyond* the limits of their available resources.[757] Mechlem contends that such an interpretation would result in the unfair scenario where, by design, poorer countries are likely to be noncompliant as a simple matter of practical circumstances.[758]

Some proponents of MELs have tried to address this unfair scenario that the core obligations concept appears to create. Craig Scott and Philip Alston, for instance, would set different requirements for wealthier states than for poorer states.[759] They assert that while there is an absolute minimum core that constitutes the basic requirements for human survival, wealthier states must also fulfill *specific* MELs, which are placed at a level higher than the absolute minimums and relates to each country's specific economic conditions and relative wealth.[760] Ultimately, however, the assertion that the there is no justification for failing to achieve MELs immediately is difficult to reconcile with the clear terms of article 2 (1), which only requires states to do what is feasible and appropriate for them to do. As expected, the ESCR Committee's assertion in this regard has been subject to heavy criticism for its apparent deviation from the plain meaning of the Covenant's text. In its most recent work, even the Committee appears to concede that there is a problem with understanding core obligations as non-derogable, immediate duties to achieve MELs without exceptions. As recently as 2016, it issued a General Comment on reproductive and sexual

754 Young (2008); Lehmann (2006).
755 Mechlem (2009) 940-945.
756 Vienna Convention on the Law of Treaties.
757 Mechlem (2009) 940-945.
758 Ibid.
759 Scott and Alston (2000) 250.
760 Ibid.

health rights wherein its statement on core obligations omitted the strong language of non-derogable duties that was present in its earlier work.[761]

In my view, the disarray about whether deprivations of MELs automatically constitute violations of core obligations are largely related to the tendency to obscure the distinction between those duties that are subject to progressive performance and those that must be performed immediately. If core obligations are understood to be nothing other than the duty to fulfill the realization of MELs, then it would be difficult to reconcile the claim that core obligations have immediate effect on the one hand, with the Covenant's allowance for progressive realization on the other. It is this erroneous construction of core obligations that gives rise to the notion that all deprivations of ESC rights conclusively indicate a failure to comply with core obligations. If, however, core obligations were to represent something other than the immediate fulfillment of MELs, then perhaps there is no conflict of interpretation.

The notion that MELs have immediate effect cannot mean that a total deprivation of ESC rights immediately or necessarily constitutes a breach of core obligations. This is due to the fact that rather than simply mirroring one another, MELs and core obligations differ in their functionality. Martin Scheinin points this out when – in his comparison of the two concepts – he rightly notes that the core obligations approach offers a methodology to operationalize minimum essential rights.[762] MELs, on the other hand, function as an indication that states bear certain core obligations *vis-à-vis* the alleviation and prevention of total deprivations.

In truth, both MELs and core obligations have immediate effect. MELs are, after all, legal rights belonging to rights bearers immediately, at all times and without delay. These ESC rights do not need to ripen or come into effect over time. For example, a person is immediately and always entitled to the right to be free from hunger, without conditions. Since all rights should correspond to duties elsewhere, the assertion that MELs are immediate is an indication that states certainly bear some obligations that are also immediate in nature, such as duties to respect and protect MELs without delay. However, this does not mean that states bear immediate or unconditional obligations to *fulfill* MELs, thus the occurrence of total deprivation alone is not enough to conclude that a state has breached its core obligations. The key to validating the claim that both MELs and core obli-

761 See General Comment No. 22: The Right to Sexual and Reproductive Health (2016) para. 49.

762 Scheinin (2013) 538.

gations have immediate effect is to distinguish between the various aspects of the state's Covenant obligations (i.e., to respect, protect and fulfill) and to clarify the extent to which each duty requires immediate actions or omissions on the part of states. The proper construction of core obligations is one that limits them to those acts that the state must immediately perform; not one that inflates all state duties to the status of core obligations.

In order to remain consistent with article 2 (1)'s allowance for progressive realization, the construction of the core obligations concepts must take into account whether it was feasible and appropriate for the state to prevent or alleviate deprivations of MELs. Some of the ESCR Committee's interpretations of the Covenant take this into account. According to its understanding of core obligations, states that fail to achieve MELs are deemed, *prima facie*, to have violated the Covenant.[763] This presumption of noncompliance arises when "any significant number of individuals is deprived of essential foodstuffs, of essential primary health care, of basic shelter and housing, or of the most basic forms of education".[764] To be sure, article 2 (1) indicates that not all deprivations of MELs constitute breaches of core obligations: it prevents holding states responsible for such deprivations if they lacked the resources to have prevented or alleviated them in the first place. Thus, the core obligation of states to refrain from causing or facilitating total deprivation as well as to prevent its onset is qualified such that these duties are binding only when the actions or omissions that they require are both feasible and appropriate. Moreover, conflating the scope of MELs and the corresponding core obligations with the limited scope of a state's obligation to fulfill runs the risk of undermining the protection of MELs by severely conditioning and restricting their contents. Since the obligation to fulfill is not absolute but rather dependent on the availability of resources by virtue of article 2 (1), restricting the contents of MELs and core obligations to the limited scope of what a state is obliged to fulfill or

---

763 General Comment No. 12: The Right to Adequate Food (1999) para. 17.

764 General Comment No. 3: The Nature of States Parties' Obligations (1990) para. 10 ("[A] minimum core obligation to ensure the satisfaction of, at the very least, minimum essential levels of each of the rights is incumbent upon every State party. Thus, for example, a State party in which any significant number of individuals is deprived of essential foodstuffs, of essential primary health care, of basic shelter and housing, or of the most basic forms of education is, prima facie, failing to discharge its obligations under the Covenant".).

ensure would mean that there is no inviolable core for ESC rights in the first place. [765]

4.2.3.4. Core Obligations Set Priorities for Realizing ESC Rights

When combined with the concept of minimum core obligations, the requirement that states dedicate the maximum of their available resources limits the flexibility that is inherent in the language of progressive realization by imposing upon states an immediate obligation to prioritize certain objectives over others. Thus, the state cannot ignore such deprivations whenever it allocates resources for the realization of ESC rights. It must alleviate or prevent such deprivations as a matter of *priority* and to the maximum extent that the availability of resources will allow.[766] In other words, the realization of ESC rights and the allocation of resources for that purpose must prioritize eradicating the total deprivation ESC rights, even if the minimum essential levels of ESC rights are yet legally definable. The drafting history of the Covenant's general limitations clause (article 4) also supports this assertion. It reveals that the proposal to protect the nature of ESC rights against all limitations was intended to prevent states from de-

765 See Lehmann (2006) 183-185 ("Following the logic of this approach, if a sufficiently wealthy state existed that could afford to meet its citizens [sic] every medically-prescribed health care need, the minimum and the maximum would be one and the same. The reverse, for the impoverished state, would of course be equally true").

766 Chenwi (2013) 753; Scott and Alston (2000) 252 ("Positive rights and the notion of core guarantees *do* have a significant prioritising function") (emphasis in original). Cf., Young (2008) 174 (cautioning that prioritizing an essential minimum core is analogous to distinguishing between the deserving and undeserving poor, which often supports rather than confronts neoliberal institutional structures, which perpetuate rather than combat poverty); Lehmann (2006) 185-193 (asserting the impossibility of locating a ranking of individual interests within a social right, such that the *right itself* requires the denial of one person's claim (beyond the minimum level) in order to grant the claim of another (below the minimum level). Instead, Lehmann argues, the full scope of protection envisioned by a right applies equally to all people, and any subsequent ranking of interests occurs exogenously within the utilitarian realm of justified limitations.).

laying the implementation of ESC rights for motives such as concentrating all their resources on economic development.[767]

Moreover, when combined with the core obligations approach, the state's duty to fulfill MELs takes on a more serious character. Scott and Alston note that the Committee's use of the term *prima facie* in reference to such cases is significant because it indicates that states that are unable to achieve immediately the absolute minimum must prove the infeasibility of guaranteeing absolute minimums by documenting their "societal poverty and patterns of wealth distribution".[768] The duty to fulfill contains an immediate obligation to do all that one can do to ensure the fulfillment of MELs as a matter of priority. In cases where nonprofits are essential for the fulfillment of MELs, the state's core obligations to fulfill MELs would indicate an immediate obligation to permit and support nonprofit provision, or to demonstrate why it was not feasible or appropriate to do so. Essentially, the immediate core obligation concept acts as a qualifier that prioritizes MELs in the protection, respect and fulfillment of social rights, rather than as an unauthorized amendment to the treaty that alters the duties of states such that they no longer correspond to the terms of the Covenant. In response to Mechlem's concerns: a harmonized construction of core obligations would mean that it is only those countries that do not dedicate the maximum of their available resources to achieving minimum essential levels – rather than simply all poorer countries – that fall out of compliance.

An additional matter of concern is whether the *manner* in which a state prioritizes the use of its resources is in line with its Covenant obligations. Since resource scarcity is the primary limitation for the realization of ESC rights, states must – at the very least – make use of their resources in a reasonable manner. The Committee of ESCR has also followed this approach at times. Due to the critical nature of these deprivations, it places the burden of the proof on the state to demonstrate that it was not in fact possible for the state to prevent their occurrence. According to its General Comments, whenever a state asserts that it lacks sufficient available resources to fulfill the minimum core of its obligations, "it must demonstrate that every effort has been made to use all resources that are at its disposition in an

767 Summary Record of the 235th Meeting, Commission on Human Rights, U. N. Economic and Social Council, UN Doc. E/CN.4/SR.235 (UN 1951) (see comments of Mr. Santa Cruz of Chile.).

768 Scott and Alston (2000) 250.

effort to satisfy, as a matter of priority, those minimum obligations."[769] In general, citing resource constraints alone does not conclusively indicate compliance or noncompliance with core obligations. Rather, a state seeking to overcome a presumption of noncompliance must demonstrate that, no matter how well-endowed its country may or may not be, it did in fact dedicate the maximum of its available resources towards alleviating total deprivation of MELs and reaching MELs *as a matter of priority*, despite not having ever reached that aim. Ultimately, the progressive realization of rights cannot be achieved in an unjust manner by, for example, deferring resources toward improving the living conditions of elite social classes, political supporters of ruling parties, or members of privileged ethnic groups.

There is still, however, the issue of reconciling states' discretion in public spending with fulfilling their core obligations. As long as states allocate their resources *with a view to* alleviating total deprivations of MELs and reaching MELs as a matter of priority, then they should enjoy a certain degree of discretion in social policy planning. First, states should be free to decide how to allocate resources between competing MEL goals. Maintaining this intentional element within the core obligations approach recognizes that some rights – such as the right to water – will need enormous investments into infrastructure in order to ensure that they can be enjoyed and to alleviate total deprivations of MELs. Therefore, a policy that directs much of the available resources into alleviating one right such that few or no resources are left for the alleviation of MEL deprivations in other areas will not constitute a breach of state duties because the state is acting with a view to alleviating total deprivation of MELs, despite not having done so evenly.

Understanding core obligations as the duty to allocate resources with a view to prioritizing MEL objectives – rather than ensuring certain minimum benefits levels – allows the state to determine for itself the best method of achieving a prioritized MEL goal. States should take into account the circumstances that are particular to their own contexts, thus benefits levels need not be the same from person to person or from country to country. Rather, the state should always aim to ensure MELs related to adequate housing, freedom from hunger, basic health care and education. This notion is exemplified by the ICESCR Committee's decision – pursuant to the ICESCR Protocol – in the *Rodríguez* case; particularly its treatment of the reduction of non-contributory disability benefits for pris-

769 General Comment No. 3: The Nature of States Parties' Obligations (1990) para. 10 (emphasis added).

oners in Spain.[770] A reduction in non-contributory benefits was deemed proportional to the cost of Mr. Rodríguez's upkeep in prison. The Committee concluded that this was a reasonable state measure because there was a change in the Mr. Rodríguez's needs, which the state – being the entity paying for his upkeep over a long period of time – was in a position to determine with a great deal of specificity and certainty. The state demonstrated that while Mr. Rodríguez was incarcerated, it was able to ensure that he received adequate housing, health care, foodstuffs and an adequate standard of living without the need to issue him non-contributory benefits. If a minimum benefits level was required, rather than the prioritized achievement of certain objectives, the state would have had to continue paying Mr. Rodríguez his disability benefits in addition to covering the costs of his upkeep in prison.

4.2.3.5. Implications for the Legality of Restrictive NGO Laws

In summary, the general core obligations of states are to refrain from allowing or causing the total deprivation of MELs and to take measures with the view of alleviating and preventing the same as a matter of priority, to the extent that such actions and omissions are both appropriate and feasible. These findings have implications for the manner in which states may regulate NGOs, particularly in least developed countries. Because a state with limited resources cannot totally eradicate deprivations of ESC rights throughout its entire country, some nonprofit entities operating within such states will be playing the critical role of alleviating the total deprivation of ESC rights for their beneficiaries. This includes nonprofit entities that provide basic medical assistance, free primary education, food and water to those who are chronically hungry or suffer from malnutrition, cash or in-kind assistance to those who are chronically poor, or housing to those who lack basic shelter. Such nonprofits would be considered essential not only to the achievement of minimum essential levels, but also to the fulfillment and discharge of the state's core obligation to ensure that no one is totally deprived of his or her ESC rights.

NGO laws that restrict the operations of this category of critical NGOs will likely constitute violations of the state's core obligations. This suggests that nonprofits that are essential for the realization and enjoyment of MELs should enjoy special legal protection against state interference, and

---

770 *Rodríguez v. Spain* para. 10.3.

not merely for the protection of their own right to associate or speak freely, but also for the sake of protecting the social rights of their beneficiaries. In practice, this could result is greater judicial scrutiny of NGO laws that tend to reduce access to funding, create complicated registration procedures, or grant public entities wide authority to interfere with or shut down nonprofit activities. For such interferences, it should not be sufficient for a state to offer blanket justifications such as protecting national security interests or maintaining public order in a generic or vague manner.

Providing special protection to these critical NGOs could also impact the patterns of nonprofit provision in a positive way. Ensuring essential nonprofit providers greater protection from state interference would incentivize nonprofit service activities to flourish the areas prioritized by core obligations. On the other hand, due to their involvement in the achievement of prioritized objectives, essential nonprofits would also bear greater responsibilities and thus may justifiably be subject to heavy regulation. The difference, however, would be that lawful government oversight must be directed toward enhancing the protection and realization of social rights, in accordance with core obligations, rather than interfering with the same.

4.3. A New Taxonomy for NGOs: Different Functional Type

Based on the analysis above, six factors can be derived from social law that are relevant for categorizing NGOs in accordance with their propensity to advance realization of social rights, to protect their enjoyment, and to fulfill state obligations. In general, social rights law requires the state to support or at the very least refrain from interfering with all nonprofit activities that are essential to the realization or enjoyment of social rights of beneficiaries. However, not all nonprofit activities that are essential to the realization of social rights will also fulfill the state's social rights obligations, thus the particularities of a state's obligations to nonprofits were vary accordingly. Social rights law, therefore, provides various levels of protection against restrictive regulatory practices and measures, in accordance with the various ways in which NGOs may advance realization, protect enjoyment and fulfill state obligations.

Within countries exhibiting sizable nonprofit sectors, these factors can combine in different ways to yield eight NGO categories or types, each representing a slightly different legal relationship between NGOs and the state. Once categorized, the varying regulatory obligations of the state with regard to nonprofit activities can be explicated, as well as the degree of protection that each type of NGO enjoys from restrictive regulatory measures. Here are the six factors:

(1) whether nonprofit activity is necessary to the realization or enjoyment of social rights, such that their activities are the sole significant cause of enjoyment or realization for an individual or groups of individuals, and alternatives are not readily available to these beneficiaries;
(2) whether nonprofit activity uses appropriate means to bring about realization/enjoyment of social rights, such that their means are both necessary for realization/enjoyments as well as compatible with principles and norms of human rights law;
(3) the level of social rights achievement reached by *nonprofit activity*;
(4) the level of social rights achievement that *the state* is required to ensure;
(5) the level of social rights achievement that the state *in fact* ensures; and
(6) whether the state and nonprofit entity work in concert to bring about realization or enjoyment of social rights.

The following subsection uses these criteria to create a new taxonomy of NGOs based on their propensity to ensure realization / enjoyment of social rights and the fulfillment of state duties.

Figure 4.2. NGO Types when MELs extend beyond Duty Horizon

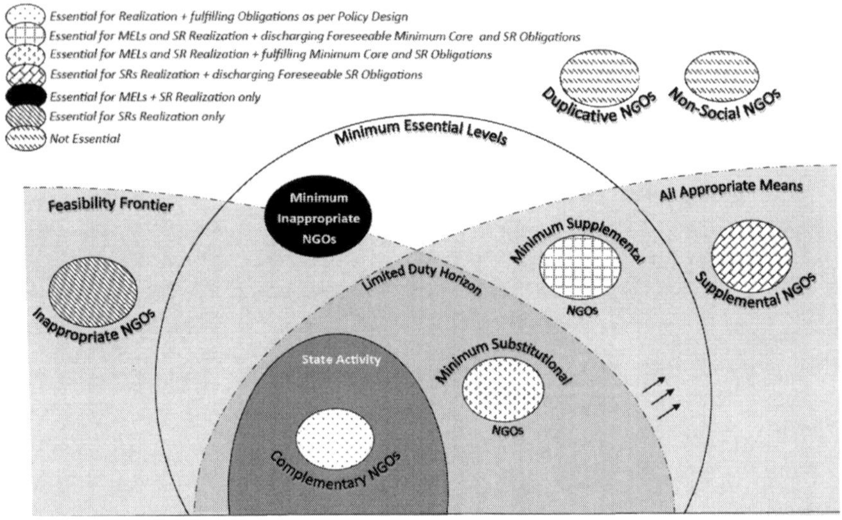

Figure 4.3. NGO Types when Duty Horizon extends beyond MELs

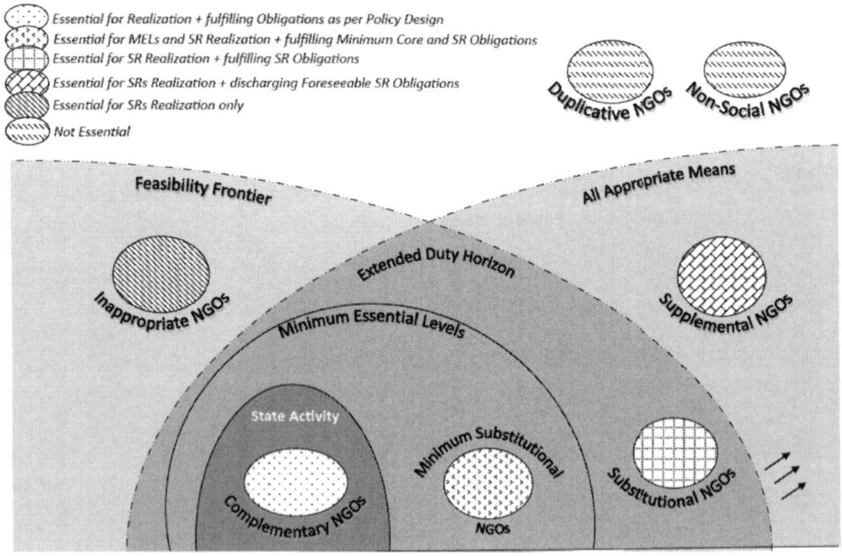

4.3.1. Non-Social NGOs, Duplicative NGOs & Inappropriate NGOs

The first two factors relate to whether nonprofit activities are essential for the realization of social rights. These criteria are legally significant because they trigger the need for an analysis of NGO-state relations from a social rights perspective. Essentiality is a function of both necessity and appropriateness. Nonprofits that are necessary for realization/enjoyment such that alternative means are not reasonably available are considered essential if their activities are also compatible with the principles and norms of human rights law. These factors have been split into separate criteria because some NGOs can feature one but not the other, thereby creating distinct categories of nonprofit activities.

Some NGOs are necessary neither for the realization of social rights nor for their enjoyment. *Non-social NGOs*, such knitting clubs or groups of antique enthusiasts, might advance social rights indirectly by promoting general wellbeing, but they are not necessary to realization and enjoyment because their activities do not pertain to social rights and their impact on social rights is simply too tenuous. The regulation of nonprofit activities that are not necessary for realization or enjoyment of social rights is simply not subject to scrutiny under social rights law, and restrictions on these types of NGOs do not present a social rights problem in the proper sense.

Duplicative NGOs – that is, those whose activities reach a level of achievement that the state already ensures – will not advance realization because the state has already done so. Nevertheless, their activities protect the enjoyment of social rights for beneficiaries that choose to engage them. An example of this may be an NGO that begins to operate a school within a community where all children already have the opportunity to attend public schools of comparable quality. For children who switch to the new school, the duplicative NGO would be protecting the enjoyment of the right to education, even though it neither advanced the right to education nor became necessary for its enjoyment. This suggests that duplicative NGOs are not fulfilling the state's social rights obligations and thus will not enjoy a great degree of protection from restrictive regulatory measures as a matter of law. However, the principle of subsidiarity, as it coincides with the overarching purpose of the ICESCR to promote human freedom, indicates that the state should refrain from interfering with duplicative NGOs unless it is necessary in order to support their work. By broadening the educational offerings that are available to children, our duplicative NGO allows for greater human freedom through the expansion of choice, which ultimately supports personal agency. Thus, the duplicative activity is valuable because it promotes human freedom, even if it is not essential to realization or enjoyment.

The next issue is whether the nonprofit activity advances the realization of social rights through appropriate means. In addition to using the maximum of available resources, article 2 (1) of the Covenant requires states to advance realization through "all appropriate means". The area where the state's maximum available resources (or all feasible means) overlap with all means that are appropriate for the realization and enjoyment of social rights represents all measures that the state is obliged to undertake. The boundary of that overlapping area marks the state's duty horizon, which expands and contracts in accordance with the availability of resources and the appropriateness of means. *Inappropriate NGOs* are those whose activities are necessary for realization or enjoyment, but do not overlap with the area of appropriate means. These activities may or may not occur within the area of maximum available resources; that is, replacing their activities may or may not be feasible for the state to do. By definition, the state is not required to ensure that these activities take place, even though they may be necessary for realization and enjoyment, because they fall beyond the state's duty horizon. Therefore, these activities do not fulfill the state's obligations. This suggests that greater regulatory restrictions may be justified in the case of inappropriate NGOs since their methods likely interfere with the rights of others, interfere with other rights of their own beneficiaries, or otherwise undermine the norms, principles or overarching objectives of the Covenant by limiting human freedom or personal autonomy. This category captures controversial NGOs whose activities advance social rights through unethical, unlawful, or otherwise inappropriate means.

Minimum inappropriate NGOs are perhaps the most controversial category of all because they advance the realization of MELs through means that are inappropriate. Both permitting and restricting their activities are rather contentious measures because of their proximity to beneficiaries whose vulnerabilities are entrenched in existential hazards. An example of such an NGO would be one that provides shelter to homeless persons in accommodations that are unfit for human habitation. This type of nonprofit activity presents a particularly challenging legal problem. On the one hand, their services are necessary to the realization of a prioritized level of social rights achievement and – in some cases – may be critical to sustaining human life and ensuring personal security. On the other hand, however, their inappropriate means may also pose a threat to the health rights of their intended beneficiaries. How far a state can go to restrict these activities will depend on the given facts of each case since the competing interests will need to be balanced in accordance with the circumstances. Restrictions against this category of NGOs are the most difficult to assess. Unfortunately, this group of NGOs is not uncommon in African LDCs, where trade-offs within MELs are a regular occurrence due to an overall lack of resources, widespread underdevelopment, and low state capacity for regulatory control.

4.3.2. Supplemental NGOs & Substitutional NGOs

Nonprofits activities that are essential for the realization or enjoyment of social rights can be distinguished further by the third, fourth and fifth criteria in accordance with their propensity to fulfill the state's social rights obligations. NGOs that fulfill the state's obligations are distinguished from those that preemptively discharge it. The starting point here is to recognize that a state is only required to realize social rights up to the level of achievement that it can feasibly ensure. The activities of *supplemental NGOs* advance the realization of social rights beyond the level of achievement required of the state. In other words, they operate beyond the state's duty horizon. When the state's duty horizon is so limited that parts of the MELs of social rights still lie beyond the horizon, NGOs that realize those MELs beyond the duty horizon are referred to as *minimum supplemental NGOs*. Unlike their duplicative and non-social counterparts, both supplemental types are essential for the realization of social rights, indicating that they come under the protection of article 2(1).

Although they advance realization, supplemental NGOs fall short of fulfilling the state's Covenant obligations because the state is not yet required to achieve the heighted level of realization that has been reached by the supplemental and minimum supplemental NGOs. Instead, these NGOs preemptively discharge what will foreseeably become the state's obligation at a later. Since the state is not yet capable of achieving the higher level of realization, foreseeable obligations have yet to ripen into standing duties. Nonetheless, they are foreseeable due to the legal expectation that states achieve realization with an intention to do so progressively rather than regressively. This underlying intention suggests that even if despite resource availability and technological advancements the state's feasibility frontier stagnates or contracts in the short term, the long-term trend of the state's duty horizon is to expand infinitely toward the ideal of reaching "full realization" in a world where "free human beings enjoy[] freedom from want and fear".[771]

When nonprofit activities fulfill the state's standing obligations, they become the functional equivalent of state activity. *Substitutional NGOs* and *minimum substitutional NGOs* advance realization of rights to a level that falls within the boundaries of the state's duty horizon, but beyond the level that the state itself ensures. In other words, these NGO types operate within the state's fulfillment gap, which is the difference between how far the state must advance realization and how far it in fact advances realization. As such, supplemental types fulfill the state's social rights obligations. In the case of minimum substitutional NGOs, the nonprofit activity and the state's fulfillment gap coincide with MELs of social rights. Since their nonprofit activities achieve MELs that the state is obliged to achieve but nonetheless does not ensure, minimum substitutional NGOs fulfill the *core obligations* of the state. This suggests that social rights law will extend special protections to supplemental NGOs – and even more protection to minimum supplemental NGOs in particular – such that they are not overburdened by regulatory restrictions.

Although I use the terms "fulfill" and "discharge" to describe how NGOs can relieve the state of the need to provide certain social rights, it should be emphasized that the obligation to realize social rights and ensure their continued enjoyment always remains with the state, even if the state explicitly involves NGOs in the provision of services. This distinction is crucial because NGOs do not bear an obligation to continue providing services or to expand their coverage. Moreover, states cannot offload their responsibilities regarding the quality of nonprofit services or the obligation to replace such services if they are terminated. As the ESCR Committee asserted in a comment on the obligation of states toward the social, economic and cultural rights of persons with disabilities, "while it is appropriate for Governments to rely on private, voluntary groups to assist person with disabilities in various ways, such arrangements can never absolve Government from their duty to ensure full compliance with their obligations under the Covenant." [772]

771 ICESCR preamble & art. 2 (1).
772 General Comment No. 5: Persons with Disabilities (1994) para. 12.

4.3.3. Complementary NGOs

The sixth factor delineates between NGOs whose activities have been incorporated into the state's social policy plan, who are referred to here as *complementary NGOs*, and the rest of NGOs who act more or less independently of the state. Since it is not clear whether the state can replace complementary activities of nonprofit actors, their essentiality is indeterminate. This reflects a fundamental difference between complementary NGOs on the one hand, and supplemental and substitutional NGOs on the other. Whereas complementary NGOs work in collaboration with the state to promote realization/enjoyment of social rights, the supplemental and substitutional varieties operate independently of the state. It is their entanglement with state activity that makes it impossible to conclude whether complementary nonprofit activities are categorically essential for the realization/enjoyment of social rights or the fulfillment/discharge of state duties. Perhaps the most that can be said is that complementary NGOs are essential for the realization/enjoyment of social rights, as well as the fulfillment/discharge of state obligations, but only as a result of the state's own policy design. However, this conclusion reveals nothing of the state's dependence upon complementary activities for the fulfillment/discharge of its own social rights obligations.

Their interdependence with the state and the complex myriad of ways in which they may be incorporated into the state's social policy plan makes it difficult to conclude with certainty whether the state depends on complementary NGOs in order to fulfill its obligations, or whether it could fulfill its obligations without them. Thus, rather than taking their essentiality for granted, the state's dependency must be assessed for each collaborative relationship between itself and a complementary NGO before a determination can be made as to whether the NGO is in fact essential. In other words, whether a complementary NGO is essential to the realization/enjoyment of social rights will depend on whether the state is able and willing to ensure its replacement in the event that its activities have been terminated, notwithstanding the fact that these complementary activities may indeed be critical to the realization/enjoyment of social rights and fulfillment/discharge of state duties as per the state's own social policy design.

Despite the indeterminate nature of their essentiality, complementary NGOs still enjoy a degree of protection against severe state interference. The subsidiarity principle indicates that states may not forcibly incorporating or totally dominating complementary NGOs. However, their integration with the state's comprehensive social policy plan also suggests that the state can exercise greater regulatory control over them than it could be able to exercise over NGOs that operate independently of the state.

Figure 4.4. Essentiality Matrix of Nonprofit Activities

	Essential for Realization or Enjoyment of Social Rights	**Essential for Realization or Enjoyment of Minimum Essential Levels**	***Not Essential for Realization or Enjoyment***
Essential for Fulfillment of Standing State Duties	Substitutional Nonprofit Activities	Minimum Substitutional Nonprofit Activities	*Duplicative Nonprofit Activities*
Essential for Preemptive Discharge of Foreseeable State Duties	Supplemental Nonprofit Activities	Minimum Supplemental Nonprofit Activities	*N/A*
Not Essential for Fulfillment or Discharge	*Inappropriate Nonprofit Activities*	*Minimum Inappropriate Nonprofit Activities*	*Non-Social Nonprofit Activities*

Essentiality of complementary nonprofit activities is indeterminate.

This depends on policy design and state's ability to replace lost complementary services.

In summary, the various NGO types have been derived from social rights law on the theory that the explicit obligations of states toward beneficiaries give rise to implicit regulatory obligations *vis-à-vis* nonprofit activities that are essential for realization or enjoyment of social rights, as well as those activities that fulfill or preemptively discharge the social rights obligations of the state. Each NGO type represents a hierarchy of legal regulatory relationships between the NGO and the state. Inappropriate NGOs that advance realization enjoy the least amount of protection and may not be protected at all if their means are so inappropriate that they violate human rights law or its underlying objectives. The subsidiarity principle ensures that duplicative NGOs enjoy a basic level of protection against restrictive NGO laws because their activities promote human freedom and personal autonomy. The next most protected type is supplemental NGOs because they are necessary for the realization of social rights, even if they do not fulfill state duties. The state must enable their activities because they preemptively discharge state obligations under the Covenant. The state must also enable the activities of substitutional NGOs; however, this category enjoys even more protection than its supplementary counterpart. Since this type fulfills the state's obligations, the state bears an additional obligation to ensure the same level of achievement through alternative means.

States must ensure that the activities of substitutional NGOs reach the required level of achievement through state-funded financial support or otherwise. Depending on the circumstances, the state could be required, for example, to replace withdrawn nonprofit activity or support nonprofit services to maintain a certain level of quality. Finally, complementary NGOs will enjoy a varying degree of protection depending on how essential they are for the realization and enjoyment of social rights and the fulfillment and discharge of Covenant duties in each particular case.

In countries with limited duty horizons, where the state is not capable of reaching MELs, the restriction of essential nonprofit activities will pose an even greater threat to the social rights of beneficiaries. While the state must support all nonprofit activities that are essential for realization and enjoyment, an NGO's protection is never absolute. In theory, all social rights can be limited in accordance with the terms of the ICESCR. However, those NGOs whose activities achieve MELs for their beneficiaries are – arguably – protected against the kinds of limitations made permissible under the Covenant. since article 4 (1) does not appear to tolerate limitations to minimum essential levels provided by the state,[773] allowing states to restricting minimum essential levels provided by nonprofit activities, *which the state would otherwise have to provide,* would effectively permit states to circumvent their Covenant obligations. This will be discussed in detail in a later chapter. Minimum supplemental NGOs enjoy a great deal of protection against restrictive regulatory measures because they achieve the minimum essential levels that the state cannot reach. However, minimum substitutional NGOs are the most protected category of all NGOs due to the fact that they are fulfilling core obligations of the state.

4.4. Conclusion

States have an obligation to do nothing less than what they can do to bring about the realization of social rights. Their minimum core obligation is to prioritize the realization of MELs. The protection of social rights is espe-

773 In order to be permissible, limitations to "the enjoyment of those rights provided by the State" must be "compatible with the nature of these [Covenant] rights"; the "nature" of social rights being synonymous with their minimum essential core. (See ICESCR art. 4; Amrei Müller, 'Limitations to and Derogations from Economic, Social and Cultural Rights', 9 Human Rights Quarterly 557 (2009).).

cially urgent in African LDCs where even prioritized objectives, such as alleviating hunger, homelessness and chronic poverty, are not within reach of the state's available resources. In this regard, nonprofit entities can be essential for the realization and protection of social rights because they bring in additional resources which are sorely needed. This raises the question whether restrictive regulation of nonprofit activities is compatible with the social rights obligations of states.

The answer to this question will depend on whether nonprofit activities are essential to the realization and enjoyment of social rights, and the fulfillment or preemptive discharge of states' obligations. NGOs can be categorized in accordingly. The resulting taxonomy renders explicit the link between realization, enjoyment, fulfillment and preemptive discharge on account of nonprofit activity on the one hand, and the permissibility of state measures that restrict nonprofit activities on the other hand. Thus, the new classification indicates that social rights law affords different kinds of NGO varying degrees of protection against restrictive regulatory measures.

Although each of these NGO types is presented separately, many of them can and often do appear simultaneously within the same society. A government may, for example, incorporate NGOs into its service plan in order to realize a portion of the MELs that it is required to ensure, while in the meantime other NGOs independently realize and ensure the enjoyment of the remainder of MELs, and still others might advance realization beyond the boundaries of MELs or the states duty horizon. For the sake of analytical simplicity, however, NGO types are examined independently in order to explicate the specific social rights obligations arising from the legal relations that bind states, NGOs and beneficiaries, as well as in order to discuss the level of protection each NGO type enjoys against restrictive regulatory measures.

5. Regulating NGOs: Limits on and Duties of the State

The present chapter asserts that the state's social rights obligations to beneficiaries give rise to implicit state obligations toward essential NGOs. In particular, the state's social rights obligations qualify the manner in which it may regulate different NGO types. Of the NGO-government relations classified in the previous chapter, only three will be addressed here: supplemental, substitutional and complementary NGOs. These are examined because they are essential both for beneficiaries' social rights and for states' Covenant obligations. Substitutional and supplemental NGOs are essential for the realization/enjoyment of social rights as well as the fulfillment/preemptive discharge of state obligations, while complementary NGOs share these features as a consequence of the state's own social policy design. In these scenarios, the state cannot fulfill its own social rights obligations to beneficiaries unless its treatment of NGOs is subject to certain legal limitations and requirements. In general, states must not obstruct the activities of these NGOs without providing adequate justification for doing so. However, the specificities of a state's regulatory duties toward a particular NGO type are shaped by that type's functional role; that is, whether NGOs in that category fulfill the state's Covenant obligations or preemptively discharge them.

I have excluded duplicative/non-social NGOs from my analysis because they are not reasonably necessary for the realization or enjoyment of social rights. Therefore, other than the general expectation that states – in observance of the subsidiarity principle – should restrain any inclination to control private actors and their affairs, no additional regulatory obligations on the part of the state can be drawn from the interaction of duplicative and non-social NGO's with beneficiaries. Inappropriate NGOs have also been excluded, but on separate grounds. While they are reasonably necessary for the realization or enjoyment of social rights, they do not do so in a way that fulfills or preemptively discharges the state's social rights obligations because they employ inappropriate means. The regulatory obligations of the state toward inappropriate NGOs are mostly limited to protecting the human rights of beneficiaries and others from third-party interference.

5.1. The Analytical Framework: Triangular Models for Social Rights

The legal relations between NGOs, the state and beneficiaries vary in accordance with the degree to which NGOs support realization and enjoyment of social rights, as well as the fulfillment or preemptive discharge of social rights obligations. The different NGO types reflect these variations. The way that these legal relations interact with one another can be examined more precisely by modeling them in a triangular formation. In particular, a triangular arrangement illustrates how one legal relationship within the model (i.e., the state-to-beneficiary relation) can affect another legal relationship within the same model (i.e., the NGO-to-state relation). The concept of triangular relations in the realization of social rights is borrowed from German social law, wherein the *sozialrechtliche Dreiecksverhältnis* model, translated by Ulrich Becker as "the social benefits delivery triangle" (Figure 5.1),[774] is used to understand the legal relationships involved when social benefits are delivered by private entities acting in collaboration with the state, as well as for examining the manner in which those legal relations influence one another.

Figure 5.1. Social Benefits Delivery Triangle.[775]

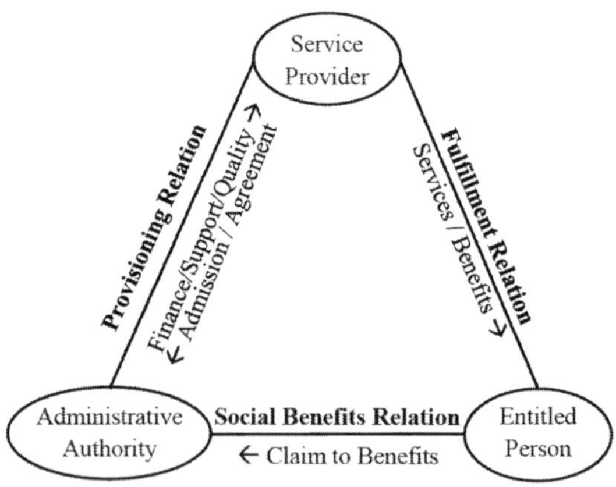

774 Ulrich Becker, 'Social Services of General Interest in Germany' in *Social Services of General Interest in the EU* (Springer 2013) 497-511.

775 Based largely on a diagram borrowed from Ulrich Becker. See ibid 503, fig. 19.1.

While legal relations within the triangular model have received considerable attention in German scholarship and jurisprudence,[776] the model is virtually non-existent in Anglo-American legal literature.[777] The World Bank has used a similar triangular model to illustrate service arrangements involving private providers, but it represents relationships of accountability and power rather than the legal relations that bind the parties.[778] The World Bank model appears to be based on the work done by Reinikka and Smith, which focuses on strengthening relationships of accountability through delegation, financing, monitoring performance and enforcing standards.[779] Edward Mac Abbey has modified this model by inserting NGOs as supportive actors into all three sectors of society.[780] Advocacy NGOs support the state's role in policy making and agenda setting; grassroots NGOs help beneficiaries and their communities – particularly poor communities – to strengthen their social capital, organize and become more civically engaged; and service NGOs provide services directly or indirectly.[781] In each of these models, the focus is on power and accountability, thus they emerge from organizational and political – rather than legal – perspectives. Since, however, the political and organizational aspects of the service delivery triangle are relevant for ascertaining the legal relations therein; this section will also draw upon those other disciplines.

The *sozialrechtliche Dreiecksverhältnis* model is based on a relationship between non-state entities and government that resembles the complementary arrangement described in the previous chapter, wherein government collaborates with private providers in order to promote the realization and enjoyment of social rights. Thus, most of Becker's translated version of the *sozialrechtliche Dreiecksverhältnis* (Figure 5.1) has been borrowed in this chapter's representation of the complementary arrangement between NGOs and the state. However, certain modifications have been made to Becker's version in order to tailor it to the particular way in which the complementary arrangement has been conceptualized here.

---

776 Becker and others (2011); Andreas Kurt Pattar, 'Sozialhilferechtliches Dreiecksverhältnis - Rechtsbeziehungen Zwischen Hilfebedürftigen, Sozialhilfeträgern Und Einrichtungsträgern', 3 Sozialrecht Aktuell 85 (2012); B 8 So 22/07 R, 102 1, (BSG 2008) (Germany).

777 For one explanation in English of the *sozialrechtliche Dreiecksverhältnis*, see Becker (2013).

778 The World Bank, *Making Services Work for Poor People* (2004) 46-80.

779 Reinikka and Smith (2004).

780 Abbey (2008).

781 Ibid 373.

In Becker's model, beneficiaries are entitled to certain rights that the state must ensure, which are referred to as the *social benefits relation*, and that legal relation between beneficiaries and the state in turn affects the legal relation between the state and private providers. In the typical case, an administrative body formally and willingly accepts private providers into a legal relationship referred to as the *provisioning relation*, whereby the administrative authority regulates and supports the private provision of services to beneficiaries. An example of this is found in Germany, where the government finances the provision of qualified services through a system of controlled compensation that relies on price regulations and service standards.[782] Complementary arrangements are advantageous for the state because governments typically lack the institutional capacity and expertise that is required in order to provide all benefits directly through public programs. Thus, it is considered more efficient for the state to collaborate with private providers in the delivery of services rather than to build up new public institutions and acquire new technical expertise.[783] Lastly, the relationship between providers and beneficiaries is based predominantly on a professional or service-based interaction, through which beneficiaries receive social services. In the complementary model, however, this relationship can also have a legal effect on the state's obligation toward the beneficiary. The obligation of the state toward the entitled person is fulfilled once the private provider delivers the service to the entitled person through the *fulfillment relation*.

The *sozialrechtliche Dreiecksverhältnis* is, however, ill-equipped to represent the legal relations that are involved in substitutional and supplemental arrangements because the *sozialrechtliche Dreiecksverhältnis* represents the complementary arrangement and it cannot be determined categorically whether complementary NGOs fulfill or discharge state duties. This difference affects the state's legal relation with NGOs, thus necessitating different representational models. Moreover, since supplemental and substitutional NGO types are more prevalent in African LDCs, the complementary triangular model is not likely to be a useful analytical tool for de-

782 Anheier and Seibel (2001) 98-109, 114-117; see also ibid 97 (noting that for a handful of large nonprofit entities called free welfare associations, "their role became deeply imprinted in the relevant social welfare legislation", such that public bodies must support their activities in the field of social assistance.).

783 Becker and others (2011) 341-342. This is also consistent with the principle of subsidiarity, which has a long history in German social provision and has been described as "the economic backbone of the German nonprofit sector." (Anheier and Seibel (2001) 72, 96-98.).

termining the NGO-to-state legal relations within African LDCs. A triangular model should accurately represent the legal relations among the parties pursuant to the ICESCR so that it is possible to conduct a systematic analysis of how states should regulate nonprofit activities, especially when those activities contribute to the fulfillment or preemptive discharge of state obligations. Therefore, new triangular models are needed to accurately represent the particularities of the other two types (Figure 5.2). In this chapter, I adopt a modified version of Becker's model as a fair representation of the complementary type, but I offer two new models for the supplementary and substitutional varieties.

Figure 5.2. Tailored Triangular Models for each NGO Type

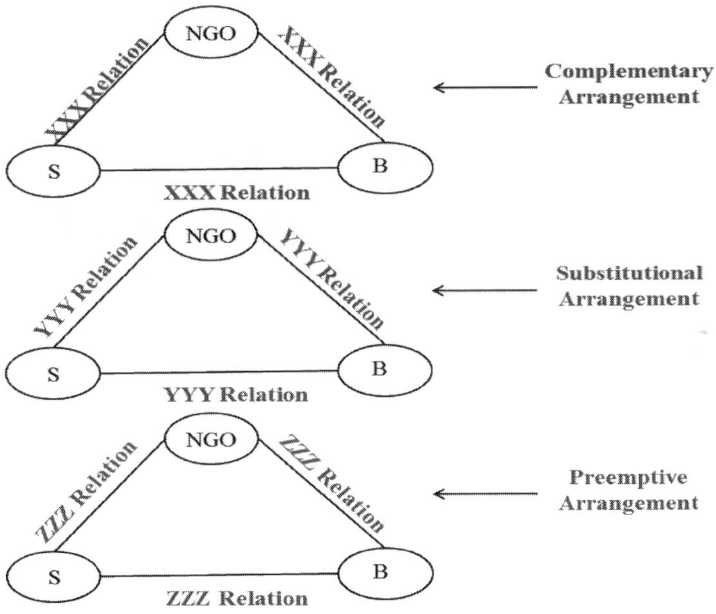

5.2. The Three Legal Relations: State-NGO-Beneficiary

All triangular models that represent the fulfillment or preemptive discharge of state duties through nonprofit activities share three basic components, which are the relationships that link the three parties. These relational components have legal attributes that are derived from the social rights law that binds the state. The most basic relational component is the

NGO-to-state relation. It concerns the functional role of nonprofit activities *vis-à-vis* the state's social rights obligations. Since NGOs varying in their functional role, the legal aspects of their relation to states will also vary. The differences explicated by the NGO taxonomy proposed in the previous chapter are important because they indicate that different regulatory obligations will correspond to different NGO types.

The legal relations in the triangular model are defined by the legal norm that binds the state. The ICESCR has been chosen as the legal framework for analysis because it serves as an international baseline for almost all countries of the world, including the vast majority of African states. Thus, in order to avoid misunderstandings, the terminology used to represent each party within the triangular model should reflect the terminology used in international human rights law. Using the labels found in Becker's translation of the *sozialrechtliche Dreiecksverhältnis* model might suggest that the law chosen – international human rights law – guarantees social rights claims that are more concrete than a reasonable reading of the law would allow. Thus, the labels used for the triangular models presented here are modified in order to avoid such misrepresentations in the context of international law.

The *sozialrechtliche Dreiecksverhältnis* model is based on the presumption that social rights claims are concretized into social benefits entitlements. In states where governments are bound to guarantee social rights that have been concretized into specific entitlements, it is appropriate to think of beneficiaries as entitled persons. Specifically, individuals can claim concrete "benefits" from the state (*social benefits relation*). In turn, this legal basis imposes an obligation upon the state to ensure the delivery of those concrete benefits, which it accomplishes by establishing certain "administrative" duties to collaborate with private providers. This results in a relationship (*provisioning relation*) through which the administrative authority (as financier and guarantor of entitled benefits and services) and the private entity (as supplier of benefits or performer of services) work together, normally under formal agreement or administrative admission, to ensure that the entitled person receives his or her benefits or services. Finally, the state's obligation is "fulfilled" once the private provider deliveries those concrete benefits to the "entitled" person (*fulfillment relation*). Each of these terms derives from a normative framework that imposes enforceable legal duties upon an administrative authority in order to guarantee concrete benefits and services to legally entitled persons. However, such arrangements are not typically found in African LDCs.

Domestic law in African LDCs often treats social rights norms as policy directives rather than as individual entitlements that correspond to enforceable state obligations.[784] As a practical matter, establishing collaborative provisioning relations are extremely costly. Although the complementary model is meant to be more economically efficient because the government need not establish its own institutions for the delivery of services,[785] it demands nonetheless a high financial commitment from the state to fund the provision of services. One does not find in Africa an abundance of domestic laws establishing concrete and justiciable social rights that amount to specific individual entitlements, coupled with enforceable corresponding duties borne by administrative agencies. Such a normative arrangement would impose unrealistic demands upon poorer states that face a scarcity of resources. Comprehensive social security schemes based on enormous financial commitments are politically unattainable in African LDCs because they would lock governments into legal obligations that they could not fulfill.

In these cases, the legal relationship between the state and the beneficiary needs another normative framework to ground the triangular relations. International or regional human rights law serves this purpose. While it remains doubtful whether human rights law clearly entitles individuals to specific benefits or services,[786] the ICESCR and the African Charter do create concrete state obligations as to the realization and enjoyment of social rights. Therefore, while the *sozialrechtliche Dreiecksverhältnis* refers to an *entitled person*, the adjusted models based on international human rights law will refer to *rights bearers* to reflect this difference (Figure 5.3).

---

784 Ssenyonjo, 'Influence of the ICESCR in Africa' 107-108.

785 Becker and others (2011) 341-342.

786 Although the ESCR Committee has recognized minimum essential cores for social and economic rights, commentators challenge the conceptual workability and legal enforceability of a minimum core. See, e.g., Young (2008).

Figure 5.3. Complementary Triangular Model.

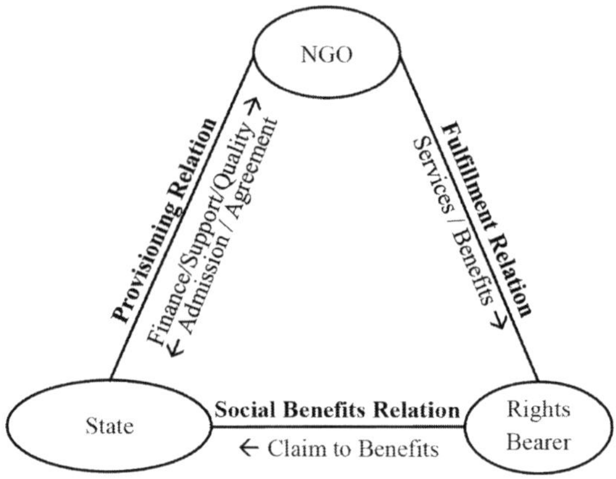

The term used for the state/governmental party within the triangular model is also modified to account for the use of international human rights law. First, for the most part, human rights law addresses *states* general rather than particular *administrative bodies* within the government. This modification takes into account the manner in which NGOs relate to all state bodies, not just the administrative arm of the state, and reflects the notion that non-administrative bodies, such as courts and legislative bodies, are also bound to protect, respect and – to the maximum extent of feasibility and appropriateness – fulfill social rights. Therefore, the state's legislation of restrictive NGO laws is as much a concern to the social rights of beneficiaries as is its administration and adjudication of such laws. To reflect these aspects, the term *state* will replace *administrative bodies*, thereby emphasizing that the social rights obligations derived from international law bind all governmental and state bodies.

Finally, the term *NGO* is used in lieu of *service provider* so as to reflect the prevalence and diversity of the non-profit sector – as appose to the private for-profit sector – in the realization of social rights for people in African LDCs. This modification allows for an analysis of NGO laws that restrict essential nonprofit activities through advocacy. For instance, NGOs may be essential for the fulfillment or preemptive discharge of state duties without providing services because they prod the government into expanding social rights protections for political minorities or other vulnerable groups by providing information about coverage gaps or social rights injuries caused by third parties.

The following sub-sections examine the ways in which states' social rights obligations – pursuant to international human rights law – determine the nature of the three legal relations that emerge when substitutional or supplementary NGOs are involved in the realization/enjoyment of social rights. The analysis looks at each of the three legal relations in turn and investigates how they affect one another under each scenario.

Figure 5.4. Triangular Models for Complementary, Substitutional and Supplementary NGOs

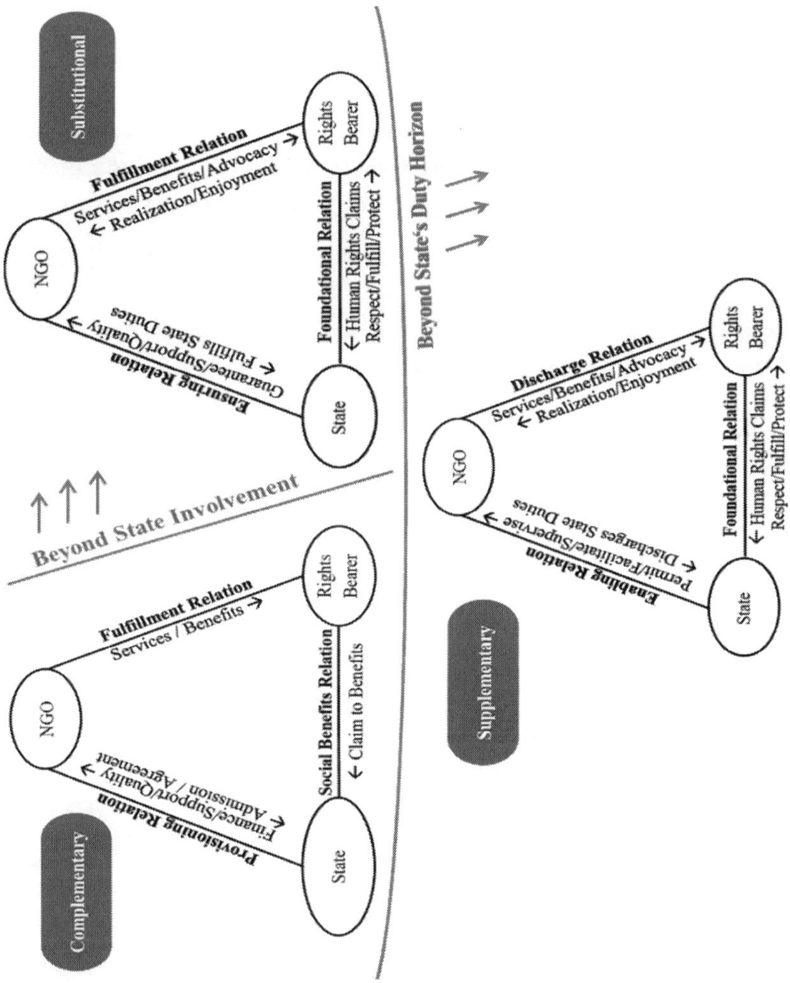

5.2.1. The Beneficiary-to-State Relation

The first relationship stretches between the state and the beneficiary. In the *sozialrechtliche Dreiecksverhältnis* it is often referred to as the *Leistungsverhältnis* (the *social benefits relation*). There, the state is generally bound by constitutional and international law to guarantee the social rights of its people.[787] Domestic laws spell out in specific and concrete terms the legal entitlements of individuals, thereby establishing their legal claims against certain administrative bodies.[788] This gives rise to the *social benefits relation* where entitled person can have a *claim to benefits* against the state.

In contrast, many people in Africa cannot lay claim to concrete social benefits and services against the state.[789] Their social rights are guaranteed at the more general level of international human rights law, and sometimes constitutional law. International law guarantees the total fulfillment of their social rights through progressive realization. Consequently, beneficiaries are *rights bearers* who have *human rights claims* against the state, rather than *entitled persons* who hold concrete *claims to benefits*. Therefore, the term *social benefits relation* should be modified so as not to suggest that international human rights law recognizes certain specific entitlements of beneficiaries.

Instead, the modified label should emphasize a chief legal function of the *social benefits relation*, which is applicable to all triangular models. German commentators note that the *social benefits relation* influences the legal relationship between the state and the provider.[790] In a sense, the state-beneficiary relationship functions as a *foundational* component of the state-provider relationship because the former augments the latter. [791] In order to emphasize this aspect of the state-beneficiary relation, the modified triangular models will use the term *foundational relation* to describe the legal relation between the beneficiary and the state. This modification applies equally to the complementary model because the complementary model also relies upon international human rights law as its foundation rather than a law that concretizes social rights into specific entitlements.

---

787 Becker and others (2011) 333.

788 Ibid.

789 See *supra*, part 0on the general problems of enforcement and justiciability regarding social rights.

790 Becker and others (2011) 333.

791 See Pattar (2012) 88.

The beneficiary's social rights correspond to certain state duties. Under international human rights law, these social rights obligations of the state include the duties to respect, protect and fulfill social rights.[792] Thus, the foundational relation in the supplementary and substitutional models exchanges *human rights claims*, which emanate from the rights bearer, with states' duties to *respect/fulfill/protect* the human rights of beneficiaries. In bilateral relations, these duties would normally be fulfilled through the state's interaction with the beneficiary. If, however, the state accepts or acquiesces to the involvement of nonprofit organizations,[793] then the state fulfills its duties to the beneficiary through its interactions with the nonprofit entity, as well as through the interactions between nonprofits and beneficiaries. Therefore, in a triangular arrangement, the foundational relation gives rise to state obligations toward the beneficiary (direct obligations) as well as obligations toward essential nonprofits (indirect obligations). The next sub-sections consider how the social rights contained within the foundational relation correspond to state duties that are performed through the NGO-to-state relation and the NGO-to-beneficiary relation.

5.2.2. The State-to-NGO Relation

In Becker's version of the *sozialrechtliche Dreiecksverhältnis*, the *social benefits relation* sets the aim and the parameters for the relationship between the administrative authority and the private provider. Becker refers to this second relationship as the *provisioning relation*.[794] The relationship between the state and the provider is initiated by some form of admission, by which the provider enters into a cooperative arrangement with the state.[795] This arrangement exhibits a greater deal of freedom and complexity than is afforded through a contractual purchase order for services. Becker notes, "Usually, the competent administrative body does not purchase the service from a private actor in a stricter sense, but it will merely create a legal basis for service provision..."[796] This "legal basis" represents the regulatory

792 See *supra*, part 0on the general social rights obligations of states.

793 As will be explained in a later sub-section, the state's acceptance or acquiesce is a basic precondition for the state's consent to be bound the legal consequences arising from triangular relations. See *infra*, part 0on the state's admission or acceptance of nonprofits as service providers.

794 Becker (2013) 504.

795 Ibid 505.

796 Ibid 504.

framework upon which the provision of services takes place while leaving a great deal of discretion in the hands of private providers. The term *provisioning relation* is useful in capturing the complex cooperative arrangements involving complementary NGOs, whereby the state regulates the quality, prices and provisioning of services, and the private entity delivers those services in exchange for public financing. However, the term should be adjusted to account for organizational frameworks that involve supplemental or substitutional NGO types, whereby NGOs and governments are not engaged in an intricate relationship of financing, price-setting and quality control.

5.2.2.1. From Provisioning Relation to Enabling / Ensuring Relations

As discussed above, the *foundational* relation between beneficiaries and the state augments the relationship between the state and NGOs. It imposes an additional obligation upon the state to support, or at the very least refrain from interfering with, the efforts of NGOs to bring about the realization or enjoyment of social rights. In other words, the state's duty to the beneficiary is what gives rise to the state's obligation to support, or at the very least permit, essential nonprofit activities. The terms of a state's obligations toward NGOs will depend on whether and how NGOs assist states in fulfilling Covenant obligations.

As discussed in the previous chapter, substitutional NGOs fulfill the state's obligations because their activities take place within an area of the duty horizon that the state does not reach.[797] In this case, substitutional NGOs are ensuring realization and enjoyment of rights that the state is under an obligation to ensure but nonetheless fails to ensure. Therefore, I have termed NGO-state relations involving substitutional NGOs the "*ensuring relation*" since the state must ensure the very same level of realization and enjoyment that the NGO is providing. In the *ensuring relation*, states are obliged to ensure the continuation and improvement of substitutional NGO activities, as well as their replacement if such activities are terminated. States bear an obligation to both support and guarantee the effects of substitutional nonprofit activities on the realization and enjoyment of social rights. The implication is that states presumably violate their duties to respect and fulfill social rights when they implement NGO laws that restrict or obstruct substitutional nonprofit activities.

797 See *supra* part 0on purposing a new taxonomy for NGOs based on new criteria.

Unlike substitutional NGOs, supplementary NGOs do not fulfill the state's obligations because supplementary nonprofit activities are conducted beyond the state's duty horizon. These are nonprofit activities that are essential for a level of realization/enjoyment that is not attainable for the state due to resource constraint; that is, beyond its duty horizon. However, since it is foreseeable that this higher level of achievement will eventually fall within the state's duty horizon, supplementary NGOs are preemptively discharging the state's foreseeable obligations before they ripen into standing duties. As such, the state's obligation toward supplemental NGOs is simply to enable them, which entails permitting and facilitating nonprofit activities, rather than to support and guarantee them as is the case with substitutional activities. While both enabling and ensuring consist of a negative obligation to abstain from obstructing nonprofit activities (i.e., to permit) as well as a positive obligation to take all appropriate and feasible measures that make it easier for NGOs to conduct their activities (i.e., to facilitate), the latter also includes an additional obligation to replace lost nonprofit activities (i.e., to guarantee) and to fill achievement gaps left behind by inadequate nonprofit activities or to extend their activities so as to guarantee a certain level of realization/enjoyment (i.e., to support). I use the term "*enabling relation*" to signify the NGO-state relationship involving supplementary NGOs so as to emphasize the obligation of states to permit and facilitate supplementary nonprofit activities and to exclude any state duties to guarantee or actively support the same.

There is evidence to suggest that some African jurists have already begun espousing this view. In *Michelo Hunsungule and Others (on Behalf of Children in Northern Uganda) v. Uganda*, the African Children's Committee considered whether the government of Uganda had violated the rights of children to the highest attainable health, as guaranteed by article 14 of the African Charter on the Rights and Welfare of Children. [798] In doing so, the African Children's Committee listed the types of governmental activities that would likely indicate a state had failed to fulfill its duties. Among those activities was, "…curtail[ing] the efforts of non-governmental organizations or other partners to contribute toward the realization of Article 14", suggesting that undermining access to NGO health services would violate the right to health.[799] By restricting the operational space of nonprofits, those same states could jeopardize existing social protection and facilitate interference with the social rights of beneficiaries. A teleological ap-

798 *Hunsungule v. Uganda.*
799 Ibid para. 75.

proach committed to the fulfillment of state duties and the protection of social rights would indicate that NGO laws may not be so restrictive that the state no longer fulfills its legal obligations toward beneficiaries. Therefore, states must permit NGOs to operate when they are essential for the realization/enjoyment of social rights (supplemental and substitutional NGOs) and enable NGOs that are essential for the fulfillment of the state's social rights obligations (substitutional NGOs). On the presumption that they breach the social rights obligations of states, measures that make it difficult for these types of NGOs to operate should be subject to heightened judicial scrutiny: their interference with nonprofit activities must be proportional to and necessary for fulfilling a legitimate state interest.

The adjustment from provisioning in the complementary model to enabling and ensuring in the supplemental and substitutional models warrants a rigorous examination of the various components that constitute the provisioning relation within the complementary model. At the general level of principles, the concept of enabling and ensuring relations remains consistent with the principle of subsidiarity by retaining components that are important for the effective realization/enjoyment of social rights. Like the provisioning relation, relations of enabling and ensuring emphasize the devolution of decision-making power away from the hands of bureaucrats and into the judgment of reasonably independent professionals,[800] which some have argued is necessary for the effective delivery of complex services that require the provision of individualized solutions for complex human problems.[801] On closer examination, however, the three concepts vary with regard to three main structural elements that define the state-to-NGO relation. In the complementary model, these three components are *admission*, *financing* and *quality assurance*. In the supplemental and substitutional models, these components are modified in order to reflect the differences between the provisioning relation and either the enabling or the ensuring relations, respectively.

5.2.2.2. From Admission to Fulfillment / Discharge of State Duties

The state's acceptance of nonprofit activities as the means of fulfilling its own social rights obligations is the cornerstone of any triangular legal relationship that fulfills social rights. Without the state's acceptance, it cannot

800 Anheier and Seibel (2001) 72.
801 Pritchett and Woolcock (2004) 195-196.

be legally bound within a triangular relation and thus it cannot acquire additional regulatory duties and limits *vis-à-vis NGOs*. For example, in the *sozialrechtliche Dreiecksverhältnis*, governments formally engage providers through agreements that define the terms of the government's support for private provisioning and the requirements for proper provisioning.[802] In the triangular model of accountability offered by Reinikka and Smith, this aspect is represented by the "compact" and can only be initiated through an act of *delegation* whereby policymakers set policy outlines and authorize private providers to carry them out.[803] The common thread is that the state has invited or endorsed the provision of services by nonprofit entities as part of its social policy program. The admission or delegation establishes a legal relationship between the state and the private provider because it represents the state's intentional commitment to fulfilling its social rights obligations through the services provided by private entities.

While this is essentially the case for complementary arrangements, it cannot be the bases of triangular legal relations involving supplementary and substitutional NGOs because governments have not given explicit consent to accept the NGOs. Nonetheless, some level of acceptance is still required in order to overcome state sovereignty and legally bind the state within such a triangular arrangement. Most African states do not have comprehensive social policy frameworks that are based on integrating NGO entities as the primary service providers within their country. Rather, NGOs operate in an *ad hoc* and voluntary manner and provide services in their capacity as informal charitable institutions. African laws that regulate NGOs, societies, charities and other such associations often create national administrative bodies that exert supervisory control. However, these laws are not part of a larger social policy framework that aims to promote social rights. Rather, in many cases, these laws represent the government's response to real or perceived political threats of an increasingly influential sector of civil society that has deep foreign connections and commitments. The act of admission signals the beginning of a collaborative and supportive provisioning relationship between the private provider and the public authority. However, without such an agreement to collaborate, there is no expressed intent from either the State or the NGO to enter into a provisioning relationship.[804]

802 Becker (2013) 505.

803 Reinikka and Smith (2004) 24-25, 29.

804 That is not to say, however, that no relationship of a legal nature exists between nonprofit providers and the state. Indeed, the state is obliged, at the very least,

The state's acceptance needs not occur by formal or explicit means. For implicit acceptance to be valid, however, it is critical that the state expresses its consent to bear additional regulatory requirements *vis-à-vis* nonprofits. This allows us to ascribe to the state acceptance of nonprofits even if its government outwardly opposes them. In supplementary and substitutional arrangements, the state's consent to the be bound by international social rights law, namely the ICESCR, serves this purpose whenever the NGO is essential for the fulfillment/preemptive discharge of the state's social rights obligations or the realization/enjoyment of beneficiaries' social rights. Thus, the state's acceptance of NGOs must be derived from its consent to bear the obligations imposed upon it by the ICESCR, thereby setting the foundation for its legal relation to essential NGOs.

A state can implicitly accept nonprofit activities simply by failing to ensure that rights are realized or enjoyed through alternative means when the state is under an obligation to ensure the same level of realization or enjoyment. Choosing not to fulfill social rights through direct state provision is not a violation of the Covenant; indeed, the Covenant explicitly recognizes the role that private actors can play in this regard. The *travaux préparatoires* of the ICESCR support this assertion, particularly in relation to article 9's guarantee of the right to social security. The drafting members rejected an amendment proposed by the representative of the USSR, which would have required that "the cost of [social security] be borne by the State or the employer or both of them."[805] They were concerned that this proposed amendment ignored the diversity of systems in different countries for financing social security; they noted that each state should be able to use the system that is best for its own circumstances, including systems that make use of private provision.[806]

There is, in effect, no obligation or expectation that states provide social security through direct state action or direct state financing. Nonetheless, states are expected to *ensure* that the social rights are respected, protected and fulfilled in accordance with the terms of the ICESCR. Thus, declining to provide services directly through public institutions is tantamount to implicitly accepting private activities whenever those activities realize so-

---

to respect the rights of the NGOs. As such, there are limitations in place regarding the extent to which the state can restrict the rights of NGOs to associate and speak freely.

805 Draft International Covenants on Human Rights: Report of the Third Committee (1957) paras. 78, 81, 84 (b).

806 Ibid.

cial rights to a level of achievement that the state is required to ensure. In this way, the state passively (and sometimes even grudgingly) embraces substitutional NGOs as actors within a triangular legal relationship because these NGOs fulfill the state's obligations under article 2 (1) of the Covenant. Thus, the state implicitly consents to being burdened with additional regulatory obligations *vis-à-vis* substitutional NGOs. The state cannot rely on these NGOs for fulfilling its social rights obligations and at the same time regulate them in a way that would obstruct the continued fulfillment of its social rights obligations. Without having explicitly or formally accepting substitutional NGOs, the state nonetheless becomes legally bound to these NGOs within a triangular relationship that fulfills the social rights of beneficiaries as well as the state's social rights obligations to those beneficiaries.

In the case of supplemental arrangements, grounding the legal relation between the state and NGOs is a bit more complicated. Unlike their substitutional counterparts, supplemental NGOs do not fulfill a state's standing obligations under article 2 (1). Rather, they discharge that which will foreseeably fall within the scope of the state's article 2 (1) obligations once the state's duty horizon expands to reflect an increase in the availability of resources. What is important to note is that the state has not yet acquired the obligation under article 2 (1) to reach the level of realization achieved by supplemental NGOs, and that it is only foreseeable rather than guaranteed that the state will in fact acquire the necessary resources in order to expand its duty horizon accordingly. Therefore, it cannot be said that these future obligations – which are unripe and unguaranteed to ripen into standing duties – are capable of giving rise today to additional regulatory obligations toward supplementary NGOs. In order for the state to bear heightened regulatory obligations *vis-à-vis* supplementary NGOs, its consent to be so burdened must have derived from some provision of the Covenant other than article 2 (1).

In this regard, article 5 (1) of the ICESCR provides the necessary basis for binding the state to supplementary NGOs within a triangular arrangement. In particular, article 5 (1) prohibits any interpretation of the ICESCR that would recognize for states a right to engage in any act that aims at the destruction of ESC rights or at their limitation to a greater extent than that which is permitted by the Covenant. In other words, state parties to the ICESCR have consented to waiving any rights that they may have had to destroy or extensively limit ESC rights that they were under no obligation to ensure. This directly contradicts any state claim that, by virtue of its sovereignty, it can lawfully obstruct NGOs even if doing so would very likely result in the destruction of or extensive limitation to the ESC rights enjoyed by beneficiaries of supplemental NGOs. Rather, states aiming to destroy or extensively limit ESC rights will need to justify or excuse such measures in a manner that is consistent with the terms, object and purpose of the Covenant. This translates into an obligation to refrain from interfering with the existing enjoyment of ESC rights unless there is a justifiable reason to do so. How states may lawfully justify such limitations is discussed in depth in the chapter that follows the present one.

The states' agreement to be bound in this way under the ICESCR could serve as the foundation for its legal entanglement with supplemental NGOs within a triangular arrangement. Supplemental NGOs are essential for the realization and enjoyment of ESC rights because the state is *unable* to ensure them. Therefore, restrictive regulatory measures that obstruct the NGO's ability to continue ensuring the realization and enjoyment of these ESC rights will amount to their destruction, which is incompatible with the state's legal commitments under article 5 (1). However, one issue remains unresolved. That is the question of whether such restrictive regulatory measures amount to an "act *aimed* at" the destruction of ESC rights, as article 5 (1) requires. This is a question of the state's purpose or intent, to the extent that it can in fact formulate intent through its lawmakers and officials. The issue here is whether restrictive NGO laws aim at destroying ESC rights, such that article 5 (1) is triggered and can serve as the foundational basis for bind states to supplemental NGOs in a triangular arrangement.

At the very least, the ordinary meaning of the phrase "aiming at" is the same as acting with the knowledge that a particular (perhaps undesired) outcome, such as the destruction of ESC rights, is likely to occur. It is not necessary that the actor desires the outcome to occur if she already knows that it is likely to occur – perhaps alongside another desired outcome – as a result of her conduct. Indeed, the actor might even sincerely hope that the undesired outcome does not occur, but nonetheless disregards the risk or certainty with which it is likely to occur in order to bring about another desired outcome. This level of intent corresponds to the *mens rea* of recklessness or knowing.

Taking it a step further, one can also aim at an undesirable outcome – the destruction of ESC rights – without knowingly doing so. In this case, the level of intent required in order to hold the actor liable would be negligence. When performing an act, all *foreseeable* outcomes that are set in motion as a result of that act fall within the range of one's aim, including unlawful outcomes such as destroying ESC rights. What matters is not whether the actor was in fact aware that an undesirable outcome stood in the path of her aim, but rather that she *should have known* it because it was a reasonably foreseeable result of her conduct. Therefore, it is only those outcomes that did not stand in the path of the actor's aim (i.e., unforeseeable results) for which she is not liable, and which are exempt from scrutiny under article 5 (1). In terms of restrictive NGO laws, this means that by virtue of consenting to article 5 (1), states have waived their right to restrain supplemental NGOs if they knew that that doing so would very likely result in the destruction of or extensive limitation to ESC rights, or if it was reasonably foreseeable that such undesirable outcomes would occur.

The notion that states cannot take measures that they *should have known* were likely to result in the destruction of or extensive limitation to ESC rights also finds support in the interpretive of work of the ESCR Committee. In one of its comments, the Committee goes so far as to assert, without making any reference at all to a mandatory level of intent, that states are noncompliant simply if their policy or legislative measures lead to "a general decline in living and housing conditions", unless they provide compensatory measures.[807] Elsewhere in its interpretive work on article 2 (1), the Committee has concluded that state measures are impermissible if there was reason for the state to known that the measures would likely have a retrogressive effect on the realization and enjoyment of social right. The Committee's work in this particular area is related to its doctrine of retrogressive measures, wherein retrogressive measures presumptively contravene the terms of the Covenant if they are implemented *deliberately*. What is interesting is that although the word 'deliberate' is weightier in terms of its intentionality than article 5 (1)'s reference to 'aiming at' destroying or extensively limiting ESC rights, the Committee nonetheless appears to understand 'deliberate' to include negligent conduct. In *Ben Djazia and Bellili v. Spain*, a decision issued by the ESCR Committee pursuant to the terms of the Optional Protocol of the ICESCR, selling public housing units to investment companies was considered a deliberately retrogressive measure although the state's purpose was not to limit the enjoyment of adequate housing.[808]

The local housing authority of Madrid sold the units because it sought to balance its budget, not because it hoped to reduce the availability of public housing. The measure was nonetheless dubbed deliberately retrogressive because the state knew or should have known that selling off pub-

807 General Comment No. 4: The Right to Adequate Housing (1991) para. 11.
808 *Ben Djazia and Bellili v. Spain* paras. 17.5-17.6.

lic housing units would very likely cause retrogression in the realization of the right to housing since "the number of public housing units available annually in Madrid was significantly fewer than the demand".[809] Naturally, the mere act of selling off public housing units is not itself an impermissible measure. However, coupled with the fact that public housing was already in short supply in Madrid, it became reasonably foreseeable that selling off public housing would result in a limitation on the right to adequate housing. Thus, the housing authority knew or *should have known* that this measure would cause a setback in the realization of adequate housing for all.

The attribution of knowledge to the state for the injurious effects of its laws is particularly significant in the context of restrictive NGO laws because NGO laws do not typically mention the social rights of beneficiaries, and in some cases government officials even express their desire that access to social services will improve by forcing NGOs into direct service provision as a result of restricting nonprofit advocacy.[810] However, where nonprofit activities are essential to the realization of social rights because the state is not capable of achieving the same level of realization, it is reasonably foreseeable that excessively restricting supplemental NGOs would result in a limitation to the enjoyment or realization of ESC rights for their beneficiaries. Moreover, allowing states to claim ignorance of these effects encourages those that seek to circumvent their Covenant responsibilities merely by issuing official statements of their desire to assist beneficiaries, despite overwhelming evidence indicating that the opposite is much more likely to occur. Thus, article 5 (1) places the state and supplemental NGOs into a triangular legal relationship, wherein the state consented to waiving its right to obstruct supplemental NGOs – in other words, the state is obliged to permit supplemental nonprofit activities that are essential for the realization and enjoyment of social rights.

In summary, the nonprofit entity that fulfills the state's obligations – the substitutional NGO – is bound to the state in a triangular relation because it acts as the functional equivalent of the state. The underlying principle is that a state cannot circumvent its social rights obligations simply by refraining from involving itself in service provision. The legal consequence is that the state's social rights obligations will have a carryover effect into its

809 Ibid para. 17.5.

810 See, e.g., Decreto Presidencial No. 74/15, No. 74/15 (Angola 2015) (stating within its first paragraph that this NGO law is meant to ensure and promote the effective participation and sustainable growth of beneficiary communities.).

regulation of private providers such that it bears additional requirements *vis-à-vis* the way that it regulates substitutional NGOs. In particular, states must generally enable (i.e., permit and facilitate) substitutional nonprofit activities as well as ensure that their positive effect on social rights continues even if the NGO ceases its activities. On the other hand, the nonprofit entity that is essential for the realization and enjoyment of rights that the state is not yet obliged to ensure – that is, supplemental NGOs – is bound to the state in a triangular relation on different grounds. It does not fulfill the state's obligation, so the state does not implicitly consent to relying on the nonprofit entity to fulfill its social rights obligations. Instead, the state's consent to waive any rights it may have had to obstruct the NGO can be derived from article 5 (1) of the Covenant, wherein states agree that they do not have the right to destroy or extensively limit ESC rights. The legal consequence is that, in general, states must permit supplemental nonprofit activities, although states are under no obligation to ensure the positive effect of such nonprofit activities on the realization and enjoyment of social rights.

5.2.2.3. From Finance to Guarantee / Permit

The second component of the provisioning relation found in the complementary model is its *financing* structure, which comprises of both reimbursement and price control mechanisms for the private provision of services. Reinikka and Smith explain that financing can enhance accountability of nonprofit provision by providing the nonprofit entity with the means to carry out its work.[811] Neither state reimbursements nor price controls are prominent features of substitutional or supplementary models – which are more common within low-income African LDCs – because NGOs in these scenarios have become integrated with the state's own social policy programs. As for *reimbursements*, most low-income African LDCs lack the resources to compensate NGOs their nonprofit activities. NGOs in African LDCs rely heavily on foreign funding rather than domestic resources. This is consistent with the supplementary and substitutional arrangements, where nonprofit activities fall beyond the range of activities that the state is willing or able to reimburse.

As for *price control* mechanisms, their primary aim is to limit the providers' fees so that services are accessible and continued provisioning is

811 Reinikka and Smith (2004).

sustainable. This is based on the presumption that private providers are for-profit entities that will heighten service fees in order to maximize their profits. The *sozialrechtliche Dreiecksverhältnis* model reflects this bias toward for-profit provision. Its structure includes regulatory instruments "concerning the fixing of tariffs and prices", in addition to the delivery and quality of services.[812] Since the state will eventually reimburse private providers for the services that they delivery to beneficiaries, price controls measures are part of the state's efforts to control its costs and ensure the financial stability of its social security system.[813] The implication here is that but-for price controls, private providers would hike up their prices so high that it would threaten the very stability of the entire social security system. This formulation of the *provisioning relation* seeks to ameliorate the risk of inhibited realization or enjoyment that is associated with profit-seeking incentives and, as such, is not appropriate for triangular models that instead envisions nonprofit provision.

Where not-for-profit entities are the predominant actors engaged in the realization and enjoyment of social rights, such as in low-income African LDCs, there is no expectation that they will charge prohibitively excessive fees, if any at all, which means there is no need for price control mechanisms. This applies to complementary arrangements, although complementary arrangements – like the *sozialrechtliche Dreiecksverhältnis* – include a financing component within the provisioning relation. Unlike the *sozialrechtliche Dreiecksverhältnis* model, however, the financing component found within the complementary model relates only the reimbursement of nonprofit provision without requiring the imposition of price control mechanisms. In the case of the enabling relation and the ensuring relation, which correspond respectively to supplemental NGOs and substitutional NGOs, the financing component is either limited or dropped all together. This is because, unlike the complementary model and the *sozialrechtliche Dreiecksverhältnis*, states in supplementary and substitutional arrangements have not indicated any intent to ensure the realization/enjoyment of rights through direct cooperation with NGOs.

In the supplemental arrangement, the state is not bound to ensure nonprofit activities, thus there is no obligation to reimburse them. The appropriate modification of the state-to-NGO relation here would be to *permit*

812 Becker (2013) 505. See also Ulrich Becker and others, 'Strukturen Und Prinzipien Der Leistungserbringung Im Sozialrecht', 1 Vierteljahresschrift für Sozialrecht (VSSR) 1 (2012) 11-21.

813 Becker and others (2012) 13-14.

nonprofit activities rather than to *finance* them. As for the substitutional arrangement, states may acquiesce to ensuring the fulfillment/enjoyment of social rights through nonprofit activities that are fully funded through external resources rather than directly funded by the state, thereby alleviating the state of any obligation to reimburse the NGOs. If, on the other hand, substitutional NGOs lack adequate funding, then there would be an obligation upon the state to choose from either funding the nonprofit activities or providing services directly through public programs in order to bridge the fulfillment gap. Thus the *financing* component is modified to merely *guaranteeing* that the social rights outcome of substitutional nonprofit activities continue to occur; meaning that the state bears an obligation to ensure the replacement of lost substitutional nonprofit activities, although it is not necessarily required to replace them through direct state action or through public funds.

5.2.2.4. From Quality to Quality / Supervise

The last structural component of the *provisioning relation* that needs to be reviewed is *quality* assurance. States that choose to engage private providers as a means of fulfilling their social rights obligations toward rights bearers are responsible for the quality of those provisions. Simply put, if the quality of those services falls below certain minimum standards of acceptability, then the state has failed to fulfill its obligation toward rights bearers. In Reinikka and Smith's accountability model, this aspect of the "compact" is enhanced through monitoring performance.[814] They posit that the greatest difficulty for states in this regard is gathering adequate and accurate information about their performance.[815]

Since private providers are stepping in for the state, the state must ensure that the quality of private services is at least as high as the quality of services which the state itself would have been obliged to provide. Conversely, states are under no obligation to ensure that the quality of privately provided services is higher than that which the state itself is obliged to provide. Since the main factor that distinguishes supplemental and substitutional NGOs is whether their activities fall within the state's duty horizon, we can expect that the duty of the state to ensure a certain standard of

814 Reinikka and Smith (2004) 25.
815 Ibid.

quality will differ depending on whether the NGO is a supplemental or substitutional entity.

In the supplemental scenario, the state's obligation to provide benefits immediately, or very soon thereafter, is limited enormously by the unavailability of resources. Many African LDCs, lacking the resources needed to provide those very services that the supplemental NGOs provide, simply bear no obligation to ensure that harmless supplemental activities of nonprofit actors are of any particular quality. That does not mean that states can turn a blind eye to medical malpractice in charitable clinics or child abuse in orphanages. The state still has an obligation to protect the human rights of beneficiaries against third party deprivation, which consequently sets the minimum quality-control standard for the private provision of social services and benefits. Thus, the third structural component for the relationship between the state and private provider has been modified from *quality* assurance to *supervision* of NGOs.

The legal outcome is different in cases involving substitutional NGOs because substitutional nonprofit activities fall within the duty horizon. This means that the substitutional NGOs are supporting realization and enjoyment to a level of achievement that is within the state's feasibility frontier. Unlike in the supplemental scenario where states lack both the obligation and ability to replace supplemental activities, states are obliged to ensure and even improve upon substitutional activities until they reach up to the level of enjoyment/realization that the state is required to achieve. Therefore, the state must guarantee a certain level of quality in the activities of substitutional NGOs. Recall, however, that human rights law protects the freedom of nonprofits to serve beneficiaries, thus substandard (but not harmful) services are protected from state obstruction. This would suggest that the state must improve upon subpar nonprofit activities rather than shut them down. The state can improve upon these activities by, for example, providing NGOs with additional resources or providing beneficiaries with additional benefits or services to supplement those suboptimal activities performed by substitutional NGOs. Since the state always retains responsibility for ensuring a certain level of quality in the case of substitutional NGOs, the substitutional model keeps the *quality* assurance label as an aspect of the *ensuring relation.*

In summary, the *provisioning relation* must be modified in order to fit the realities of nonprofit activities that are more commonly found in low-income African LDCs, namely substitutional and supplemental arrangement, because *admission*, *financing*, and *quality control* are not always prominent structural components of these arrangements. States' social rights obligations are limited by the availability of resources at their disposal. As such, states facing resource scarcities will have minimal social rights obligations. Entering into comprehensive, collaborative and supportive provisioning relations with NGOs – which is characteristic of complementary arrangements – is not required by international law, and is likely beyond the capacity of low-income African LDCs in terms of their resources. Consequently, the complementary triangular model has been modified such that the state-to-NGO relation involving substitutional NGOs is now referred to as the *ensuring relation*, and its structural components are *guaranteeing*, *supporting* and *quality* assurance. As for supplemental NGOs, their relation to the state is more properly labelled the *enabling relation*, and its structural components consist of *permitting*, *facilitating* and *supervising NGOs*.

5.2.3. The NGO-to-Beneficiary Relation

The last legal relationship links the beneficiary to the NGO. In the complementary model, this is called the *fulfillment relation* (or *Erfüllungsverhältnis* in the *sozialrechtliche Dreiecksverhältnis*) because it relates to the state's social rights obligation toward the entitled person. In Reinikka and Smith's triangular model, the relationship between provider and beneficiary is referred to in a very different way because their model does not represent the legal relations between parties. Reinikka and Smith call this the "client power" relation, which reflects their concern with the power of beneficiaries to hold providers accountable for the quality of their services. However, what is most important for our analysis is that it is through this relationship that social rights are realized or enjoyed.[816] In the complementary

816 Furthermore, emphasizing that the NGO-to-beneficiary relation marks the moment of realization or enjoyment has the added benefit of leaving the door open for considering the horizontal application of social rights law, thereby carrying with it the potential for a social justice perspective. It is not only the state that bears responsibilities toward the beneficiary. Private actors also bear their own responsibilities towards beneficiaries when they willfully engage in the business of realizing and enjoying social rights. This perspective gains some support from the preamble of the ICESCR and articles 25, 26 and 27 of the African Charter on Human and Peoples' Rights. (Peters (2016) *Beyond Human Rights: The Legal Status of the Individual in International Law*; Clapham (2013) *Human Rights and Non-State Actors*.) One theoretical framework that underpins this perspective is the notion that both private law and international law are undergoing a process of constitutionalization. (Jan Klabbers, Anne Peters and Geir Ulfstein, *The Con-*

model, it represents the point at which the state's obligations to the beneficiary are fulfilled. While Reinikka and Smith pull the state out of the provider-to-beneficiary relation, the social rights models pulls the state back into the equation by emphasizing the fulfillment of its legal obligations.

Since substitutional NGOs fulfill the standing obligations of states to beneficiaries, it is appropriate to maintain the same label for substitutional NGOs. Therefore, the NGO-to-beneficiary relation in the substitutional model retains the term *fulfillment relation*. In supplemental arrangements, however, nonprofit activities do not fulfill the standing obligations of the state because supplemental activities take place beyond the state's duty horizon. Thus, the moment that supplemental nonprofit activities achieve the realization or enjoyment of social rights for the beneficiary does not coincide with the moment that the state's social rights obligations to the beneficiary are fulfilled. While the NGO-to-beneficiary relation represents the realization or enjoyment of social rights, it signals something other than the moment of fulfillment in a supplemental arrangement. Instead, the NGO-to-beneficiary relation is the site at which the state's foreseeable obligations are *preemptively discharged* rather than the moment at which the state's standing duties are fulfilled. The label representing the NGO-to-beneficiary relation within the supplemental model thus reflects this modification.

5.3. Summary

The triangular model is an analytical tool that can be used to examine the legal relations that bind the state, NGOs and beneficiaries, as well as the

---

stitutionalization of International Law (Oxford University Press 2011); Hans- W. Micklitz (ed), *Constitutionalization of European Private Law*, vol 22 (Oxford University Press 2014).) This perspective is embedded with a strong social justice orientation, which resonates with the post-colonial Africanist paradigm. It views social rights as representing more than merely entitlements to specific services and benefits. Rather, "their influence should infuse the entire legal system, including the legal rules and doctrines that allocate social benefits and economic resource benefits in private relationships such as family law, property law and contract law." (Sandra Liebenberg, 'Direct Constitutional Protection of Economic, Social and Cultural Rights in South Africa' in Danwood Mzikenge Chirwa and Lilian Chenwi (eds), *The Protection of Economic, Social and Cultural Rights in Africa: International, Regional and National Perspectives* (Cambridge University Press 2016) 305-337, 325.).

manner in which those legal relations influence one another. In the *sozialrechtliche Dreiecksverhältnis* and the complementary model, the state designs a larger social policy framework wherein its social rights obligations are fulfilled through coordination with the activities of non-state actors. This kind of arrangement is consistent with the state's international obligations under the ICESCR because the Covenant does not require the state to fulfill social rights obligations exclusively through direct state action.[817] While the complementary model is more prevalent in advanced industrial economies, it does not represent a triangular arrangement that is typically found in low-income African LDCs. Thus, there is a need for new triangular models that more accurate represent the functional role of NGOs in African LDCs, and the legal consequences thereof. The new models proposed in this chapter correspond with the characteristics of supplemental and substitutional NGOs, and thereby reflect the specific ways in which the social rights obligations of states toward beneficiaries determine the regulatory obligations of the state toward NGOs.

817 Alston and Quinn (1987) 182-183.

6. Evaluating NGO Laws: Unlawful Restrictions on Social Rights?

The previous chapters have argued that certain NGOs are essential for the realization/enjoyment of beneficiaries' social rights as well as the fulfillment/preemptive discharge of states' duties, indicating that state measures that restrict essential NGOs may breach states' social rights obligations and limit the social rights of beneficiaries. In general, the ICESCR prohibits restricting Covenant rights, including the social rights guaranteed therein. Textual evidence coupled with a teleological interpretation of the Covenant as well as the *travaux préparatoires* all indicate the same.[818] This suggests that restrictions upon nonprofit activities that are essential for the realization and enjoyment of social rights are also generally prohibited because it is reasonably foreseeable that they will result in limitations to the ESC rights of beneficiaries. Such restrictions would undoubtedly undermine precisely those conditions that have become necessary for the enjoyment or realization of social rights, as well as the Covenant's overarching purpose of achieving human freedom and human security for all.

Nevertheless, as discussed in the previous chapter, restricting NGOs will be reasonable or even necessary at times in order to protect the rights of beneficiaries. The issue that now remains is whether the resulting restriction on social rights is permissible. The present chapter addresses the following question: to what extent does the Covenant permit NGO laws that result in restrictions on the enjoyment or realization of beneficiaries' social rights? The answer depends on the type of restriction being imposed, the legitimacy of the state's aim in imposing such restrictions, and whether the restrictions are proportional to the state's objective.

818 See *supra* part 0on the subsidiarity principle as a component of the ICESCR's overarching purpose (discussing the Covenant's aim to protect and achieve human freedom, which would be inconsistent with any interpretation of the Covenant that recognizes a general right of the state to restrict ESC rights).

6.1. Three Types of Restrictions: Obstructions, Derogations and Limitations

The ICESCR contemplates at least three different ways that ESC rights may be restricted. These can be distinguished by whether they interfere with the realization of rights or with their enjoyment. Realization and enjoyment have different but related meanings: Realization marks the moment when a rights bearer begins to exercise or enjoy a right; thus, enjoyment is the consequence of realization. Enjoyment continues until there is an interruption in the exercise of a right or in the ability to exercise it. The effects of restricting enjoyment are unlike the effects of restricting realization. For example, while the latter might result in a withdrawal of existing services, the former is characterized by the lost opportunity to provide new services or to expand coverage for existing services. Furthermore, limiting the existing enjoyment of rights can result in extraordinary personal harm because people tend to plan around and rely on the continued enjoyment of their rights, which is neither unreasonable nor unforeseeable when their right to the "continuous improvement of living conditions" is taken into account.[819]

Nonprofit activities are essential for the realization of social rights when they are preparatory in nature, in that they achieve the necessary preconditions for the enjoyment of a right without directly bringing about its enjoyment. Examples of nonprofit activities that are essential for realization but not for enjoyment include training medical staff, building educational facilities, informing beneficiaries about existing services, and advocating for the expansion of services. On the other hand, nonprofit activities that are essential for enjoyment are typically direct service provision programs. The manner in which states regulate NGOs that are essential for the realization/enjoyment of social rights can result in one of three types of restrictions to the social rights of beneficiaries.

The enjoyment of social rights can be *destroyed* (i.e., derogated from) or *limited*, while the realization of rights can be *obstructed*. The destruction of a right occurs when the state totally derogates from it by completely suspending its enjoyment or making it practically impossible to continue enjoying the right. Limitations are less damaging because they do not amount to a total destruction. Rather, rights bearers can continue to enjoy their rights, although they are constrained in their ability to do so, or in the manner in which they choose to enjoy their rights. Finally, the realization of rights may be totally or partially obstructed by state measures that

819 ICESCR art. 11 (1).

make it either impossible or highly unlikely that certain unrealized rights will become enjoyable in the foreseeable future.

Distinguishing between whether an NGO law interferes with the enjoyment of rights or with their realization is important because the Covenant treats these restrictions differently in terms of their permissibility. Article 4 is the Covenant's general limitations clause. It addresses the permissibility of limiting the enjoyment of Covenant rights. Here is the text of article 4 in its entirety:

> The State Parties to the present Covenant recognize that, in the enjoyment of those rights provided by the State in conformity with the present Covenant, the State may subject such rights only to such limitations as are determined by law only in so far as this may be compatible with the nature of these rights and solely for the purpose of promoting the general welfare in a democratic society.

Article 2 (1) relates to obstructing the realization of ESC rights, rather than limiting their enjoyment. Although this provision neither directly nor explicitly concerns the obstruction of realization, its terms clearly imply certain criteria for their permissible use. For convenience, the text of article 2 (1) is reproduced here:

> Each State Party of the present Covenant undertakes to take steps, individually and through international assistance and cooperation, especially economic and technical, to the maximum of available resources, with a view to achieving progressively the full realization of the rights recognized in the present Covenant by all appropriate means, including particularly the adoption of legislative measures.[820]

Unlike how article 4 permits limitations of rights under certain circumstances, article 2 (1) relates primarily to the duties of states to realize ESC rights. However, by defining the boundaries of the state's obligations to realize social rights, it implicitly carves out legitimate grounds for obstructing realization attained by state or non-state actors. Namely, states are only required to realize social rights through means that are both appropriate and feasible. Therefore, it must be permissible for states to obstruct or forgo the realization of social rights when it would be infeasible or inappropriate to do so. While article 4 limits the state's power to restrict rights, article 2 limits the state's obligation to realize rights.[821]

---

820 Ibid art. 2(1).

821 See Saul, Kinley and Mowbray (2014) 246-247.

Article 2 (1) should not be used to evaluate the lawfulness of limiting the enjoyment of ESC rights that have already been realized. The drafting history of articles 2 (1) and 4 indicates that drafting members who supported the adoption of a general limitations clause reasoned that it was patently inappropriate to use article 2 as a general limitations clause because doing so would allow broad and unrestricted limitations on ESC rights. One report on the matter noted,

> The provision of the general article [which eventually became article 2] should, in their view, relate only to the general level of attainment of the rights and should not be invoked by States as grounds for detailed limitations on them. The general article did not indicate what limitations could be legitimate and it was necessary to state clearly that limitations would be permissible only in certain circumstances and under certain conditions. [822]

While article 4 provides the criteria for permissible limitations, article 5 describes what qualifies as a forbidden limitation. Article 5 relates to the destruction of Covenant and non-Covenant rights, as well as to the use of limitations beyond those explicitly permitted by the Covenant. It generally protects Covenant and non-Covenant rights against derogations and extensive limitations. Article 5 (1) states:

> Nothing in the present Covenant may be interpreted as implying for any State, group or person any right to engage in any activity or to perform any act aimed at the destruction of any of the rights or freedoms recognized herein, or at their limitation to a greater extent than is provided for in the present Covenant.

This provision relates to the abuse of rights, whereby one party might claim that, in order to realize its own rights, the rights of others must be violated. Article 5 (1) prohibits all such derogations, as well as limitations that fail to conform to the requirements of article 4.

Article 5 (2) is directed toward the protection of *non-Covenant* rights against certain derogations and restrictions, as well as preserving higher

822 Report to the Economic and Social Council on the Eigth Session of the Commission (1952) para. 155.

standards of protection for ESC rights that might exist at the national level.[823] Here is the text of article 5 (2):

> No restriction upon or derogation from any of the fundamental human rights recognized or existing in any country in virtue of law, conventions, regulations or custom shall be admitted on the pretext that the present Covenant does not recognize such rights or that it recognizes them to a lesser extent.

Article 5 (2) essentially forbids limiting or destroying non-Covenant rights on the grounds that the Covenant does not explicitly recognize them. States still may restrict non-Covenant rights, but they will need another reason to do so. In considering the permissibility of limitations under the African Charter, the African Commission similarly recognizes a "general rule that no one has the right to engage in any activity or perform any act aimed at the destruction of any of the rights and freedoms recognised elsewhere."[824]

The term "fundamental rights" should not be understood to mean the minimum level of protection. The *travaux préparatoires* reveal that proponents of the adopting the provisions found in article 5 (2) sought to protect existing standards of protection that *exceeded* those guaranteed by the Covenant.[825] Even some of those who opposed the provision when it was proposed did so because,

> ...[they] thought it inconceivable that any State ratifying the covenant would use it as a pretext to abridge the rights and freedoms already exercised and guaranteed within its territory if the covenant should impose lesser obligations in a particular sphere.[826]

Rather than thinking of "fundamental rights" in this context as minimum standards, it is more accurate to understand the term to mean rights that are recognized by law or perhaps by color of law. Thus, if, by virtue of domestic law, a state attains higher levels of realization for ESC rights than the Covenant requires (e.g., high-value cash transfers to each household; debt forgiveness for all student loans), and recognizes those levels of real-

823 The *travaux preparatoires* indicate that this provision was proposed with the aim of protecting rights enjoyed to a greater extent under national law than was provided for by the Covenant. (Ibid paras. 149-150.).

824 *Prince v. South Africa*, Comm. No. 255/2002 (ACmHPR 2004) para. 43.

825 Report to the Economic and Social Council on the Eigth Session of the Commission (1952) para. 150.

826 Ibid para. 151.

ization as the fulfillment of legal rights even though they are not explicitly guaranteed by the Covenant (e.g., a right to basic income; a right to free higher education), then it cannot justify arbitrarily restricting those rights on the grounds that the Covenant did not explicitly oblige the state to guarantee those rights in the first place. Again, the state still may restrict those rights and regress from levels of realization already attained, but it will need to identify another (legitimate) reason for doing so. Lastly, article 5 (2) tends to support the ESCR Committee's doctrine against the use of retrogressive measures. If this provision represents the unwillingness of member states to condone the limitation and restriction of rights not even mentioned within the Covenant, it stands to reason that the Covenant does not take lightly the use of retrogressive measures against Covenant rights.

6.2. *The Permissibility of Limiting NGO-Provided Rights*

It will undoubtedly be necessary at times for states to limit non-state activities that provide social rights in order, for example, to promote general welfare or fulfill the state's obligation to protect the rights of others. Yet, article 5 (1) appears to forbid the use of limitations beyond those permitted by the Covenant, and the general limitations clause - article 4 - does not explicitly permit limitations on rights provided by non-state actors. Without the ability to limit rights provided by nonprofits, the ability of states to regulate NGOs on legitimate grounds would be compromised. For instance, a devious nonprofit entity might provide basic services, like delivering food, in exchange for sworn loyalty from beneficiaries in support of a particular political agenda. In such cases, it would be unthinkable that the Covenant would require states to permit inappropriate NGO activities on the pretext that article 4 does not explicitly authorize such limitations. Such an interpretation would clearly undermine the Covenant's commitment to the interconnectedness of all human rights in general,[827] and to the protection of all peoples' right to self-determination in particular.[828] How, then, could the Covenant be interpreted such that the limitation of rights provided by NGOs is permitted, subject to certain restrictions?

827 ICESCR preamble.
828 Ibid art. 1.

In my view, since essential NGOs, such as those that play a substitutional role, are acting as the functional equivalent of the state in terms of fulfilling the state's social rights obligations, it would stand to reason that the Covenant would similarly restrict state efforts to limit those social rights enjoyed by beneficiaries of essential NGOs. To come to this conclusion, one must look carefully at the ordinary meaning of the texts found in articles 4, 5 and 2 (1) within their contexts and in accordance with the object and purpose of the Covenant.

6.2.1. The Permissibility of Limiting ESC Rights in General

As mentioned above, the state can restrict social rights in one of three ways: by derogating (destroying) from or limiting the enjoyment of rights, or by obstructing their realization. The Covenant provides some guidance as to the lawfulness of such restrictions by providing specific and general restrictions upon Covenant rights, as well as by defining the boundaries of permissibility.

6.2.1.1. Specific Limitations Clauses of the ICESCR: Article 13 (3) and (4)

Some articles of the ICESCR specifically limit Covenant rights, such as those relating to trade unions[829] and the rights of non-nationals in developing states.[830] No specific limitations have been placed directly upon social rights. There are, however, specific limitations placed on the right to establish private schools and the right to select a private education for one's own children. Article 13 (3) limits the freedom of parents to choose non-public schools for their children by requiring that they choose only schools that "conform to such minimum standards as may be laid down or approved by the State". In the fourth paragraph of article 13, the freedom of private parties to create educational institutions are

> subject always to the observance of the principles set forth in paragraph 1 of this Article [art. 13] and to the requirement that the education given in such institutions shall conform to such minimum standards as may be laid down by the State.

829 Ibid art. 8.
830 Ibid art. 2 (3).

Although these are limitations on rights that are not social rights, they may interfere with the right to education, particularly when access to public schools is rather limited. Placing such restrictions on educators and parents can limit the scope of education that is available to potential students. When alternative education of comparable quality is available to potential students, then such a limitation on the right to education is minimal or nonexistent. Thus, the only limitations that need to be evaluated are those imposed upon the rights of educators and parents, which can be done according to the provisions of article 13 (3) and (4). If, however, the private school is essential to the realization or enjoyment of education because the state has failed to ensure alternative means of acquiring education, then the permissibility of the resulting limitation on the right to education must also be evaluated.

Consider the example of Ethiopia's NGO law, which targets nonprofits receiving more than 10% of their funding from a foreign source – which constitutes a large share of the nonprofits in Ethiopia – by forbidding them from promoting human rights. Like article 13 of the ICESCR, the African Children's Charter[831] forbids state interference with the private establishment of schools, as long as such schools observe the child's right to education and conform to minimum educational standards set by the Ethiopian government.[832]One could hardly argue that prohibiting the promotion of human rights qualifies as a minimum educational standard because Ethiopia's NGO law neither explicitly contemplates basic childhood education nor indicates any legislative intent to advance the education of children. This kind of legislation is plainly a violation of the freedom of private actors to establish and maintain private schools.

Since article 13 does not address secondary interferences with ESC rights, it lacks the necessary safeguards for evaluating such limitations. It does not, for example, try to protect the nature of the right to education or require that all limitations serve the public welfare. Therefore, the indirect interference with the right to education must be evaluated in accordance with the general clauses of the ICESCR, which address the permissibility of restrictions on ESC rights. A major attribute of this approach is that ESC rights will always enjoy the minimum baseline of protection that is built into the general clauses. For example, in a state where the availability

831 Ratified on Oct. 2, 2002. ('Ratification Table: African Charter on the Rights and Welfare of the Child' (*African Union*) <http://www.achpr.org/instruments/child/ratification/>.).

832 African Children's Charter art. 11 (7); ICESR art. 4.

of free public education is severely limited, the state cannot set minimum standards of education so high that they effectively prohibit the establishment of nonprofit schools that would have otherwise provided at least some basic form of education where there was none at all. Article 13 (3) and (4) protect the right to education by ensuring the education that is available to students is only of a good quality. It allows states to exclude private schools of lesser quality when public education of a better quality is readily available. However, when public schools are a rarity, using article 13 to obstruct the establishment of private education would tend to degrade or limit the right to education, thereby triggering a need to apply the protective provisions of the general clauses that relate to restricting Covenant rights.

6.2.1.2. Permissibility of Limitations According to the African Charter

As for the African Charter, it does not explicitly limit ESC rights. Its text imposes neither specific limitations on ESC rights, nor any general limitations clause. The African Commission understands this to mean that it should be very cautious when permitting states to restrict Charter rights:

> The spirit behind the absence of such a general limitation must be understood as the desire to avoid abusive restriction of rights, a restriction which will be applied only under very limited and legally circumscribed conditions.[833]

The Commission has declared "a general principle that applies to all rights" that "[g]overnments should avoid restricting rights" and that "[n]o situation justifies the wholesale violation of human rights", thereby effectively restricting the permissible use of limitations and totally rejecting the general use of derogations.[834] Thus, when the Commission infers from the Charter the permissible use of limitations, it does so in a restrictive man-

833 *Groupe De Travail v. DRC*, para. 66.

834 *Media Rights Agenda, Constitutional Rights Project, Media Rights Agenda and Constitutional Rights Project v. Nigeria*, Comm. Nos. 105/93, 128/94, 130/94 and 152/96 (ACmHPR 1998) para. 65; see also, *Amnesty International, Comité Loosli Bachelard, Lawyers' Committee for Human Rights, Association of Members of the Episcopal Conference of East Africa v. Sudan*, Comm. Nos. 48/90, 50/91, 52/91 and 89/93 (ACmHPR 1999) paras. 80 & 82.

ner.[835]Consequently, the Commission has read into the Charter the twin principles of proportionality and necessity for all limitations in order to restrict their permissible use.[836] It notes that,

> The reasons for possible limitations must be founded in a legitimate State interest and the evils of limitations of rights must be strictly proportionate with and absolutely necessary for the advantages which are to be obtained.[837]

Furthermore, in defining the permissibility of limitations, the Commission has ensured the protection of fundamental rights guaranteed under international law,[838] as well as what appears to be a core minimum of enjoyment against total derogation.[839]As for the legitimacy of the state's reason for limiting rights, article 27 (2) of the African Charter offers some guidance. It states:

> The rights and freedoms of each individual shall be exercised with due regard to the rights of others, collective security, morality and common interest.

This clause suggests that states are likely justified in restricting rights if they do so for one of these reasons. The Commission likewise recognizes these particular purposes as "[t]he only legitimate reasons for limitations".[840] Noting that the Charter does not feature a general derogations clause, the Commission concluded that "limitations on the rights and freedoms enshrined in the Charter cannot be justified by emergencies or special circumstances."[841]

---

835 *Groupe De Travail v. DRC* para. 66; *Media Rights Agenda and Others v. Nigeria* para. 69.
836 *Groupe De Travail v. DRC* para. 66.
837 *Media Rights Agenda and Others v. Nigeria* para. 69.
838 *Amnesty International and Others v. Sudan* para. 80; *Groupe De Travail v. DRC* para. 67.
839 *Media Rights Agenda and Others v. Nigeria* para. 70.
840 Ibid para. 68.
841 Ibid para. 67.

6.2.2. Articles 4 and 5 Do Not Forbid the Limitation of NGO-Provided Rights

Article 4's explicit reference to "rights provided by the State" as well as its silence as to rights provided by non-state actors, leaves one wondering whether limitations on rights provided by NGOs are permissible, forbidden or restricted in any way. On the one hand, article 4 could be interpreted as a blanket prohibition of all limitations on rights provided by NGOs. This, however, is at odds with the purpose and object of the Covenant since it would effectively allow all NGOs – including inappropriate NGOs – to escape regulatory control as long as they provide some ESC rights. On the other hand, since article 4 does not explicitly restrict limitations on social rights provided by nonprofit entities, one may arrive at the opposite conclusion: limitations on rights provided by NGOs are *always* permitted. Analysts who neglect the impact that NGO restrictions can have on social rights are unwittingly aligned with this approach. Both interpretations are extreme and have undesirable consequences. They either create a loophole for predatory or exploitative nonprofits by protecting them against state regulation as long as they also provide some ESC rights for some beneficiaries, or they suggest that states have unbridled authority to limit social rights as long as non-state actors provide them. These conclusions are incompatible with meaning of article 4, in light of its context[842] and the object and purpose of the Covenant.

Readings of article 4 that forbid or permit all limitations of social rights provided by NGOs are based on the same error of interpretation: the notion that the application of a law in one area of context (rights provided by the state) automatically excludes or necessitates its application in another context (rights provided by NGOs). Instead, to determine whether and to what extent the Covenant permits limitations on rights provided by NGOs, it is necessary to look beyond the text of article 4 and to consider other parts of the Covenant as well as its purpose and object. The ESCR Committee has emphasized, "the Covenant's limitation clause, article 4, is primarily intended to protect the rights of individuals rather than to per-

842 Note that article 4 must be read in conjunction with article 5 (1), which generally forbids the limitation of rights beyond the extent to which the Covenant already permits. This precludes an interpretation of article 4 whereby states are permitted to wield unlimited power to restrict social rights as long as those rights are provided by NGOs.

mit the imposition of limitations by States."[843] Likewise, the limitation clause should take a beneficiary-centered approach in order to prioritize the protection of rights rather than to serve as a technical means for NGOs to escape regulatory control or for states to circumvent their Covenant obligations. Ultimately, the answer to the question, "when are limitations to rights provided by NGOs permissible?" must remain compatible with the norms and principles of the Covenant.

It cannot be interpreted from article 4 that the use of limitations under all circumstances other than when rights are provided by the State is simply forbidden. Even the ordinary meaning of the text in this article does not require such a conclusion. The phrase "in the enjoyment of *those rights provided by the State* in conformity with the present Covenant"[844] has been inserted into a line of text that establishes the criteria for the permissibility of limitations, thus it has the grammatical function of qualifying the statement into which it was inserted rather than being itself qualified. In this case, the qualification serves to confine the range of limitations that are of concern to only those limitations that affect rights provided by the state. It would be a mistake to understand it the other way around, namely as indicating that it is only those rights provided by the state that may be subject to limitations. In other words, article 4 restricts the range of limitations that are of concern rather than the range of rights that may be limited. Therefore, limitations affecting rights provided by non-state actors are not forbid; they are simply not of concern to this article.

This narrowed scope of concern is reaffirmed by the words, "...the State may subject such rights only to such limitations as are determined by law..." Here, the term "only" precedes the words "to such limitations ..." and does not precede the words "such rights", thereby indicating that it is the range of limitations that are being restricted rather than the range of rights that may be limited. This leaves the door open to an interpretation of article 4 whereby limitations on rights provided by non-state actors might be permissible.

However, article 4's silence on the matter should not be understood to mean that all limitations on NGO-provided rights are permissible, without due regard to their proportionality *vis-à-vis* the legitimacy of the state's underlying interests or the extent to which such rights are limited. Making no mention of limitations to rights provided by non-state actors, article 4

843 General Comment No. 14: The Right to the Highest Attainable Standard of Health (2000) para. 28.

844 (Emphasis added.).

neither explicitly permits nor forbids the use of such limitations. Yet, as a practical matter, when NGOs are prevalent and essential to social rights and to the fulfillment or preemptive discharge of state duties, the state must be able to regulate them to a certain extent, even if – at times – regulatory restrictions result in a limitation to the ESC rights of their beneficiaries.

Similarly, a combined literal reading of articles 4 and 5 (1) might appear at first glance to permit all limitations or the complete destruction of ESC rights, as long as it was not the state's aim to do so, and as long as the rights effected were provided by non-state actors.[845] This is essentially what is happening in African states. In general, existing NGO laws that restrict nonprofit activities do not appear to aim at the destruction or limitation of social rights. In fact, many of these laws do not mention social rights at all, which suggests that lawmakers are not considering the negative impact that they could have on the enjoyment and realization of social rights. Some might even argue that restrictive NGO laws would *enhance* social rights by forcing NGOs to focus predominantly on service provision instead of advocacy. Thus, these laws can inadvertently result in restrictions to the enjoyment and realization of social rights. In such cases, the limitation on social rights is indirect because lawmakers seek primarily to control NGOs or limit their political influence rather than to interfere with the social rights of their beneficiaries.

Technically speaking, this kind of inadvertent limitation on ESC rights is not forbidden according to a literal reading of article 4 (which does not address rights provided by NGOs) and article 5 (1) (which forbids only those acts that aim at restricting ESC rights). However, one should not arrive at such a conclusion lightly. Adjudicators should be careful to vet out cases in which the state knew or should have known that restricting NGOs would result in an interference with the social rights of beneficiaries. A heighten level of scrutiny is especially appropriate when the NGOs are essential for the realization/enjoyment of social rights or for the fulfillment/preemptive discharge of state duties. Moreover, a heightened level of judicial scrutiny in this regard would incentivize lawmakers to ensure that

845 This is because article 4 does not explicitly forbid limitations on rights provided by non-state actors, and because article 5 (1) only explicitly forbids acts *aimed at* the destruction or extensive limitation of ESC rights, thereby leaving open the issue of whether acts that only inadvertently bring about the same effects are therefore permissible.

they are reasonably informed about the impact that their laws will likely have on the realization and enjoyment of ESC rights.

Although as a practical matter, states must be able to limit NGO-provided rights to a certain extent, article 5 (1) disqualifies all interpretations of the Covenant that would permit any act aimed at limiting ESC rights to a greater extent than is permitted by article 4 and the specific limitations clauses. How, then, can the Covenant be interpreted such that it permits limitations on NGO-provided rights – subject to certain restrictions – but also remains consistent with the terms of article 5 (1)? The solution is to ground such an interpretation squarely within the scope of article 4. In other words, in order to be consistent with the requirements of article 5 (1), limitations imposed upon rights provided by NGOs are permissible to the extent that their permissibility can be derived from the existing general limitations clause. As such, I propose that article 4 applies analogously to limitations imposed upon NGO-provided rights whenever those rights are provided by substitutional or supplemental NGOs, or by their minimum NGO counterparts, because those rights are treated as the functional equivalent of rights provided by the state. Under this interpretation, the ICESCR limits how restrictive NGO laws are allowed to be such that any resulting interference with the enjoyment or realization of social rights must satisfy the requirements of article 4.

6.2.3. Article 4 Can Be Used Analogously for NGO-Provided Rights

The preliminary question is whether the text of article 4 indicates that its provisions should *never* be applied to the limitation of rights provided by non-state actors; that is, whether it forbids its analogous application to rights provided by NGOs. While at first glance the text of article 4 might appear to restrict its application to rights provided by the state, further investigation reveals that this is not the case. The ordinary meaning of those words in the context of the surrounding words indicates that a different interpretation is proper.

Although the text of article 4 includes the phrase "those rights provided by the State in conformity with the present Covenant", it is not clear whether the meaning of this phrase is to prohibit the use of restrictions on rights provided by non-state actors. For example, the meaning of this phrase might be to exclude the use of limitations on rights not yet provided such as those not yet realized or enjoyed. Likewise, the meaning of the phrase could be that it excludes the use of limitations on rights provided in conformity with other Covenants, such as the ICCPR. To understand the meaning of this phrase, one must look beyond the four corners of the Covenant.

The Committee on ESC rights has not provided much guidance on the meaning or underlying reasoning of article 4, let alone any guidance on this particular issue. The drafting history, however, provides some guidance. It seems that excluding from the applicable scope of article 4 those rights provided by non-state actors was barely within the drafters' range of awareness, let alone forming part of their intent. The members of both the Third Committee of the General Assembly and the Commission on Human Rights paid virtually no attention to this question. There is, however, one exception. During general debates of the Third Committee on the general provisions of the ICESCR as they had been drafted by the Commission on Human Rights, Miss Marsh of Canada noted that she would have preferred that article 4 be amended so that the words "those rights provided by the State" would have been deleted.[846] However, she did not submit an official amendment, and the issue was neither discussed nor raised again. The Third Committee adopted article 4 unanimously,[847] without any changes, and without discussing or fully considering whether the rights provided by non-state actors should be subject to limitations and whether the use of such limitations should be restricted. Earlier drafting history also reveals the uncontroversial nature of the words "rights provided by the State". They were accepted by the Commission without any debate about their meaning.[848]

The drafting history of how this phrase was originally proposed and why it was partly amended provides more insight into its meaning. The phrase first appeared during the seventh session of the Human Rights Commis-

846 Miss Marsh would have removed the words "in the enjoyment of those rights provided by the State in conformity with this Covenant, the State may..." and inserted in its place "in ensuring the enjoyment of the rights set forth in this Covenant, they may..." (Summary Record of the 1185th Meeting, Third Committee, U. N. General Assembly, UN Doc. A/C.3/SR.1185 (UN 1962) para. 18.).

847 Summary Record of the 1206th Meeting, Third Committee, U. N. General Assembly, UN Doc. A/C.3/SR.1206 (UN 1962) para. 53.

848 Summary Record of the 306th Meeting, Commission on Human Rights, U. N. Economic and Social Council, UN Doc. E/CN.4/SR.306 (UN 1952); Draft International Covenants on Human Rights: Report of the Third Committee (1955); Summary Record of the 308th Meeting (1952); Summary Record of the 234th Meeting, Commission on Human Rights, U. N. Economic and Social Council, UN Doc. E/CN.4/SR.234 (UN 1951); Summary Record of the 235th Meeting (1951); Summary Record of the 236th Meeting (1951).

sion. It was part of the original proposal for a general limitations clause proposed by the representative of the United States.[849] That proposal was the following:

> Each State Party to the Covenant recognizes that in the enjoyment of those rights provided by the State in conformity with this Part of the Covenant, the State may subject such rights only to such limitations as are determined by law and solely for the purpose of securing due recognition and respect for the rights and freedoms of others and of meeting the just requirements of morality, public order and the general welfare in a democratic society.[850]

The phrase "rights provided by the State in conformity with this Part of the Covenant" was by no means an absentminded insertion. It was noted by the Chairman of the Commission that the United States' proposal was "obviously" drafted in the same way as existing limitations provisions within the Covenant.[851] Likewise, the United States by its own admission mimicked the text of article 29 of the Universal Declaration of Human Rights.[852] However, while much of the United States' proposal was copied verbatim from the pre-existing texts, none of those pre-existing texts included language that restricted their application to rights provided by states. This language was deliberately added to the United States' proposal for a particular purpose. That purpose, however, was not to exclude from article 4's scope of application those rights provided by non-state actors.

The first and perhaps primary purpose of inserting this phrase was to distinguish between limitations on rights already being enjoyed (i.e., provided by the state) and those not yet realized (i.e., *not yet* provided by the state), rather than distinguishing between rights provided by the state and those provided by non-state actors. There was concern among some members, including the United States, that the way in which article 2 and the substantive articles had been formulated, the Covenant imposed upon

---

849 Summary Record of the 234th Meeting (1951).

850 United States Proposal Relating to the General Clause Concerning Economic, Social and Cultural Rights, Commission on Human Rights, U. N. Economic and Social Council, UN Doc. E/CN.4/610/Add.2 (UN 1951).

851 Summary Record of the 234th Meeting (1951); Report to the Economic and Social Council on the Seventh Session of the Commission on Human Rights, Commission on Human Rights, U. N. Economic and Social Council, UN Doc. E/CN.4/640 (UN 1951) annex I (articles 13-16 of the draft international covenant include specific limitations for certain civil and political rights).

852 Summary Record of the 234th Meeting (1951).

states an ever-increasing duty to realize ESC rights that – once realized – were absolute and could never be limited. The general limitations clause was meant to allow states some degree of freedom to limit rights once they've already been realized, which was simply beyond the scope of article 2's leniency. In defense of her delegation's proposal for a general limitations clause, Mrs. Roosevelt – the representative of the United States – explained the following:

> ...each of the articles on economic, social and cultural rights so far adopted began with the words: "The States Parties to this Covenant recognize the right of everyone...": those rights were thus set forth in absolute, unqualified form.
> ...The United States delegation proposed the inclusion in the part of the Covenant dealing with economic, social and cultural rights of a general recognition that rights, when provided by the State, would not necessarily be absolute, but might be subject to the limitations mentioned in article 29 of the Universal Declaration of Human Rights.[853]

The second reason for the insertion appears to have been driven by the geopolitical divides of that era. Throughout the drafting history,[854] a division among drafting members is evident as to whether ESC rights should be treated differently than civil and political rights, and this historical context provides another explanation for the insertion of the lines "provided by the State". Although a single unified Covenant was the instrument originally intended for guaranteeing all human rights, certain members (chief among them, the delegation from the United States) sought to separate the two categories of rights into distinct legal spheres. However, very likely due to heavy resistance from those opposing such a measure (lead primarily by the delegation from the USSR), those who sought to distance ESC rights from civil and political rights were only able to do so through a series of small changes. These changes began with moving the ESC rights into their own section within a unified draft Covenant and ended with each category of rights being separated its own distinct legal instrument. In the middle of this process, while ESC rights were still to be guaranteed within a unified Covenant, albeit within its own section and subject to its own general provisions, the United States proposed the adoption of a general limitations clause exclusively for ESC rights. The USSR and others who

853 Ibid (emphasis in original.).
854 Ibid; Summary Record of the 235th Meeting (1951); Summary Record of the 236th Meeting (1951).

opposed the move argued fervently that a general limitations clause for ESC rights was both unnecessary – because it was difficult to imagine when it would ever be appropriate to limit ESC rights – and dangerous – because it threatened to render ESC rights completely meaningless. These members believed that ESC rights had already been severely weakened as a result of, *inter alia*, being separated from civil and political rights within the Covenant and being subjected to the language of "progressive realization".

From this historical vantage point, it stands to reason that the line "rights provided by the State in conformity with this Part of the Covenant" was inserted by the United States delegation not for the purpose of fully allowing or completely prohibiting the limitation of ESC rights provided by non-state actors, or even for the purpose of restricting the application of article 4 to rights provided only by state actors. Rather, it was very likely the result of efforts by the United States and its supporters on the Commission to create a general limitations clause that would apply *only to ESC rights* (i.e., "...this Part of the Covenant...") and not to civil and political rights. The operative phrase here is not "those rights provided by the State", but rather "provided by the State *in conformity with this Part of the Covenant*".[855]

Ultimately, neither the text of the Covenant nor the drafting history precludes the analogous application of article 4 to limitations on rights provided by non-state actors. Moreover, bringing the limitation of rights provided by NGOs within the purview of article 4 would extend much needed protection to the rights of beneficiaries against extensive state interferences, particularly when NGOs are essential for the realization and enjoyment of social rights or the alleviation of their total deprivation. Therefore, I propose extending the scope of article 4 such that it applies to state measures that restrict NGOs whenever those NGOs are substitutional, supplemental or the minimum form of either type.

6.2.4. Using Article 4 to Restrict Limitations on NGO-Provided Rights

The previous sub-section argues that states are allowed to limit rights provided by NGOs. If applied analogously, article 4 would not only permit

855 (Emphasis added.) This was later changed to "...in conformity with the present Covenant" once ESC rights were separated from civil and political rights and placed into their own Covenant.

the use of limitations on rights provided by NGOs, but it would also restrict their use. Limitations must be (1) determined by law, (2) compatible with the nature of the rights being limited, and (3) implemented solely for the purpose of promoting the general welfare in a democratic society.

The first requirement ensures that states do not arbitrarily impose limitations on right provided by NGOs. This rules out arbitrary limitations of rights and makes it procedurally (and perhaps politically) more cumbersome for states to limit ESC rights. Procedurally speaking, the legislative process that gives rise to NGO laws would normally fulfill this requirement. However, it is questionable whether the substantive provisions constitute lawful limitations under article 4 if rather than directly limiting ESC rights they merely grant governmental officials unfettered discretion to do so indirectly by shutting down NGOs, freezing their financial accounts or denying them important licenses, access to beneficiaries in need, or access to foreign funding. For example, Uganda's former NGO law, the Non-Governmental Organisations Registration Act (2009), authorized a public body called the National Board of Non-Governmental Organistions to dissolve NGOs for a number of reasons as well as "any other reason the Board considers necessary in the public interest."[856] The words 'public interest' are left undefined. Setting aside the question of whether all NGOs in Uganda are helpful to beneficiaries,[857] the very fact that the Uganda is a poor country with high poverty rates and inadequate governmental social protection schemes indicates that at least some nonprofit activities will be essential for beneficiaries.[858] Thus, while it is reasonable and in fact necessary for the government to regulate NGOs in order to protect beneficiaries

856 The Non-Governmental Organisations Registration Regulations, 2017 No. 22 (Uganda 2017) § 17(3)(e).

857 See *Human Development in Uganda: Meeting Challenges and Findinal Solutions*, World Bank, (2009) 44 <http://documents.worldbank.org/curated/en/659361468175487874/Uganda-Human-development-in-Uganda-Meeting-challenges-and-finding-solutions>; Susan Dicklitch and Doreen Lwanga, 'The Politics of Being Non-Political: Human Rights Organizations and the Creation of a Positive Human Rights Culture in Uganda', 25 Human Rights Quarterly 482 (2003); *Uganda - the Role of Nongovernmental Organizations and Community-Based Groups in Poverty Alleviation*, World Bank (1994) <http://documents.worldbank.org/curated/en/363831468765338754/Uganda-The-role-of-nongovernmental-organizations-and-community-based-groups-in-poverty-alleviation>.

858 Uganda is both a low-income and least developed country with a national poverty rate averaging 19.7 %, and 42 % in northern Uganda. (*Poverty Maps of Uganda*, World Bank (2018) 18 <http://documents.worldbank.org/curated/en/456801530034180435/Poverty-Maps-of-Uganda> .).

against inappropriate conduct, very restrictive NGO laws will likely impede nonprofit activities that do in fact assist portions of the population who are in need of assistance and whom the government does not reach. Such interferences with social rights must comply with the requirements of article 4, which means they must be determined by law. In cases involving substitutional or supplemental NGOs, granting the Board virtually unfettered discretion to decide when NGOs were to be dissolved was tantamount to allowing limitations to social rights to be determined by public officials rather than by law. Uganda has since enacted a new NGO law whereby only courts of law now have the power to involuntarily dissolve NGOs.[859]

These kinds of laws do not state clearly the manner in which the social rights of beneficiaries may be limited, thus limitations are not *determined* by law, even though they are *consistent* with the law that regulates NGOs. Yet, as the drafting history reveals,[860] there is a clear distinction between the phrases 'determined by law' and 'consistent with law', the latter being less stringent than the former because it allows limitations to be determined by acts of governmental officials acting in accordance with NGO laws rather than being determined by the law itself. The requirement is that the law – rather than a governmental official – determines whether and how a limitation on the rights provided by NGOs will occur. Lawmakers must have intended to limit the rights of beneficiaries through NGO regulations. Inadvertent limitations are not permissible.

Article 4's second requirement is that limitations must remain compatible with the nature of the rights being limited. The meaning of this is that although restrictions on NGOs may limit social rights, those limitations must not extinguish the nature of the ESC rights that are being limited. This criterion is critical for ensuring that limitations do not cross the line and become full derogations by entirely destroying the substance of a right. Some commentators have noted the difficulty in imagining any limitation to social rights that would still be compatible with the nature of those rights.[861] It is unclear, for instance, how a state might limit the right to health or freedom from hunger in such a way that remains compatible with the nature of those rights. It is even more difficult to imagine how limiting the very essential core of a social right would still be compatible

859 The Non-Governmental Organisations Act, No 5 of 2016 (Uganda) arts. 48 & 50.

860 Summary Record of the 236th Meeting (1951).

861 Alston and Quinn (1987) 202-203.

with the nature of that right since minimum essential levels reflect the nature of Covenant rights, thus restricting them would be tantamount to obliterating the nature of those rights. For that reason, some have argued that limitations affecting minimum essential levels are impermissible because they cannot satisfy the requirements of article 4. [862]

At the very least, ensuring the nature of social rights must include refraining from causing their complete destruction and alleviating their total deprivation. This constitutes the core obligation of the state. Consequently, in the context of substitutional and supplemental NGOs, article 4 forbids the use of NGO laws that are so restrictive that the social rights of beneficiaries are completely destroyed. However, the case of minimum substitutional and minimum supplemental NGOs is of particular significance in this regard because these NGOs alleviate the total deprivation of social rights, and they are essential to their alleviation because the state does not and/or cannot ensure the same. Therefore, their activities respectively fulfill or preemptively discharge the positive core obligations of states.

Consider, as an example, how Ethiopia's NGO law nearly completely destroys a part of the child's right to education that is provided by NGOs. In addition to being a party to the ICESCR, Ethiopia has also signed and ratified regional human rights instruments, including the African Charter [863] and the African Children's Charter[864]. Like article 13 of the ICESCR, the African Children's Charter recognizes the child's right to education, as well as "the liberty of individuals and bodies to establish and direct educational institutions".[865] Consider now the example of an NGO that establish schools for children with foreign funding. Under Ethiopia's NGO law, such a school is forbidden from promoting human rights.[866] This prohibition directly violates Ethiopia's commitments under the international human rights law, which – as the African Children's Charter mandates – includes ensuring that education

---

862 Müller (2009) 575, 579-583.

863 Ratified June 15, 1998. ('Ratification Table: African Charter on Human and Peoples' Rights' (*African Union*) <http://www.achpr.org/instruments/achpr/ratification/>).

864 Ratified Oct. 2, 2002. ('Ratification Table: African Charter on the Rights and Welfare of the Child'(*African Union*)).

865 African Children's Charter art. 11 (1) & (7).

866 Charities and Societies Proclamation No 621/2009 (Ethiopia).

> foster[s] respect for human rights and fundamental freedoms, with particular reference to those set out in the provisions of various African instruments on human and peoples' rights and international human rights declarations and conventions.[867]

The obligation to strengthen respect for human rights through education is also part of the ICESCR.[868] This feature of Ethiopia's NGO law directly and intentionally destroys a part of the right to education, which is the right to an education that strengthens respect for human rights.

Once total deprivation is alleviated for the beneficiaries, the state then bears the negative core obligation of refraining from totally destroying those minimum levels of achievement. This indicates that article 4 forbids *any* limitations on rights provided by minimum substitutional and minimum supplemental NGOs, even if in the unlikely event that doing so would promote the general welfare. This is not to say, however, that the state cannot regulate or limit these NGOs. It may indeed do so, but only to the extent that such regulatory measures do not impose a limitation on the social rights of beneficiaries. Although this rule might sound rather extreme, it is quite sensible. It is difficult to imagine a scenario in which promoting the general welfare would require restricting nonprofit activities that are vital to alleviating the total deprivation of social rights, especially when these NGOs are not minimum *inappropriate* NGOs. The regulation of minimum inappropriate NGOs is permitted through a combined reading of articles 2 (1) and article 4, which will be discussed later on in this chapter.

The last requirement of article 4 is that the limitations serve the purpose of promoting the general welfare in a democratic society. This is difficult to interpret because of its broad meaning. Unlike limitations clauses found in the ICCPR, article 4 of the ICESCR does not explicitly permit limitations for any reason other than "promoting general welfare in a democratic society."[869] Although it is unclear what precisely is meant by "general welfare", the drafting history reveals that this language was inserted as a means of preventing arbitrary and oppressive limitations of rights, such as those that would occur under a dictatorship. [870] Furthermore, there is reason to believe that the limitation of ESC rights such that particularly vul-

867 African Children's Charter art. 11 (2) (b).

868 ICESCR art. 13.

869 Ibid art. 4.

870 Draft International Covenants on Human Rights: Report of the Third Committee (1962) para. 89; see also Müller (2009) 575.

nerable individuals are disproportionately injured never promotes the general welfare. [871]

Lastly, implicit within article 4 is a requirement that the severity of limitations be proportional to the gravity of the state's legitimate aim. This can be garnered from the article's protection of the nature of rights, as well as its restrictive and protective tone. The drafting history also supports this conservative approach to permitting limitations.[872] This suggests that the greater the limitation is on a particular right, the greater the societal need must be for its limitation. In other words, not only must article 4 limitations be necessary for promoting the general welfare, but their severity should also be appropriate. [873] These requirements are based on the principle of proportionality, which is a common featured of other areas of human rights law, and has been recognized by both the African Commission and the ESCR Committee.[874] The ESCR Committee has recognized the proportionality test as an inherent component of assessing article 4 limitations. It attributes the proportionality requirement to article 5 (1), noting that "the least restrictive alternative must be adopted where several types of limitations are available."[875]

6.3. Permissibility of Obstructing the Realization of Rights by NGOs

As to the permissibility of obstructing the realization of social rights by NGOs, one must look to article 2 (1), which only requires state to states achieve the realization of social rights through appropriate and feasible

---

871 Müller (2009) 574.

872 Proponents of including a general limitations clause expressed the need to constrain the use of limitations such that the inevitable limitations that arise as a consequence of practical obstacles to realization would not pose a disproportionate threat to the ESC rights. (See, e.g., Draft International Covenants on Human Rights: Report of the Third Committee (1955) 3 (Mr. Hoare of the United Kingdom argued that the intent of a general limitations clause "was precisely to limit such limitations by states that were permissible only in certain circumstances and under certain conditions"); ibid 5 (likewise, Mr. Juvigny of France agreed with Mr. Hoare of the UK in concluding that a general limitations clause was necessary to protect ESC rights against extensive limitations.).

873 Müller (2009) 583-584.

874 See General Comment No. 21: The Right of Everyone to Take Part in Cultural Life (2009) para. 19; *Prince v. South Africa* para. 43.

875 General Comment No. 14: The Right to the Highest Attainable Standard of Health (2000) para. 29.

means. This would indicate that if the state obstructed efforts by NGOs to realize social rights inappropriately, or "inappropriate NGOs", such a restriction would be permissible under the terms of article 2 (1). Supplemental and substitutional NGOs, however, may not be restricted in the same way because, by definition, they realize social rights only by means that are appropriate.

Article 2 (1) establishes the obligations of the state such that states are not required to realize social rights to a level of achievement beyond that which they are capable of achieving. The article allows for progressive realization by all appropriate means and within the maximum of available resources. Although the explicit terms of article 2 (1) concern defining the scope of the state's duties, its open-ended language of progress, appropriateness and availability of resources suggests that the scope of the state's duties are rather dynamic. In this way article 2 (1) obligations can indirectly accommodate certain restrictions on the realization of social rights. Thus, states may pause the progression of realization in order to cease using inappropriate means, or due to resource constraints.

Article 2 (1) is not a limitations clause *per se*, but rather a dynamic obligations clause that allows the duties of states to shrink or expand in accordance with the availability of resources or the appropriateness of means. Technically, it is not the case that article 2 (1) permits limitations on the realization of rights provided by nonprofit entities, but rather that it does not burden states with the obligation of allowing nonprofit entities to advance realization at all times, under all circumstances and by any means they choose. More importantly, restricting realization does not automatically constitute to a limitation on social rights because rights must first be enjoyed before they can be limited. If the restriction were causing limitations on social rights, then it would need to be scrutinized under article 4. Thus, restrictions on nonprofit activities that are essential for the realization of social rights but not for their enjoyment, such as preparatory activities or those related to advocacy, are subject to review under the terms of article 2 (1).

Having rendered the state's duty to adopt a particular manner of realization dependent upon whether those means are both appropriate and feasible, article 2 (1) indirectly empowers states to restrict activities that would nonetheless lead to advancements in realization if they are inappropriate or infeasible. In other words, states are free to block the nonprofit entities if (1) those activities advance realization of social rights through inappropriate means, or (2) it is too costly for the state to permit their activity in the first place. Note that this is a more lenient standard for the permissibility of obstructions than the criteria set up by article 4 regarding limitations. The Covenant appears to be much more forgiving of restrictions on the realization of rights not yet enjoyed (i.e., pursuant to requirements of articles 2 (1) and 5) than it is of restrictions on the enjoyment of rights that have already been realized (i.e., according to the terms of article 4).

It is difficult to imagine how it might be infeasible for a state to permit nonprofit activities. It costs virtually nothing to permit nonprofit activities to take place. Of course, the state's policing and administrative costs would increase as the number of active NGOs increase within its territory, but these costs are probably negligible. Thus, barring unusual circumstances, states may not obstruct nonprofit activities that advance realization on account of resource constrains. This leaves open the issue of whether it is appropriate to allow nonprofit activities to advance the realization of social rights. And this in turn depends on whether the nonprofit activities themselves are appropriate.

At the very least, nonprofit activities will be appropriate if they are reasonably likely to advance realization in a manner that is consistent with the norms and principles of human rights law. Therefore, one reason that nonprofit activities may be deemed inappropriate is if they result in an interference with other human rights or the rights of others, which would be inconsistent with article 5 (2)'s indication that the Covenant generally does not support the derogation from or limitation of non-Covenant rights, as well as with the preamble's recognition of the interconnectedness of all human rights. In these instances, it would be permissible under article 2 (1) for the state to obstruct the realization of rights by these inappropriate means. For example, although forcibly subjecting women to medical treatments upon their husbands' requests might have been deemed appropriate in the past, it is no longer considered to be so today, and an NGO that engages in such practices may be restricted by the state, even at the cost of limiting the health "benefits" to the women. Such a limitation does not fall into the scope of article 4's requirements because it is not within the duty of the state – according to article 2 (1) – to ensure the realization of the right to health through such inappropriate means. In other words, no justification is needed to restrict an inappropriate medical procedure when the state is under no obligation to ensure its provision in the first place.

6.3.1. The Doctrine of Deliberately Retrogressive Measures

In its reading of article 2 (1), the ESCR Committee has articulated a doctrine on the use of "retrogressive measures", which it has applied when states use resource constraints as a justification for restricting rights. Although resource constraints are not typically the grounds for restricting NGOs, this can be the reason that states cite if they do not extend financial assistance to NGOs that fulfill their social rights obligations, such as substitutional NGOs and – potentially – complementary NGOs. The problem with the ESCR Committee's doctrine of retrogressive measures, however, is that it evaluates the permissibility of limitations on account of resource constraints under a more lenient standard than that which is established under article 4.

Retrogressive measures are those that would directly or indirectly diminish, or threaten to diminish, the enjoyment of Covenant rights.[876] This line of reasoning is developed from the Committee's understanding of how article 2 (1) emphasizes progressive realization and the use of maximum available resources. [877] Although social rights may be realized progressively rather than immediately, interpreting these words to mean that states can advance leisurely toward the fulfillment of social rights or that there are no time limits whatsoever placed upon their fulfillment would be tantamount to gutting Covenant obligations of all their meaningful content. This is why the Committee has reasoned that states must "move as expeditiously and effectively as possible towards that goal," [878] and then from there has concluded that retrogressive measures are presumably impermissible. According to the Committee, the state's use of deliberately retrogressive measures raises a rebuttable presumption that states are failing to fulfill their article 2 (1) obligations to achieve full realization in a progressive manner.

---

876 See General Comment No. 4: The Right to Adequate Housing (1991) para. 11 ("a general decline in living and housing conditions, directly attributable to policy and legislative decisions by States parties, and in the absence of accompanying compensatory measures, would be inconsistent with the obligations under the Covenant"). Economic, Social and Cultural Rights, United Nations High Commissioner for Human Rights, U. N. Economic and Social Council, UN Doc. E/2017/70 (UN 2017) para. 23.

877 General Comment No. 13: The Right to Education (1999) para. 45; General Comment No. 14: The Right to the Highest Attainable Standard of Health (2000) para. 32; General Comment No. 15: The Right to Water (2003) para. 19; General Comment No. 19: The Right to Social Security (2007) para. 42.

878 General Comment No. 3: The Nature of States Parties' Obligations (1990) para. 9.

The Committee notes that retrogressive measures can only be impermissible when they are deliberate. This comes from the notion that the Covenant's command to take steps "with a view to achieving progressively" ESC rights suggests that an element of intention, rather than conduct, is associated with this obligation.[879]This means that states are not required to achieve full realization along a linear path of ever-increasing achievements. Rather, achieving the realization of social rights may stall, or even regress at times, as long as it is the *intention* of states to achieve full realization in a progressive manner. Therefore, the problem with retrogressive measures arises when the state implements them deliberately, thereby triggering a presumption that article 2 (1) obligations have been breached.[880]

Once a presumption of breach has been raised, it may be rebutted because not all deliberately retrogressive measures violate the terms of the Covenant. The Covenant is sensitive to the limited capacity of states, which makes it difficult for them to sustain ever-increasing socio-economic outcomes and may at times leave them with few choices other than to pull back service levels or administer austerity measures. However, retrogressive measures should be avoided and used only as a last resort when sufficient resources are no longer available to sustain or increase existing levels of socio-economic achievement. In this regard, the Committee insists,

> If any deliberately retrogressive measures are taken, the State party has the burden of proving that they have been introduced after the most careful consideration of all alternatives and that they are fully justified by reference to the totality of the rights provided for in the Covenant and in the context of the full use of the state party's maximum available resources.[881]

In this way, the Committee has elaborated a doctrine for retrogressive measures, whereby a rebuttable presumption is raised against the lawfulness of deliberately retrogressive measures.

---

879 Ibid.

880 Cf., Craven (1995) (arguing that the Committee has not gone far enough to recognize deliberately retrogressive measures as *prima facie* violations; instead it "comes close to this position but does so in an excessively tentative and ambiguous manner.").

881 General Comment No. 13: The Right to Education (1999) para. 45. See also General Comment No. 3: The Nature of States Parties' Obligations (1990) para. 9; General Comment No. 15: The Right to Water (2003) para. 19; General Comment No. 19: The Right to Social Security (2007) para. 42.

6.3.2. Retrogressive Measures Should Meet the Criteria of Article 4

The ESCR Committee has limited the application of its doctrine to cases in which states have restricted the enjoyment of Covenant rights due to resource constraints. Moreover, very little insight has been provided into the application of article 4. Consequently, state measures that limit the enjoyment of social rights on account of resource constraints are considered under the retrogressive measures doctrine rather than under article 4. By insisting that retrogressive measures be evaluated under article 2 (1) rather than article 4, the Committee implies that restrictions on rights due to resources constraints are not the same as limitations. Consequently, resource-related restrictions are subject to a set of criteria that is more lenient than that which is established under article 4. When states reduce their financial support for essential NGOs, or when they decline to provide additional assistance although it is needed, the enjoyment of ESC rights provided by NGOs may be limited. As such, these limitations on ESC rights provided by NGOs qualify as article 4 limitations and should not suddenly fall under a more lenient standard of review simply because the government asserts that it lacks the resources to support the NGOs. The state's claim that it lacks adequate resources should be viewed with enormous suspicion when NGOs also fulfill the state's social rights obligations.

While the retrogressive measures doctrine requires the state to prove that resource-related restrictions on ESC rights were taken only after careful consideration of alternative measures, article 4 forbids the use of limitations unless they are implemented by law. And while the doctrine requires states to prove that retrogressive measures are fully justified by reference to the totality of Covenant rights and the maximal use of available resources, article 4 requires that limitations remain compatible with the nature of the rights being limited and that they promote the general welfare in a democratic society. The standards of article 4 are much more demanding than the Committee's doctrine as they require the involvement of some law-making process, and they suggest that some minimum level of rights must always be protected against limitations, even limitations motivated by resources constraints. In contrast to these high standards, the Committee has developed a list of factors to take into consideration when evaluating a state's justification[882] of retrogressive measures as well as the state's claim

882 In 2007, the Committee laid out a list of factors to consider when assessing whether the use of deliberately retrogressive measures is justified, in regards to respecting the right to social security. (General Comment No. 19: The Right to

that the unavailability of resources[883] is the reason for resorting to retrogressive measures.

While the retrogressive measures doctrine might be appropriate for evaluating the state's failure to advance realization or it's obstruction of realization by non-state actors, its use is improper for assessing the lawfulness of limitations to the enjoyment of rights already realized. Limitations on the enjoyment of rights must be assessed under the stricter standard of article 4 because they can cause greater harm to rights bearers since people tend to rely on and plan their lives around the expectation that existing standards of living will not suddenly and substantially decline. By subjecting restrictions on the enjoyment of existing Covenant rights under the relaxed standards imposed by article 2 (1), the Committee's doctrine of retro-

---

Social Security (2007) para. 42.) The Committee notes that it will take into account whether:
(a) there was reasonable justification for the action;
(b) alternatives were comprehensively examined;
(c) there was genuine participation of affected groups in examining the proposed measures and alternatives;
(d) the measures were directly or indirectly discriminatory;
(e) the measures will have a sustained impact on the realization of the right to social security, an unreasonable impact on acquired social security rights or whether an individual or group is deprived of access to the minimum essential level of social security; and
(f) whether there was an independent review of the measures at the national level.
(Id.).

883 In the event that a state cites resource constraints as justification for using retrogressive measures, the Committee indicated that it would consider:
(a) the country's level of development;
(b) the severity of the alleged breach, in particular whether the situation concerned the enjoyment of the minimum core content of the Covenant;
(c) the country's current economic situation, in particular whether the country was undergoing a period of economic recession;
(d) the existence of other serious claims on the State party's limited resources; for example, resulting from a recent natural disaster or from recent internal or international armed conflict.
(e) whether the State party had sought to identify low-cost options; and
(f) whether the State party had sought cooperation and assistance or rejected offers of resources from the international community for the purposes of implementing the provisions of the Covenant without sufficient reason
(An Evaluation of the Obligation to Take Steps to the "Maximum of Available Resources" under an Optional Protocol to the Covenant: Statement, Committee on Economic, Social and Cultural Rights, U.N. Doc E/C.12/2007/1 (UN 2007) para. 10.).

gressive measures circumvents the protection built into the Covenant for the enjoyment of existing rights.

Some commentators question why all types of restrictions should not be treated as limitations under article 4. They argue that this distinction is unreasonable and less compatible with the purpose of the Covenant than a unified approach that treats all restrictive measures as article 4 limitations.[884] Alston and Quinn point out the risk that states would readily argue that any restriction on rights is a retrogressive measure in order to circumvent the hefty requirements of article 4. [885] They argue that resource-motivated constraints should be considered article 4 limitations on policy grounds. Doing so would make it more difficult for states to implement such measures, thereby reducing the likelihood that they will implement resource-motivated constraints in the first place.[886] Müller offers a unified approach under which a certain minimum core of each right would be protected against all limitations and retrogressive measures, without regard to resource constraints.[887]

Notwithstanding these concerns, the text of the Covenant supports the assertion that restricting the enjoyment of rights due to the unavailability of resources is not a violation of states' duties *per se*. However, that is not an excuse for removing from article 4's scrutiny all limitations that are due to resource constraints. To the contrary, they must be subject to article 4's scrutiny because doing so provides an additional safeguard to rights bearers that is absent from article 2 (1). In effect, once states fulfill the requirement of article 2 (1) by demonstrating that they in fact it lacks the necessary resources to ensure continued enjoyment of ESC rights, they are permitted to implement cutbacks or austerity measures that limit enjoyment. However, article 2 says nothing about the quality of the cutbacks or how these limitations should be designed. States could distribute financial assistance to NGOs in a transparent and legally determined manner that optimizes the enjoyment / realization of social rights rather than, for example, through patrimonial systems that fosters corruption and clientelism.

Article 4 is helpful in this regard because it requires that the limitations are compatible with the nature of the rights, which means that they must

884 Müller (2009) 585-591; Alston and Quinn (1987) 205-206.
885 Alston and Quinn (1987) 205.
886 Ibid 205-206; cf., Saul, Kinley and Mowbray (2014) 246-247 (reasoning that progressive realization and limitations on rights are distinct concepts, suggesting that articles 2 and 4 can be applied independently.).
887 Müller (2009).

avoid totally depriving ESC rights. This suggests that MELs should be protected from cutbacks as a matter of priority.[888] Article 4's requirements that the cutbacks be determined by law excludes arbitrariness or discretionary decision-making on the part of government officials about where and how to limit rights due to budget constraints. Where and how limitations will be made must be *legally* determinable, meaning administrative officers must follow objective criteria set by the law. Lastly, cutbacks to the enjoyment of rights must be designed and implemented in a way that promotes the general welfare, rather than privileging a select few, meaning that the brunt of the burden of austerity measures must not be placed upon vulnerable, historically disadvantaged or politically powerless groups. Without the additional layer of protection provided by article 4, austerity measures can do more harm to ESC rights than is needed to protect the financial sustainability of the state – at worst, a legitimate need for austerity measures can be exploited by political elites as a pretext to oppress undesirable or opposing groups when they are already made vulnerable by difficult financial times.

Treating all restrictions as though they were article 4 limitations does not appear consistent with the explicit text of the Covenant. However, the proper distinction is not restricted to whether limitations are taken on account of resource constraints, as the Committee has suggested. Rather, analysts must consider whether the restriction is a limitation on the enjoyment of rights and should be handled by article 4, or an obstruction to their realization and thus is thus governed by article 2 (1). Taken all together, the terms of articles 2, 4, and 5 indicate that limitations on the enjoyment of rights are subject to the special standard articulated in article 4, while other kinds of restrictions are either forbidden (i.e., measures that destroy or extensively limit rights) or permissible under a lower threshold of tolerance (i.e., obstructing or forgoing the realization of rights).

6.4. Balancing Rights Claims: Beneficiaries, NGOs and the Rights of Others

At times, it will be reasonable to restrict nonprofit activities that are essential for the realization or enjoyment of social rights if those nonprofit activities simultaneously injure the rights of others. In the taxonomy of NGO

888 See Christine Kaufmann, 'The Covenants and Financial Crises' in Daniel Moeckli, Helen Keller and Corina Heri (eds), *The Human Rights Covenants at 50: Their Past, Present, and Future* (Oxford University Press 2018) 303-333, 318-319.

types, the most difficult scenario for a state to address is the regulation of minimum inappropriate NGOs. These are NGOs that are essential for the realization of the minimum essential levels of social rights because the state has not yet ensured them, however they do so by means that are inappropriate. Restricting these NGOs will limit the very nature of the beneficiaries' social rights, triggering scrutiny under article 4. Yet, the state must assess the injury that their inappropriate means are causing and protect the rights of beneficiaries and others from interference. For example, a minimum inappropriate NGO could provide emergency health services to a community that lacks access to any other medical services, but it may restrict access to these nonprofit services to only members of a particular religious group. Setting aside the legality of such private forms of discrimination, it is inappropriate for the state to tolerate a scenario wherein the discriminatory provision of services is the only reasonably available means of realization/enjoyment, particularly in the field of MELs. Article 2 (2) of the ICESCR, article 26 of the ICCPR, and still more instruments of international law strictly forbid such discriminatory practices in the public sphere, yet when private actors are fulfilling public obligations, their discriminatory practices become part of the public sphere such that states bear an obligation to correct it. In such a scenario, a state would bear competing obligations that derive from competing rights claims: the claims of the NGO's beneficiaries to the highest attainable health, versus the claim of those denied services on account of their religion to the equal enjoyment of their rights, and particularly the MELs thereof.

Resolving this problem from a perspective that is only concerned with the rights of NGOs is fairly straightforward. The ICCPR guarantees the NGO's right to free association, but this is not an absolute rights as it may be limited "by law" when it would be "necessary in a democratic society in the interest of … the protection of the rights and freedoms of others."[889] With this specific limitation built into the same provision that guarantees the right to free association, the state could reasonably restrict the activities of the inappropriate minimum NGO because its methods are discriminatory. However, since articles 5 (2) of both the ICCPR and the ICESCR require states to consider how their measures affect non-Covenant rights, a social rights perspective must be integrated into the associational rights approach.

From an integrative perspective, however, the problem becomes more complicated. The state is stuck between competing obligations: to permit

889 ICCPR art. 22 (1)-(2).

the NGO to operate for the sake of its associational rights, to enable the NGO to operate for the sake of those enjoying minimum essential levels, and to restrict the NGO in defense of those suffering from unlawful discrimination. Resolving this dilemma requires a nuanced approach when regulating inappropriate (minimum) NGOs that properly balances of competing rights claims made by the NGO, by those receiving medical services and by those suffering from discrimination.

6.4.1. The Permissibility of Limiting ESC Rights to Protect the Rights of Others

At first glance, the ICESCR may not appear to support balancing competing rights claims. The text of the general limitations clause, article 4, only permits limitations to social rights for the purpose of promoting general welfare. Promoting "public order", "national security", "public health or morals" or "the rights and freedoms of others" are not explicitly recognized as legitimate grounds for article 4 limitations. The *travaux préparatoires* reveal that a proposal to include most[890] of these alternative terms was rejected by the drafters in favor of the singular legitimate aim of promoting general welfare. Commentators have argued that this suggests that the term "general welfare" should be understood in the narrowest sense so as to exclude these other rejected terms.[891] Indeed, some representatives rejected the idea of limiting rights on the grounds of public order or public morals, in part because these were vague terms that were difficult to interpret and in part because it was difficult to imagine a scenario wherein social rights would need to be limited in order to secure public order or morals.[892]

But why shouldn't "general welfare in a democratic society" include protecting the rights and freedoms of others? The text of article 5 (1) indicates that the aim of destroying or extensively limiting Covenant rights is never a lawful or legitimate cause for any state or non-state actor. This implies that the state acts legitimately when it limits nonprofit activities that aim to destroy or extensively limit Covenant rights of others, even if those

890 All terms were rejected except for 'national security', which was never proposed. (Müller (2009) 573.).

891 Alston and Quinn (1987).

892 See Draft Interntional Covenants on Human Rights: Annotations, U.N. Secretary-General, U.N. General Assembly, UN Doc. A/2929 (UN 1955) paras. 51-52.

NGOs would have also contributed to the realization/enjoyment of ESC rights for their own beneficiaries. This supports the assertion that states may at times limit ESC rights in order to protect the rights of others.

A closer look at the drafting history also supports this interpretation. When proposed, the general limitations clause was understood to be important precisely because it provided states with a way to balance competing rights claims.[893] It is rather likely that the drafters voted to exclude an explicit reference to protecting the rights of others because they considered it an inherent aspect of "promoting the general welfare in a democratic society". It is clear from the *travaux préparatoires* that some state representatives considered limiting ESC rights in order to respect the rights of others as being an obvious limitation recognized within democratic societies.[894] One state representative went so far as to declare that respecting the rights of others was "obviously" a limitation upon all rights that was "perfectly clear and justified" and one that "arose naturally in democratic societies".[895] Others reasoned that limiting ESC rights in order to protect the rights of others was already inherently authorized by the provision that was eventually renumbered as article 5 (1).[896] It is not obvious from the drafting history that, in a scenario where one person's rights are destroyed or extensively limited in the course of another fulfilling his or her own rights, the state is prohibited from interfering in these private affairs for the purpose of balancing the competing rights claims – taking instead a Darwinian approach of 'survival of the fittest'.

Upon closer examination, it appears that those who opposed including "protecting the rights of others" into the general limitations clause as an independent ground for limitations either did not see the added benefit of explicitly doing so, or were concerned that mentioning it independently of promoting the general welfare would have undesirable consequences.

893 Summary Record of the 236th Meeting (1951) (see comments by Mrs. Roosevelt of the United States of America, which submitted the porposal for a general limitations clause in order to "restrict[] the rights of the individual only so far as was necessary to protect the rights of others".).

894 Summary Record of the 235th Meeting (1951) (see the comments of state representatives from France and Uruguay).

895 Summary Record of the 234th Meeting (1951) 21 (comments of the state representative from Uruguay, Mr. Ciasullo).

896 Summary Record of the 235th Meeting (1951) (see comments of Mr. Eustathiades of Greece, wherein he asserts that art. 18 (1) - which was later renumbered art. 5 (1) - recognized limitations based on respecting the rights of others. See also comments of Mr. Santa Cruz of Chile).

Most drafting members who opposed including "protecting the rights of others" represented the developing countries of that time, and in particular former colonial territories. They were concerned primarily with the right of peoples to self-determination. These representatives feared that the general limitations clause, and in particular limiting ESC rights for the purpose of protecting the rights of others, would totally invalidate the right of self-determination. Mr. Santa Cruz of Chile explained this sentiment during the 307th meeting of the Commission of Human Rights:

> There was one right, however, which would be completely nullified by that [general limitations] clause: the right of peoples and nations to self-determination... The Commission had recognized that that right included permanent sovereignty of the peoples over their natural wealth and resources and had gone on to say that in no case might a people be deprived of its own means of subsistence on the grounds of any rights that might be claimed by other States. A general limitations clause which stated that limitations could be imposed on that right on the grounds of recognition of and respect for the rights of others made that right completely inoperative, since it was obvious that there would always be a conflict of interests in that field between an underdeveloped country or colonial territory and the highly industrialized Powers which had gained control over their natural resources.[897]

It was not their assertion that the general welfare did not include protecting the rights of others, or that protecting the rights of others was not a legitimate and sometimes necessary reason for limiting ESC rights. Rather, members were concerned that explicitly enumerating the protection of the rights of others within a general limitations clause would establish it as an independent ground for limiting ESC rights that was *distinct from* – rather than part of – promoting the general welfare. They feared that such an interpretation would permit limitations that were potentially inconsistent with promoting the general welfare. State actions that limit or deprive the masses of very basic levels of realization and enjoyment in order to advance the realization of ESC rights for a few privileged individuals hardly resembles a measure that promotes the general welfare, and particularly within a post-colonial democratic society, although it technically protects the rights of others. There is no reason to conclude from the drafting history that promoting the general welfare within a democratic society excludes

897 Draft International Covenants on Human Rights: Report of the Third Committee (1955) 7.

protecting the rights of others whenever doing so would in fact promote the general welfare rather than undermine it.

In my view, the terms of the Covenant permit state measures that balance competing rights claims. In addition to prohibiting state acts that aim to destroy or extensive limit ESC rights, the second function of article 5 (1) is to allow states to balance claims arising from competing rights. By denying individuals the right to destroy or extensively limit the ESC rights of others, article 5 (1) implicitly legitimizes state measures that limit ESC rights in order to protect the rights of others. The *travaux préparatoires* support this assertion. Some drafting members expressed the view that article 5 (1) alone or in combination with articles 4 and 5 (2) allowed for a balancing of community interests and individual interests, as well as balancing the need to limit one right in order to protect another.

For example, while discussing how to balance the right to health against the right of individuals to be free of forced medical treatment, the drafting committee rejected a proposal that would have included a specific limitations clause to authorize the use of "compulsory medical treatments" but only when it was "provided by law and for reasons of public health", and only to the extent that such a law did not go "beyond the limits imposed by respect for the human person."[898] In rejecting the proposal, some members reasoned that articles 4 and 5 of the ICESCR, as well as article 7 of the ICCPR[899], were capable of protecting individuals against affronts to human dignity and prohibiting extremely inappropriate means of ensuring the right to health.[900] Likewise, in an earlier drafting meeting of the Commission on Human Rights, members expressed the view that article 5 (1) fully covered the issue of protecting the rights of others.[901] The suggestion here is that articles 4 and 5, independently or in conjunction with one another, adequately authorize and equip the state for the task of properly balancing competing interests and rights claims.

Whenever the interests of NGOs are in conflict with those of beneficiaries, a balance must be struck between them. The duty of the state to regu-

898 Draft International Covenants on Human Rights: Report of the Third Committee (1957) paras. 148, 156 (l).

899 Article 7 of the ICCPR prohibits torture, cruel, inhuman or degrading treatment or punishment, particularly in relation to conducting medical or scientific experiments without securing the subject's free consent.

900 Draft International Covenants on Human Rights: Report of the Third Committee (1957) para. 155.

901 Report to the Economic and Social Council on the Eigth Session of the Commission (1952) para. 157.

late NGOs for the protection of beneficiaries' rights must be weighed against the duty of the state to respect the rights of NGOs. In order to do so, courts should take into account the rights of both parties whenever it evaluates whether NGO laws are too restrictive. If courts seek to protect the rights of only one party, they may inadvertently sanction the deprivation of rights belonging to the other. Still, it is not evident from the text of the Covenant *how* and *to what extent* ESC rights should be limited, such that the rights of others are adequately protected. How should competing interests that arise from different human rights claims be addressed and prioritized? Beyond prioritizing the alleviation of total deprivation, it is far from clear how these claims should be balanced against one another. In practice, courts find some way to resolve compete rights claims, but not all courts take a beneficiary centered approach when considering restrictions placed on NGOs, sometimes even failing to do so when the NGOs pose a threat to the rights of their beneficiaries.

The following sub-section reviews two related cases from courts in Uganda in order to provide some examples of judicial efforts to balance competing rights claims between NGOs and their beneficiaries, and what has happened when they refrain from doing so entirely. These cases are not meant to provide a comprehensive review of case law in Uganda or to be representative of any jurisdiction in Africa. Rather, they are illustrative of two opposing judicial paths that courts can take: one in which the interests of beneficiaries are taken into account, and another in which they are not.

6.4.2. Balancing Competing Rights: Examples from the Courts of Uganda

Although the following decisions constitute separate cases, each involves the same NGO that is called Caring for Orphans, Widows and the Elderly (COWE). The government tried to shut down COWE on the basis that it had allegedly stolen money from its beneficiaries. Many complained that COWE was operating a large-scale fraudulent scheme in which funds collected from thousands of beneficiaries went missing, although it was never conclusively determined whether it was the NGO or its employees that were responsible for the missing funds.[902] Upon being informed of the allegations against COWE, the NGO Board – a public supervisory body in

902 *Balikowa & Anor v. Uganda*, 2012 UGHCCRD 2, Criminal Appeal No. 003 of 2011 (UGHC 2012) (Uganda); Richard M. Kavuma, 'Ugandan Financial Fraud Victims: Still Fighting for Compensation Years Later' *The Guardian* (Jan. 13,

Uganda – revoked the NGOs' registration without giving it an opportunity to be heard. COWE lodged two complaints: a first lawsuit in which it sought relief in the form of the reinstatement of its registration, and a second lawsuit for monetary damages. COWE won in both suits.

In the first case, *Kaggwa Andrew & 5 Others v. Honorable Minister of Internal Affairs*, the court found that the NGO Board's order to de-register COWE was null and void; it ordered the Board to reinstate COWE's registration.[903] The court reasoned that the Board's failure to afford COWE an opportunity to be heard before revoking its registration was patently unlawful because it violated COWE's fundamental right to due process. The court did not consider whether it was justifiable for the Board to act so hastily in revoking COWE's registration, likely due to the fact that the government did not make an appearance to defend itself or to provide any evidence. The court did not once take into account the state's obligation to protect the public or COWE's beneficiaries, or whether the Board's drastic measures were necessary in order to protect the public and the beneficiaries against substantial and irreparable injury. Without considering why the state limited the NGO's right to be heard, the court could not balance the competing interests. Thus, it predictably concluded that the state's decision to de-register COWE was unlawful because it clearly limited the NGO's right to be heard.

In the second case, *Cowe (U) & Cowe LTD v. Attorney General* the court took notice of the state's duty to protect the public against unscrupulous NGOs, but nonetheless failed to balance the competing interests.[904] Instead, it discussed at length the importance of COWE's right to a fair hearing, and offered only a mere acknowledgement of the state's duty to protect the public.

This time, the government made an appearance to defend itself. It argued that the NGO Board cancelled COWE's registration "on grounds of public interest" in order to protect the public against COWE's allegedly fraudulent conduct. While the court certainly recognized that the state was dealing with competing rights claims, it does not appear to have consid-

2016) <https://www.theguardian.com/global-development-professionals-network/2016/jan/13/ugandan-victims-still-fighting-for-compensation-years-late-cowe>.

903 *Kaggwa Andrew & 5 Others v. Hno Minister of Internal Affairs*, 2002 UGHC 21, HCT-00-CV-MC-0105 OF 2002 (UGHC 2002) (Uganda).

904 *Cowe (U) & Cowe Ltd v. Attorney General*, 2015 UGHCCD 78, HCT-00-CV-CS-O194-2004 (UGHC 2015) (Uganda).

ered whether and how the state's obligation to protect the public might limit COWE's procedural rights. The court writes,

> I agree with the submission of Counsel for the defendant that the NGO Board was exercising its duty in protecting the public when it revoked the plaintiff's certificate of registration and stopped all its operations. However, the NGO Board also owed a duty to the 1st plaintiff [COWE] in ensuring that it followed due process before such revocation in order to ensure fairness and control over any possible damage/loss that would most likely follow the revocation. When the NGO Board denied the 1st plaintiff its constitutional right to be heard before reaching the decision to revoke the Certificate of Registration, in my view, it breached the duty of care. The right to be heard is a fundamental procedure that any administrative body or tribunal is expected to observe and uphold; it embraces a whole notion of fair procedure and due process, and any decision reached in breach of this rule is void.[905]

The judge did not explain how she balanced the state's duty toward the NGO with its duty to protect the public, or whether the threat of harm to the NGO was greater than the treat of harm to the ESC rights of its "beneficiaries". She did not offer much any analysis as to how these duties relate to one another. At best, one can only speculate the court's reasoning was that although the state's duty of care to the public might have justified revoking COWE's registration and obstructing its operations, it did not justify the state's failure to follow proper procedures to ensure due process prior to taking such action. However, this says nothing of instances in which the state must act quickly to stop extraordinarily harmful activities of NGOs in order to protect the rights of beneficiaries, especially when the injury to beneficiaries could be as harmful as depriving them of their ability to realize or enjoy minimal levels of social rights.

It is clear that without a thorough consideration of the rights of beneficiaries to be protected against exploitation and abuse, the court can neither balance the rights involved nor begin to examine how the NGO's rights might be justifiably limited.

This was more or less a superficial acknowledgement of the rights of beneficiaries without affording them any weight in the balance. Having no counterweighing rights in the balance, the court understandably prioritized the fundamental right of COWE to be heard in all circumstances and ruled in COWE's favor. The court writes,

905 Ibid.

> The right to be heard is a fundamental procedure that any administrative body or tribunal is expected to observe and uphold; it embraces a whole notion of fair procedure and due process, and *any decision reached in breach of this rule is void.*[906]

In both cases, neither court thoroughly balanced the competing duties of the state, or engaged in a theoretical consideration of how the duty to protect the beneficiary might at times be jeopardized if the state were always and categorically bound to fulfill its duty to provide the NGO with an opportunity to be heard. The result was that the courts conceptualized an unqualified and absolute state duty to provide NGOs an opportunity to be heard.[907] I do not mean to suggest that the outcome of the case was incorrect; indeed, the right to be heard is of paramount importance. I only intend to illustrate that the courts' analyses lacked any meaningful consideration of another set of very important rights: the social rights of beneficiaries, which includes the right to be free from exploitation that interferes with their realization and enjoyment of an adequate standard of living. Of course, even if the court had taken a beneficiary-centered approach, it still may have come to the same conclusion. The point is, however, without having even considered the rights of beneficiaries, the possibility of protecting those rights was also lost.

6.5. Conclusion

In summary, restrictive NGO laws can be evaluated as limitations on ESC rights whenever it is reasonably foreseeable that they will bring about an interference with the enjoyment or realization of ESC rights. When NGOs

---

906 Ibid (emphasis added).

907 In yet another lawsuit involving COWE, an appellate court departed from this rigid view and concluded that COWE was not entitled to an opportunity to be heard before Uganda's central bank froze its financial accounts. The court was persuaded by a *prima facie* finding that COWE was acting criminally and that there was a substantial risk that allowing the NGO time to withdrawing its funds from the account would cause injury to depositors (i.e, its supposed 'beneficiaries'). (*Bank of Uganda v. Caring for Orphans, Widows & Elderly Ltd.*, 2009 UGCA 36, Civil Appeal No.35 of 2007 (UGCA 2009) (Uganda).) Although the *Kaggwa Andrew* and *Cowe (U)* courts strictly enforced the state's obligation to provide COWE with an opportunity to be heard, the *Bank of Uganda* court would not automatically impose procedural rules, emphasizing instead the need to guard against those who seek to abuse intended safeguards.

are essential for the realization or enjoyment of ESC rights – because the state is unwilling or unable to ensure the same – then it is reasonably foreseeable that restrictive NGO laws that obstruct these nonprofit activities will limit or even destroy ESC rights. As limitations on social rights, restrictive NGO laws that obstruct (minimum) substitutional and supplemental NGOs must be evaluated under article 4 because these NGOs are essential for the enjoyment of certain ESC rights. State restrictions on NGOs are permissible under article 4 when they are determined by law, they are consistent with the nature of the rights – suggesting they do not destroy the rights in question – and they promote the general welfare within a democratic society, which includes balancing rights claims and protecting the rights of others.

Protecting the rights of others is a legitimate state aim for limitations on ESC rights as long as doing so still promotes the general welfare within a democratic society. This means that states may limit nonprofit activities that are essential for the enjoyment of ESC rights in order to protect the rights of others or to protect non-ESC rights of beneficiaries against unscrupulous NGO activities. Moreover, article 2 (1) permits limiting the realization of social rights when NGOs would have done so through inappropriate means. In this way, articles 2 (1) and 4 permits state efforts to protect beneficiaries against inappropriate NGOs – even those that are essential for the realization and enjoyment of minimum essential levels.

Determining whether restrictive NGO laws are permissible is not an exact science. Judges will have to balance competing rights claims on a case-by-case basis. However, adjudicators should be wary of restrictive NGO laws that obstruct nonprofit activities when such activities are *essential* for the realization or enjoyment of ESC rights. Applying heightened level of scrutiny in these cases would be appropriate, such as the scrutiny required by article 4. In this way, a beneficiary-centered approach can have an insulating or legitimizing effect on the limitation of liberal rights claimed by NGOs,[908] and at the same time protect beneficiaries as well as the NGOs that help them against obstructive state interference.

908 See Marius Pieterse, 'The Legitimizing/Insulating Effect of Socio-Economic Rights' 22 Canadian Journal of Law & Society/La Revue Canadienne Droit et Société 1 (2007) (arguing that states can use socio-economic rights to curb or limit liberal rights (e.g., freedom to contract or private law), thereby ensuring all individuals in a society have meaningful access to social protection.).

7. Conclusion: NGO Regulations and Aid Efficacy

All over the world, NGOs have seen a dramatic growth in their numbers in recent decades. They were celebrated as a promising supplement to official development aid and as a more direct means for funders to reach beneficiaries. However, anti-NGO sentiments have been steadily emerging. One scholar described this growing critical voice as "a movement" and "a force with which to be reckoned".[909]Perhaps unsurprisingly, governments across the globe have also become wary of NGOs, and in particular of their financial dependence on foreign entities, which often includes foreign states. There is some credence to these concerns. Despite all the social development efforts that have been made over the course of decades, progress has been rather slow in Africa. The reasons for this are varied and multifaceted. Yet, what is certain is that NGOs and state efforts to restrict them are only one part of a larger and more complex process directed toward social development and social welfare. It is worthwhile seeing the bigger picture as well. To that end, this chapter does two things. First, it summarizes the theoretical and doctrinal findings of this dissertation regarding the manner in which restrictive NGO regulations can interfere with the social rights of beneficiaries. Second, it seeks to contextualize the way in which restrictive NGO laws interfere with social rights by asking the much broader questions that is of relevance to the social wellbeing of beneficiaries: why hasn't social development worked in Africa?

Regulating NGOs for the Protection of Social Rights

A legal trend has been developing across Africa that aims to restrict civil society organizations and NGOs.[910] Many express their concern that the cornerstones of a free civil society – namely the rights to associate and speak freely – are coming under attack. A less common concern among scholars is that such state measures might also threaten the social rights of beneficiaries. These stakes are even higher in least developed countries – most of which are located in sub-Saharan Africa – where restrictive NGO

909 Jenkins (2012) 464.
910 International Center of Not-for-Profit Law, 'Introductory Overview' (2010) 7-8.

laws are likely to push people even further into poverty and exacerbate their vulnerability. Consider the case of Angola, which was home to 462 NGOs by 2008,[911] and which was ranked in 2015 as the least sustainable environment in sub-Saharan Africa for civil society organizations.[912] Civil society organizations from Angola have been concerned that the government's harassment and intimidation of human rights defenders undermined the defense of social rights.[913] The ESCR Committee shared this concern in its Concluding Observations for Angola in 2008 where it "urge[d] the State party to establish legal guarantees to enable NGOs to carry out their activities for the promotion and protection of economic, social and cultural rights without arbitrary interferences."[914] The Committee does not, however, make the link between the state's Covenant obligations toward beneficiaries and its treatment of NGOs that are involved in the realization and enjoyment of ESC rights.

A human rights analysis of restrictive NGO laws should focus on the social wellbeing of beneficiaries, especially when least developed countries are concerned. In this regard, the ICESCR guarantees rights related to social security, health, education, housing and an adequate standard of living. While these rights are enshrined in the Covenant, giving them the status of legal rights, their full realization requires a great deal of effort and resources on the part of states. This is particularly challenging for least developed countries, where the availability of resources is rather limited. It is for this reason that the Covenant qualifies the corresponding obligations of states. In essence, states are required to do all of and only that which they are capable of doing in order to bring about the realization of social rights. To this aim, article 2 (1) of the ICESCR imposes upon states a general obligation to use all appropriate means to the maximum of their available resources. This means that a state that lacks the capacity to reach a par-

---

911 Core Document Forming Part of the Reports of States Parties: Angola, International Human Rights Instruments, United Nations, HRI/CORE/AGO/2008 (UN 2008) para. 78.

912 United States Agency for International Development (USAID), *The 2014 CSO Sustainability Index: Central and Eastern Europe and Eurasia* (2014) xvii.

913 'Committee on Economic, Social and Cultural Rights Hears from Human Rights Institutions and Civil Society from the United Kingdom, the Former Yugoslav Republic of Macedonia, and Angola.' *United Nations Office of the High Commission for Human Rights* (13 June 2016) <https://www.ohchr.org/EN/NewsEvents/Pages/DisplayNews.aspx?NewsID=20087&LangID=E>.

914 Concluding Observations on the Third Period Report on Angola (2008) para. 13.

ticular level of social rights achievement will not have violated the Covenant if it can prove "that every effort has been made to use all the resources at its disposition".[915] The obligation to use the maximum of available resources implies that a distinction must be made between states that are unwilling to fulfill their obligations, and those that are unable to do so. Similarly, the Committee notes that "[a] State which is unwilling to use the maximum of its available resources for the realization of the right to health is in violation of its obligations", rather than one that merely lacks the resources to do so. [916]

Moreover, states are under no obligation to achieve full realization immediately. Instead, article 2 (1) of the ICESCR only requires that they take steps in that direction with the view of achieving full realization progressively. This, however, is far from a license for states to circumvent their obligations. Indeed, the ESCR Committee has cautioned that article 2 (1) cannot be construed in such a manner as to render it devoid of all meaning or consequence.[917] The term "progressive" favors the speedy realization of rights, such that states are required "to move as expeditiously and effectively as possible toward that goal."[918] To fulfill this obligation, states must "take steps" that are "deliberate, concrete and targeted" through the use of "all appropriate means, including … legislative measures". [919] These steps must be taken in "good faith".[920]

On the one hand, the language of progressive realization provides the states with some leeway to achieve social rights incrementally over time. On the other hand, the call for using all appropriate means and the maximum of available resources indicates that states may not delay the realization of social rights and that they must do all that they can do to achieve that aim. In this sense, the social rights obligation of states is a dynamic concept that grows over time as though it were an expanding horizon that depends on a country's given circumstances. How, then, should the state's

915 General Comment No. 3: The Nature of States Parties' Obligations (1990) para. 10.

916 General Comment No. 14: The Right to the Highest Attainable Standard of Health (2000) para. 47.

917 General Comment No. 3: The Nature of States Parties' Obligations (1990) para. 9.

918 Ibid; General Comment No. 12: The Right to Adequate Food (1999) para. 14.

919 General Comment No. 3: The Nature of States Parties' Obligations (1990) paras. 2-3.

920 General Comment No. 15: The Right to Water (2003) paras. 40-41.

social rights obligations be calculated when NGOs with external funding sources enter into the picture?

In least developed countries, such NGOs do not draw on the state's limited resources because they depend mostly on foreign funders. Consequently, their nonprofit activities can expand the realization of social rights beyond the state's own duty horizon. Such NGOs could be referred to as *supplemental* NGOs because their activities supplement that of the state. In another scenario, nonprofits can realize social rights within the state's duty horizon – meaning that they achieve a level of realization that the state is capable of achieving, and therefore is obliged to achieve. These NGOs can be called *substitutional* NGOs because they substitute for the state by fulfilling the state's outstanding social rights obligations. In each scenario, the contours of the state's social rights obligations are shaped by the fact that these NGOs are stepping in to realize social rights that the state cannot – or simply does not – ensure.

The manner in which nonprofit activities can affect the state's social rights obligations depends on whether the nonprofit activities are essential for the realization or enjoyment of social rights, or for the fulfillment of the state's social rights obligations. When nonprofit activities are a significant way for people to realize and enjoy their social rights, they become part of a triangular relationship that involves the state and beneficiaries. This triangular relationship has a legal character: The state owes social rights obligations to beneficiaries whose rights are in turn realized through nonprofit activities. The task that remains is to clarify the terms of the legal relationship between nonprofits and the state.

Nonprofits that substitute for the state in the fulfillment of social rights obligations are those that are essential for a level of realization that the state is obliged to ensure but nonetheless does not ensure. In such a case, the state's duty to fulfill social rights requires not only that it permits and facilitates nonprofit activities, but also that it ensures their replacement if these activities were to come to an end. If, on the other hand, nonprofit activities are supplementing for the state in that they achieve a level of realization that lies beyond the state's duty horizon, then the state's duty to respect social rights requires only that it permits and facilitates such supplemental nonprofit activities, without the additional requirement of ensuring their continuation. The reason for this is that the state was never required to achieve the same level of realization reached by supplemental nonprofits. Finally, a state's duty to protect the rights of beneficiaries against third party interference requires that it takes reasonable measures to ensure that NGOs are not harming the rights of their beneficiaries, or – under separate legal grounds – the rights of others.

From a regulatory perspective, this means that states must provide some oversight to ensure that beneficiaries are not harmed or exploited by unscrupulous NGOs or scammers posing as NGOs. Yet, states cannot exert so much regulatory control that beneficial nonprofit activities are hampered or obstructed. This balance is rather difficult to define *a priori* by law because it depends on a variety of political, social and economic factors. Rather, states must enjoy a certain degree of discretion in determining how best to regulate NGOs while also respecting the social rights of beneficiaries. However, when state measures that affect NGOs are so restrictive as to constitute limitations on ESC rights, these state actions must comply with the rules on limitations. There will undoubtedly be times when it is appropriate for states to restrict NGOs, even if doing so would limit the enjoyment or realization of social rights for their beneficiaries. This would be the case, for example, when an NGO is harming one group in order to benefit another. In these scenarios, however, the state's authority to limit the social rights of beneficiaries is subject to certain limitations. Articles 2 (1), 4 and 5 of the ICESCR provide guidance on when and how the state may limit Covenant rights.

Article 4 is of particular interest because it is the Covenant's general limitations clause. According to its terms, states may limit Covenant rights only when such limitations are determined by law, serve the general welfare and remain consistent with the nature of the rights being affected. Although article 4 permits limitations to social right under limited circumstances, it does not address the limitation of *NGO-provided* rights. In fact, it makes explicit reference to rights provided by states, thereby appearing to exclude from its scope of application the limitation of rights provided by non-state actors. However, such a conclusion would lead to results that are incompatible with the object and purpose of the Covenant: depending on which perspective one takes, this would mean either that states may *never* limit rights provided by NGOs or that they can *always* limit rights provided by NGOs. Instead, when NGOs function as either a substitute for the state in the fulfillment of state obligations or as a supplement of the state in the realization of social rights, it seems fair and reasonable to apply article 4 analogously to any state measures that would limit the social rights *provided by NGOs*. The drafting history of ICESCR also supports such an analogous treatment of article 4.

The lawfulness of state measures that restrict nonprofit activities that are essential for the *realization* of social rights but not for their enjoyment are evaluated under a different legal standard. Such nonprofit activities are preparatory in nature: they do not result in the immediate attainment of rights, but they set up the preconditions that are necessary for those rights to be realized and therefore enjoyed. An example of nonprofit activities that are essential only for realization would be training teachers or advocating for safer health care standards. Direct service provision, on the other hand, could constitute an activity that is essential for the enjoyment of social rights. Article 2 (1) indicates when the state may restrict nonprofit activities that are essential only for realization. The state's power to restrict such nonprofit activities is limited to instances when nonprofit activities employ inappropriate means. Article 4 would not be applicable in this case because it only refers to the *limitations* of social rights, which must first be enjoyed before they can be limited.

Adjudicating the Lawfulness of NGO Laws

The main argument of this dissertation has been that restrictive NGO laws can become incompatible with the states' social rights obligations whenever NGOs are essential for the realization or enjoyment of social rights. However, one might wonder about the practical significance of these findings, which lies in their potential application in courts of law. Judicial evaluations of how governments treat or regulate NGOs that are essential for the enjoyment of social rights, or for the fulfillment of a state's social rights obligations, should address the issue of whether the state is circumventing or neglecting its social rights obligations by restricting nonprofit activities. One way to do this is to use a heightened level of scrutiny to evaluate restrictive NGO laws whenever courts determine that the nonprofit activities being restricted are essential for the enjoyment of social rights. Restricting such essential activities will result in limitations to the enjoyment of social rights, and whenever states limit the enjoyment of social rights, the standard established under article 4 of the ICESCR applies. This standard is a form of heightened scrutiny: governments must demonstrate that restricting nonprofit activities that are essential for the enjoyment of social rights is *necessary* for the promotion of the general welfare, and they must ensure that such restrictive measures remain consistent with the nature of the social rights being affected. On the other hand, if the realization of social rights is being limited rather than their enjoyment, then adjudicators should apply a different standard of scrutiny, which is based on article 2 (1) of the ICESCR. The article 2 (1) standard permits states to restrict or obstruct nonprofit activities that are essential for the realization of social rights only when such activities employ inappropriate means.

Admittedly, the practical utility of some of these legal findings will depend on politically determined facts. For example, whether an NGO is a substitutional nonprofit entity that can benefit from the protection of heightened judicial scrutiny depends on whether the state is obliged to achieve the level of realization that the NGO has already achieved through its activities, which in turn depends on the predominantly political question of whether the state is in fact using the maximum of its available resources. However, this is important mostly for cases in which the legal question is whether the state must replace lost nonprofit activities. If the only legal issue to be resolved is whether the state must permit an NGO's operations, then a court only needs to certify that the nonprofit entity satisfies the qualifications for being recognized as a *supplemental* NGO. These qualifications are less strict because they require merely that the NGO is essential for the realization/enjoyment of social rights, but not necessarily the fulfillment of the state's social rights obligations. This determination does not depend on the predominantly political question of whether the state is capable of achieving the level of realization that the NGO has already achieved, but rather on the factual question of whether the state is indeed ensuring the same level of achievement for beneficiaries – regardless of whether it is required to do so. If NGOs are providing services that the state simply does not provide, and if their activities are both appropriate and essential for their enjoyment or realization, then these nonprofits are generally protected against obstructive state measure, unless the state can justify its restrictive measures under article 4 of the ICESCR. In such a case, a court could apply heightened scrutiny without needing to take on the problematic role of asking and answering political questions.

While this dissertation began with an observation about LDCs in sub-Saharan African states, its doctrinal findings are generalizable to other regions and other states because it relies predominantly on international human rights law. The regulation of nonprofit providers in the global North could be examined using the same analytical framework. For example, although nonprofits may not be essential for the fulfillment of states' social rights obligations in industrialized welfare states, supplemental NGOs – those that provide services beyond that which the state is required to ensure – are still essential for the realization and enjoyment of certain social rights. This is true because the full realization of social rights is an expanding, dynamic ideal rather than a fixed, predetermined level of achievement. There is no cap on how far social rights achievements can go, thus supplemental NGOs exist even in the wealthiest of states. These NGOs should also fall under the protection of the ICESCR, and courts should ensure that state efforts to restrict or obstruct them are subject to the appropriate level of scrutiny.

The aim of this doctoral thesis has been to examine in a systematic manner the legal consequences of restrictive NGO laws on the social rights of beneficiaries. This has been a primarily doctrinal and theoretical contribution to the legal scholarship. In reality, however, the enjoyment and realization of social rights through nonprofit activities both succeeds and fails within the messiness of the everyday life as well as the larger political, economic and social contexts of developing countries. The remainder of this closing chapter is an attempt to contextualize the work of this dissertation within the larger framework of foreign aid, its processes and its efficacy *vis-à-vis* the enjoyment and realization of social rights through nonprofit means.

Foreign Aid and its Impact on the Capabilities of NGOs

Although massive amounts of foreign aid have been directed toward African states, social development indicators continue to rank African peoples among the world's most impoverished.[921] Even some long-term and targeted aid programs have not been effective in reducing poverty on the continent.[922] Likewise, even though some African governments depend heavily on foreign aid,[923] whether foreign assistance has been effective for

921 World Development Indicators Database, Gross Domestic Product 2015 (World Bank 2015) <http://databank.worldbank.org/data/download/GDP.pdf> (African countries are among poorest nations; Africa ranks as the poorest region of the world).

922 For instance, in evaluating the outcome of the International Monetary Fund's (IMF) poverty reduction strategy in Sub-Saharan Africa over the last fifteen years, one report found that while the wealthiest Africans got wealthier, the IMF's poverty reduction strategy "neither reduced poverty headcount, nor raised the income share of the poorest quintile". (Daouda Sembene, International Monetary Fund, *Poverty, Growth, and Inequality in Sub-Saharan Africa: Did the Walk Match the Talk under the Prsp Approach?* (IMF 2015) 6 <https://www.imf.org/external/pubs/ft/wp/2015/wp15122.pdf>.).

923 By 2015, fourteen countries received foreign aid that amounted to 10 percent of their Gross National Income (GNI). Five of those countries received aid that amounted to at least a fifth of their GNI, and aid received by one country amounted to more than half its GNI. (Geographical Distribution of Financial

social development continues to be a controversial topic that is subject to mixed criticism.[924]

In terms of social welfare, the lowest performing states are also characterized by their high reliance on foreign aid.[925] African countries that rely heavily on foreign aid – namely Ethiopia, Burundi, Rwanda, Senegal and Zambia – exhibit low and falling life expectancy, poor secondary school enrolment, relatively weak states and low levels of public spending on health and education.[926] On the other hand, countries that rely more extensively on tax revenues (Kenya, Namibia, South Africa and Zimbabwe) and mineral exports (Botswana) than on foreign aid are the best performing welfare regimes in sub-Saharan Africa.[927] While it is always difficult to determine causality and its direction, many explanations have been offered to make sense of this low return on aid.[928]

Some critics offer structural arguments by pointing out the unfavorable financial or economic conditions of African countries. One study of the least developed African countries asserts that doubling oversees development aid only hurts lesser developed countries.[929] This is because each country has a specific absorption capacity for aid, beyond which additional assistance can overwhelm existing projects.[930] On the other hand, LDCs in

Flows to Developing Countries, Development Co-operation Report, and International Development Statistics, Net ODA Received (% of GNI) (Development Assistance Committee of the Organisation for Economic Co-operation and Development <www.oecd.org/dac/stats/idsonline>.).

924 See Evelyn Wamboye, Abel Adekola and Bruno S. Sergi, 'Foreign Aid, Legal Origin, Economic Growth and Africa's Least Developed Countries', 14 Progress in Development Studies 335 (2014).

925 See Ian Gough and Miriam Abu Sharkh, 'Financing Welfare Regimes: Mapping Heterogeneous Revenue Structures' 20 International Journal of Social Welfare 280 (2011) 286; Gough and Abu Sharkh (2010).

926 Gough and Abu Sharkh (2011) 286-287 (comparing revenue sources); Gough and Abu Sharkh (2010) (comparing welfare regime performances). However, while Ghana also relies heavily on foreign aid, it performs better than its peers because it benefits from higher literacy rates among its youth. (Ibid.).

927 Gough and Abu Sharkh (2011) 286-287 (comparing revenue sources); Gough and Abu Sharkh (2010) (comparing welfare regime performances).

928 See generally, Bräutigam and Knack (2004).

929 Wamboye, Adekola and Sergi (2014) 351.

930 Elliot R. Morss, 'Institutional Destruction Resulting from Donor and Project Proliferation in Sub-Saharan African Countries' 12 World Development 465 (1984).

Africa carry significant debt,[931] which can undermine their progress. In many states, more domestic expenditure is dedicated to repaying foreign debts than funding health care or other essential services.[932] Blaming poor governance and corruption, other analysts point to the vices associated with receiving "free" money. Proponents of this argument claim that direct aid fosters corruption in governments and has led to the mass misappropriation of aid money rather than to the advancement of social welfare outcomes in Africa.[933]

Some direct their criticism toward foreign donors, asserting that the manner in which they have influenced and directed development programming has undermined the efforts made by developing states to promote welfare within their countries.[934] The problem is not so much foreign aid in and of itself, but rather the *way* in which foreign aid is delivered.[935] In one example, the UN Committee on the Rights of the Child (CRC) expressed its concern that aid money from the United Kingdom was funding private, for-profit providers of primary education in developing countries. The Committee cautioned, "Rapid increase in the number of such schools may contribute to sub-standard education, less investment in free and quality public schools, and deepened inequalities in the recipient countries", and urged the UK to "ensure that its international development cooperation supports the recipient States in guaranteeing the right to free compulsory primary education for all." [936]

Furthermore, foreign donors are criticized for exerting too much thematic control over development projects. For example, Lisa McIntosh

931 Between 2011 and 2012, the average external debt stock of LDCs in Africa was 30% of GNI, with the range extending from 93% in Sao Tome and Principe to 18% in Rwanda and Guinea. (United Nations Under-Secretary-General and High Representative for LDCs, LLDCs and SIDS, *Extreme Poverty Eradication in the Least Developed Countries and the Post-2015 Development Agenda* (2014) 74, Table A9.).

932 Nancy Erbe and others, 'Negotiating and Mediating Peace in Africa' 9 Pepperdine Dispute Resolution Law Journal 457 (2008).

933 See, e.g., Dambisa Moyo, *Dead Aid: Why Aid Is Not Working and How There Is Another Way for Africa* (Allen Lane 2009) 52-57.

934 See, e.g., Tomaševski (2001).

935 Bräutigam and Knack (2004) (finding that "high levels of aid are associated with declines in the quality of governance" in sub-Saharan Africa but recommending that "the current system of institutions and incentives must be changed" rather than reducing overall levels of aid.).

936 Concluding Observations on the Fifth Periodic Report of the United Kingdom of Great Britain and Northern Ireland, U.N. Committee on the Rights of the Child, U.N. Doc. CRC/C/GBR/CO/5 (UN 2016) para. 16-17.

Sundstrom argues that foreign assistance to NGOs in Russia was much more likely to be ineffective when it was employed to promote norms that were specific to special societal contexts rather than universally embraced norms.[937] This is a particular concern for NGOs that receive official aid – that is, funds for foreign governments or other political bodies.[938] Michael Edwards and David Hulme find that although such an arrangement does not necessarily lead to foreign thematic control of NGO programming, the risk still exists and can be managed through a partnership approach to funding.[939]

Donors are also scrutinized for setting up inadequate safeguards – or none at all – against the potentially negative consequences of their aid. This line criticism relies in part on instances in which donors have failed to secure their funds against fraud. For example, fraud cost Britain 1.04 million pounds in 2015 to 2016.[940] Foreign donors are blamed for funding projects in developing countries without adequately considering the negative consequences that intended beneficiaries may have to face. For instance, although private for-profit schools provide education for a "low" fee, one commentator argues that the use of aid money to privatize education in developing countries could deepen inequalities along lines of class, gender and able-bodiedness: very poor families would only send some of their children to school, to the detriment of girls and disabled children, while families who are even poorer would be totally underserved.[941] Moreover, in some instances, the quality of services funded by foreign donors has been challenged, such that the very efficacy of their programs is called

937 Lisa McIntosh Sundstrom, 'Foreign Assistance, International Norms, and NGO Development: Lessons from the Russia Campaign' 59 International Organization 419 (2005).

938 Michael Edwards and David Hulme, 'Too Close for Comfort? The Impact of Official Aid on Nongovernmental Organizations' 24 World Development 961 (1996).

939 Ibid 969.

940 Tom Esslemont, ''Tougher Scrutiny' of Britain's Aid Spending Sees Steep Rise in Fraud Bill' *Thomas Reuters Foundation* (Sept. 22, 2016) <http://news.trust.org/item/20160922131353-jxpbs>.

941 Prachi Srivastava, 'Low-Fee Private Schooling: What Do We Really Know? Prachi Srivastava Responds to the Economist' (Oxfam Aug. 11, 2015) <http://oxfamblogs.org/fp2p/its-complicated-or-low-fee-private-schooling-what-do-we-really-know/>. See also, Oliver Balch, 'UN Criticises UK for Spending Aid Money on for-Profit Private Schools' *The Guardian* <https://www.theguardian.com/sustainable-business/2016/jun/14/un-criticises-uk-government-millions-aid-money-private-schools-developing-countries>.

into question.[942] For example, the United Kingdom's Independent Commission for Aid Impact announced in 2012 that while the UK had substantially expanded school enrolment in three East African countries by issuing 1 billion pounds of bilateral aid, "the quality of education being provided to most children is so low that a large majority is failing to achieve basic literacy and numeracy."[943]

Advocates of locally-led development have criticized the top-down structure and professionalization of the aid industry, and have urged donors to put people and beneficiaries at the center of aid.[944] Although it is now widely acknowledged that there is a great need for aid at the community level and that more projects should ensure local participation, donors continue to pour their funds into large international NGOs. Between 2010 and 2014, local NGOs across the globe received only 1.6% of all humanitarian aid given to NGOs during the same period.[945] Critiques continue to urge greater support for local NGOs, arguing that Big Aid is part of the problem.[946]

Some commentators have pointed to the tendency of donors to impose conditionalities upon aid recipients.[947] This was similarly the case with development loans. During the 1980s, structural adjustment programs required recipients of development loans to cut social welfare spending and

942 E.g., Srivastava (2015).

943 DFID's Education Programmes in Three East African Countries, Independent Commission for Aid Impact, (UK 2012) 1 <https://icai.independent.gov.uk/wp-content/uploads/DFIDs-Education-Programmes-in-Three-East-African-Countries-Final-Report-3.pdf>.

944 *The World Humanitarian Summit: Putting People at the Centre*, ACT Alliance (2015) <http://actalliance.org/wp-content/uploads/2015/12/J3734-ACT-Alliance-position-paper-for-World-Humanitarian-Summit_AW.pdf>.

945 *Focus on Local Actors, the Key to Humanitarian Effectiveness*, International Federation of Red Cross and Red Crescent Societies, (World Disaster Report, 2015) 105 <https://ifrc-media.org/interactive/wp-content/uploads/2015/09/1293600-World-Disasters-Report-2015_en.pdf>.

946 Bibi van der Zee, 'Less Than 2% of Humanitarian Funds 'Go Directly to Local NGOs'' *The Guardian* (Oct. 16, 2015) <https://www.theguardian.com/global-development-professionals-network/2015/oct/16/less-than-2-of-humanitarian-funds-go-directly-to-local-ngos>; Imogen Wall, ''We Are Demanding Change': The Somali Woman Taking on International NGOs' *The Guardian* (Mar. 21, 2016) <https://www.theguardian.com/global-development-professionals-network/2016/mar/21/degan-ali-somali-woman-taking-on-the-humanitarian-system>.

947 Bräutigam and Knack (2004) 261-262; Moyo (2009) 38-44.

liberalize markets from government interference.[948] Such conditionalities challenge the autonomy of African states, rendering their policymakers nearly powerless to prioritize development projects in a manner that they see fit. Some argue that policy-oriented conditionalities led African state officials to become "passive", since the prospect of receiving substantial aid packages created "negative incentives to disagree with the donors".[949]

Some conditionalities require the acceptance of foreign technical assistance, which undermines the transfer of governance skills to African governments because it "limits a central (or local) government's ability to learn skills for more effectively managing and administering."[950] Consequently, a decline in government capacity and the elimination of public subsidies has led to a reduction in social services, especially in education and health care, as well as intensified food insecurities. [951] This has generated more space for the expansion of non-state social provision.

Foreign aid dependency, especially when perpetuated through the extensive imposition of conditionalities, tends to undercut democratic participation within receiving states. One writer describes aid dependency as "a state of mind, where aid recipients lose their capacity to think for themselves and thereby relinquish control."[952] When aid dependency systematically inflates the political influence of foreign donors within a receiving state, the legitimacy and competence of state bodies may be called into question. Within an international political system based on the primacy of nation-states, a global developmental approach that undermines the political capacity and legitimacy of a nation-state seems to cut against developmental aims by perpetuating dysfunctionality and asymmetry.

Still others draw upon all of the aforementioned criticisms to contextualize NGOs within international and historical governance practices, so as

948 J. Barry Riddell, 'Things Fall Apart Again: Structural Adjustment Programmes in Sub-Saharan Africa' 30 The Journal of Modern African Studies 53 (1992) 57-58. See also Joel R. Paul, 'Do International Trade Institutions Contribute to Economic Growth and Development?' 44 Virginia Journal of International Law 285 (2003) 319 ("The International Monetary Fund and foreign banks often insist that as a condition for further loans, developing countries must cut social services to balance their budgets, accelerate privatization, and eliminate trade barriers").

949 Bräutigam and Knack (2004) 261-262.

950 Ibid.

951 See Riddell (1992) 58.

952 Bräutigam and Knack (2004) 257 (quoting Rehman Sobhan).

to exam critically the "aspirational capabilities" of NGOs.[953] Reflecting upon NGO interventions that address HIV/AIDS in Africa, Hakan Seckinelgin writes,

> In short, without a doubt there are interesting and effective interventions implemented by NGOs. However, in many of these instances these interventions are based on immediate relief and are not able to engage with long-term issues. Furthermore, they are conditioned by changing international funding interests and frames. Therefore, while it is clear that that relief is an important issue, at present these NGO interventions are providing fragmented relief with a short-term vision based on the international governance of the disease that is not able to engage with the sociocultural conditions of the disease.[954]

Others are far more critical of the economic and political environment within which NGOs operate. Alan Fowler posits that the world presently operates within a global system of social welfare that is misaligned with the overarching values of social welfare.[955] In this regard, he asserts sharply that the function of aid has become to "contribute to the security of capital investment and to the stability of Southern regimes which maintain the environment necessary to produce returns on them."[956] Fowler refers to this phenomenon as the "globalization of social welfare" and places the onus on NGOs in Africa to "reappraise their long-term strategies and role within the continent", "renegotiate their position with governments" and "recognize that in global terms their resources are negligible in relation to the forces that cause and maintain poverty".[957] Similarly, Terje Tvedt criticizes NGO supporters for neglecting to consider how global power relations and structural forces frame the organizational landscape of NGOs.[958] He proposes that NGO scholarship should focus on power and integration through a universal analytical approach that he terms "the new interna-

953 Hakan Seckinelgin, 'Who Can Help People with HIV/AIDS in Africa? Governance of HIV/AIDS and Civil Society' 15 Voluntas 287 (2004).

954 Ibid 301-302.

955 Fowler (1995).

956 Ibid 66.

957 Ibid 67.

958 Terje Tvedt, *Angels of Mercy or Development Diplomats?: NGOs & Foreign Aid* (Africa World Press 1998).

tional social system", which reflects the interaction between foreign donors, states, development NGOs and beneficiaries.[959]

Likewise, albeit from historical and post-colonial perspectives, Issa Shivji argues that the shortcomings of development aid in Africa, and particularly of foreign NGOs in Africa, are contemporary symptoms of an older colonial ailment.[960] He contends NGOs and the donor community promote African development and globalization without critically examining the African context. Shivji posits that globalism is a modern articulation of neo-imperialism, that—in Africa—it relies upon existing political and economic legacies of colonialism, and that it aims to advance a neo-liberal agenda for the benefit of wealthier nations and individuals. While encouraging NGOs to engage African intellectuals in academic discourse, Shivji poses the thought-provoking question: "But how can you make poverty history without understanding the 'history of poverty'?"[961] Others have echoed this concern, arguing that NGOs must "think outside existing institutional culture… mainly by acknowledging that the causes of poverty and vulnerability must be understood, and that the study of power relations becomes a key part of the analysis."[962]

Makau Mutua argues that international human rights NGOs are "ideological analogues, both in theory and in method, of the traditional civil rights organizations that preceded them in the West", and stresses that western industrialized nations provide the moral, financial and social sources upon which INGOs continue to draw support.[963] The Boards of INGOs, he contends, are "dominated by Westerns", and that a "tapestry of social and business ties, drawn from leading Americans who believe in liberal values and their internationalization through the human rights regime, underlines the agenda of INGOs."[964] Mutua delivers a damning conclusion and urges readers to initiate in earnest a postliberal society. He writes,

959 Terje Tvedt, 'Development NGOs: Actors in a Global Civil Society or in a New International Social System?' 13 Voluntas 363 (2002).

960 Shivji (2006).

961 Ibid 43.

962 *Focus on Culture and Risk,* International Federation of Red Cross and Red Crescent Societies, (World Disaster Report, 2014) 94 <http://www.ifrc.org/Global/Documents/Secretariat/201410/WDR%202014.pdf>.

963 Mutua, 'Human Rights International NGOs: A Critical Evaluation' 151, 153.

964 Ibid 154-155.

> The facade of neutrality, the fiction that INGOs do not seek the establishment of a particular political system, in this case, a liberal democracy, must be abandoned immediately. No one should be expected to believe that the scheme of rights promoted by INGOs does not seek to replicate a vision of society based on the industrial democracies of the North. Only after openly conceding that INGOs indeed have a specific political agenda can discussions be had about the wisdom, problems, and implications for the advocacy of such values.[965]

This critical perspective is also reflected in the domestic laws that restrict and target human rights NGOs. Consider, as well, Ethiopia's restrictive NGO law,[966] which operates by foreignizing NGOs that most people would normally think of as Ethiopian organizations. It does this by categorizing all NGOs receiving more than 10% of their funds from foreign sources as foreign entities, without regard to any other factor. For example, an NGO run entirely by and for Ethiopian citizens and receives 85% of its funding from domestic sources would still be considered a foreign NGO, and would thus be barred from promoting human rights. Painting otherwise apparently local NGOs as foreign entities offers political elites an ideological advantage with political currency in post-colonial societies. It allows African governments to position themselves dialectically as the protectors of state sovereignty and national independence in opposition to agents of foreign interests (i.e., the NGOs), who are suspected of following neo-imperialistic agendas on behalf of foreign handlers.

All together, these writers represent a critical voice that contextualizes NGOs within larger systems and structures in order to examine their shortcomings and capabilities. They remind us that any understanding of the ways in which NGOs can realize or interfere with the social rights of their beneficiaries is incomplete without considering this larger context. Despite these complexities, we should remain mindful of the wellbeing of beneficiaries, who are often among the most vulnerable members of society in terms of social development and social wellbeing. This could not be more urgent than at a time when space for civil society continues to shrink across the globe. While states must certainly be held accountable for the fulfillment of their social rights obligations to the poor who live within their territories, we should not allow the ideal of an international order consisting of equally powerful and sovereign nation-states lock our analysis

965 Ibid 159.
966 Charities and Societies Proclamation No 621/2009 (Ethiopia).

into a rigid focus on the territorial obligations of states, such that we fail to acknowledge when other states and non-state actors are responsible for social harms. A beneficiary-centered approach encourages a critical perspective by keeping what is important at the forefront of analysis. In this way, the fate of NGOs, states and others remain firmly tied to the wellbeing of the poor.

8. References

Table of Cases

African Commission on Human and Peoples' Rights

Civil Liberties Organisation V. Nigeria, Comm. No. 129/94 (ACmHPR 1995)

Free Legal Assistance Group and Others V. Zaire (Drc), Comm. Nos. 25/89, 47/90, 56/91, 100/93 (ACmHPR 1996)

Media Rights Agenda, Constitutional Rights Project, Media Rights Agenda and Constitutional Rights Project V. Nigeria, Comm. Nos. 105/93, 128/94, 130/94 and 152/96 (ACmHPR 1998)

Amnesty International, Comité Loosli Bachelard, Lawyers' Committee for Human Rights, Association of Members of the Episcopal Conference of East Africa V. Sudan, Comm. Nos. 48/90, 50/91, 52/91 and 89/93 (ACmHPR 1999)

Sir Dawda K. Jawara V. Gambia (the), Comm. No. 147/95-149/96 (ACmHPR 2000)

Mouvement Burkinabé Des Droits De L'homme Et Des Peuples V. Burkina Faso, 204/97 (ACmHPR 2001)

Social and Economic Rights Action Center and Center for Economic and Social Rights V. Nigeria, Communication No. 155/96 (ACmHPR 2001)

Purohit and Moore V. Gambia, 241/01 (ACmHPR 2003)

Prince V. South Africa, Comm. No. 255/2002 (ACmHPR 2004)

Zimbabwe Human Rights NGO Forum V. Zimbabwe, 254/02 (ACmHPR 2006)

Sudan Human Rights Organisation & Centre on Housing Rights and Evictions V. Sudan, Comm. Nos. 279/03, 296/05 (ACmHPR 2009)

Egyptian Initiative for Personal Rights & Interrights V. Egypt Comm. No. 323/06 (ACmHPR 2011)

Egyptian Initiative for Personal Rights and Interights V. Egypt, Comm. No. 323/2006 (ACmHPR 2013)

Monim Elgak, Osman Hummeida and Amir Suliman V. Sudan, Communication 379/09 (ACmHPR 2014)

Groupe De Travail Sur Les Dossiers Judiciaires Stratégiques V. Democratic Republic of Congo, Comm. No. 259/2002 (ACmHPR 2015)

The Nubian Community in Kenya V. The Republic of Kenya, 317/06 (ACmHPR 2015)

African Committee of Experts on the Rights and Welfare of the Child

Institute for Human Rights and Development in Africa and Other on Behalf of Children of Nubian Decent in Kenya V. Kenya, No. 002/Com/002/2009 (ACmERWC 2011)

Michelo Hunsungule and Others (on Behalf of Children in Northern Uganda) V. Uganda, Communication No. 1/2005 (ACmERWC 2013)

Centre for Human Rights, University of Pretoria and La Rencontre Africaine Pour La Defense Des Droits De L'homme V. Senegal, (ACmERWC 2014)

European Court of Human Rights

Golder V. United Kingdom, Application no. 4451/70 (ECtHR 1975)

X and Y V. The Netherlands, 8 EHRR 235, 8978/80 (ECtHR 1985)

Inter-American Court of Human Rights

Velasquez Rodriguez V. Honduras, (Ser. C) No. 4 (IACrtHR 1988)

International Cases

Case Concerning Ahmadou Sadio Diallo (Republic of Guinea V. Democratic Republic of the Congo), 2010 I.C.J. Rep. 639, (ICJ 2010)

Idg V. Spain,U.N. Doc. E/C.12/55/D/2/2014, Communiciation No. 2/2014 (CESCR 2015) (U.N.)

Rodríguez V. Spain,U.N. Doc. E/C.12/57/D/1/2013, Communiciation No. 1/2013 (CESCR 2016) (U.N.)

Ben Djazia and Bellili V. Spain,U.N. Doc. E/C.12/61/D/5/2015, Communiciation No. 5/2015 (CESCR 2017) (U.N.)

National Cases

Germany

B 8 So 22/07 R, 102 1, (BSG 2008) (Germany)

South Africa

Government of the Republic of South Africa and Others V. Grootboom and Others, 1 SA 46, CCT 11/00 (CC 2000) (South Africa)

National Association of Welfare Organisations and Non-Governmental Organisations and Others V. Mec of Social Development, Free State and Others, 2010 ZAFSHC 73, 1719/2010 (Free St. High Ct. 2010) (South Africa)

National Association of Welfare Organization and Non-Governmental Organizations and Others V. Mec for Social Development, Free State and Others 2011 ZAFSHC 84, 1719/2010 (Free St. High Ct. 2011) (South Africa)

National Association of Welfare Organisations and Non-Governmental Organisations and Others V. Mec for Social Development, Free State and Others 2013 ZAFSHC 49, 1719/2010 (Free St. High Ct. 2013) (South Africa)

National Association of Welfare Organisations and Non-Governmental Organisations and Others V. Mec for Social Development, Free State and Others 2014 ZAFSHC 127, 1719/2010 (Free St. High Ct. 2014) (South Africa)

Mokoena and Others V. Mec Gauteng Department of Health: Mahlangu N.O, 2016 ZALCJHB 98, J 352/16 (Labour Ct. Johannesburg 2016) (South Africa)

Uganda

Centre for Health Human Rights & Development & Others V. Attorney General,UGCC 4, Petition No. 16 of 2011 (CC 2012) (Uganda)

Bank of Uganda V. Caring for Orphans, Widows & Elderly Ltd., 2009 UGCA 36, Civil Appeal No.35 of 2007 (UGCA 2009) (Uganda)

Kaggwa Andrew & 5 Others V. Hno Minister of Internal Affairs, 2002 UGHC 21, HCT-00-CV-MC-0105 OF 2002 (UGHC 2002) (Uganda)

Balikowa & Anor V. Uganda, 2012 UGHCCRD 2, Criminal Appeal No. 003 of 2011 (UGHC 2012) (Uganda)

Cowe (U) & Cowe Ltd V. Attorney General, 2015 UGHCCD 78, HCT-00-CV-CS-O194-2004 (UGHC 2015) (Uganda)

United States

Pierce V. Society of Sisters, 268 U.S. 510, (Supreme Ct. 1925) (United States)

Griswold V. Connecticut, 381 U.S. 479, (Supreme Ct. 1965) (United States)

Table of Laws

Treaties

International

Covenant on the Elimination of All Forms of Racial Discrimination (adopted Dec. 21, 1965, entered into force Jan. 4, 1969) 660 UNTS 195 (CERD)

International Covenant on Civil and Political Rights (adopted 16 December 1966, entered into force Mar. 23, 1976) 999 UNTS 171 (ICCPR)

International Covenant on Economic, Social and Cultural Rights (adopted 16 December 1966, entered into force Jan. 3, 1976) 993 UNTS 3 (ICESCR)

Vienna Convention on the Law of Treaties (adopted May 23, 1969, entered into force Jan. 27, 1980) 1155 UNTS 331 (VCLT)

International Covenant on the Elimination of All Forms of Discrimination Against Women (adopted Dec. 18, 1979, entered into force Sept. 3, 1981) 1249 UNTS 13 (ICEDAW)

International Covenant on the Rights of the Child (adopted Nov. 20, 1989, entered into force Sept. 2, 1990) 1577 UNTS 3 (ICRC)

Optional Protocol to the International Covenant on Economic, Social and Cultural Rights (adopted 10 Dec. 2008, entered into force May 5, 2013) 2922 UNTS 27 (OP-ICESCR)

Regional

African Charter on Human and Peoples' Rights (adopted 27 June 1981, entered into force Oct. 21, 1986) 21 ILM 58 (ACHPR)

African Charter on the Rights and Welfare of the Child (adopted 11 July 1990, entered into force Nov. 29, 1999) OAU Doc. CAB/LEG/24.9/49 (ACRWC)

Protocol to the African Charter on Human and Peoples' Rights on the Rights of Women in Africa (adopted July 11, 2003, entered into force Nov. 25, 2005) AU Doc. CAB/LEG/66.6 (P-ACHPRRWA)

Resolutions and Declarations

International

UNGA, Draft International Covenant on Human Rights and Measures of Implementation: Future Work of the Commission on Human Rights (Dec. 4, 1950) UN Doc. A/RES/421(V)

UNGA, Inclusion in the International Covenant or Covenants on Human Rights of an Article to the Right of Peoples to Self-Determination (Feb. 5, 1952) UN Doc. A/RES/545 (VI)

UNGA, World Conference on Human Rights (Dec. 20, 1993) UN Doc. A/RES/48/121

UNGA, Universal Declaration of Human Rights (December 10, 1948) UN Doc A/810 (UDHR)

UNGA, Protection of Persons with Mental Illness and Improvement of Mental Health Care (Dec. 17, 1991) U.N. Doc. A/RES/46/119

UNCHR, The Limburg Principles on the Implementation of the International Covenant on Economic, Social and Cultulral Rights (Jan. 8, 1987) UN Doc. E/CN.4/1987/17 (The Limburg Principles)

Vienna Declaration and Programme of Action (July 12, 1993) U.N. Doc. A/CONF.157/23

Regional – African Commission on Human and Peoples' Rights

ACmHPR, Pretoria Declaration on Economic, Social and Cultural Rights in Africa, ACHPR/Res. 73 (Dec. 7, 2004)

ACmHPR, Resolution on the Health and Reproductive Rights of Women in Africa (May 16-30, 2007) ACHPR/Res. 110

ACmHPR, Resolution on Access to Health and Needed Medicines in Africa (Nov. 24, 2008) ACHPR/Res. 141

ACmHPR, Resolution on the Optional Protocol to the International Covenant on Economic, Social and Cultural Rights (May 2, 2012) ACHPR/Res. 223

ACmHPR, Resolution on the Right to Adequate Housing and Protection from Forced Evictions (Oct. 9-22, 2012) ACHPR/Res. 231

ACmHPR, Resolution on the Right to Water Obligations (Feb. 28, 2015) ACHPR/Res. 300

ACmHPR, Resolution on the Right to Education in Africa (Apr. 20, 2016) ACHPR/Res. 346

ACmHPR, Resolution on the Situation of Human Rights Defenders in Africa (May 22, 2017) ACHPR/Res. 376 (LX)

Other International Authorities

ACmHPR, Guidelines on Freedom of Association and Assembly in Africa <http://www.icnl.org/news/2017/ACHPR%20Guidelines%20english.pdf>

ACmHPR, Principles and Guidelines on the Implementation of Economic, Social and Cultural Rights in the African Chart on Human and Peoples' Rights <http://www.achpr.org/files/instruments/economic-social-cultural/achpr_instr_guide_draft_esc_rights_eng.pdf>

CESCR, General Comment No. 1: Reporting by States Parties (UN 1989) U.N. Doc. E/C.12/1989/5, Annex III

CESCR, General Comment No. 3: The Nature of States Parties' Obligations (UN 1990) U.N. Doc. E/1991/23

CESCR, General Comment No. 4: The Right to Adequate Housing (UN 1991) U.N. Doc. E/1992/23

CESCR, General Comment No. 5: Persons with Disabilities (UN 1994) U.N. Doc. E/1995/22

CESCR, General Comment No. 6: The Economic, Social and Cultural Rights of Older Persons (UN 1995) U.N. Doc. E/C.12/1995/16

CESCR, General Comment No. 7: The Right to Adequate Housing - Forced Evictions (UN 1997) U.N. Doc. E/1998/22, annex IV

CESCR, General Comment No. 8: The Relationship between Economic Sanctions and Respect for Economic, Social and Cultural Rights (UN 1997) U.N. Doc. E/C.12/1997/8

CESCR, General Comment No. 9: The Domestic Application of the Covenant (UN 1997) U.N. Doc. E/1998/24

CESCR, General Comment No. 12: The Right to Adequate Food (UN 1999) U.N. Doc. E/C.12/1999/5

CESCR, General Comment No. 13: The Right to Education (UN 1999) U.N. Doc. E/C.12/1999/10

CESCR, General Comment No. 14: The Right to the Highest Attainable Standard of Health (UN 2000) U.N. Doc. E/C.12/2000/4

CESCR, General Comment No. 15: The Right to Water (UN 2003) U.N. Doc. E/C.12/2002/11

CESCR, General Comment No. 18: The Right to Work (UN 2006) U.N. Doc. E/C.12/GC/18

CESCR, General Comment No. 19: The Right to Social Security (UN 2007) U.N. Doc. E/C.12/GC/19

CESCR, General Comment No. 21: The Right of Everyone to Take Part in Cultural Life (UN 2009) U.N. Doc. E/C.12/GC/21

CESCR, General Comment No. 22: The Right to Sexual and Reproductive Health (UN 2016) U.N. Doc. E/C.12/GC/22

CRC, General Comment No. 5: General Measures of Implementation of the Covenant on the Rights of the Child (UN 2003) U.N. Doc. CRC/GC/2003/5

HRC, General Comment No. 31: The Nature of the General Legal Obligation Imposed on States Parties to the Covenant (UN 2004) U.N. Doc. CCPR/C/21/Rev. 1/Add.13

UNGA, Responsibility of States for Internationally Wrongful Acts (Jan. 28, 2002) U.N. Doc. A/RES/56/83 (Annex)

National Constitutions

Constitution of Uganda (1995; rev. 2005)
Constitution of South Africa (1996)

National Legislation, Regulations and Bills

Angola

Decreto Presidencial No. 74/15, Lei No. 74/15 (Angola 2015)
Lei Das Associações Privadas, Lei No 6/2012 (Angola 2012)

Eritrea

A Proclamation to Determine the Administration of Non-Governmental Organizations, Proclamation No 145/2005 (Eritrea 2005)

Ethiopia

Charities and Societies Proclamation No 621/2009 (Ethiopia 2009)

Kenya

Non-Governmental Organizations Co-Ordination Act, No 19 of 1990 (Kenya 1990)
The Statute Law (Miscellaneous Amendemendments) Act, 1991, No 14 of 1991 (Kenya 1991)
The Statute Law (Miscellaneous Amendemendments) Act, 1992, No 11 of 1992 (Kenya 1992)
The Statute Law (Miscellaneous Amendments) Bill. 2013, Bill No 32 (Kenya 2013)

Portugal

Associações Secretas, Lei No 1901 (Portugal 1935)

Sierra Leone

Non-Government Organisations Policy Regulations (Sierra Leone 2009)

Uganda

The Non-Governmental Organisations Registration (Amendment) Act, No 25 of 2006 (Uganda 2006)

The Non-Governmental Organisations Act, No 5 of 2016 (Uganda 2016)

The Non-Governmental Organisations Registration Regulations, 2009 No. 19 (Uganda 2009)

The Non-Governmental Organisations Registration Regulations, 2017 No. 22 (Uganda 2017)

The Non-Governmental Organisations Regulations, No. 22 of 2017 (Uganda 2017)

The Non-Governmental Organisations Bill, 2015, Bill No 10 (Uganda 2015)

Official Government Documents

International

CESCR, An Evaluation of the Obligation to Take Steps to the "Maximum of Available Resources" under an Optional Protocol to the Covenant: Statement (UN 2007) U.N. Doc E/C.12/2007/1

CESCR, Concluding Observations on the First through Third Period Reports on Ethiopia (UN 2012) UN Doc. E/C.12/ETH/CO/1-3

CESCR, Concluding Observations on the Initial and Second Period Report of Djibouti (UN 2013) UN Doc. E/C.12/DJI/CO/1-2

CESCR, Concluding Observations on the Third Period Report on Angola (UN 2008)

CESCR, Concluding Observations on the Fourth and Fifth Period Report of Angola (UN 2015) UN Doc. E/C.12/UGA/CO/4-5

CESCR, Concluding Observations on the Initial Period Report of Uganda (UN 2015) UN Doc. E/C.12/UGA/CO/1

CESCR, Human Rights Defenders and Economic, Social and Cultural Rights (UN 2017) U.N. Doc. E/C.12/2016/2

CRC, Concluding Observations on the Fifth Periodic Report of the United Kingdom of Great Britain and Northern Ireland (UN 2016) U.N. Doc. CRC/C/GBR/CO/5

Commission for Social Development, UNESC, Emerging Issues: Social Protection (UN 2010) UN Doc. E/CN.5/2011/8

International Human Rights Instruments of the UN, Core Document Forming Part of the Reports of States Parties: Angola (UN 2008) UN Doc. HRI/CORE/AGO/2008

Third Committee, UNGA, Summary Record of the 1185th Meeting (UN 1962) UN Doc. A/C.3/SR.1185

Third Committee, UNGA, Summary Record of the 1206th Meeting (UN 1962) UN Doc. A/C.3/SR.1206

Third Committee, UNGA, Summary Record of the 363rd Meeting (UN 1951) UN Doc. A/C.3/SR.363

UNCHR, UNESC, Report to the Economic and Social Council on the Seventh Session of the Commission on Human Rights (UN 1951) UN Doc. E/CN.4/640

UNCHR, UNESC, Report to the Economic and Social Council on the Eigth Session of the Commission (UN 1952) UN Doc. E/CN.4/669

UNCHR, UNESC, Summary Record of the 234th Meeting (UN 1951) UN Doc. E/CN.4/SR.234

UNCHR, UNESC, Summary Record of the 235th Meeting (UN 1951) UN Doc. E/CN.4/SR.235

UNCHR, UNESC, Summary Record of the 236th Meeting (UN 1951) UN Doc. E/CN.4/SR.236

UNCHR, UNESC, Summary Record of the 237th Meeting (UN 1951) UN Doc. E/CN.4/SR.237

UNCHR, UNESC, Summary Record of the 306th Meeting (UN 1952) UN Doc. E/CN.4/SR.306

UNCHR, UNESC, Summary Record of the 307th Meeting (UN 1952) UN Doc. E/CN.4/SR.307

UNCHR, UNESC, Summary Record of the 308th Meeting (UN 1952) E/CN.4/SR.308

UNCHR, UNESC, United States Proposal Relating to the General Clause Concerning Economic, Social and Cultural Rights (UN 1951) UN Doc. E/CN.4/610/Add.2

UNGA, Draft International Covenants on Human Rights: Report of the Third Committee (UN 1955) UN Doc. A/3077

UNGA, Draft International Covenants on Human Rights: Report of the Third Committee (UN 1962) UN Doc. A/5365

UNGA, Draft International Covenants on Human Rights: Report of the Third Committee (UN 1963) UN Doc. A/5655

UNHCHR, UNESC, Economic, Social and Cultural Rights (UN 2017) UN Doc. E/2017/70

UNSG, UNGA, Draft Interntional Covenants on Human Rights: Annotations (UN 1955) UN Doc. A/2929

Regional

AU, Social Policy Framework for Africa (AU 2008) AU Doc. CAMSD/EXP/4(1)

AU, Common African Position (CAP) on the Post-2015 Development Agenda (AU 2014)

Regional Committee for Africa, World Health Organization, The Role of the Community in Improving Maternal, Newborn and Child Health in the Who Africa Region (UN 2007) UN Doc. AFR/RC57/16 (b)

National

Department of Social Development, Ministry of Social Development, Policy on Financial Awards to Service Providers (South Africa 2003) <http://www.dsd.gov.za/index2.php?option=com_docman&task=doc_view&gid=34&Itemid=39>

Independent Commission for Aid Impact, DFID's Education Programmes in Three East African Countries (United Kingdom 2012) <https://icai.independent.gov.uk/wp-content/uploads/DFIDs-Education-Programmes-in-Three-East-African-Countries-Final-Report-3.pdf>

Bibliography

Books, Book Chapters, Encyclopedias and Theses

Encyclopedia of Twentieth-Century African History (Routledge 2003)

Alexander, Larry, 'What Is the Problem of Judicial Review?' in Carrecedo, José Rubio (ed), *Political Philosophy: New Proposals for New Questions* (Franz Steiner Verlag 2007) 173-181

Alston, Philip, ''Not-a-Cat' Syndrome: Can the International Human Rights Regime Accommodate Non-State Actors?' in Alston, Philip (ed), *Non-State Actors and Human Rights* (Oxford University Press 2005) 3-36

Anheier, Helmut K. and Salamon, Lester M., *The Nonprofit Sector in the Developing World: A Comparative Analysis* (Manchester United Press 1998)

Anheier, Helmut K. and Salamon, Lester M., 'The Nonprofit Sector in Comparative Perspective' in Powell, Walter W. and Steinberg, Richard (eds), *The Nonprofit Sector: A Research Handbook* (2nd edn, Yale University Press 2006) 89-114

Anheier, Helmut K. and Seibel, Wolfgang, *The Nonprofit Sector in Germany: Between State, Economy, and Society* (Manchester University Press 2001)

An-Na'īm, Abdullahi Ahmed., 'Introduction: Expanding Legal Protection of Human Rights in African Contexts' in Na'īm AAA (ed), *Human Rights under African Constitutions: Realizing the Promise for Ourselves*(University of Pennsylvania Press, Incorporated 2003) 1

Awortwi, Nicholas and Walter-Drop, Gregor, 'Governance Below the State: Non-State Social Protection Services in Africa' in Awortwi, Nicholas and Walter-Drop, Gregor (eds), *Non-State Social Protection Actors and Services in Africa: Governance Below the State* (Routledge 2018) 1-24

Balanda, Mikuin L., 'African Charter on Human and Peoples' Rights' in Ginther, Konrad and Benedek, Wolfgang (eds), *New Perspectives and Conceptions of International Law: An Afro-European Dialogue* (Springer-Verlag 1984) 134-146

Barrientos, Armando, 'Social Protection' in Currie-Adler, Bruce and others (eds), *International Development: Ideas, Experience & Prospects* (Oxford University Press 2014) 188-203

Becker, Ulrich, 'Social Services of General Interest in Germany' in *Social Services of General Interest in the EU* (Springer 2013) 497-511

Ben-Ari, Rephael H., *The Normative Position of International Non-Governmental Organizations under International Law: An Analytical Framework* (Martinus Nijhoff 2012)

Bevan, Philippa, 'The Dynamics of Africa's in/Security Regimes' in Gough, Ian and Wood, Geof (eds), *Insecurity and Welfare Regimes in Asia, Africa and Latin America: Social Policy in Development Contexts* (Cambridge University Press 2004)

Biegon, Japhet, 'The Inclusion of Socio-Economic Rights in the 2010 Constitution: Conceptual and Practical Issues' in Biegon, Japhet and Musila, Godfrey M. (eds), *Judiciary Watch Report: Judicial Enforcement of Socio-Economic Rights under the New Constitution : Challenges and Opportunities for Kenya*, vol 10 (Kenya Section of the International Commission of Jurists 2011)

Bourdieu, Pierre and Wacquant, Loïc J. D., *An Invitation to Reflexive Sociology* (University of Chicago Press 1992)

Brownlie, Ian, *Brownlie's Principles of Public International Law* (8th edn, Oxford University Press 2012)

Cammett, Melanie and MacLean, Lauren M., 'Introduction' in Cammett, Melanie and MacLean, Lauren M. (eds), *The Politics of Non-State Welfare* (Cornell University Press 2014) 1-16

Cammett, Melanie and MacLean, Lauren M. (eds), *The Politics of Non-State Welfare* (Cornell University Press 2014)

Chapman, Audrey R. and Russell, Sage (eds), *Core Obligations: Building a Frameowrk for Economic, Social and Cultural Rights* (Intersentia 2002)

Chilcote, Ronald H. (ed), *Protest and Resistance in Angola and Brazil: Comparative Studies* (University of California Press 1972)

Clapham, Andrew, 'Non-State Actors' in Moeckli, Daniel and others (eds), *International Human Rights Law*(Oxford University Press 2010) 561-582

Clapham, Andrew (ed), *Human Rights and Non-State Actors*, vol 5 (Edward Elgar Publishing Limited 2013)

Craven, Matthew, *The International Covenant on Economic, Social and Cultural Rights: A Perspective on Its Development* (Brownlie, Ian (ed) Oxford University Press 1995)

Curtin, Philip and others, *African History* (Little Brown 1978)

Devereux, Stephen and Getu, Melese, 'The Conceptualisation and Status of Informal and Formal Social Protection in Sub-Saharan Africa' in Devereux, Stephen and Getu, Melese (eds), *Informal and Formal Social Protection in Sub-Saharan Africa*(Fountain Publishers 2013) 1-8

Devereux, Stephen and Getu, Melese (eds), *Informal and Formal Social Protection in Sub-Saharan Africa* (Fountain Publishers 2013)

Dobler, Gregor, 'Private Vices, Public Benefits? Small Town Bureaucratisation in Namibia' in Peters, Anne and Handschin, Lukas (eds), *Conflict of Interest in Global, Public and Corporate Governance* (Cambridge University Press 2012) 217-232

Dorman, Sara R., 'Inclusion and Exclusion: NGOs and Politics in Zimbabwe' (Doctoral Thesis, University of Oxford 2001)

Esping-Andersen, Gøsta, *The Three Worlds of Welfare Capitalism* (Princeton University Press 1990)

Ferguson, James, *Global Shadows: Africa in the Neoliberal World Order* (Duke University Press 2006)

Fisher, Julie, *Nongovernments: NGOs and the Political Development of the Third World* (Kumarian Press 1998)

Fitzmaurice, Malgosia, 'Interpretation of Human Rights Treaties' in Shelton, Dinah (ed), *The Oxford Handbook of International Human Rights Law* (Oxford University Press 2013) 739-771

Fowler, Alan, 'NGOs & the Globalization of Social Welfare: Perspectives from East Africa' in Therklindsen, Ole and Semboja, Joseph (eds), *Service Provision under Stress in East Africa: The State, NGOs & People's Organizations in Kenya, Tanzania & Uganda* (Centre for Development Research 1995)

Gagakuma, Wisdom and Samuel, Zigiju, 'Effectiveness of Capacity Building Programs in Fragile States: The Ethiopia Case' in Olowu, Dele and Chanie, Paulos (eds), *State Fragility and State Building in Africa: Cases from Eastern and Southern Africa* (Springer International Publishing 2015) 113-134

Gilbert, Neil and Gilbert, Barbara, *The Enabling State* (Oxford University Press 1989)

Gough, Ian, 'Welfare Regimes in Development Contexts: A Global and Regional Analysis' in Gough, Ian and others (eds), *Insecurity and Welfare Regimes in Asia, Africa and Latin America*(Cambridge University Press 2004) 15-47

Gough, Ian, 'Mapping Social Welfare Regimes Beyond the OECD' in Cammett, Melanie and MacLean, Lauren M. (eds), *The Politics of Non-State Welfare* (Cornell University Press 2014) 17-30

Harriss, John, 'Development Theories' in Currie-Adler, Bruce and others (eds), *International Development: Ideas, Experience & Prospects* (Oxford University Press 2014) 35-49

Hebo, Mamo, ''Giving Is Saving': The Essence of Reciprocity as an Informal Social Protection System among the Arsii Oromo, Southern Ethiopia' in Devereux, Stephen and Getu, Melese (eds), *Informal and Formal Social Protection in Sub-Saharan Africa* (Fountain Publishers 2013) 9-42

Inman, Robert P., 'Markets, Governments, and the "New" Political Economy' in Auerbach, Alan J. and Feldstein, Marin (eds), *Handbook of Public Economics*, vol 2 (1987) 647-776

Ishumi, Abel G. M., 'Provision of Secondary Education in Tanzania: Historical Background and Current Trends' in Therklindsen, Ole and Semboja, Joseph (eds), *Service Provision under Stress in East Africa: The State, NGOs & People's Organizations in Kenya, Tanzania & Uganda* (Centre for Development Research 1995) 153

Jayawickrama, Nihal, *The Judicial Application of Human Rights Law: National, Regional and International Jurisprudence* (Cambridge University Press 2002)

Jordan, Lisa and van Tuijl, Peter (eds), *NGO Accountability: Politics, Principles and Innovations* (Earthscan 2006)

Kälin, Walter and Künzli, Jörg, *The Law of International Human Rights Protection* (Oxford University Press 2009)

Kaufmann, Christine, 'The Covenants and Financial Crises' in Moeckli, Daniel and others (eds), *The Human Rights Covenants at 50: Their Past, Present, and Future*(Oxford University Press 2018) 303-333

King, Jeff, *Judging Social Rights* (Dyzenhaus D and Tomkins A eds, Cambridge University Press 2012)

Klabbers, Jan and others, *The Constitutionalization of International Law* (Oxford University Press 2011)

Klare, Karl, 'Critical Perspectives on Social and Economic Rights, Democracy and Separation of Powers' in García, Helena Alviar and others (eds), *Social and Economic Rights in Theory and Practice: Critical Inquiries* (Routledge 2015) 3-22

Krsticevic, Viviana and Griffey, Brian, 'Interim Measures' in Langford, Malcolm and others (eds), *The Optional Protocol to the International Covenant on Economic, Social and Cultural Rights: A Commentary* (Pretoria University Law Press 2016) 293-326

Kufuor, Kofi O., *The African Human Rights System: Origin and Evolution* (Palgrave Macmillan US 2010)

Kumar, Ashwani, 'The Question of the Poor' in Taylor, Rupert (ed), *Third Sector Research* (Springer 2010) 281-298

Kwesiga, Jassy B. and Namisi, Harriet, 'Issues in Legislation for NGOs in Uganda' in Jordan, Lisa and van Tuijl, Peter (eds), *NGO Accountability: Politics, Principles and Innovations* (Earthscan 2006) 81-92

Levy, Brian and Kpundeh, Sahr John (eds), *Building State Capacity in Africa: New Approaches, Emerging Lessons* (World Bank Publications 2004)

Liebenberg, Sandra, *Socio-Economic Rights: Adjudication under a Transformative Constitution* (Juta & Co. 2010)

Liebenberg, Sandra, 'Direct Constitutional Protection of Economic, Social and Cultural Rights in South Africa' in Chirwa, Danwood M. and Chenwi, Lilian (eds), *The Protection of Economic, Social and Cultural Rights in Africa: International, Regional and National Perspectives* (Cambridge University Press 2016) 305-337

Makau, B. M., 'Dynamics of Partnership in the Provision of General Education in Kenya' in Therklindsen, Ole and Semboja, Joseph (eds), *Service Provision under Stress in East Africa: The State, NGOs & People's Organizations in Kenya, Tanzania & Uganda*(Centre for Development Research 1995) 87

Manji, Firoze, 'The Depoliticisation of Poverty' in Manji, Firoze (ed), *Development and Rights* (Oxfam GB 1998) 12-33

Mberu, Blessing and others, 'Internal Migration, Urbanization and Slumbs in Sub-Saharan Africa' in Groth, Hans and May, John F. (eds), *Africa's Population: In Search of a Demographic Dividend* (Springer 2017) 315-332

McCorquodale, Robert, 'Non-State Actors and International Human Rights Law' in Joseph, Sarah and McBeth, Adam (eds), *Research Handbook on International Human Rights Law* (Edward Elgar 2010) 91-114

Mertus, Julie A., *Bait and Switch: Human Rights and U.S. Foreign Policy* (2d edn, Routledge 2008)

Micklitz, Hans- W. (ed), *Constitutionalization of European Private Law*, vol 22 (Oxford University Press 2014)

Moeckli, Daniel, 'Interpretation of the ICESCR: Between Morality and State Consent' in Moeckli, Daniel and others (eds), *The Human Rights Covenants at 50: Their Past, Present, and Future* (Oxford University Press 2018) 48-74

Moyo, Dambisa, *Dead Aid: Why Aid Is Not Working and How There Is Another Way for Africa* (Allen Lane 2009)

Munishi, Gaspar K., 'Social Services Provision in Tanzania: The Relationship between Political Development Strategies and NGO Participation' in Therklindsen, Ole and Semboja, Joseph (eds), *Service Provision under Stress in East Africa: The State, NGOs & People's Organizations in Kenya, Tanzania & Uganda* (Centre for Development Research 1995) 141

Murray, Rachel and Long, Debra, *The Implementation of the Findings of the African Commission on Human and Peoples' Rights* (Cambridge University Press 2015)

Murungi, John, *An Introduction to African Legal Philosophy* (Lexington Books 2013)

Mutua, Makau, 'Human Rights International NGOs: A Critical Evaluation' in Welch, Jr., Claude E. (ed), NGOs *and Human Rights: Promise and Performance* (University of Pennsylvania Press 2001) 151-166

Mutzenberg, Patrick, 'NGOs: Essential Actors for Embedding the Covenants in the National Context' in Moeckli, Daniel and others (eds), *The Human Rights Covenants at 50: Their Past, Present, and Future* (Oxford University Press 2018) 75-95

Mwebe, Henry, 'The Impact of Privatisation on Socio-Economic Rights and Services in Africa: The Case of Water Privatisation in South Africa' (Master's Thesis, University of Pretoria 2004)

Nassali, Maria, *Beating the Human Rights Drum: Applying Human Rights Standards to NGOs' Governance* (Pretoria University Law Press 2015)

Neuman, Gerald L., 'Subsidiarity' in Shelton, Dinah (ed), *The Oxford Handbook of International Human Rights Law* (Oxford University Press 2013) 345-359

Oakland, William H., 'Theory of Public Goods' in Auerbach, Alan J. and Feldstein, Marin (eds), *Handbook of Public Economics*, vol 2 (1987) 485-535

Odongo, Godfrey O. and Musila Godfrey M., 'Direct Constitutional Protection of Economic, Social and Cultural Rights in Kenya's 2010 Constitution' in Chirwa, Danwood M. and Chenwi, Lilian (eds), *The Protection of Economic, Social and Cultural Rights in Africa: International, Regional and National Perspectives* (Cambridge University Press 2016) 338-371

Okoth-Ogendo, H. W. O., 'Human and Peoples' Rights: What Point Is Africa Trying to Make?' in Cohen, Ronald and others (eds), *Human Rights and Governance in Africa* (Univeristy Press of Florida 1993) 74-86

Okoye, Ada Obianuju, 'The Role of Law in the Development of Nonprofit Sector in Nigeria and South Africa' (University of Cape Town 2006)

Oloka-Onyango Joe, 'Ngo Struggles for Economic, Social, and Cultural Rights in Utake: A Ugandan Perspective' in Mutua, Makau (ed), *Human Rights NGOs in East Africa: Political and Normative Tensions* (University of Pennsylvania Press 2009) 75-111

Olukoshi, Adebayo O., *The Politics of Opposition in Contemporary Africa* (Stylus Pub Llc 1998)

Pacific United Nations Economic Social Commission for Asia, *Sustainable Social Development in a Period of Rapid Globalization: Challenges, Opportunities and Policy Options* (United Nations Publications 2002)

Passi, Fabius, O., 'The Rise of Peoples' Organizations in Primary Education in Uganda' in Therklindsen, Ole and Semboja, Joseph (eds), *Service Provision under Stress in East Africa: The State, NGOs & People's Organizations in Kenya, Tanzania & Uganda* (Centre for Development Research 1995) 209

Peter, Chris M., 'Coming of Age: NGOs and State Accountability' in Mutua, Makau (ed), *Human Rights NGOs in East Africa: Political and Normative Tensions*

(University of Pennsylvania Press 2009) 305-318

Peters, Anne, *Jenseits Der Menschenrechte: Die Rechtsstellung Des Individuums Im Völkerrecht* (Mohr Siebeck Tübingen 2014)

Peters, Anne, *Beyond Human Rights: The Legal Status of the Individual in International Law*, vol 126 (Cambridge University Press 2016)

Quashigah, Edward K., 'Legitimate Governance: The Pre-Colonial African Perspective' in Quashigah, Edward K.and Okafor, Obiora C. (eds), *Legitimate Governance in Africa: International and Domestic Legal Perspectives* (Springer Netherlands 1999) 43-66

Ramcharan, Bertrand G., 'The Concept and Dimensions of the Right to Life' in Ramcharan, Bertrand G. (ed), *The Right to Life in International Law*, vol 3 (Martinus Nijhoff 1985) 1-32

Reinikka, Ritva and Smith, Nathanael, *Public Expenditure Tracking Surveys in Education* (International Institute for Educational Planning 2004)

Robinson, Mark and White, Gordon, 'The Role of Civic Organizations in the Provision of Social Services: Towards Synergy' in Mwabu, Germano and others (eds), *Social Provision in Low-Income Countries* (Oxford University Press 2001) 79 - 100

Rodley, Nigel S., 'The Role and Impact of Treaty Bodies' in Shelton, Dinah (ed), *The Oxford Handbook of International Human Rights Law* (Oxford University Press 2013) 621-648

Rosas, Allan, 'Internal Self-Determination' in Tomuschat, Christian (ed), *Modern Law of Self-Determination* (Martinus Nijhoff 1993) 225-252

Rosas, Allan, 'The Right of Self-Determination' in Eide, Asbjørn and others (eds), *Economic, Social and Cultural Rights: A Textbook* (2nd rev. edn, Martinus Nijhoff 2001) 79-86

Saul, Ben and others, *The International Covenant on Economic, Social and Cultural Rights: Commentary, Cases and Materials* (1 edn, Oxford University Press 2014)

Scheinin, Martin, 'Economic and Social Rights as Legal Rights' in Eide, Asbjørn and others (eds), *Economic, Social and Cultural Rights: A Textbook* (2nd rev. edn, Martinus Nijhoff 2001) 41-62

Scheinin, Martin, 'Core Rights and Obligations' in Shelton, Dinah (ed), *The Oxford Handbook of International Human Rights Law* (Oxford University Press 2013) 527-540

Scheinin, Martin, 'Indirect Protection of Economic, Social and Cultural Rights in International Law' in Chirwa, Danwood M. and Chenwi, Lilian (eds), *The Protection of Economic, Social and Cultural Rights in Africa: International, Regional and National Perspectives* (Cambridge University Press 2016) 72-87

Scott, James C., *Seeing Like a State: How Certain Schemes to Improve the Human Condition Have Failed* (Yale University Press 1998)

Scott, T. Jeffrey, 'Evaluating Development-Oriented NGOs' in Welch, Jr., Claude E. (ed), NGOs *and Human Rights: Promise and Performance*(University of Pennsylvania Press 2001) 204-221

Scruggs, Lyle and others, 'Implementation of the Human Right to Social Security around the World: A Preliminary Analysis of National Social Protection Laws' in Minkler, Lanse (ed), *The State of Economic and Social Human Rights: A Global Review* (Cambridge University Press 2013) 117-134

Seibel, Wolfgang, 'The Function of Mellow Weakness: Nonprofit Organizations as Problem Nonsolvers in Germany' in James, Estelle (ed), *The Nonprofit Sector in International Perspective: Studies in Comparative Culture & Policy* (Oxford University Press 1989) 177-192

Seibel, Wolfgang, *Funktionaler Dilettantismus: Erfolgreich Scheiternde Organisationen Im "Dritten Sektor" Zwischen Markt Und Staat* (Nomos-Verlag-Ges. 1992)

Sepúlveda, M. Magdalena, *The Nature of the Obligations under the International Covenant on Economic, Social and Cultural Rights* (Intersentia 2003)

Sewanyana, Livingstone, *Comparative Experiences of NGO Regulatory Frameworks: Eastern and Southern Africa* (Verlag Dr. Kovac 2017)

Sewanyana, Livingstone 'Towards an Enabling NGO Regulatory Framework in Uganda: Comparative Experiences from Eastern and Southern Africa' (Doctoral Thesis Unversity of Capetown 2014)

Shivji, Issa G., *The Concept of Human Rights in Africa* (Codesria Book Series 1989)

Spicker, Paul, *Principles of Social Welfare: An Introduction to Thinking About the Welfare State* (Routledge 1988)

Ssenyonjo, Manisuli, *Economic, Social and Cultural Rights in International Law* (2d edn, Hart Publishing 2016)

Ssenyonjo, Manisuli, 'Influence of the ICESCR in Africa' in Moeckli, Daniel and others (eds), *The Human Rights Covenants at 50: Their Past, Present, and Future* (Oxford University Press 2018) 99-123

Steiner, Henry J. and others, *International Human Rights in Context: Law, Politics, Morals* (3d edn, Oxford University Press 2008)

Teamey, Kelly, *Whose Public Action? Analysing Inter-Sectoral Collaboration for Service Delivery* (2007)

Teshome, Amdissa and others, 'Governance Characteristics and Policy Relevance of Informal Social Protection Services in Ethiopia: When the State Is Willing but Not Able' in Awortwi, Nicholas and Walter-Drop, Gregor (eds), *Non-State Social Protection Actors and Services in Africa: Governance Below the State* (Routledge 2018) 25-43

Therklindsen, Ole and Semboja, Joseph 'A New Look at Service Provision in East Africa' in Therklindsen, Ole and Semboja, Joseph (eds), *Service Provision under Stress in East Africa: The State, NGOs & People's Organizations in Kenya, Tanzania & Uganda* (Centre for Development Research 1995)

Tomaševski, Katarina, 'International Development Finance Agencies' in Eide, Asbjørn and others (eds), *Economic, Social and Cultural Rights: A Textbook* (2nd rev. edn, Martinus Nijhoff 2001) 403-413

Tomuschat, Christian, *Human Rights: Between Idealism and Realism* (2d edn, Oxford University Press 2008)

Tvedt Terje, *Angels of Mercy or Development Diplomats?: NGOs & Foreign Aid* (Africa World Press 1998)

Weisbrod, Burton Allen (ed), *The Voluntary Nonprofit Sector: An Economic Analysis* (Lexington Books 1977)

Williams, David, 'The Study of Development' in Currie-Adler, Bruce and others (eds), *International Development: Ideas, Experience & Prospects* (Oxford University Press 2014) 21-34

Williams, Lucy A., 'Resource Questions in Social and Economic Rights Enforcement: A Preliminary View' in García Helena A. and others (eds), *Social and Economic Rights in Theory and Practice: Critical Inquiries* (Routledge 2015) 43-64

Wood, Geof, 'States without Citizens: The Problem of the Franchise State' in Hulme, David and Edwards, Michael (eds), NGOs, *States and Donors: Too Close for Comfort?* (Macmillan 1997) 79-92

Wood, Geof, 'Informal Security Regimes: The Strength of Relations' in Gough, Ian and others (eds), *Insecurity and Welfare Regimes in Asia, Africa and Latin America* (Cambridge University Press 2004) 49-87

Journal Articles

A-Rahman, A., Jacquet, Gabrielle A. and Hassan, Nada, 'The State of Emergency Care in the Republic of the Sudan' 4 African Journal of Emergency Medicine 55 (2014)

Abbey, Edward Mac, 'Constructive Regulation of Non-Governmental Organizations' 48 The Quarterly Review of Economics and Finance 370 (2008)

Abom, Bill, 'Social Capital, NGOs, and Development: A Guatemalan Case Study' 14 Development in Practice 342 (2004)

Abrams, Philip, 'Notes on the Difficulty of Studying the State (1977)' 1 Journal of Historical Sociology 58 (1988)

Acharya, Amitav, 'Norm Subsidiarity and Regional Orders: Sovereignty, Regionalism, and Rule-Making in the Third World' 55 International Studies Quarterly 95 (2011)

Ackson, Tulia, 'Justiciability of Socio-Economic Rights in Tanzania' 23 African Journal of International and Comparative Law 359 (2015)

Adeniran, Akingbolahan, 'Non-Profit Privatization of the Management of Nigerian Public Schools: A Legal and Policy Analysis' 53 Journal of African Law 249 (2009)

Alston, Philip and Quinn, Gerard, 'The Nature and Scope of States Parties' Obligations under the International Covenant on Economic, Social and Cultural Rights' 9 Human Rights Quarterly 156 (1987)

Anderson, Robert T., 'Voluntary Associations in History' 73 American Anthropologist 209 (1971)

Banks, Nicola and others 'NGOs, States, and Donors Revisited: Still Too Close for Comfort?' 66 World Development 707 (2015)

Bartel, Ann P. and Thomas, Lacy Glenn, 'Direct and Indirect Effects of Regulation: A New Look at Osha's Impact' 28 The Journal of Law and Economics 1 (1985)

Batley, Richard, 'Engaged or Divorced? Cross-Service Findings on Government Relations with Non-State Service-Providers' 26 Public Administration and Development 241 (2006)

Batley, Richard, 'Structures and Strategies in Relationships between Non-Government Service Providers and Governments' 31 Public Administration and Development 306 (2011)

Becker, Ulrich and others, 'Strukturen Und Prinzipien Der Leistungserbringung Im Sozialrecht' 5 Vierteljahresschrift für Sozialrecht (VSSR) 323 (2011)

Becker, Ulrich and others, 'Strukturen Und Prinzipien Der Leistungserbringung Im Sozialrecht' 1 Vierteljahresschrift für Sozialrecht (VSSR) 1 (2012)

Bell Jr., Derrick A., 'Serving Two Masters: Integration Ideals and Client Interests in School Desegregation Litigation' 85 Yale Law Journal 470 (1976)

Bereketeab, Redie, 'Conceptualizing Civil Society in Africa: The Case of Eritrea' 5 Journal of Civil Society 35 (2009)

Brass, Jennifer N., 'Blurring Boundaries: The Integration of NGOs into Governance in Kenya' 25 Governance 209 (2012)

Brass, Jennifer N., 'Why Do NGOs Go Where They Go? Evidence from Kenya' 40 World Development 387 (2012)

Bratton, Michael, 'The Politics of Government-NGO Relations in Africa' 17 World Development 569 (1989)

Bräutigam, Deborah A. and Knack, Stephen, 'Foreign Aid, Institutions, and Governance in Sub-Saharan Africa' 52 Economic Development and Cultural Change 255 (2004)

Brodhead, Tim, 'NGOs: In One Year, out the Other?' 15 World Development 1 (1987)

Burger, Ronelle, 'Reconsidering the Case for Enhancing Accountability Via Regulation' 23 Voluntas 85 (2012)

Carozza, Paolo G., 'Subsidiarity as a Structural Principle of International Human Rights Law' 97 American Journal of International Law 38 (2003)

Chenwi, Lilian, 'Unpacking "Progressive Realisation", Its Relation to Resources, Minimum Core and Reasonableness, and Some Methodological Considerations for Assessing Compliance' 46 De Jure 742 (2013)

Chinzara, Zivanemoyo and others, 'Growth and Development Finance Required for Achieving Sustainable Development Goals (Sdgs) in Africa' 29 African Development Review 15 (2017)

Chirwa, Danwood Mzikenge, 'The Doctrine of State Responsibility as a Potential Means of Holding Private Actors Accountable for Human Rights' 5 Melbourne Journal of International Law 1 (2004)

Cornwall, Andrea and Nyamu-Musembi, Celestine, 'Putting the "Rights-Based Approach" to Development in Perspective' 25 Third World Quarterly 1415 (2004)

Craig, Scott and Macklem, Patrick, 'Constitutional Ropes of Sand or Justiciable Guarantees? Social Rights in a New South African Constitution' 141 University of Pennsylvania Law Review 1 (1992)

Dennis, Michael J. and Stewart, David P., 'Justiciability of Economic, Social and Cultural Rights: Should There Be an International Complaints Mechanism to Adjudicate the Rights to Food, Water, Housing, and Health?' 98 American Journal of International Law 462 (2004)

Dicklitch, Susan and Lwanga, Doreen, 'The Politics of Being Non-Political: Human Rights Organizations and the Creation of a Positive Human Rights Culture in Uganda' 25 Human Rights Quarterly 482 (2003)

Dinokopila, Bonolo Ramadi, 'The Justiciability of Socio-Economic Rights in Botswana' 57 Journal of African Law 108 (2013)

Dupuy, Kendra and others, 'Hands Off My Regime! Governments' Restrictions on Foreign Aid to Non-Governmental Organizations in Poor and Middle-Income Countries' 84 World Development 299 (2016)

Edmonds, Kevin, 'Beyond Good Intentions: The Structural Limitations of NGOs in Haiti' 39 Critical Sociology 439 (2012)

Edwards, Michael and Hulme, David, 'Too Close for Comfort? The Impact of Official Aid on Nongovernmental Organizations' 24 World Development 961 (1996)

Eisenberg, Pablo, 'Forum - Looking Ahead: What Is the Future for the Nonprofit World' 8 International Journal of Not-for-Profit Law 81 (2005)

Elone, Jeanne, 'Backlash against Democracy: The Regulation of Civil Society in Africa' 7 Democracy and Society (2010)

Erbe, Nancy and others, 'Negotiating and Mediating Peace in Africa' 9 Pepperdine Dispute Resolution Law Journal 457 (2008)

Ferreira, Nick, 'Feasibility Constraints and the South African Bill of Rights: Fulfilling the Constitution's Promise in Conditions of Scarce Resources' 129 South African Law Journal 274 (2012)

Flikke, Geir, 'Resurgent Authoritarianism: The Case of Russia's New NGO Legislation' 32 Post-Soviet Affairs 103 (2016)

Forman, Lisa and others, 'Conceptualising Minimum Core Obligations under the Right to Health: How Should We Define and Implement the 'Morality of the Depths'' 20 The International Journal of Human Rights 531 (2016)

Garton, Jonathan, 'The Judical Review of the Decision of Charity Trustees' 20 Trust Law International 160 (2006)

George, Tayo O. and others, 'Effective Service Delivery of Nigeria's Public Primary Education: The Role of Non-State Actors' 15 Journal of African Development 221 (2013)

Gill, Timothy M, 'Unpacking the World Cultural Toolkit in Socialist Venezuela: National Sovereignty, Human Rights and Anti-NGO Legislation' 38 Third World Quarterly 621 (2017)

Gough, Ian and Abu Sharkh, Miriam, 'Global Welfare Regimes: A Cluster Analysis' 10 Global Social Policy 27 (2010)

Gough, Ian and Abu Sharkh, Miriam, 'Financing Welfare Regimes: Mapping Heterogeneous Revenue Structures' 20 International Journal of Social Welfare 280 (2011)

Grabosky, Peter N., 'Using Non-Governmental Resources to Foster Regulatory Compliance' 8 Governance 527 (1995)

Griffin, Elizabeth, 'The Ethical Responsibilities of Human Rights NGOs' 15 International Journal of Not-for-Profit Law 5 (2013)

Gugerty, Mary Kay, 'The Effectiveness of NGO Self-Regulation: Theory and Evidence from Africa' 28 Public Administration and Development 105 (2008)

Gutto, Shadrack B. O., 'Beyond Justiciability: Challenges of Implementing/Enforcing Socio-Economic Rights in South Africa' 4 Buffolo Human Rights Law Review 79 (1998)

Hailu, Daniel and Northcut, Terry, 'Ethiopia's Social Protection Landscape: Its Surface and Underlying Structures' 56 International Social Work 828 (2012)

Hearn, Julie, 'African NGOs: The New Compradors?' 38 Development and Change 1095 (2007)

Hern, Erin, 'In the Gap the State Left: Policy Feedback, Collective Behavior, and Political Participation in Zambia' 52 Studies in Comparative International Development 510 (2017)

Holcombe, Randall G., 'A Theory of the Theory of Public Goods' 10 Review of Austrian Economics 1 (1997)

Ibrahim, Barbara Lethem, 'States, Public Space, and Cross-Border Philanthropy: Observations from the Arab Transitions' 17 International Journal of Not-for-Profit Law 72 (2015)

Inglis, Tom, 'Empowerment and Emancipation' 48 Adult Education Quarterly 3 (1997)

International Center of Not-for-Profit Law, 'Introductory Overview' 12:2 International Journal of Not-for-Profit Law 5 (2010)

Jenkins, Garry W., 'Nongovernmental Orgainzations and the Forces against Them: Lessons of the Anti-NGO Movement' 37 Brook Journal of International Law 459 (2012)

Jheelan, Navish, 'The Enforceability of Socio-Economic Rights' 2 European Human Rights Law Review 146 (2007)

Kahssay, Jihan A, (Note) 'Lessons Learned from Somalia: Retuning to a Humanitarian-Based Humanitarian Intervention' 19 UC Davis Journal of International Law & Policy 113 (2012)

Kamat, Sangeeta, 'The Privatization of Public Interest: Theorizing NGO Discourse in a Neoliberal Era' 11 Review of International Political Economy 155 (2004)

Khoza, Sibonile, 'Promoting Economic, Social and Cultural Rights in Africa: The African Commission Holds a Seminar in Pretoria: Recent Developments' 4 African Human Rights Law Journal 334 (2004)

Kok, Maryse C. and others, 'Optimising the Benefits of Community Health Workers' Unique Position between Communities and the Health Sector: A Comparative Analysis of Factors Shaping Relationships in Four Countries' 12 Global Public Health 1404 (2017)

Korpi, Walter, 'An Augmented Rational-Action Analysis of the Origins and Path Dependency of Welfare State Institutions in Western Countries' 13 Rationality and Society 235 (2001)

Lehmann, Karin, 'In Defense of the Constitutional Court: Litigating Socio-Economic Rights and the Myth of the Minimum Core' 22 American University International Law Review 163 (2006)

Little, Kenneth L., 'The Role of the Secret Society in Cultural Specialization' 51 American Anthropologist 199 (1949)

Little, Kenneth L., 'The Organisation of Voluntary Associations in West Africa / Les Associations Volontaires En Afrique Occidentale' 9 Civilisations 283 (1959)

MacLean, Lauren M., 'Neoliberal Democratisation, Colonial Legacies and the Rise of the Non-State Provision of Social Welfare in West Africa' 44 Review of African Political Economy 358 (2017)

Manji, Firoze and O'Coill, Carl, 'The Missionary Position: NGOs and Development in Africa' 78 International Affairs 567 (2002)

Mapuva, Jephias and Muyengwa-Mapuva, Loveness, 'A Critique of the Key Legislative Framework Guiding Civil Liberties in Zimbabwe' 15 Potchefstroom Electronic Law Journal 125 (2012)

Marcinkutė, Lina, 'The Role of Human Rights NGOs: Human Rights Defenders or State Soverignty Destroyers?' 4 Baltic Journal of Law & Politics 52 (2011)

Mathews, Jessica T., 'Power Shift' 76 Foreign Affairs 50 (1997)

Mayhew, Susannah H., 'Hegemony, Politics and Ideology: The Role of Legislation in NGO-Governmental Relations in Asia' 41 Journal of Development Studies 727 (2005)

McBeth, Adam, 'Privatising Human Rights: What Happens to the State's Human Rights Duties When Services Are Privatised?' 5 Melbourne Journal of International Law 133 (2004)

Mechlem, Kerstin, 'Treaty Bodies and the Interpretation of Human Rights' 42 Vanderbilt Journal of Transnational Law 905 (2009)

Milward, H. Brinton and Provan, Keith G., 'Governing the Hollow State' 10 Journal of Public Administration Research and Theory 359 (2000)

Moellendorf, Darrel, 'Reasoning About Resources: Soobramoney and the Future of Socio-Economic Rights Claims' 14 South African Journal on Human Rights 327 (1998)

Morss, Elliot R., 'Institutional Destruction Resulting from Donor and Project Proliferation in Sub-Saharan African Countries' 12 World Development 465 (1984)

Mubangizi, John Cantius, 'The Constitutional Protection of Socio-Economic Rights in Selected African Countries: A Comparative Evaluation' 2 African Journal of Legal Studies 1 (2006)

Müller, Amrei, 'Limitations to and Derogations from Economic, Social and Cultural Rights' 9 Human Rights Quarterly 557 (2009)

Mutua, Makau, 'Human Rights in Africa: The Limited Promise of Liberalism' 51 African Studies Review (2008)

Najam, Adil, 'The Four-C's of Third Sector-Government Relations: Cooperation, Confrontation, Complementarity, and Co-Optation' 10 Nonprofit Management & Leadership 375 (2000)

Nolan, Aoife, 'Addressing Economic and Social Rights Violations by Non-State Actors through the Role of the State: A Comparison of Regional Approaches to the 'Obligation to Protect'' 9 Human Rights Law Review 225 (2009)

Nxumalo, Nonhlanhla and others, 'Community Health Workers, Recipients' Experiences and Constraints to Care in South Africa – a Pathway to Trust' 28 AIDS Care 61 (2016)

O'Leary, Susan, 'Grassroots Accountability Promises in Rights-Based Approaches to Development: The Role of Transformative Monitoring and Evaluation in NGOs' 36 Accounting, Organizations and Society 21 (2017)

Oloka-Onyango, Joe, 'Reinforcing Marginalized Rigths in an Age of Globalization: International Mechanisms, Non-State Actors, and the Struggle for Peoples' Rights in Africa' 18 American University International Law Review 851 (2002-2003)

Olsen, William C., 'The Empire Strikes Back: Colonial "Discipline" and the Creation of Civil Society in Asante' 30 History in Africa 223 (2003)

Ordor, Ada Okoye, 'The Non-Profit Sector in the Context of Law in Development in Africa' 58 Journal of African Law 45 (2014)

Pattar, Andreas Kurt, 'Sozialhilferechtliches Dreiecksverhältnis - Rechtsbeziehungen Zwischen Hilfebedürftigen, Sozialhilfeträgern Und Einrichtungsträgern' 3 Sozialrecht Aktuell 85 (2012)

Paul, Joel R., 'Do International Trade Institutions Contribute to Economic Growth and Development?' 44 Virginia Journal of International Law 285 (2003)

Petras, James, 'NGOs: In the Service of Imperialism' 29 Journal of Contemporary Asia 429 (1999)

Pieterse, Marius, 'Health Care Rights, Resources and Rationing' 124 South African Law Journal 514 (2007)

Pieterse, Marius, 'The Legitimizing/Insulating Effect of Socio-Economic Rights' 22 Canadian Journal of Law & Society/La Revue Canadienne Droit et Société 1 (2007)

Pieterse, Marius, 'Relational Socio-Economic Rights' 25 South African Journal on Human Rights 198 (2009)

Piotrowicz, Maria and Cianciara, Dorota, 'The Role of Non-Governmental Organizations in the Social and the Health System' 67 Przeglad Epidemiologiczny 69 (2013)

Pritchett, Lant and Woolcock, Michael, 'Solutions When the Solution Is the Problem: Arraying the Disarray in Development' 32 World Development 191 (2004)

Reading, Joshua P., (Note) 'Who's Responsible for This? Globalization of Healthcare in Developing Countries' 17 Indiana Journal of Global Legal Studies 367 (2010)

Riddell, J. Barry, 'Things Fall Apart Again: Structural Adjustment Programmes in Sub-Saharan Africa' 30 The Journal of Modern African Studies 53 (1992)

Robertson, Robert E., 'Measuring State Compliance with the Obligation to Devote the "Maximum Available Resources" to Realizing Economic, Social and Cultural Rights' 16 Human Rights Quarterly 693 (1994)

Rutzen, Douglas, 'Aid Barriers and the Rise of Philanthropic Protectionism' 17:1 International Journal of Not-for-Profit Law 5 (2015)

Salamon, Lester M., 'Of Market Failure, Voluntary Failure, and Third-Party Government: Toward a Theory of Government-Nonprofit Relations in the Modern Welfare State' 16 Journal of Voluntary Action Research 29 (1987)

Salamon, Lester M., 'The Rise of the Nonprofit Sector' 73 Foreign Affairs 109 (1994)

Salamon, Lester M., 'Introduction: The Nonprofitization of the Welfare State' 26 Voluntas 2147 (2015)

Salamon, Lester M. and Anheier, Helmut K., 'Social Origins of Civil Society: Explaining the Nonprofit Sector Cross-Nationally' 9 Voluntas 213 (1998)

Samuelson, Paul A., 'The Pure Theory of Public Expenditure' 36 The Review of Economics and Statistics 387 (1954)

Scheinin, Martin, 'Terrorism and the Pull of 'Balancing' in the Name of Security' EUI Working Papers Law 55 (2009)

Schmitz, Hans Peter, 'A Human Rights Based Aproach (HRBA) in Practice: Evaluating NGO Development Efforts' 44 Polity 523 (2012)

Scott, Craig, 'Interdependence and Permeability of Human Rights Norms: Towards a Partial Fusion of the International Covenants on Human Rights' 27 Osgoode Hall Law Journal 769 (1989)

Scott, Craig and Alston, Philip, 'Adjudicating Constitutional Priorities in a Transnational Context: A Comment on Soobramoney's Legacy and Grootboom's Promise' 16 South African Journal on Human Rights 206 (2000)

Seckinelgin, Hakan, 'Who Can Help People with HIV/AIDS in Africa? Governance of HIV/AIDS and Civil Society' 15 Voluntas 287 (2004)

Seibel, Wolfgang, 'Successful Failure' 39 American Behavioral Scientist 1011 (1996)

Shelton, Dinah, 'Hierarchy of Norms and Human Rights: Of Trumps and Winners' 65 Saskatchewan Law Review 301 (2002)

Shelton, Dinah, 'Subsidiarity and Human Rights Law' 27 Human Rights Law Journal 4 (2006)

Shivji, Issa G., 'The Silences in the NGO Discourse' 31 African Development 22 (2006)

Silberberg, Mina, 'Balancing Autonomy and Dependence for Community and Nongovernmental Organizations' 72 Social Service Review 47 (1998)

Simmons, P. J. , 'Learning to Live with NGOs' 112 Foreign Policy 82 (1998)

Skogly, Sigrun, 'The Requirement of Using the 'Maximum of Available Resources' for Human Rights Realisation: A Question of Quality as Well as Quantity?' 12 Human Rights Law Review 393 (2012)

Sundstrom, Lisa McIntosh, 'Foreign Assistance, International Norms, and NGO Development: Lessons from the Russia Campaign' 59 International Organization 419 (2005)

Tinta, Mónica Feria, 'Justiciability of Economic, Social and Cultural Rights in the Inter-American System of Protection of Human Rights: Beyond Traditional Paradigms and Notions' 29 Human Rights Quarterly 431 (2007)

Trilsch, Mirja, 'What's the Use of Socio-Economic Rights in a Constitution? – Taking a Look at the South African Experience' 42 Verfassung und Recht in Übersee / Law and Politics in Africa, Asia and Latin America 552 (2009)

Tvedt, Terje, 'Development NGOs: Actors in a Global Civil Society or in a New International Social System?' 13 Voluntas 363 (2002)

Udombana, Nsongurua J., 'Between Promise and Performance: Revisiting States' Obligations under the African Human Rights Charter' 40 Stanford Journal of International Law 105 (2004)

Udombana, Nsongurua J., 'Social Rights Are Human Rights: Actualizing the Rights to Work and Social Security in Africa' 93 Cornell International Law Journal 181 (2006)

Waldron, Jeremy, 'A Rights-Based Critique of Constitutional Rights' 13 Oxford Journal of Legal Studies 18 (1993)

Wamboye, Evelyn and others, 'Foreign Aid, Legal Origin, Economic Growth and Africa's Least Developed Countries' 14 Progress in Development Studies 335 (2014)

Whitfield, Lindsay and Fraser, Alastair, 'Negotiating Aid: The Structural Conditions Shaping the Negotiating Strategies of African Governments' 15 International Negotiation 341 (2010)

Wietzke, Frank-Borge, 'Historical Origins of Uneven Service Supply in Sub-Saharan Africa: The Role of Non-State Providers' 50 The Journal of Development Studies 1614 (2014)

Woods, Dwayne, 'Elites, Ethnicity, and 'Home Town' Associations in the Côte D'ivoire: An Historical Analysisof State-Society Links' 64 Africa: Journal of International African Institute 465 (1994)

Young, Dennis R., 'Alternative Models of Government-Nonprofit Sector Relations: Theoretical and International Perspectives' 29 Nonprofit and Voluntary Sector Quarterly 149 (2000)

Young, Katharine G., 'The Minimum Core of Economic and Social Rights: A Concept in Search of Content' 33 Yale Journal of International Law 113 (2008)

Reports and Working Papers

ACT Alliance, *The World Humanitarian Summit: Putting People at the Centre* (2015) <http://actalliance.org/wp-content/uploads/2015/12/J3734-ACT-Alliance-position-paper-for-World-Humanitarian-Summit_AW.pdf>

African Commission on Human and Peoples' Rights, *42nd Activity Report of the African Commission on Human and Peoples' Rights* (2017) <http://www.achpr.org/files/activity-reports/42/42nd_activity_report_eng.pdf>

Batley, Richard and Mcloughlin Claire, Governance and Social Development Resource Centre, *State Capacity and Non-State Service Provision in Fragile and Conflict-Affected States* (2006) <http://www.gsdrc.org/docs/open/eirs3.pdf>

Beegle, Kathleen and others, World Bank Group, *Poverty in a Rising Africa* (2016) <https://openknowledge.worldbank.org/bitstream/handle/10986/22575/9781464807237.pdf?sequence=10&isAllowed=y>

Bratton, Michael, Institute for Development Research, *Civil Society and Political Transition in Africa* 6 (1994) <https://www.issuelab.org/resources/19673/19673.pdf>

Corbett, Justin, Local to Global Protection, *Learning from the Nuba: Civilan Resilience and Self-Protection During Conflict* (2011) <http://www.local2global.info/wp-content/uploads/SK_Nuba_L2GP_report_final.pdf>

Courtis, Christian, International Commission of Jurists & Inter-American Institute of Human Rights, *Commentary on the Optional Protocol to the International Covenant on Economic, Social and Cultural Rights* (2008) <https://www.icj.org/wp-content/uploads/2009/07/Commentary-OP-ICESCR-publication-2009-eng.pdf>

Dade, Saide, *The Dimension of NPI in Mozambique: A Satellite Account Perspective* (2009) <http://ccss.jhu.edu/wp-content/uploads/downloads/2011/10/Mozambique_SatelliteAccount_2009.pdf>

Directory of Development Organizations: Resource Guide to Development Organizations and the Internet (vol Africa 2010) <https://www.ecoi.net/file_upload/1002_1264767399_uganda.PDF & https://www.ecoi.net/file_upload/1002_1264708453_botswana.PDF>

Freedom House, *Populists and Autocrats: The Dual Threat to Global Democracy* (2017) <https://freedomhouse.org/sites/default/files/FH_FIW_2017_Report_Final.pdf>

Institut National de la Statistique *Compte Satellite Des Institutions Sans but Lucratif: De L'année 2011* (2014) <http://ccss.jhu.edu/wp-content/uploads/downloads/2015/01/Cameroon_SatelliteAccount_2014.pdf>

International Commission of Jurists, *Courts and the Legal Enforcement of Economic, Social and Cultural Rights: Comparative Expereinces of Justiciability* (2008) <https://www.humanrights.ch/upload/pdf/080819_justiziabilitt_esc.pdf>

International Federation of Red Cross and Red Crescent Societies, *Focus on Culture and Risk* (2014) <http://www.ifrc.org/Global/Documents/Secretariat/201410/WDR%202014.pdf>

International Federation of Red Cross and Red Crescent Societies, *Focus on Local Actors, the Key to Humanitarian Effectiveness* (2015) <https://ifrc-media.org/interactive/wp-content/uploads/2015/09/1293600-World-Disasters-Report-2015_en.pdf>

Kiai, Maina, U.N. Special Rapporteur on the Rights to Freedom of Peaceful Assembly and of Association, *Annual Report: Comparative Study of Enabling Environments for Businesses and Associations* A/70/266 (2015)

Kiai, Maina, U.N. Special Rapporteur on the Rights to Freedom of Peaceful Assembly and of Association, *Analysis on International Law, Standards and Principles Applicable to the Foreign Contributions Regulation Act 2010 and Foreign Contributions Regulation Rules 2011* (2016)

Kreienkamp, Julia, Global Governance Institute, *Responding to the Global Crackdown on Civil Society* (2017) <https://www.ucl.ac.uk/global-governance/downloads/policybriefs/policy-brief-civil-society>

NEPAD Planning and Coordinating Agency, UN Economic Comission for Africa, *Mobilizing Domestic Financial Resources for Implementing Nepad National and Regional Programmes & Projects: Africa Looks Within* (2014) <http://www.un.org/africarenewal/sites/www.un.org.africarenewal/files/DRM_ENGLISH_REPRO_OP.pdf>

Organization for Economic Cooperation and Development, *Aid at a Glance: Flows of Official Development Assistance to and through Civil Society Organizations in 2011* (2013) <http://www.oecd.org/dac/peer-reviews/Aid%20for%20CSOs%20Final%20for%20WEB.pdf>

Salamon, Lester M. and Toepler Stefan, Center for Civil Society Studies, *The Influence of the Legal Environment on the Development of the Nonprofit Sector,* No. 17 (2000)

Sembene, Daouda, International Monetary Fund, *Poverty, Growth, and Inequality in Sub-Saharan Africa: Did the Walk Match the Talk under the Prsp Approach?* (IMF 2015) <https://www.imf.org/external/pubs/ft/wp/2015/wp15122.pdf>

Stevens, Mike and others, World Bank, *Governance: The World Bank's Experience* (1994) <http://documents.worldbank.org/curated/en/711471468765285964/pdf/multi0page.pdf>

Tawfik, Youssef, Northrup Robert and Prysor-Jones Suzanne, Academy for Educational Development, *Utilizing the Potential of Formal and Informal Private Practitioners in Child Survival: Situation Analysis and Summary of Promising Interventions* (2002) <http://pdf.usaid.gov/pdf_docs/Pnacp202.pdf>

Trémolet, Sophie, Building Partnerships for Development in Water & Sanitation, *Adapting Regulation to the Needs of the Poor: Experience in 4 East African Countries* (2006) <https://www.ircwash.org/sites/default/files/Tremolet-2006-Adapting.pdf>

United Nations Committee for Development Policy, *List of Least Developed Countires (as of June 2017)* (2017) <https://www.un.org/development/desa/dpad/wp-content/uploads/sites/45/publication/ldc_list.pdf>

United Nations Conference on Trade and Development (UNCTAD), *The Path to Gradution and Beyond: Making the Most of the Process* (2016) <http://unctad.org/en/PublicationsLibrary/ldc2016_en.pdf>

United Nations Development Programme, *The Zimbabwean Non-Governmental Orgnizations Bill 2004 and International Human Rights Law/Standards: Issues, Analysis and Policy Recommendations* (UNDP 2004)

United Nations Educational, Scientific and Cultural Organization (UNESCO), *The World Needs Almost 69 Million New Teachers to Reach the 2030 Education Goals* (2016) <http://unesdoc.unesco.org/images/0024/002461/246124e.pdf>

United States Agency for International Development (USAID), *The 2013 CSO Sustainability Index: The Middle East and North Africa* (2013)

United States Agency for International Development (USAID), *The 2014 CSO Sustainability Index: Central and Eastern Europe and Eurasia* (2014)

United Nations Under-Secretary-General and High Representative for LDCs, LLDCs and SIDS, *Extreme Poverty Eradication in the Least Developed Countries and the Post-2015 Development Agenda* (2014) <http://unohrlls.org/custom-content/uploads/2014/10/State-of-the-Least-Developed-Countries-Report-2014.pdf>

World Bank, *Taking on Inequality* <https://openknowledge.worldbank.org/bitstream/handle/10986/25078/9781464809583.pdf?sequence=24&isAllowed=y>

World Bank, *Uganda - the Role of Nongovernmental Organizations and Community-Based Groups in Poverty Alleviation* (1994) <http://documents.worldbank.org/curated/en/363831468765338754/Uganda-The-role-of-nongovernmental-organizations-and-community-based-groups-in-poverty-alleviation>

World Bank, *Human Development in Uganda: Meeting Challenges and Findinal Solutions* (2009) <http://documents.worldbank.org/curated/en/659361468175487874/Uganda-Human-development-in-Uganda-Meeting-challenges-and-finding-solutions>

World Bank, *Managing Risk, Promoting Growth: Developing Systems for Social Protection in Africa* (2012) <https://openknowledge.worldbank.org/handle/10986/23744>

World Bank, *Making Services Work for Poor People* (vol 2004 2004) <https://openknowledge.worldbank.org/bitstream/handle/10986/5986/WDR%202004%20-%20English.pdf?sequence=1&isAllowed=y>

World Health Organization, *Partnerships for Safer Health Service Delivery: Evaluation of Who African Partnerships for Patient Safety 2009-2014* WHO/HIS/SDS/2015.13 (2015) <http://www.who.int/patientsafety/implementation/apps/evaluation-report.pdf>

World Bank, *Poverty Maps of Uganda* (2018) <http://documents.worldbank.org/curated/en/456801530034180435/Poverty-Maps-of-Uganda>

Z., Ali and others, Sudanese Medical Association UK & Ireland, *Oncology Services in Sudan: Realities and Ambitions, Conference Report* (2013)

News Articles

'29 NGOs Banned in Crackdown' *New Zimbabwe* (14 Feb 2012) <http://www.newzimbabwe.com/news-7189-29+NGOs+banned+in+crackdown/news.aspx>

'Anti-Torture NGO El-Nadeem Rejects Health Ministry's Reasons for Shutdown' *Ahram Online* (Feb. 25, 2016) <http://english.ahram.org.eg/NewsContent/1/64/188500/Egypt/Politics-/Antitorture-NGO-ElNadeem-rejects-health-ministrys-.aspx>

'Egypt's Health Ministry Orders Shutdown of Anti-Torture NGO El-Nadeem' *Ahram Online* (Feb. 17, 2017) <http://english.ahram.org.eg/NewsContent/1/0/187869/Egypt/0/Egypts-health-ministry-orders-shutdown-of-antitort.aspx>

'Egypt Dissolves 57 NGOs for Brotherhood Links' *Middle East Monitor* (Sept. 7, 2015) <https://www.middleeastmonitor.com/20150907-egypt-dissolves-57-ngos-for-brotherhood-links/>

'Egypt Government Seizes More Hospitals, Firms Owned by Muslim Brotherhood' *Ahram Online* (June 23, 2016) <http://english.ahram.org.eg/NewsContent/1/64/226670/Egypt/Politics-/Egypt-government-seizes-more-hospitals,-firms-owne.aspx>

'Egyptian Court Approves Asset Freezes in High-Profile NGO Trial' *Thomson Reuters Foundation* (Sept. 17, 2017) <http://news.trust.org/item/20160917125847-us9sg>

'Three International Schools Shut Down, 28 Warned' *Egypt Independent* (Apr. 20, 2016) <http://www.egyptindependent.com/news/three-international-schools-shut-down-28-warned>

'Health Fears as Sudan Expels NGOs' *Aljazeera* (5 Mar. 2009) <http://www.aljazeera.com/news/africa/2009/03/200935174114968814.html>

'NGO Expulsion to Hit Darfur's Displaced' *IRIN News* (Khartoum, 9 Mar. 2009) <http://www.irinnews.org/news/2009/03/09/ngo-expulsion-hit-darfurs-displaced>

'Sudan Expels 10 Aid NGOs and Dissolves 2 Local Groups' *Sudan Tribune* (4 Mar. 2009) <http://www.sudantribune.com/spip.php?article30382>

'UN Lauds New Tool Enabling Individual Complainst on Economic, Social and Cultural Rights' *UN News Centre* (Feb. 6, 2013) <http://www.un.org/apps/news/story.asp?NewsID=44081#.WJMqCZUzVaS>

'Kenya 'Deregisters' NGOs in Anti-Terror Clampdown' *BBC* (19 Dec. 2014) <https://www.bbc.com/news/world-africa-30494259>

'S. Sudan Parliament Passes NGOs Bill, Gives Requirements for Relief Agencies' *Sudan Tribune* (12 Mar. 2015) <http://www.sudantribune.com/spip.php?article54953>

'Social Solidarity Ministry Shutters at Least 39 More NGOs, over 400 Closed This Year' *Mada Masr* (July 8, 2015) <https://www.madamasr.com/en/2015/07/08/news/u/social-solidarity-ministry-shutters-at-least-39-more-ngos-over-400-closed-this-year/>

'South Sudan Oil Revenue at $3.38 Bln, Hit by Conflict and Price Falls' *Reuters* (3 Jan. 2015) <http://www.reuters.com/article/southsudan-crude-idUSL6N0UI02D20150103>

'South Sudan Risks 'Catastrophe' with New Aid Agency Law, Warn NGOs' *The Guardian* (14 May 2015) <http://www.theguardian.com/global-development/2015/may/14/south-sudan-aid-agency-law-risks-catastrophe-warn-ngos>

'South Sudan Tables NGOs Bill for the Second Time' *Sudan Tribune* (20 Jan. 2016) <http://www.sudantribune.com/spip.php?article57749>

'South Sudanese President Signs NGO Bill into Law' *Sudan Tribune* (11 Feb. 2016) <http://sudantribune.com/spip.php?article57988>

Balch, Oliver, 'UN Criticises UK for Spending Aid Money on for-Profit Private Schools' *The Guardian* <https://www.theguardian.com/sustainable-business/2016/jun/14/un-criticises-uk-government-millions-aid-money-private-schools-developing-countries>

Charbonneau Louis, 'Sudan Expulsion of NGOs Leave Aid Gap - UN' *Reuters* (9 Mar. 2009) <https://www.reuters.com/article/idUSN09481219>

Elbagir, Yousra, 'Patients over Politics: Sudanese Breast Cancer Clinic That Beat Sanctions' *The Guardian* (1 Oct. 2016) <https://www.theguardian.com/world/2016/oct/01/patients-over-politics-sudanese-breast-cancer-clinic-that-beat-sanctions>

Esslemont, Tom, ''Tougher Scrutiny' of Britain's Aid Spending Sees Steep Rise in Fraud Bill' *Thomas Reuters Foundation* (Sept. 22, 2016) <http://news.trust.org/item/20160922131353-jxpbs>

Fortin, Jacey, 'Power Struggles Stall South Sudan's Recovery' *New York Times* (31 May 2016) <http://www.nytimes.com/2016/05/31/world/africa/south-sudan-struggles-to-collect-taxes-after-years-of-war.html>

Hassan, Amro, 'This Group Stood up to Egypt's Crackdown on Human Rights Organizations' *Los Angeles Times* (Apr. 5, 2015) <http://www.latimes.com/world/middleeast/la-fg-egypt-dissident-crackdown-20160405-story.html>

Hodal, Kate, 'UN Warns Universal Education Goal Will Fail without 69 Million New Teachers' *Guardian* (5 Oct. 2016) <https://www.theguardian.com/global-development/2016/oct/05/un-universal-education-goal-fail-69-million-new-teachers-unesco>

Kavuma, Richard M., 'Ugandan Financial Fraud Victims: Still Fighting for Compensation Years Later' *The Guardian* (Jan. 13, 2016) <https://www.theguardian.com/global-development-professionals-network/2016/jan/13/ugandan-victims-still-fighting-for-compensation-years-late-cowe>

Patinkin, Jason 'It's Like Florence Nightingale's Time': South Sudan's Public Services Collapse' *The Guardian* (27 May 2016) <http://www.theguardian.com/global-development/2016/may/27/south-sudan-public-services-collapse-juba-teaching-hospital-like-florence-nightingale-time>

Srinath, Ingrid and Tiwana, Mandeep, 'Civil Society: Only the Clampdown Is Transparent' *The Guardian* (Sept. 12, 2010) <https://www.theguardian.com/commentisfree/libertycentral/2010/sep/12/civil-society-millennium-development-goals>

Srivastava, Prachi, 'Low-Fee Private Schooling: What Do We Really Know? Prachi Srivastava Responds to the Economist' (Oxfam Aug. 11, 2015) <http://oxfamblogs.org/fp2p/its-complicated-or-low-fee-private-schooling-what-do-we-really-know/>

van der Zee, Bibi, 'Less Than 2% of Humanitarian Funds 'Go Directly to Local NGOs'' *The Guardian* (Oct. 16, 2015) <https://www.theguardian.com/global-development-professionals-network/2015/oct/16/less-than-2-of-humanitarian-funds-go-directly-to-local-ngos>

Wall, Imogen, ''We Are Demanding Change': The Somali Woman Taking on International NGOs' *The Guardian* (Mar. 21, 2016) <https://www.theguardian.com/global-development-professionals-network/2016/mar/21/degan-ali-somali-woman-taking-on-the-humanitarian-system>

Press Releases

Egypt: Unprecedented Crackdown on NGOs, Amnesty International, (Mar. 23, 2016) <https://www.amnesty.org/en/press-releases/2016/03/egypt-unprecedented-crackdown-on-ngos/>

Committee on Economic, Social and Cultural Rights Hears from Human Rights Institutions and Civil Society from the United Kingdom, the Former Yugoslav Republic of Macedonia, and Angola, UNHCHR, (13 June 2016) <https://www.ohchr.org/EN/NewsEvents/Pages/DisplayNews.aspx?NewsID=20087&LangID=E>

Maina Kiai Tells Conference That Civil Society Is "under Attack" in Africa, Free Assembly, (Nov. 25, 2013) <http://freeassembly.net/wp-content/uploads/2013/11/Media-statement-Kiai-warns-civil-society-under-attack-in-Africa.pdf>

Non-Governmental Organizations Suspensions, U.S. Embassy Kenya, (4 Nov. 2015) <https://ke.usembassy.gov/non-governmental-organizations-suspensions/>

Statement Attributable to the Spokesperson for the UN Secretary-General United Nations, (5 Mar. 2009) <https://unamid.unmissions.org/statement-attributable-spokesperson-un-secretary-general-0>